Research and Publication Ethics

Principles and Practices

Noushad Husain

SHIPRA

₹595
US$ 20
ISBN: 978-93-91978-50-1

2024
First Published in India

Research and Publication Ethics: Principles and Practices

Published by:
SHIPRA PUBLICATIONS
LG 18-19, Pankaj Central Market
I.P. Ext., Patparganj, Delhi 110092, India
11 47322068, 2223 5152/6152; 96500 28065
info@shiprapublication.com
www.shiprapublication.com

The Author Gratefully Acknowledges
His Indebtedness to
God
For His Mercy

Dedicated to

My Wife **Razda Khan** and

My Sons **Arsh Husain** & **Areeb Husain**

Preface

Research ethics *are the ethics of the planning, conduct and reporting of research.*

Publication ethics *are the ethical standards, policies, and guidelines set to ensure the integrity, quality and validity of published research.*

Research is the cornerstone of progress and innovation. It shapes our understanding of the world, drives advancements in various fields and influences decision-making processes that impact society. However, with such influence comes a great responsibility to uphold ethical standards throughout the research journey.

In an age of rapid information dissemination and an ever-expanding body of knowledge, the importance of ethics in research and publication cannot be overstated. Ethical principles not only safeguard the integrity of the research process but also uphold the trust of the public, peers and institutions in the scientific and scholarly endeavours that shape our understanding of the world.

Research and publication ethics are essential aspects of the academic and scientific community that ensure the integrity, transparency and credibility of research and scholarly publications. Research and publication ethics ensure the integrity of scientific inquiry and the validity of research findings. Ethical practices prevent the fabrication, falsification, and plagiarism of data, which are essential for maintaining the credibility and trustworthiness of scientific knowledge.

This book aims to provide a clear and accessible framework for understanding and addressing the ethical challenges that researchers and authors encounter throughout their academic journey. From the inception of an idea to the publication of results, from the responsible conduct of research to the dissemination of findings, we will delve into a wide range of ethical topics, including authorship, plagiarism, data management, peer review, conflicts of interest, and more.

This book is a comprehensive exploration of the fundamentals of research and publication ethics. It is a guide for those who are embarking on their research journey, a reference for seasoned scholars and an invitation to all who seek to understand and uphold the ethical principles that underpin the pursuit of knowledge. Within the content of this book, we will delve into the complexities, challenges, and ethical dilemmas that researchers, authors, editors, and reviewers encounter throughout their academic and scientific careers.

This book is organised to provide a logical progression through the various facets of research and publication ethics. It is a flexible resource for both students and professionals because each chapter is made to stand alone for quick reference. We hope the book will be found as a beneficial companion on the academic path, whether you are a beginner researcher looking for fundamental knowledge or a seasoned scholar hoping to enhance your grasp of ethical concerns.

In addition to this, I would also like to point out that the book is very pertinent in today's society, where the value of research integrity is becoming increasingly recognized. For anyone who aspires to advance one's knowledge, this book is a vital resource since it offers concrete advice on how to perform and publish research in an ethical manner.

First, I thank a lot of my indebtedness to God for His Mercy', because without the mercy of God, the present book could not have been completed. God gave me a direction, knowledge, support and patience to write this book.

I would like to take this opportunity to thank my father Mr. Zakir Husain and mother Mrs. Aiysha Begum, who are always a source of inspiration for my academic work. I would also like to thank my wife Razda Khan and my beloved sons Arsh Husain and Areeb Husain because without the help and support of my family members, this would not have been possible.

I would also like to extend my gratitude to the countless researchers, educators and professionals who have contributed to the development of ethical standards in academia and beyond. Their dedication to upholding the highest ethical standards enriches the intellectual and moral fabric of our society.

As we will embark on this journey through the valuable content of this book, let us remember that ethical conduct in research and publication is not a burden but a privilege — a privilege that allows us to contribute to the advancement of knowledge, to foster trust in our communities and to leave a lasting legacy for generations to come.

Thank you for joining us on this exploration of research and publication ethics. May it serve as a guiding light in your scholarly endeavours.

In the end, I am thankful to Mr. D. Kumar, Shipra Publications, for the meticulous processing of the manuscript and give the book a nice look

Prof. (Dr.) Noushad Husain
Principal
Maulana Azad National Urdu University
College of Teacher Education
Bhopal (Madhya Pradesh)

Contents

List of Figures

1

Introduction to Philosophy

From the very beginning man has been continuously trying to know and understand the mystery of the Universe around him. He is trying to know the relationship with the physical world on one side and social world on the other. It requires keen observation, critical study and deep thinking. It is philosophy, which has been very useful and helpful to know the nature of man, his origin and relationship with nature, his aspirations and the tool he uses to achieve his aims.

Life and philosophy are so closely related that it is said that if there is life, there would be some philosophy of it also. The function of philosophy is to refine the interests of an individual. With this, it studies the views of the people. The differences in the views of people are quite natural.

Philosophy is wisdom, means knowledge. Knowledge is related to education. Philosophy directs so many things in life. Likewise, it directs the education also. It is philosophy which co-ordinates the activities of the individual, including education, which depends on philosophy.

1.1. Meaning of Philosophy

The term philosophy has a Greek origin. The word philosophy can be traced to the Greek word *'philosophia'* which is made up of the words – *'philos'* (meaning love) and *'sophia'* (meaning wisdom). So, the philosophy means *'love of wisdom'* or *'love of truth'*. Philosophy deals with the general problems of life. Traditionally, philosophy refers to a set of opinions, customs, beliefs and ideas about the nature of reality, truth and values. According to westerners, philosophy is a method of analysis, clarification and criticisms.

Philosophy deals with the questions of reality, knowledge and value. It is theoretical and practical. It is related to theoretical questions like - what is life? What is value? Where did man come from? Where does he go? and other practical questions like 'What kind of life is worth living'?

Philosophy plays the most important role in determining the nature of any education. Although the nature of man and different inventions of science affect the nature of any education, still the role of philosophy for the same is the most important. Since, the creation of man, different efforts have been made to understand man, his origin, his aim, his diverse relationships and his destiny. Man is endowed with the quality of critical thinking and is always contemplating about the environment around him. The process of his ideas and thinking is Philosophy. There is no aspect of human life and human activity which is differentiated from philosophy.

Etymological Meaning of Philosophy: The term philosophy is derived from two Greek words – "*Philos*" and "*Sophia*". Philos means "*Love*" and Sophia means "*Wisdom*". So, the word philosophy means "*love of wisdom*". It is concerned with a search for eternal truth and the man who engages himself in this search is called a Philosopher. Wisdom consists in knowledge plus the ability to utilize it properly in different situations. Thus, philosophy gives the man that wisdom with the help of which he understands the whole universe, it's nature and purpose, it's relations to himself and all the people around him.

Specific Meaning of Philosophy: To be precise and definite, one may call philosophy as that deep thinking and meditation which concern itself to the God, the soul and the nature. Henderson and his colleagues have well said, "*Philosophy is a rigorous, disciplined and guarded analysis of some most difficult problems which man has ever faced.*" Some examples of philosophical problems are: What is knowledge? What is world? Who has created the world? Is there God? Who am I? What is the aim of my life? Why should I live? All these are the topics of philosophical thinking and ultimate realization.

1.2. Concept of Philosophy

Philosophy is an attempt to answer the ultimate questions of life. It is a search of knowledge and wisdom. Philosophy explores the things, makes critical study of problems related to our experience. It is concerned to solve the puzzles of life. Philosophy actually influences the conduct of life. It goes deep into secrets and unknown things. Philosophy helps us to inquire new light about life, gives new ways and new hopes. It defines the most complicated problems and situations to life.

The concept of philosophy is dynamic. It changes with the change of time. During the course of centuries, the meaning attached to it and subject matter of this branch of knowledge has undergone many changes. In order to arrive at the meaning of philosophy you will have to discuss its problems, attitude, method, process, conclusion and results. In brief, philosophy is philosophical process of solving some characteristic problems through characteristic methods from a characteristic attitude and arriving at a characteristic conclusions and results.

Philosophy may be concluded indispensable for every aspect of life. It is not only love of wisdom but also stands for love of knowledge and ultimate reality. Thus, philosophy is an organized search of knowledge.

Since times immemorial there have been various pursuits of unfolding the mysteries of the universe, birth and death, sorrow and joy. Various ages have produced different thoughts throwing light upon the mystic region. The ultimate truth is yet to be found out. This eternal quest for truth lends to the origin of philosophy. A love of wisdom is the essence for any philosophic investigation.

The following sentences will help to develop the concept of philosophy:

- Philosophy is a personal attitude towards life and the universe.
- Philosophy is a method of reflective thinking and reasoned enquiry.
- Philosophy is an attempt to gain a view of the whole.

- Philosophy is the logical analysis of language and the clarification of the meaning of words and concepts.
- Philosophy is a group of problems as well as theories about the solution of these problems.
- Philosophy is related to educational theories and provides suitable solutions to educational problems.
- Philosophy directs education by providing some guidelines.
- Philosophy provides us answers and gives directions to the educational ideas, beliefs and problems.
- Philosophy is helpful and essential for the analysis of educational principles.

1.3. Definitions of Philosophy

Philosophy has been defined by various scholars from various angles. Philosophy according to them is nothing but an endeavor to bring about a consistent explanation of the different realities around us. Let us quote some definitions:

Wikipedia, *"discipline concerned with questions of how one should live (ethics); what sorts of things exist and what are their essential natures (metaphysics); what counts as genuine knowledge (epistemology); and what are the correct principles of reasoning (logic)".*

American Heritage Dictionary, *"investigation of the nature, causes, or principles of reality, knowledge, or values, based on logical reasoning rather than empirical methods".*

Penguin English Dictionary, *"the study of the ultimate nature of existence, reality, knowledge and goodness, as discoverable by human reasoning".*

Word Net, *"the rational investigation of questions about existence and knowledge and ethics".*

Kernerman English Multilingual Dictionary, *"the search for knowledge and truth, especially about the nature of man and his behavior and beliefs".*

Microsoft Encarta Encyclopedia, *"the rational and critical inquiry into basic principles."*

Oxford Dictionary of Philosophy, *"the study of the most general and abstract features of the world and categories with which we think: mind, matter, reason, proof, truth, etc."*

Coleridge,*"Science of sciences".*

Arstippus,*"The ability to feel at ease in any society".*

Dewey,*"Whenever philosophy has been defined, it has been assumed that it signified achieving a wisdom that would influence the conduct of life".*

Plato,*"He who has a taste for every sort of knowledge and is curious to learn and is never satisfied may be termed as philosopher".*

Radhakrishnan,*"Philosophy is the logical inquiry into the nature of reality".*

Bacon,*"Philosophy is the great mother of science".*

Fichte, *"Philosophy is the science of Knowledge."*

Herbert Spencer, *"Philosophy is concerned with everything as a universal science."*

Immanuel Kant, *"Philosophy is the science and criticism of cognition"*.

Plato, *"Philosophy aims at the knowledge of the eternal, of the essential nature of things"*.

Aristotle, *"Philosophy is the science which investigates the nature of being as it is in virtue of its own nature."*

Comte, *"Philosophy is the science of sciences"*.

Dr. Paulsen, *"Philosophy is the sum total of all scientific knowledge"*

Merriam Webster, *"the study of ideas about knowledge, truth, and the nature and meaning of life."*

According to Wikipedia, *"Philosophy is the study of general and fundamental questions about existence, knowledge, values, reason, mind, and language."*

Aristipus (435-356 B.C), *"Philosophy is the ability to feel at ease in any society"*.

Brightman, *"Philosophy may be defined as the attempt to think truly about human experience as a whole and to make our whole experience intelligible"*.

Cicero, Marcus Tullius, *"Philosophy is the mother of all arts and the true medicine of mind"*.

Henderson, *"Philosophy is a search for a comprehensive view of nature, an attempt at universal explanation of nature of thing."*

Russel, Bertrand,*"Philosophy is to be studied not for the sake of any definite answers to its questions.... But rather for the sake of the questions themselves, because these questions enlarge our conception of what is possible... but above all because the mind also is rendered great and becomes capable of that union with the universe which constitutes its heist goal."*

R. W. Seller, *"philosophy is persistent attempt to gain insight into the nature of the world and of ourselves by means of systematic reflections"*.

Of these definitions some emphasize the critical aspect of philosophy, while others lay emphasis upon its synthetic aspect. Some examples of these two types of definitions of philosophy are as follows:

I. Philosophy is a critical method of approaching experience.
- Edgar S. Brightman, *"Philosophy is essentially a spirit or method of approaching experience rather than a body of conclusions about experience"*.
- Duccase,*"Where I limited to one line of my answer to it, I should say that philosophy is general theory of criticism"*.

II. Philosophy is a comprehensive synthetic science.
- Leighton,*"Philosophy, like science, consists of insights arrived at as a result of systematic reflection"*.
- Herbert Spencer, *"Philosophy is concerned with everything as a universal science"*.

There are "eight" consensus definitions of philosophy. These should be consulted whenever the need to define philosophy arises. They are;

1. Philosophy as the Love of Wisdom: This definition represents the etymological definition of philosophy. Philosophy was formed from the two Greek words of *"Philein"* and *"Sophia"*. The former means *"love"* while the latter means *"wisdom"*; so together, they construct the etymology of philosophy, *"love of wisdom"*. However, it is noteworthy to emphasize that this definition of philosophy which is the most appropriate of all, was coined by *"Pythagoras"*, a pre-Socratic philosopher who postulated *"numbers"* as the unifying principle of the universe. This definition expresses the craving and desire of the philosopher to want to discover the right application of knowledge.

2. *Philosophy as the Search for Reality*: This definition draws its potency from, and is related to *"metaphysics"*- a major branch of philosophy. It emphasizes the role of the philosopher in discovering the principles of life and existence, as well as transcendence i.e., going beyond the natural.

3. *Philosophy as the Search for Truth*: This definition is the representation of *"epistemology"* in philosophy as one of its main branches. It emphasizes the continuous drive of the philosopher in his quest for knowledge and truth; as well as the principles and presuppositions guiding their operation.

4. *Philosophy as the Search for Value or the Best Forms of Life*: This definition falls within the domain of *"ethics"*— the third major branch of philosophy. It shows what the moral philosopher aims at achieving within human society and how he intends to create stability in an unstable world.

5. *Philosophy as the Rational Study of Nature*: This definition is an emphasis on the cosmological speculation by the pre-Socratic philosophers of ancient Greek tradition. This very act of propounding what the primordial substance or unifying principle of the universe could be, was what pioneered the dawn of the philosophical enterprise in about 600 B.C. by Thales.

6. *Philosophy as the Critical Discussion of Received Ideas*: This definition which represents *"dialectical argumentation"* as a major part of the nature of philosophy was introduced by "Plato"- a contemporary of Socrates. Together, dialectics is an important concept in both their philosophies; the act of question and answer that is rigorous and critical. This was their way of discovering deep rooted truths. This definition appraises "logic" as a tool of philosophy.

7. *Philosophy as the Concern with the Problems of Human Existence*: This definition is an expression of the effort of philosophers in their journey of wanting to transform and change the world, by solving the numerous problems of human existence. They try to do this by prescribing norms and viable theories, which when applied, are positioned in the direction of changing the world positively; thus, solving the problems of existence. "Karl Marx" is an advocate of this philosophical definition.

8. *Philosophy as a Reflection on Human Experience*: This definition which is very relevant and prominent in ancient Chinese and Indian philosophies, asserts the fact that one's life experiences will invariably affect one's philosophy about life. A turbulent life experience like poverty, for example, will tend to make one advocate ideologies that can curb such, in people's lives in general.

1.4. Nature of Philosophy

The literal meaning of Philosophy is the *'love of wisdom'* and it enquires into the human reality finding rational conception of our being. The nature of philosophy can be said to be purely scientific as it incorporates curious discovery of human reality and integrates with other sciences like Psychology, Sociology, Physics, Political Science, amongst others to understand various philosophical questions. Through the 6 branches of Philosophy, i.e., Metaphysics, Epistemology, Logic, Ethics, Political Philosophy and Aesthetics, it sets out to harmonize sciences to understand the human mind and the world.

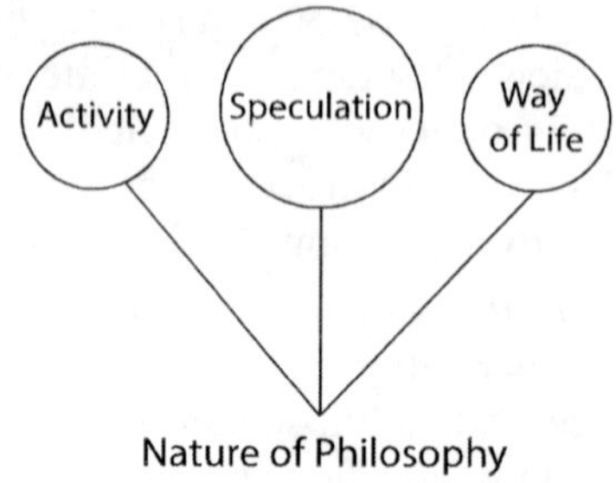

Figure 1.1 *Nature of Philosophy*

Nature of philosophy is discussed below:

1. Philosophy as an Activity: Levison states that "philosophy is first of all an activity of a certain kind and only secondarily a subject matter consisting of definite body of literature." In its real sense, philosophy is a mental activity, involving the problems of human life, its nature and purpose.

2. Philosophy as Speculation: Since the earliest of recorded history, individuals have speculated about the nature of reality and of meaning of life itself. In doing so, these persons have dealt with one of the most basic but also most pervasive concerns of human existence. The history of philosophy records the efforts of ancient Indian thinkers like the vedic seers and sages, Sankara, Aristotle, Locke, Kant, Dewey and others. These philosophers and many others have speculated about the nature of reality. When they recounted or recorded their speculations, they attempted to describe the nature of reality. Based upon their insight into reality, philosophers have also sought to prescribe values and ideals.

3. Philosophy as a way of Life: The derivation of the word states that philosophy means love of wisdom. Wisdom is regarded as knowledge for the conduct of life and philosophy is valued as a way of life. Everyone in his life thinks about the existence, about nature of world, God, his relation to his environment of things and people. During the course he develops genuine philosophy of life and tries to live in accordance with it. Thus, philosophy becomes a way of life.

1.5. Scope of Philosophy

The general scope of philosophy is very vast. Within its scope, we discuss soul, God, mystic powers, the origin of the universe, its expansion and development, truth, morality, aesthetics and logic. The subject Philosophy can be divided into three major divisions and these three major divisions of philosophy are particularly important in the various aspects of education.

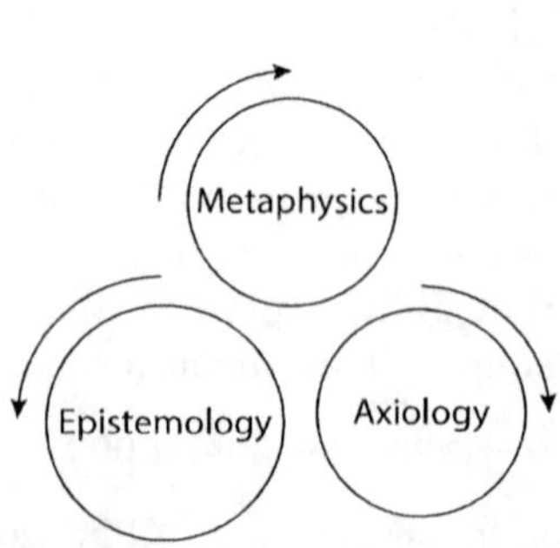

Figure 1.2 *Scope of Philosophy*

1. Metaphysics: Metaphysics is that branch of philosophy, which deals with the nature of reality. Metaphysics tries to answer the question, "What is real?" The purpose of education is to explain 'reality' to the students. Is there a purpose in life? Does life have a meaning? Is there a set of enduring principles that guide the operation of the universe?" etc. It was Aristotle who developed the study of Metaphysics.

2. *Epistemology*: Whereas metaphysics is concerned with the nature of reality, Epistemology focuses on our knowledge of this reality. Epistemology deals with the theory concerning the various aspects of knowledge and its acquisition. Epistemology tries to answer, "How do we get knowledge? How does a man know what is real? Knowledge is of different types – revealed knowledge (revelation), intuitive knowledge (intuition), empirical knowledge (experience), rational knowledge (reason) and authoritative knowledge (authority sources).

3. *Axiology*: Axiology is that branch of Philosophy, which is concerned with values. It is an attempt to discover and recommend principles for deciding what actions and qualities are most worthwhile and why they are so. Axiology has two major sub divisions – Ethics and Aesthetics. Ethics is concerned with good and bad, right and wrong and approval and disapproval as well as virtue and vice. Aesthetics is inquiry into the nature of what is beautiful or ugly and why it is so. Axiology is the source of the aim of education. All education and all form of schooling are integrated with values of life. Consciously or unconsciously, teachers are agents of value development and transmission.

1.6. Branches of Philosophy

Western philosophy can be divided into six branches that have assumed various importance over time. These branches of philosophy are discussed below:

1.6.1. Metaphysics

Metaphysics can be defined as the study of *"ultimate reality"* in all ramifications. Its etymology as a word was coined from the Greek phrase *"meta-ta-physika"* meaning *"beyond the physical"*; and it was done by "Andronicus of Rhodes"- a student of Aristotle. Metaphysics is further subdivided into three arms, which are:

- *Ontology*: the study of being (being qua being)
- *Cosmology*: the study of the nature of the universe
- *Cosmogony*: the study of the origin of the universe

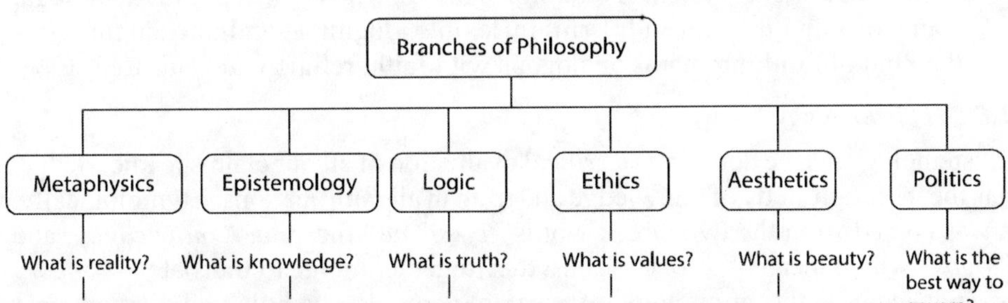

Figure 1.3 *Mind Map of Branches of Philosophy*

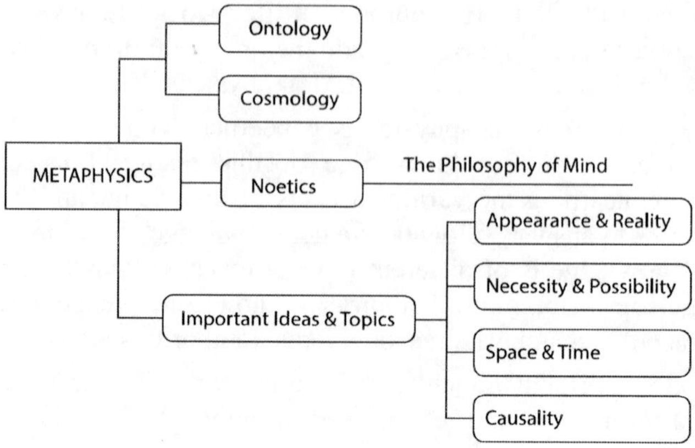

Figure 1.4 *Mind Map of Metaphysics*

Furthermore, metaphysics has two major schools of thought, which are:

- *Idealism*: This school postulates that reality is intrinsically ideal, spiritual, abstract, and the likes. Philosophers of this school are called "idealists"; e.g. Parmenides.
- *Materialism*: This school postulates that reality is intrinsically material, physical, concrete, and the likes. Philosophers of this school are called "materialists"; e.g. Democritus.

In addition, there are the concepts of "being metaphysical" "being a metaphysician"; as well as "traditional metaphysical thinking".

- *Being Metaphysical*: One is said to be "metaphysical" when one examines the past, analyses the present and uses such idea to speculate or predict the future.
- *Being a Metaphysician*: A metaphysician is a philosopher who adopts either the idealist or materialist orientation, and then uses it to express his views about the universe. For example, Hegel is a metaphysician of the idealist orientation while Karl Marx is a metaphysician of the materialist orientation.
- *Traditional Metaphysical Thinking*: This is when one upholds a thought frame of mind that is rigid, firm, inflexible, dogmatic and unchanging. It is the kind of thinking that is analogous with faith, religion and culture.

1.6.2. Epistemology

Epistemology can be defined as a critical evaluation of all our claims to knowledge. It is the thorough study of knowledge and truth in all ramifications. Etymologically, it was coined from the two Greek words *"episteme"* meaning *"knowledge"*, and *"logos"* which means *"theory"*. Thus, they together merge to translate as *"theory of knowledge"*- the etymology of epistemology. Epistemology has two main schools of thought which are:

i. *Rationalism*: This school postulates that knowledge is acquired via reasoning (the mind) alone. Hence, it upholds "a priori knowledge"- knowledge via reasoning and perception by the mind as the standard form of knowledge. Philosophers of this school are called "rationalists"; e.g. Plato.
ii. *Empiricism*: This school postulates that knowledge is the product of the senses (five senses) alone. Thus, it upholds "empirical knowledge" and "a posteriori knowledge"- knowledge obtained through sense perception and experience respectively as the ideal form of knowledge. Philosophers of this school are called "empiricists"; e.g. Aristotle.

Also, there are some other schools of thought in epistemology, like:

- *Scepticism*: This school of thought plays a very major role in the advancement of epistemology due to its nature and vocation. Scepticism postulates that nothing can be known at all, and knowledge is impossibility. The two brands of scepticism are; "universal scepticism"- knowledge is impossible; and "mitigated scepticism"- knowledge is partially possible. Philosophers of this school are called "sceptics"; e.g. Gorgias, Pyrrhoe.t.c.
- *Relativism*: This school of thought says that knowledge is a function of the individual; and that the individual is the standard for knowledge. Philosophers of this school are called "relativists". For example; Protagoras whom postulated the philosophical dictum "homo mensura" meaning, man is the measure (determinant) of all things.

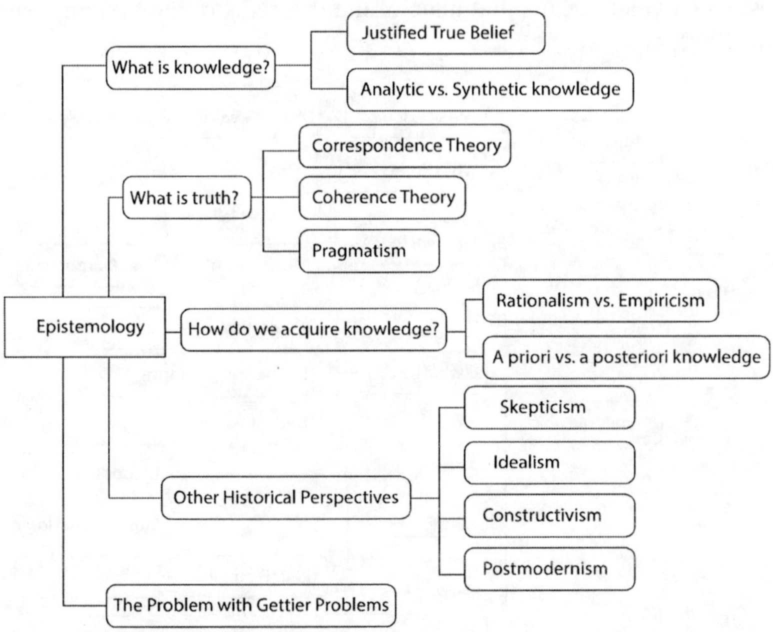

Figure 1.5 *Mind Map of Epistemology*

In addition, we have some important concepts that matter a lot in epistemology, such as:

- *Universals*: This represents the essences and intrinsic nature of beings which are general and objective of their particular individual members. There are three brands of universals, which are exaggerated realism, moderate realism and nominalism.
- *Abstraction*: This is the mental act of stripping individual and particular beings of their specific traits and then extracting their essences (universals).

1.6.3. Logic

Logic (from the Greek "logos", which has a variety of meanings including word, thought, idea, argument, account, reason or principle) is the study of reasoning, or the study of the principles and criteria of valid inference and demonstration. It attempts to distinguish good reasoning from bad reasoning. Aristotle defined logic as *"new and necessary reasoning"*, "new" because it allows us to learn what we do not know, and "necessary" because its conclusions are inescapable. It asks questions like "What is correct reasoning?", "What distinguishes a good argument from a bad one?", "How can we detect a fallacy in reasoning?"

Logic investigates and classifies the structure of statements and arguments, both through the study of formal systems of inference and through the study of arguments in natural language.

Logical systems should have three things:

i. consistency (which means that none of the theorems of the system contradict one another);

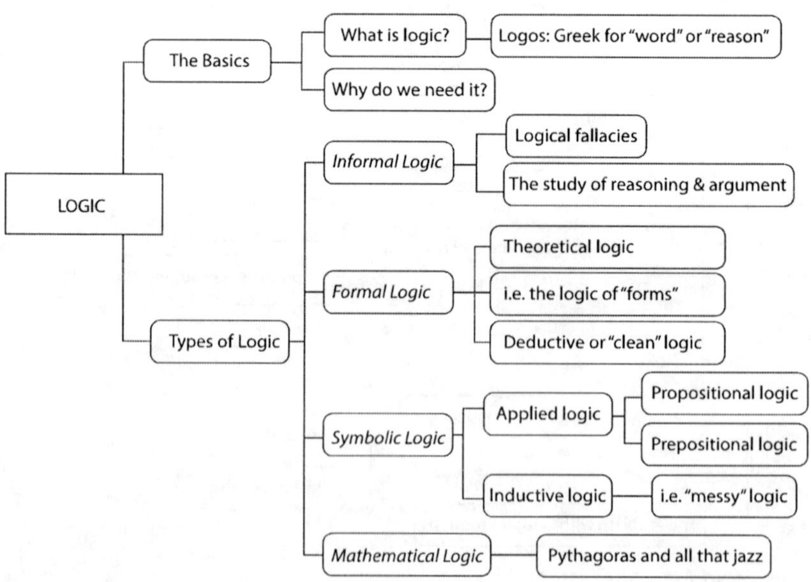

Figure 1.6 *Mind Map of Logic*

ii. soundness (which means that the system's rules of proof will never allow a false inference from a true premise); and
iii. completeness (which means that there are no true sentences in the system that cannot, at least in principle, be proved in the system).

1.6.3.1. Types of Logic

Logic can be divided into:

1. Formal Logic: Formal Logic is what we think of as traditional logic or philosophical logic, namely the study of inference with purely formal and explicit content (i.e., it can be expressed as a particular application of a wholly abstract rule), such as the rules of formal logic that have come down to us from Aristotle.

2. Informal Logic: Informal Logic is a recent discipline which studies natural language arguments, and attempts to develop a logic to assess, analyze and improve ordinary language (or "everyday") reasoning.

3. Symbolic Logic: Symbolic Logic is the study of symbolic abstractions that capture the formal features of logical inference. It deals with the relations of symbols to each other, often using complex mathematical calculus, in an attempt to solve intractable problems traditional formal logic is not able to address.

It is often divided into two sub-branches:

- Predicate Logic: a system in which formulae contain quantifiable variables.
- Propositional Logic (or Sentential Logic): a system in which formulae representing propositions can be formed by combining atomic propositions using logical connectives, and a system of formal proof rules allows certain formulae to be established as theorems.

4. Mathematical Logic: Both the application of the techniques of formal logic to mathematics and mathematical reasoning, and, conversely, the application of mathematical techniques to the representation and analysis of formal logic.

The earliest use of mathematics and geometry in relation to logic and philosophy goes back to the Ancient Greeks such as Euclid, Plato and Aristotle. Mathematics-related doctrines include:

- Logicism: perhaps the boldest attempt to apply logic to mathematics, pioneered by philosopher-logicians such as Gottlob Frege and Bertrand Russell, especially the application of mathematics to logic in the form of proof theory, model theory, set theory and recursion theory.
- Intuitionism: the doctrine which holds that logic and mathematics does not consist of analytic activities wherein deep properties of existence are revealed and applied, but merely the application of internally consistent methods to realize more complex mental constructs.

5. Deductive Logic: Deductive reasoning concerns what follows necessarily from given premises (i.e., from a general premise to a particular one). An inference is deductively valid if (and only if) there is no possible situation in which all the premises are true and the conclusion false. However, it should be remembered that a false premise can possibly lead to a false conclusion.

Deductive reasoning was developed by Aristotle, Thales, Pythagoras and other Greek philosophers of the Classical Period. At the core of deductive reasoning is the syllogism (also known as term logic), usually attributed to Aristotle), where one proposition (the conclusion) is inferred from two others (the premises), each of which has one term in common with the conclusion. For example:

> Major premise: *All humans are mortal.*
> Minor premise: *Socrates is human.*
> Conclusion: *Socrates is mortal.*
>
> An example of deduction is:
> *All apples are fruit.*
> *All fruits grow on trees.*
> *Therefore, all apples grow on trees.*

6. Inductive Logic: Inductive reasoning is the process of deriving a reliable generalization from observations (i.e., from the particular to the general), so that the premises of an argument are believed to support the conclusion, but do not necessarily ensure it.

Many philosophers, including David Hume, Karl Popper and David Miller, have disputed or denied the logical admissibility of inductive reasoning. In particular, Hume argued that it requires inductive reasoning to arrive at the premises for the principle of inductive reasoning, and therefore the justification for inductive reasoning is a circular argument.

An example of *strong induction* (an argument in which the truth of the premise would make the truth of the conclusion probable but not definite) is:

> *All observed crows are black.*
> Therefore:
> *All crows are black.*

An example of *weak induction* (an argument in which the link between the premise and the conclusion is weak, and the conclusion is not even necessarily probable) is:

> *I always hang pictures on nails.*
> Therefore:
> *All pictures hang from nails.*

7. Modal Logic: Modal Logic is any system of formal logic that attempts to deal with modalities (expressions associated with notions of possibility, probability and necessity). Modal Logic, therefore, deals with terms such as "eventually", "formerly", "possibly", "can", "could", "might", "may", "must", etc.

Modalities are ways in which propositions can be true or false. Types of modality include:

- Alethic Modalities: Includes possibility and necessity, as well as impossibility and contingency. Some propositions are impossible (necessarily false), whereas others are contingent (both possibly true and possibly false).
- Temporal Modalities: Historical and future truth or falsity. Some propositions were true/false in the past and others will be true/false in the future.
- Deontic Modalities: Obligation and permissibility. Some propositions ought to be true/false, while others are permissible.
- Epistemic Modalities: Knowledge and belief. Some propositions are known to be true/false, and others are believed to be true/false.

8. Propositional Logic: Propositional Logic (or Sentential Logic) is concerned only with sentential connectives and logical operators (such as "and", "or", "not", "if ... then ...", "because" and "necessarily"), as opposed to Predicate Logic (see below), which also concerns itself with the internal structure of atomic propositions.

9. Predicate Logic: Predicate Logic allows sentences to be analyzed into subject and argument in several different ways, unlike Aristotelian syllogistic logic, where the forms that the relevant part of the involved judgments took must be specified and limited (see the section on Deductive Logic above). Predicate Logic is also able to give an account of quantifiers general enough to express all arguments occurring in natural language, thus allowing the solution of the problem of multiple generality that had perplexed medieval logicians.

For instance, it is intuitively clear that if:

Some cat is feared by every mouse then it follows logically that: *All mice are afraid of at least one cat*

But, because the sentences above each contain two quantifiers ('some' and 'every' in the first sentence and 'all' and 'at least one' in the second sentence), they cannot be adequately represented in traditional logic.

Predicate Logic was initially developed by Gottlob Frege and Charles Peirce in the late 19th Century, but it reached full fruition in the Logical Atomism of Whitehead and Russell in the 20th Century (developed out of earlier work by Ludwig Wittgenstein).

10. Fallacies: A logical fallacy is any sort of mistake in reasoning or inference, or, essentially, anything that causes an argument to go wrong. There are two main categories of fallacy, Fallacies of Ambiguity and Contextual Fallacies:

- *Fallacies of Ambiguity*: a term is ambiguous if it has more than one meaning. There are two main types:
    - i. *equivocation*: where a single word can be used in two different senses.
    - ii. *amphiboly*: where the ambiguity arises due to sentence structure (often due to dangling participles or the inexact use of negatives), rather than the meaning of individual words.

- *Contextual Fallacies*: which depend on the context or circumstances in which sentences are used. There are many different types, among the more common of which are:
    - *i.* *Fallacies of Significance*: where it is unclear whether an assertion is significant or not.
    - *ii.* *Fallacies of Emphasis*: the incorrect emphasis of words in a sentence.
    - *iii.* *Fallacies of Quoting Out of Context*: the manipulation of the context of a quotation.
    - *iv.* *Fallacies of Argumentum ad Hominem*: a statement cannot be shown to be false merely because the individual who makes it can be shown to be of defective character.
    - *v.* *Fallacies of Arguing from Authority*: truth or falsity cannot be proven merely because the person saying it is considered an "authority" on the subject.
    - *vi.* *Fallacies of Arguments which Appeal to Sentiments*: reporting how people feel about something in order to persuade rather than prove.
    - *vii.* *Fallacies of Argument from Ignorance*: a statement cannot be proved true just because there is no evidence to disprove it.
    - *viii.* *Fallacies of Begging the Question*: a circular argument, where effectively the same statement is used both as a premise and as a conclusion.
    - *ix.* *Fallacies of Composition*: the assumption that what is true of a part is also true of the whole.
    - *x.* *Fallacies of Division*: the converse assumption that what is true of a whole must be also true of all of its parts.
    - *xi.* *Fallacies of Irrelevant Conclusion*: where the conclusion concerns something other than what the argument was initially trying to prove.
    - *xii.* *Fallacies of Non-Sequitur*: an argumentative leap, where the conclusion does not necessarily follow from the premises.
    - *xiii.* *Fallacies of Statistics*: statistics can be manipulated and biased to "prove" many different hypotheses.

11. Paradoxes: A paradox is a statement or sentiment that is seemingly contradictory or opposed to common sense and yet is perhaps true in fact. Conversely, a paradox may be a statement that is actually self-contradictory (and therefore false) even though it appears true. Typically, either the statements in question do not really imply the contradiction, the puzzling result is not really a contradiction, or the premises themselves are not all really true or cannot all be true together.

It can be argued that there are four classes of paradoxes:

- *Veridical Paradoxes*: which produce a result that appears absurd but can be demonstrated to be nevertheless true.
- *Falsidical Paradoxes*: which produce a result that not only appears false but actually is false.
- *Antinomies*: which are neither veridical nor falsidical, but produce a self-contradictory result by properly applying accepted ways of reasoning.
- *Dialetheias*: which produce a result which is both true and false at the same time and in the same sense.

1.6.4. Ethics

Ethics which is also known as moral philosophy is a normative and prescriptive discipline which is concerned with the justification of the principles of morality. This is because it is concerned with what "ought" to be the case as regards the implementation of morality and its codes. Ethics has several definitions, but the most accepted one is, ethics is, *"the normative science of human conduct"*. Its etymology is gotten from the Greek words *"Ethika"*- morals; and *"Ethos"*- custom. Ethics has two main branches, which are highlighted thus:

1. Meta-Ethics: This is the branch of ethics which deals with the analysis and clarification of ethical terms such as "good", "bad", "virtue", "vice", "justice" and so on. The major challenge in meta-ethics is the question of "how do we come to know a good or bad action"? In this regard, four meta-ethical theories have sprung up in order to solve this problem, which are; Naturalism, Anti-naturalism, Emotivism, Prescriptivism.

2. Normative Ethics: This branch of ethics is at its very core. This is because it basically deals with the norms, principles and standards of human behaviour. The major challenge in normative ethics, is the question of, "what is the moral standard"? In this regard, eight platforms which are assumed to be the solution (the moral standard), whether individually or collectively, have been proposed, they are; Social custom, Law, Revelation, Conscience, Pleasure, Universalizability, Intuition, Right Reason.

1.6.4.1. Ethical School of Thoughts

Furthermore, ethics has several schools of thought and concepts. However, only a few would be highlighted, thus:

Utilitarianism: This ethical school of thought advocates the dictum of "the greatest happiness for the greatest number". Hence, for something to be seen as morally good, it must be in favour and benefit of the largest number of people. E.g., if a mall has been hijacked by an armed man, and all it takes to save the people is a face to face struggle by a judo black belter; the judoka must do it even if it means that he would die alongside the hijacker. At least everyone, except him, would be saved. The proponents of this school are "Jeremy Bentham" and "John Stuart Mill".

Hedonism: This ethical school of thought advocates "pleasure" as the moral standard. Hence, any and everything which gives pleasure is morally good. In simpler words, actions that would inadvertently lead to pain are morally bad while those that would give pleasure in the long run are morally good. "Epicurus" is a proponent of this school.

Egoism: This ethical school of thought says that every action which is perpetuated by man is done out of selfish desires. Hence, anything done by man is done, due to the fact that he knows that he is going to benefit from it either directly or indirectly in the future.

Intuitionism: This ethical school of thought postulates that moral goodness cannot be explained, but only can be recognised in things and it is through

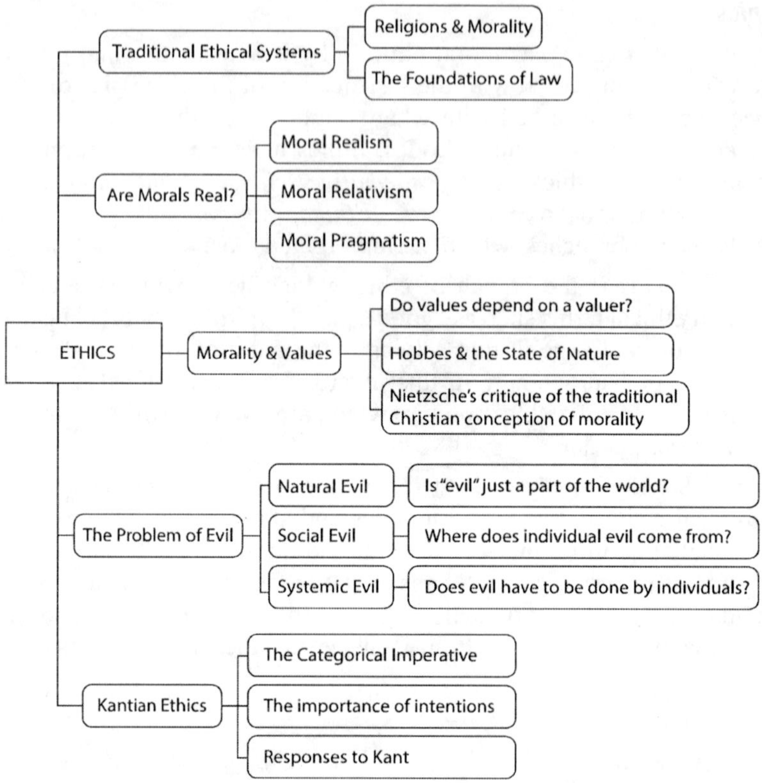

Figure 1.7 *Mind Map of Ethics*

"intuition" that we can recognise moral goodness. A proponent of this school is George Edward Moore.

1.6.5. Aesthetics

Aesthetics is the branch of philosophy concerned with the nature and appreciation of art, beauty and good taste. It has also been defined as *"critical reflection on art, culture and nature"*. The word *"aesthetics"* derives from the Greek *"aisthetikos"*, meaning *"of sense perception"*. Along with Ethics, aesthetics is part of axiology (the study of values and value judgments).

In practice, we distinguish between aesthetic judgments (the appreciation of any object, not necessarily an art object) and artistic judgments (the appreciation or criticism of a work of art). Thus, aesthetics is broader in scope than the philosophy of art. It is also broader than the philosophy of beauty, in that it applies to any of the responses we might expect works of art or entertainment to elicit, whether positive or negative.

Aestheticians ask questions like *"What is a work of art?"*, *"What makes a work of art successful?"*, *"Why do we find certain things beautiful?"*, *"How can things of very different categories be considered equally beautiful?"*, *"Is there a*

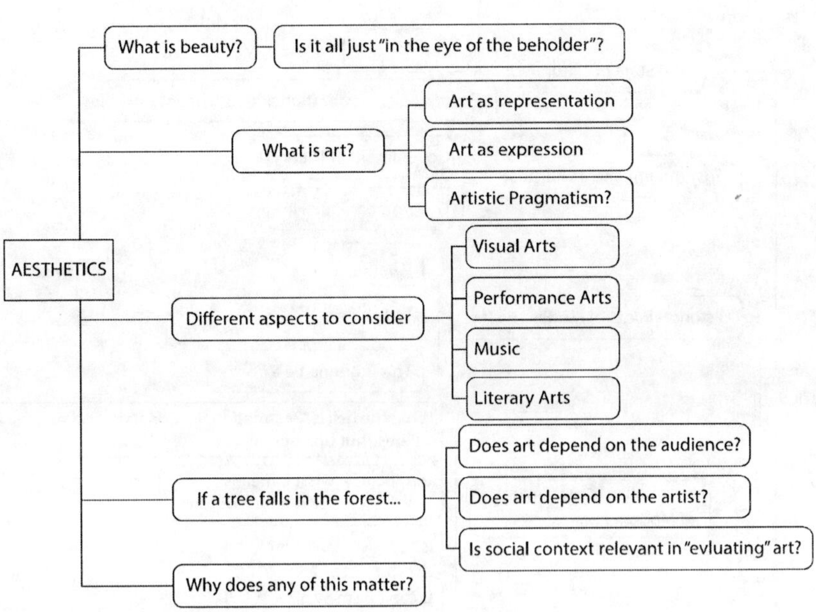

Figure 1.8 *Mind Map of Aesthetics*

connection between art and morality?", "Can art be a vehicle of truth?", "Are aesthetic judgments objective statements or purely subjective expressions of personal attitudes?", "Can aesthetic judgments be improved or trained?"

In very general terms, it examines what makes something beautiful, sublime, disgusting, fun, cute, silly, entertaining, pretentious, discordant, harmonious, boring, humorous or tragic.

1.6.6. Politics or Political Philosophy

Combining the two fields of Politics and Philosophy, Political Philosophy studies political government, laws, liberty, justice, rights, authority, political states and systems, ethics, and more. It explores the concepts of why we need governments, the role of played by governments, what are its constituents, amongst others.

Political philosophy is the study of fundamental questions about the state, government, politics, liberty, justice and the enforcement of a legal code by authority. It is Ethics applied to a group of people, and discusses how a society should be set up and how one should act within a society. Individual rights (such as the right to life, liberty, property, the pursuit of happiness, free speech, self-defense, etc.) state explicitly the requirements for a person to benefit rather than suffer from living in a society.

Political philosophy asks questions like: *"What is a government?", "Why are governments needed?", "What makes a government legitimate?", "What rights and freedoms should a government protect?", "What duties do citizens owe to a legitimate government, if any?" and "When may a government be legitimately overthrown, if ever?"*

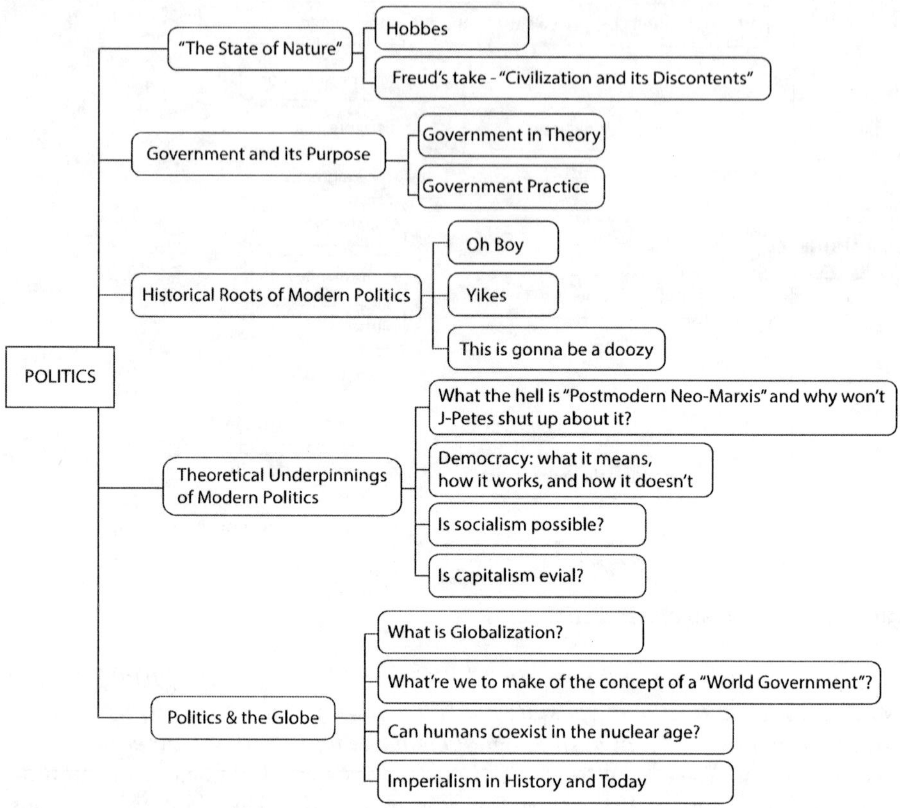

Figure 1.9 *Mind Map of Politics*

1.6.7. Political Schools of Thought

Major school of thoughts of Political Philosophy include:

- Anarchism
- Capitalism
- Communism
- Communitarianism
- Conservatism
- Contractarianism
- Egalitarianism
- Fascism
- Feminism
- Liberalism
- Libertarianism
- Marxism
- Nationalism
- Socialism
- Totalitarianism

1.7. Why Study Philosophy

- Philosophy imparts skills that will be valued by any future employer.
- Philosophy enhances our problem-solving capacities by contributing to our ability to organize ideas and issues, and to extract what is essential from masses of information.
- Philosophy help us to distinguish between different viewpoints and to discover common ground among them.
- Philosophy help us to appreciate a variety of perspectives so they can be synthesized into a unified whole.

- Philosophy helps to eliminate ambiguities and vagueness from your speech, and enables us to present what is distinctive about our position through the use of systematic argumentation.
- Philosophy develops our ability to explain and communicate difficult material.
- Philosophy enhances our persuasive powers by providing training in the construction of clear formulations, good arguments, and apt examples that allow us to forcefully articulate and defend our points of view.
- Philosophy teaches good interpretive, comparative, argumentative, and descriptive writing skills that will allow us to communicate ideas in a clear and powerful way.
- Philosophy is uniquely well-suited to preparing students for law school.
- Philosophy teaches us to think analytically, to write and speak clearly and persuasively, to evaluate evidence, to construct and present sound arguments, to recognize flaws in opposing arguments, and to have a deep sense of justice—skills which are essential to the legal profession.
- Philosophy is one of the best ways into graduate or medical school.
- Philosophy's lessons of analytical thinking, clear expression, and good writing are indispensable to the graduate student in any discipline.
- Philosophy's lessons of the rational evaluation of evidence, analytical problem-solving, isolating the essential elements from complex bodies of data, and thinking in a holistic manner are skills essential to anyone entering the medical profession.
- Philosophy's critical skills offer the best defense against foolishness and falsehoods.
- Philosophy allows us to see through cultural and intellectual fads.
- Philosophy protects us from the often empty posturing of politicians.
- Philosophy insulates us from the often inane prattling of media pundits and commentators.
- Philosophy defends us from the slippery claims of advertisers and salespeople.
- Philosophy protects us from foolish opinions and everyday nonsense.
- Philosophy is one of the best ways of enriching our life, even as it prepare us for life.
- Philosophy broadens the range of things that we can understand and enjoy.
- Philosophy makes a substantial contribution to our expressive powers.
- Philosophy enhances our self-knowledge, foresight, and sense of direction in life.
- Philosophy provides special pleasures of insight to our reading and conversation.
- Philosophy can lead to self-discovery, an expansion of consciousness, and self-renewal.
- Philosophy nurtures individuality and self-esteem.
- Philosophy brings us into contact with the most important and fundamental human questions.
- Philosophy helps us to live a more fully human life by demanding that us confront these questions.

2

Introduction to Research

Research is defined as the creation of new knowledge and/or the use of existing knowledge in a new and creative way so as to generate new concepts, methodologies and understandings. This could include synthesis and analysis of previous research to the extent that it leads to new and creative outcomes. Some people consider research as a movement, a movement from known to unknown. It is actually a voyage of discovery. Research is a careful investigation or inquiry specifically through a search for new facts in any branch of knowledge. It is an original contribution to the existing knowledge making for its advancement.

Research begins when we want to know something. Research is concerned with increasing our understanding. Research is a systematic investigation of a subject in order to find something new. Research is the collection and evaluation of information about a particular subject. The overarching purpose of research is to answer questions and generate new knowledge. Research is a systematic inquiry to describe, explain, predict and control the observed phenomenon. Research is a process to discover new knowledge.

2.1. What is Research?

Simply put, research is the process of discovering new knowledge. This knowledge can be either the development of new concepts or the advancement of existing knowledge and theories, leading to a new understanding that was not previously known. A formal definition of research is *"Research is a systematic investigation (i.e., the gathering and analysis of information) designed to develop or contribute to generalizable knowledge"*

The word *"research"* originated from the old French word *"recerchier"* meaning to search and search again. It literally implies repeating a search for something and implicitly assumes that the earlier search was not exhaustive and complete in the sense that there is still scope for improvement. Research in common parlance refers to a search for knowledge. It may be defined as a scientific and systematic search for pertinent information on a specific topic/area. In fact, research is an art of scientific investigation.

2.2. Definitions of Research

Research can be defined as:

1. According to Cambridge Advanced Learner's Dictionary, *"Research is a detailed study of a subject, especially in order to discover (new) information or reach a (new) understanding"*

2. According to Dictionary reference.com, *"Research is a diligent and systematic inquiry or investigation into a subject in order to discover or revise facts, theories, applications, etc."*
3. According to Merriam-Webster's Online Dictionary, *"Research is a studious inquiry or examination; especially: investigation or experimentation aimed at the discovery and interpretation of facts, revision of accepted theories or laws in the light of new facts, or practical application of such new or revised theories or laws."*
4. According to Advanced Learner's Dictionary, *"Research is a careful investigation or inquiry especially through search for new facts in any branch of knowledge."*
5. According to Redman and Mory, *"Research is a systematized effort to gain new knowledge."*
6. According to Clifford Woody, *"Research comprises defining and redefining problems, formulating hypothesis or suggested solutions; collecting, organising and evaluating data; making deductions and reaching conclusions; and at last carefully testing the conclusions to determine whether they fit the formulating hypothesis."*
7. According to Coombes, *"Research is a tool for getting you from point A to point B. You wish to prove an idea – research it. You wish to disprove an idea – research it. You think that fact ABC is incorrect – research it, or that fact ABC is correct – research it. Research is simply a method for investigating and collecting information".*
8. According to Gina Wisker, *"Research is about asking and beginning to answer questions, seeking knowledge and understanding of the world and its processes, and testing assumptions and beliefs."*
9. Research can be defined as, *"A systematic investigation (i.e., the gathering and analysis of information) designed to develop or contribute to generalizable knowledge."*
10. Research is to, *"extend human knowledge of the physical, biological, or social world beyond what is already known."*
11. The Advanced Learner's Dictionary of Current English lays down the meaning of research as *"a careful investigation or inquiry especially through search for new facts in any branch of knowledge".*
12. According to the American sociologist Earl Robert Babbie, *"Research is a systematic inquiry to describe, explain, predict, and control the observed phenomenon. Research involves inductive and deductive methods."*

2.3. Why to Do Research?

Research is used to find things out, reaffirm the results of previous work, solve new or existing problems, support existing theories or develop new theories. A research may also be an expansion on previous work in the field. In order to test the validity of instruments, procedures, or experiments, research may replicate elements of prior research. The primary purposes of research are: documentation, discovery and interpretation or the research and development of methods and systems for the advancement of knowledge. Research has one fundamental characteristic i.e. it uses scientific methods to produce evidence and results. It does this by following rules, so that findings do not depend upon the personal views of the researchers.

The purpose of research is to:

- Review or synthesize existing knowledge;
- Investigate existing situations or problems;
- Provide solutions to problems;
- Explore and analyze general issues;
- Construct or create new procedures or systems;
- Explain new phenomena;
- Generate new knowledge or
- a combination of any of the above.

2.4. Process of Scientific Research

Scientific knowledge is advanced through a process known as the scientific method. Basically, ideas (in the form of theories and hypotheses) are tested against the real world (in the form of empirical observations), and those observations lead to more ideas that are tested against the real world, and so on. In this sense, the scientific process is circular. We continually test and revise theories based on new evidence.

Two types of reasoning are used to make decisions within this model: Inductive and Deductive.

1. Inductive Reasoning: In inductive reasoning, we go from the specific to the general. We make many observations, discern a pattern, make a generalization and infer an explanation or a theory.

2. Deductive Reasoning: In deductive reasoning, we go from the general - the theory- to the specific - the observations. Deductive reasoning starts out with a general statement or hypothesis and examines the possibilities to reach a specific logical conclusion.

These processes (Inductive & Deductive Reasoning) are inseparable, like inhaling and exhaling, but different research approaches place different emphasis on the deductive and inductive aspects.

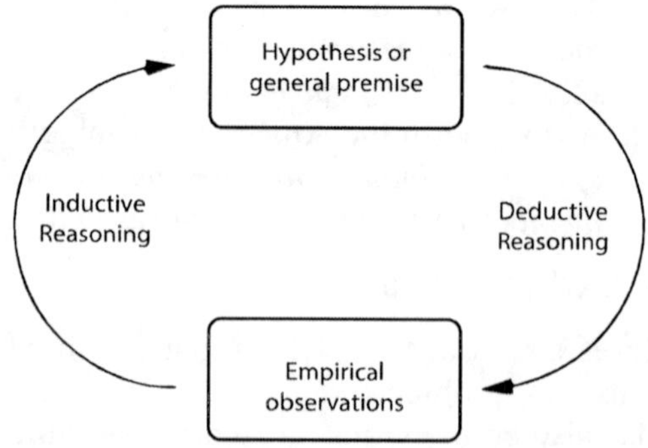

Figure 2.1 *Research Relies on Both Inductive and Deductive Reasoning*

2.5. Scientific Method

Research is different than other forms of discovering knowledge because it uses a systematic process called the Scientific Method. The scientific method consists of observing the world around us and creating a hypothesis about relationships in the

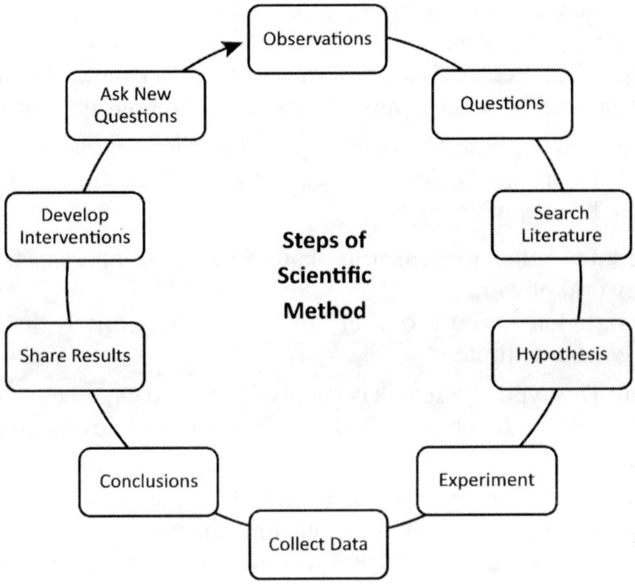

Figure 2.2 *Steps of Scientific Method*

world. A hypothesis is an informed and educated prediction or explanation about something. Part of the research process involves testing the hypothesis and then examining the results of these tests as they relate to both the hypothesis and the world around us. When a researcher forms a hypothesis, these acts like a map through the research study. It tells the researcher which factors are important to study and how they might be related to each other or caused by a manipulation that the researcher introduces (e.g., a program, treatment or change in the environment). With this map, the researcher can interpret the information he/she collects and can make sound conclusions about the results.

Research can be done with human beings, animals, plants, other organisms and inorganic matter. In short, the term 'Research' refers to *"the systematic method consisting of defining the problem, formulating a hypothesis, collecting the facts or data, analyzing the facts and reaching certain conclusions either in the form of solution(s) towards the concerned problem or in certain generalizations for some theoretical framework."*

2.6. Types of Knowledge Contributed by Research

Gall, Borg and Gall (1996) proposed four types of knowledge that research contributed to education as follows:

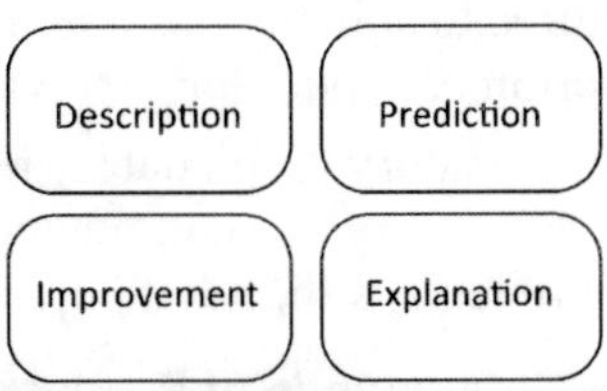

Figure 2.3 *Types of Knowledge Contributed by Research*

1. Description: Results of research can describe natural or social phenomenon, such as its

form, structure, activity, change over time, relationship to other phenomena. The descriptive function of research relies on instrumentation for measurement and observations. The descriptive research results in our understanding of what happened. It sometimes produces statistical information about aspects of education.

2. Prediction: Prediction research is intended to predict a phenomenon that will occur at time Y from information at an earlier time X. In educational research, researchers have been engaged in:

- Acquiring knowledge about factors that predict students' success in school and in the world of work
- Identifying students who are likely to be unsuccessful so that prevention programs can be instituted.

3. Improvement: This type of research is mainly concerned with the effectiveness of intervention. The research approach includes experimental design and evaluation research.

4. Explanation: This type of research subsumes the other three: if the researchers are able to explain an educational phenomenon, it means that they can describe, can predict its consequences, and know how to intervene to change those consequences.

2.7. Purpose of Research

There are three purposes of research:

1. Exploratory: As the name suggests, exploratory research is conducted to explore a group of questions. The answers and analytics may not offer a final conclusion to the perceived problem. It is conducted to handle new problem areas which haven't been explored before. This exploratory process lays the foundation for more conclusive research and data collection.

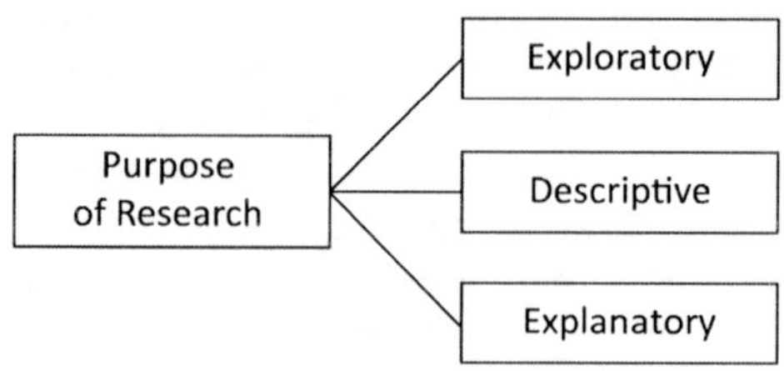

Figure 2.4 *Purpose of Research*

2. Descriptive: Descriptive research focuses on expanding knowledge on current issues through a process of data collection. Descriptive studies are used to describe the behavior of a sample population. In a descriptive study, only one variable is required to conduct the study. The three main purposes of descriptive research are describing, explaining, and validating the findings.

3. Explanatory: Explanatory research or causal research is conducted to understand the impact of certain changes in existing standard procedures. Conducting experiments is the most popular form of casual research.

2.8. Significance of Research

1. Research inculcates scientific and inductive thinking and it promotes the development of logical habits of thinking and organization.

2. The role of research in every fields of life has greatly increased in modern times.
3. Research provides the basic for nearly all Government policies.
4. Research has its special significance in solving various operational and planning problems.
5. Research is equally important for social scientists in studying social relationships and in seeking answers to various social problems.

2.9. Characteristics of Research

Some desirable characteristics of research are given below:

- The research should focus on priority problems.
- The research should be systematic. It emphasizes that a researcher should employ a structured procedure.
- The research should be logical. Without manipulating ideas logically, the scientific researcher cannot make much progress in any investigation.
- The research should be reductive. This means that the findings of one researcher should be made available to other researchers to prevent them from repeating the same research.
- The research should be replicable. This asserts that there should be scope to confirm the findings of previous research in a new environment and different settings with a new group of subjects or at a different point in time.
- The research should be generative. This is one of the valuable characteristics of research because answering one question leads to generating many other new questions.
- The research should be action-oriented. In other words, it should be aimed at reaching a solution leading to the implementation of its findings.
- The research should follow an integrated multidisciplinary approach, i.e., research approaches from more than one discipline are needed.
- The research should be participatory, involving all parties concerned (from policymakers down to community members) at all stages of the study.
- The research must be relatively simple, timely and time-bound, employing a comparatively simple design.
- The research must be as much cost-effective as possible.
- The results of the research should be presented in formats most useful for administrators, decision-makers, business managers or the community members.

2.10. Features/ Criteria of Good Scientific Research

Scientific research should satisfy the following criteria:

1. The purpose of the research should be clearly defined and common concepts be used.
2. The research procedure used should be described in sufficient detail to permit another researcher to repeat the research for further advancement, keeping the continuity of what has already been attained.

3. The procedural design of the research should be carefully planned to yield results that are as objective as possible.
4. The researcher should report with complete frankness, flaws in procedural design and estimate their effects upon the findings.
5. The analysis of data should be sufficiently adequate to reveal its significance and the methods of analysis used should be appropriate. The validity and reliability of the data should be checked carefully.
6. Conclusions should be confined to those justified by the data of the research and limited to those for which the data provide an adequate basis.
7. Greater confidence in research is warranted if the researcher is experienced, has a good reputation in research and is a person of integrity.

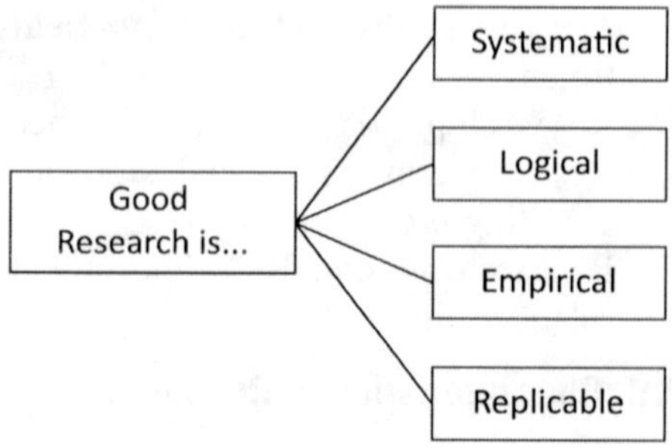

Figure 2.5 *Qualities of a Good Research*

In other words, we can state the qualities of a good research as under:

- *Good Research is Systematic*: It means that research is structured with specified steps to be taken in a specified sequence in accordance with the well-defined set of rules. Systematic characteristic of the research does not rule out creative thinking but it certainly does reject the use of guessing and intuition in arriving at conclusions.
- *Good Research is Logical*: This implies that research is guided by the rules of logical reasoning and the logical process of induction and deduction are of great value in carrying out research. Induction is the process of reasoning from a part to the whole whereas deduction is the process of reasoning from some premise to a conclusion which follows from that very premise. In fact, logical reasoning makes research more meaningful in the context of decision making.
- *Good Research is Empirical*: It implies that research is related basically to one or more aspects of a real situation and deals with concrete data that provides a basis for external validity to research results.
- *Good Research is Replicable*: This characteristic allows research results to be verified by replicating the study and thereby building a sound basis for decisions.

2.11. Aims and Objectives of Research

One of the most important aspects of a thesis, dissertation, research paper or research project is the correct formulation of the aims and objectives. This is because aims and objectives will establish the scope, depth and direction that the research will ultimately take.

Research Aims: A research aim describes the main goal or the overarching purpose of the research project.A research aim is usually formulated as a broad statement of the main goal of the research and can range in length from a single sentence to a short paragraph.

Research Objectives: Where a research aim specifies what the study will answer, research objectives specify how the study will answer it.They divide the research aim into several smaller parts, each of which represents a key section of the research project. Research objectives describe concisely what the research is trying to achieve.

Importance of Research Objectives

- They define the research since it provides meaning to the research.
- A research is meaningless without research objectives as is the same for any other task.
- They aid in the formulation of hypothesis.
- They are a guideline on which the researcher conducts the study. In every step of research, the researcher uses objectives to be more specific.
- It also helps in narrowing down the research and provides a focal point.
- The development of research methodology also depends on them.
- They also guide to the conduction of a valid and reliable research study.
- They also summarize the research to the readers and to the researcher. The researcher and the reader know by reading the research objectives what the author wants to accomplish.
- It also saves the time of the researcher because he/she avoids collection of unnecessary data.
- They also provide a step-by-step guideline that makes the research well-planned and sequential.

Difference Between Research Aims and Objectives

- The research aim focus on what the research project is intended to achieve; research objectives focus on how the aim will be achieved.
- Research aims are relatively broad; research objectives are specific.
- Research aims focus on a project's long-term outcomes; research objectives focus on its immediate, short-term outcomes.
- A research aim can be written in a single sentence or short paragraph; research objectives should be written as a numbered list.

How to Write Research Aims and Objectives

There are some basic principles to write the research aims and objectives.

Research Aims

Research aim should be made up of three parts that answer the below questions:

- *Why is this research required?* The first question, why, provides context to the research project.
- *What is this research about?* The second question, what, describes the aim of the research.

How are you going to do it? The last question, how, acts as an introduction to the research objectives which will immediately follow.

Research Objectives

Each of the research objectives should be SMART:

- *Specific* – is there any ambiguity in the action you are going to undertake, or is it focused and well-defined?
- *Measurable* – how will you measure progress and determine when you have achieved the action?
- *Achievable* – do you have the support, resources and facilities required to carry out the action?
- *Relevant* – is the action essential to the achievement of your research aim?
- *Timebound* – can you realistically complete the action in the available time alongside your other research tasks?

In addition to being SMART, the research objectives should start with a verb that helps communicate researcher's intent. Common research verbs include:

Table 2.1 *Research Verbs to Use in Research Aims and Objectives*

Understanding *(Understanding and organizing information)*	***Applying*** *(Solving problems using information)*	***Analyzing*** *(Reaching conclusion from evidence)*	***Synthesizing*** *(Breaking down into components)*	***Evaluating*** *(Judging merit)*
Review	Interpret	Analyze	Propose	Appraise
Identify	Apply	Compare	Design	Evaluate
Explore	Demonstrate	Inspect	Formulate	Compare
Discover	Establish	Examine	Collect	Assess
Discuss	Determine	Verify	Construct	Recommend
Summarize	Estimate	Select	Prepare	Conclude
Describe	Calculate	Test	Undertake	Select
	Relate	Arrange	Assemble	

Table 2.1 showing common research verbs which should ideally be used at the start of a research aim or objective.

2.12. Classification of Research

Research can be classified on the basis of:

1. Uses or Outcomes
2. Purpose or Depth of Scope
3. Type of Data Used
4. Degree of Manipulation of Variables
5. Type of Inference
6. Time in Which Research is Carried Out
7. Sources of Information
8. How the Data is Obtained

2.12.1. Types of Research on the basis of Uses or Outcome

Following are the different types of research on the basis of purpose.

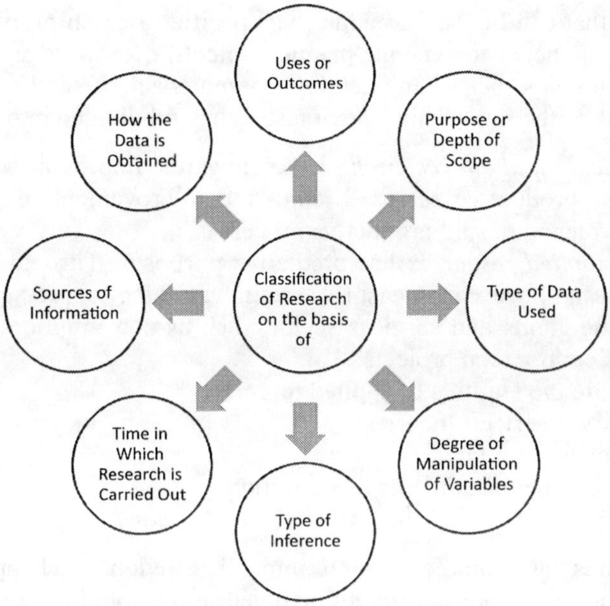

Figure 2.6 *Classification of Research*

Pure Research or Theoretical Research

Pure research is theoretical type not a practical one. Pure research is the knowledge of facts and theories to give us satisfaction of knowledge and understanding. It discovers general principles for a problem solution. Theoretical research, also referred to as pure or basic research, focuses on generating knowledge, regardless of its practical application. Here, data collection is used to generate new general concepts for a better understanding of a particular field or to answer a theoretical research question. Results of this kind are usually oriented towards the formulation of theories and are usually based on documentary analysis, the development of mathematical formulas and the reflection of high-level researchers. For example, a philosophical dissertation, since the aim is to generate new approaches from existing data without considering how its findings can be applied or implemented in practice. Following are some of the features of pure research.

- It keeps the foundation of initial study.
- It discovers new facts.
- It gives theoretical reports for solution.

Applied Research

Applied research is the implementation of theoretical study upon a problematic situation. It applied its theories and facts to know about the nature of the problem and give a concrete shape for the solution. Here, the goal is to

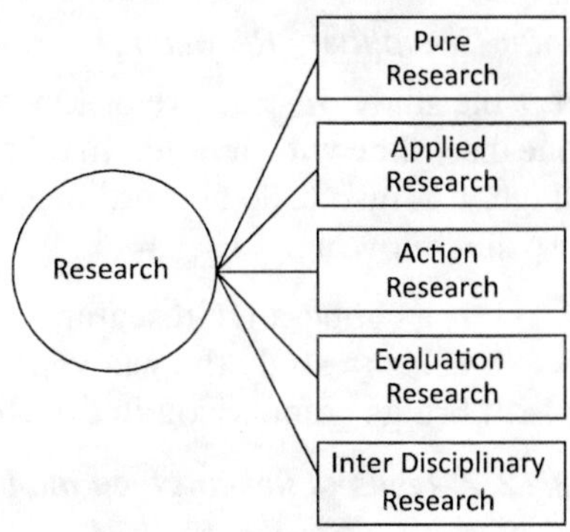

Figure 2.7 *Types of Research on the Basis of Uses or Outcome*

find strategies that can be used to address a specific research problem. Applied research draws on theory to generate practical scientific knowledge, and its use is very common in fields such as engineering, computer science and medicine. This is practical work in the field. This type of research is subdivided into two types:

- *Technological applied research*: looks towards improving efficiency in a particular productive sector through the improvement of processes or machinery related to said productive processes.
- *Scientific applied research*: has predictive purposes. Through this type of research design, we can measure certain variables to predict behaviours useful to the goods and services sector, such as consumption patterns and viability of commercial projects.

  Following are the features of applied research:
  - It tests and verifies theories
  - It discovers new facts
  - It gives immediate answer to a question

Action Research

Action research is based on the taking of immediate action on a happening, event or situation. The researcher is actively involved in the solution of the problems. Features of action research are as under:

- It is quick service oriented
- It is taking immediate action
- It is sensitive to time and place

Evaluation Research

This type of research is an evaluation of some programs working for the construction of problematic areas. It is the dankness of implemented programmes about their effects and positive solution. There are three main types of evaluation:

- Concurrent evaluation-means continuous process
- Phase or periodic evaluation-stage wise.
- Terminal evaluation-Evaluation after the completion of the programme.

Inter Disciplinary Research

It is the study of structure or functions of a particular discipline or comparison of one discipline with another. In other words, it is the comparison of a developmental stage. It is also called co-ordinate research. Features of inter disciplinary research are the following:

- It is a cooperative research
- It helps in study the whole phenomena
- It brings comparison in different disciplines

2.12.2. Types of Research on the basis of Purpose or Depth of Scope

Exploratory Research: Exploratory research is used for the preliminary investigation of a subject that is not yet well understood or sufficiently researched. It serves

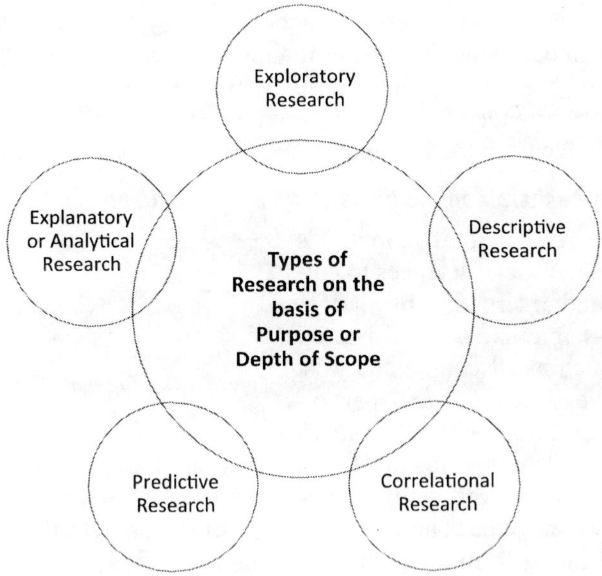

Figure 2.8 *Types of Research on the basis of Purpose or Depth of Scope*

to establish a frame of reference and a hypothesis from which an in-depth study can be developed that will enable conclusive results to be generated. Because exploratory research is based on the study of little-studied phenomena, it relies less on theory and more on the collection of data to identify patterns that explain these phenomena. For example, an investigation of the role social media in the perception of self-image.

Descriptive Research: The primary objective of descriptive research is to define the characteristics of a particular phenomenon without necessarily investigating the causes that produce it. In this type of research, the researcher must take particular care not to intervene in the observed object or phenomenon, as its behaviour may change if an external factor is involved. For example, investigating how the public census of influential government officials differs between urban and non-urban areas.

Explanatory or Analytical Research: Explanatory research is the most common type of research method and is responsible for establishing cause-and-effect relationships that allow generalizations to be extended to similar realities. It is closely related to descriptive research, although it provides additional information about the observed object and its interactions with the environment. For example, investigating the brittle behaviour of a specific material when under compressive load.

Correlational Research: The purpose of this type of scientific research is to identify the relationship between two or more variables. A correlational study aims to determine whether a variable change, how much the other elements of the observed system change.

Predictive Research: Predictive research goes further by forecasting the likelihood of similar situation occurring elsewhere. It aims to generalize from the analysis by predicting certain phenomenon on the basis of hypothesized, general relationships. Predictive research provides 'how', 'why', and 'where' answers to current events as well as to similar events in the future.

2.12.3. Types of Research on the basis of Type of Data Used

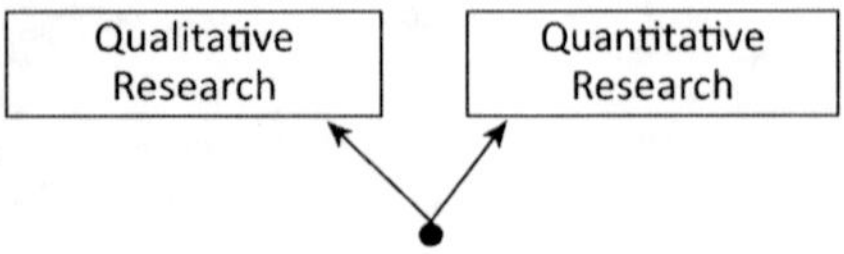

Figure 2.9 *Types of Research on the basis of Type of Data Used*

Qualitative Research: Qualitative methods are often used in the social sciences to collect, compare and interpret information, has a linguistic-semiotic basis and is used in techniques such as discourse analysis, interviews, surveys, records and participant observations. In order to use statistical methods to validate their results, the observations collected must be evaluated numerically. Qualitative research, however, tends to be subjective, since not all data can be fully controlled. Therefore, this type of research design is better suited to extracting meaning from an event or phenomenon (the 'why') than its cause (the 'how'). For example, examining the effects of sleep deprivation on mood.

Quantitative Research: Quantitative research study delves into a phenomenon through quantitative data collection and using mathematical, statistical and computer-aided tools to measure them. This allows generalized conclusions to be projected over time. For example, conducting a computer simulation on vehicle strike impacts to collect quantitative data.

2.12.4. Types of Research on the basis of Degree of Manipulation of Variables

Experimental Research: It is about designing or replicating a phenomenon whose variables are manipulated under strictly controlled conditions in order to identify or discover its effect on another independent variable or object. The phenomenon to be studied is measured through study and control groups, and according to the guidelines of the scientific method. For example, randomized controlled trial studies for measuring the effectiveness of new pharmaceutical drugs on human subjects.

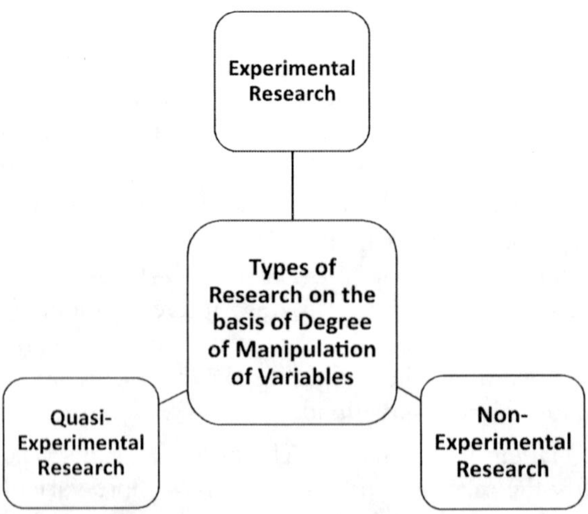

Figure 2.10 *Types of Research on the basis of Degree of Manipulation of Variables*

Non-Experimental Research: Also known as an observa-

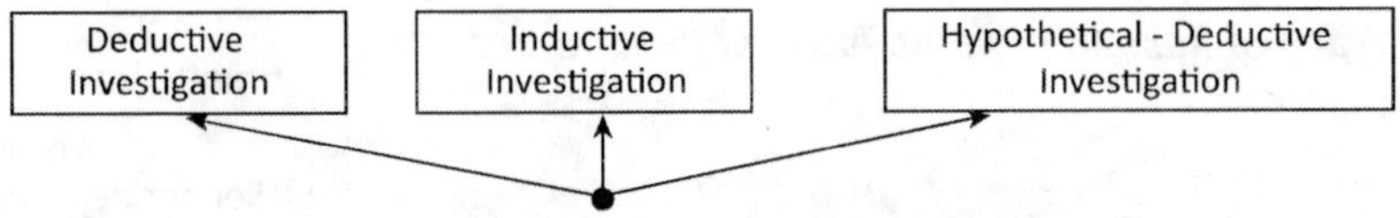

Figure 2.11 *Types of Research on the basis of Type of Inference*

tional study, it focuses on the analysis of a phenomenon in its natural context. As such, the researcher does not intervene directly, but limits their involvement to measuring the variables required for the study. Due to its observational nature, it is often used in descriptive research. For example, a study on the effects of the use of certain chemical substances in a particular population group can be considered a non-experimental study.

Quasi-Experimental Research: It controls only some variables of the phenomenon under investigation and is therefore not entirely experimental. In this case, the study and the focus group cannot be randomly selected, but are chosen from existing groups or populations. This is to ensure the collected data is relevant and that the knowledge, perspectives and opinions of the population can be incorporated into the study. For example, assessing the effectiveness of an intervention measure in reducing the spread of antibiotic-resistant bacteria.

2.12.5. Types of Research on the basis of Type of Inference

Deductive Investigation: In this type of research, reality is explained by general laws that point to certain conclusions; conclusions are expected to be part of the premise of the research problem and considered correct if the premise is valid and the inductive method is applied correctly.

Inductive Investigation: In this type of research, knowledge is generated from an observation to achieve a generalization. It is based on the collection of specific data to develop new theories.

Hypothetical-Deductive Investigation: It is based on observing reality to make a hypothesis, then use deduction to obtain a conclusion and finally verify or reject it through experience.

2.12.6. Types of Research on the basis of Time in Which Research is Carried Out

Longitudinal Study (also referred to as Diachronic Research): It is the monitoring of the same event, individual or group over a defined period of time. It aims to track changes in a number of variables and see how they evolve over time. It is often used in medical, psychological and social areas. For example, a cohort study that analyses changes in a particular indigenous population over a period of 15 years.

Cross-Sectional Study (also referred to as Synchronous Research): Cross-sectional research design is used to observe phenomena, an individual or a group of research subjects at a given time.

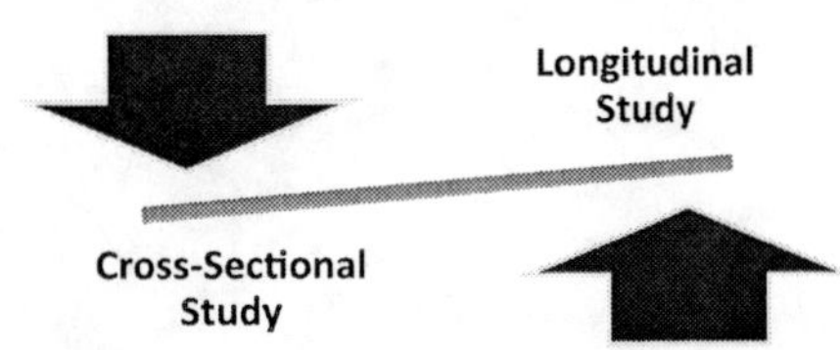

Figure 2.12 *Types of Research on the basis of Time*

2.12.7. Types of Research on the basis of the Sources of Information

Primary Research: This fundamental research type is defined by the fact that the data is collected directly from the source, that is, it consists of primary, first-hand information.

Secondary Research: Unlike primary research, secondary research is developed with information from secondary sources, which are generally based on scientific literature and other documents compiled by another researcher.

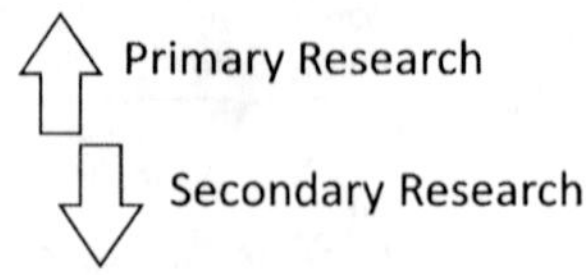

Figure 2.13 *Types of Research on the basis of the Sources of Information*

2.12.8. Types of Research on the basis of How the Data is Obtained

Documentary (cabinet): Documentary research, or secondary sources, is based on a systematic review of existing sources of information on a particular subject. This type of scientific research is commonly used when undertaking literature reviews or producing a case study.

Field: Field research study involves the direct collection of information at the location where the observed phenomenon occurs.

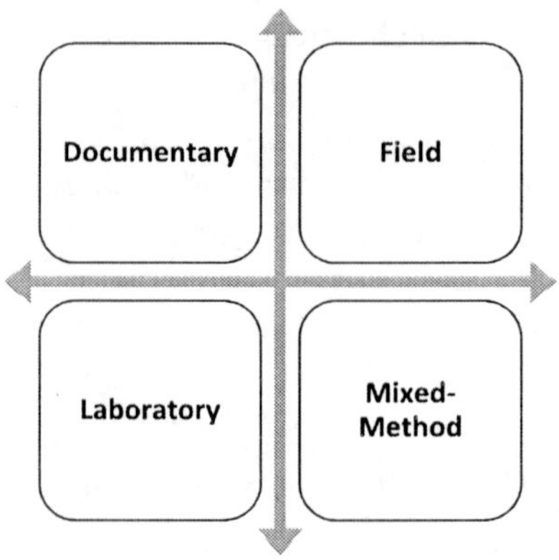

Figure 2.14 *Types of Research on the basis of How the Data is Obtained*

Laboratory: Laboratory research is carried out in a controlled environment in order to isolate a dependent variable and establish its relationship with other variables through scientific methods.

Mixed-Method: Mixed research methodologies combine results from both secondary (documentary) sources and primary sources through field or laboratory research.

3

Introduction to Research Philosophy

The idea that there are different views of the world and the processes that operate within it, is part of what is known as philosophy. Philosophy is concerned with views about how the world works and, as an academic subject, focuses, primarily, on reality, knowledge and existence. Our individual view of the world is closely linked to what we perceive as reality. On a day-to-day basis outside of our academic work, it would be unusual to think often about the way we perceive reality and the world around us. However, in relation to research, it is very important to realize how researcher perceive reality. Researcher's individual perception of reality affects how he gain knowledge of the world and how he acts within it. This mean that researcher's perception of reality and how he gains knowledge, will affect the way in which he conducts the research.

3.1. Research Philosophy

Research philosophy deals with the source, nature and development of knowledge. Research philosophy refers to the development of knowledge adopted by the researchers in their research. It is the theory that used to direct the researcher for conducting the procedure of research design, research strategy, questionnaire design and sampling. It is very important to have a clear understanding of the research philosophy so that we could examine the assumptions about the way we view the world, which are contained in the research philosophy we choose, knowing that whether they are appropriate or not.

All research has a philosophical perspective. Research philosophy is defined as the development of research assumption, its knowledge, and nature. Research philosophy presents the nature of the research, the type of data associated with its, the understanding of the sources of the data and theoretical approaches to analyze it. In simple terms, a research philosophy is belief about the ways in which data about a phenomenon should be collected, analysed and used.

The term research philosophy refers to a system of beliefs and assumptions about the development of knowledge. Whether researchers are consciously aware of them or not, at every stage in their research they will make a number of types of assumption. These include assumptions about human knowledge (*epistemological assumptions*), about the realities they encounter in their research (*ontological assumptions*) and the extent and ways their

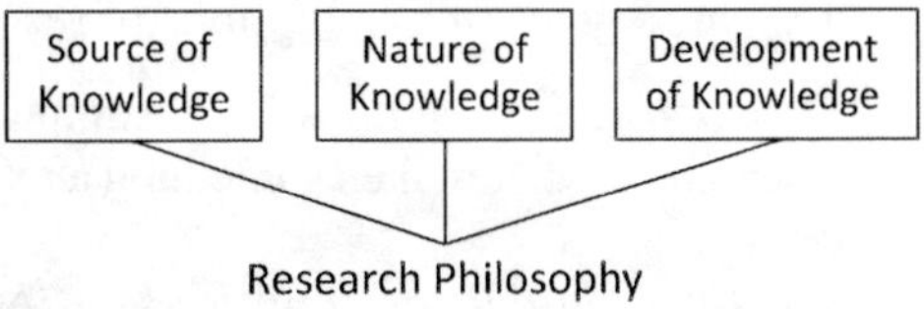

Figure 3.1 *Meaning of Research Philosophy*

own values influence their research process (*axiological assumptions*). These assumptions inevitably shape how they understand their research questions, the methods they use and how they interpret their findings. A well-thought-out and consistent set of assumptions will constitute a credible research philosophy, which will underpin researcher's methodological choice, research strategy and data collection techniques and analysis procedures.

3.2. Definitions of Research Philosophy

- According to Saunders (2012), *"the term research philosophy refers to 'a system of beliefs and assumptions about the development of knowledge"*.
- According to Collis and Hussey (2014), *"A research philosophy is a framework that guides how research should be conducted based on ideas about reality and the nature of knowledge."*
- According to Bryman (2012), *"A research philosophy refers to the set of beliefs concerning the nature of the reality being investigated."*

3.3. Need and Significance of Research Philosophy to Researchers

The need and significance of research philosophy to researchers can be understand by the following three reasons:

- By understanding research philosophy, the researcher may refine and clarify the research method to be used in their study and consequently help the researchers to gather their evidence and to answer their research questions.
- The knowledge of research philosophy will enable to assist the researchers with different types of methodologies and as such avoiding inappropriate and unrelated works.
- By understanding the basic meaning of research philosophy and understanding its advantages and benefits, it helps the researcher to be more creative and exploratory in their method of research.

3.4. Assumptions of Research Philosophy/ Branches of Research Philosophy/ Ways of Thinking about Research Philosophy/ Philosophical Realms

Research philosophy is generally an overarching term denoting *'the school of thought that underpins the development of knowledge and the nature of that knowledge in relation to research'*. There are three philosophical realms directly involved in research, namely, ontology, epistemology and axiology. In other word, we can say that there are three major ways of thinking about research philosophy, which are: ontology, epistemology and axiology.

The three types of assumptions of research philosophy are:

- *Ontological assumptions* – Assumptions regarding the reality faced in the research or what makes something a reality, and how a researcher can understand existence.
- *Epistemological assumptions* – Assumptions associated with human knowledge or what forms valid knowledge, whether it can be known, and how a researcher can get it and transfer it.

- *Axiological assumptions* – These are assumptions about the level of influence of the researcher's values on the research process or what is essential and valuable in the research.

Each of them carries significant differences which will have an impact on the way we consider the research procedures. Further, these assumptions help a researcher to design the research questions, choose appropriate methods and influence the interpretation of findings. These assumptions altogether form the research philosophy of the study. Now, we will discuss these three branches/ways of thinking/realms/ assumptions or branches of research philosophy in detail.

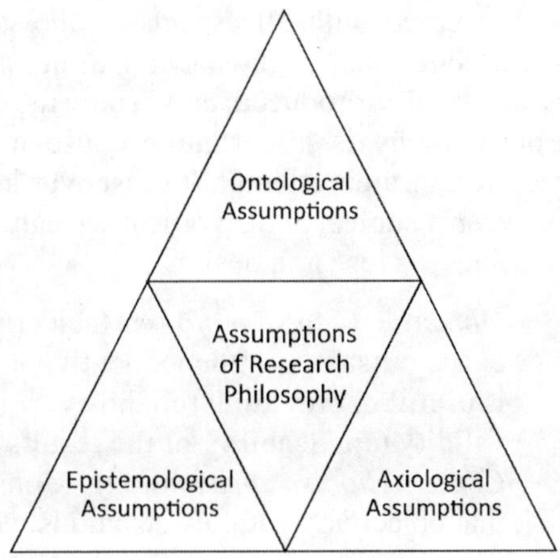

Figure 3.2 *Assumptions of Research Philosophy*

3.4.1. Ontology

Ontology *"is concerned with nature of reality"*. The first branch is ontology, or the 'study of being', which is concerned with what actually exists in the world about which humans can acquire knowledge. Ontology helps researchers recognize how certain they can be about the nature and existence of objects they are researching. For instance, what 'truth claims' can a researcher make about reality? Who decides the legitimacy of what is 'real'? How do researchers deal with different and conflicting ideas of reality?

- *Realist ontology*: Realist ontology relates to the existence of one single reality which can be studied, understood and experienced as a 'truth'; a real world exists independent of human experience.
- *Relativist ontology*: Relativist ontology is based on the philosophy that reality is constructed within the human mind, such that no one 'true' reality exists. Instead, reality is 'relative' according to how individuals experience it at any given time and place.

3.4.1.1. Ontological Assumption

The ontological assumption is the assumption made by a researcher regarding the nature of reality. Here reality means the study area or a subject domain. Your assumption about the nature of reality (ontology) decides how you view the subject domain or the research area, which in turn influences what you want to research (what research questions to ask or what research objectives to study).

3.4.2. Epistemology

Epistemology *"concerns what constitutes acceptable knowledge in a field of study."* The second branch is epistemology, the 'study of knowledge'. Epistemology is concerned with all aspects of the validity, scope and methods of acquiring knowledge, such as a) what constitutes a knowledge claim; b) how can knowledge be acquired or produced; and c) how the extent of its transferability can be assessed. Epistemology is important because it influences how researchers frame their research in their attempts to discover knowledge. By looking at the relationship between a subject and an object we can explore the idea of epistemology and how it influences research design.

- *Objectivist epistemology*: Objectivist epistemology assumes that reality exists outside, or independently, of the individual mind. Objectivist research is useful in providing reliability (consistency of results obtained) and external validity (applicability of the results to other contexts).
- *Constructionist epistemology*: Constructionist epistemology rejects the idea that objective 'truth' exists and is waiting to be discovered. Instead, 'truth', or meaning, arises in and out of our engagement with the realities in our world. That is, a 'real world' does not pre-exist independently of human activity or symbolic language. The value of constructionist research is in generating contextual understandings of a defined topic or problem.
- *Subjectivist epistemology*: Subjectivist epistemology relates to the idea that reality can be expressed in a range of symbol and language systems, and is stretched and shaped to fit the purposes of individuals such that people impose meaning on the world and interpret it in a way that makes sense to them. The value of subjectivist research is in revealing how an individual's experience shapes their perception of the world.

3.4.2.1. Epistemological Assumption

The epistemological assumption is an assumption made by a researcher regarding knowledge. What forms valid and reliable knowledge? How do we acquire and communicate it?

3.4.3. Axiology

Axiology *"studies judgements about value"*. Axiology is the third branch of philosophy that studies judgements about the value. Specifically, axiology is engaged with assessment of the role of researcher's own value on all stages of the research process. Axiology primarily refers to the 'aims' of the research. This branch of the research philosophy attempts to clarify if you are trying to explain or predict the world, or are you only seeking to understand it. In simple terms, axiology focuses on what do you value in your research. This is important because your values affect how you conduct your research and what do you value in your research findings.

3.4.3.1. Axiological Assumption

The axiological assumption is an assumption made by a researcher regarding the influence of values and beliefs on the research. The researcher tries to be free from values and beliefs intruding into the research or positively considers and acknowledges values and beliefs influencing the research process and the conclusions. Sometimes we need to decide on whether the values and beliefs of the research respondents should be considered or not. Researchers argue that it is very tough to keep ourselves free from the influence of values and beliefs. For instance, as a researcher you might have come across your supervisor/guide saying "parametric test is stronger than non-parametric", "qualitative data gives in-depth understanding about a phenomenon than quantitative data". What are these assumptions? They are the aspects of research your advisor values more.

3.5. Research Paradigm

As a researcher, one will face the fundamental question of what philosophical structure and direction he should give his enquiry. In order to carry out any research, researcher should first understand the core philosophical position that underpins the research method he is planning to adopt. This is known as the research paradigm.

To determine a researcher's position on the three major realms of philosophy, research paradigms have been introduced. A research paradigm is defined as *'a philosophical framework or set of beliefs that guides action on research'*. It usually reflects a researcher's assumptions and portrays diverse philosophical perspectives.

3.5.1. What is Research Paradigm?

A research paradigm is an approach or a model or a pattern to conduct research. It is a framework of thoughts or beliefs or understandings within which theories and practices operate. It acts as a function of how a researcher thinks about the development of knowledge. In simple words, a research paradigm is a process of creating a blueprint of research.

3.5.2. Definitions of Research Paradigm

Bryman and Bell (2011) define a paradigm as, *"a cluster of beliefs, and dictates in a particular discipline to influence what should be studied, how research should be done and how results should be interpreted."*

3.5.3. Types of Research Paradigm

Research paradigm can be divided into four types discussed below:

3.5.3.1. Positivist Paradigm

Positivism (or objectivism, empiricism, reductionism, hypothetico-deductive). Auguste Comte first named this paradigm during the Enlightenment period. Positivists believe that the external world is ordered and regular and that there is an objective reality (or truth) with specific patterns, which can be predicted or explained through theories or laws. The generalisability of objective results is central to empiricism. Positivists view knowledge as value-free without the influence of researchers. As illustrated in Figure-3.4, positivists mostly carry out theory-based research using deductive reasoning as part of the scientific method, i.e., starting

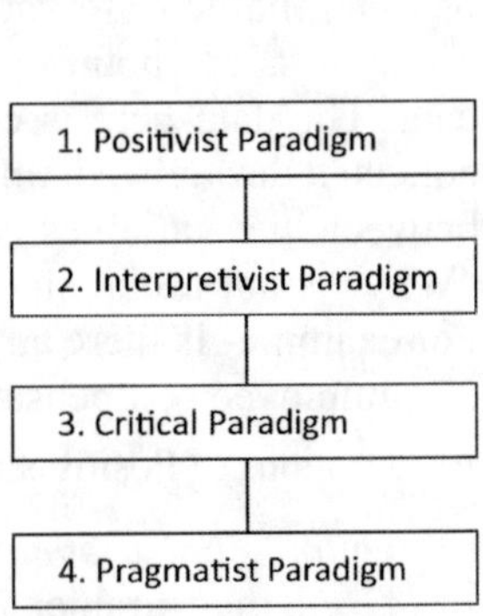

Figure 3.3 *Types of Research Paradigm*

from identifying a theory, through formulating a hypothesis and collecting data, to confirm a pattern with generalisation; however, some researchers might begin their study with data observation by means of inductive reasoning.

As a philosophy, positivism adheres to the view that only "factual" knowledge gained through observation (the senses), including measurement, is trustworthy. In positivism studies the role of the researcher is limited to data collection and interpretation in an objective way. In these types of studies research findings are usually observable and quantifiable.

Positivism depends on quantifiable observations that lead to statistical analyses. It has been noted that "as a philosophy, positivism is in accordance with the empiricist view that knowledge stems from human experience. It has an atomistic, ontological view of the world as comprising discrete, observable elements and events that interact in an observable, determined and regular manner".

The five main principles of positivism research philosophy can be summarized as the following:

- There are no differences in the logic of inquiry across sciences.
- The research should aim to explain and predict.
- Research should be empirically observable via human senses. Inductive reasoning should be used to develop statements (hypotheses) to be tested during the research process.
- Science is not the same as the common sense. The common sense should not be allowed to bias the research findings.
- Science must be value-free and it should be judged only by logic.

Positivists believe that there is a single reality which can be measured and known. Therefore, quantitative methods are used to measure this reality. Positivism in research is a philosophy that is closely associated with the idea of fact-based investigation. A research-based on positivism philosophy follows a rigorous method of systematic investigation of data sources. It believes that only "factual" knowledge gained through observation including measurement is reliable. In positivism, the role of the researcher is limited to data collection and interpretation. It depends on quantifiable observations that lead to statistical analyses. In positivism-based researches, a hypothesis is proposed which is proved using statistical analysis of data. The data here is collected through questionnaires (primary analysis) or is collected through existing data sources (secondary analysis). Here the relationship between two variables is established and the reason for relationship or answer to "Why" is not found since positivism believes in the existence of a single reality. For example- Is there any significant relationship between employee performance and employee compensation?

Assumptions of Positivism: Positivism leads to the following four sets of assumptions:

- *Ontological assumptions (nature of reality)*: There is one defined reality, fixed, measurable, and observable. *Realist Ontology* - assumes that there are real world objects apart from the human knower. In other words, there is an objective reality.

- *Epistemological assumptions (knowledge)*: Genuine knowledge is objective and quantifiable. The goal of science is to test and expand theory. *Representational Epistemology* - assumes people can know this reality and use symbols to accurately describe and explain this objective reality.
- *Axiological assumptions (role of values)*: Objectivity is good, and subjectivity is inherently misleading.
- *Methodological assumptions (research strategies)*: Using quantitative research methods such as experiments, quasi-experiments, exploratory and analytical models, case studies, and so on—which require objective measurement and analysis—is the only acceptable method to generate valid knowledge.

Characteristics of Research Located Within the Positivist Paradigm: The following summary should help you to understand the basic characteristics of research that is normally located within the Positivist paradigm:

- A belief that theory is universal and law-like generalisations can be made across contexts.
- The assumption that context is not important
- The belief that truth or knowledge is 'out there to be discovered' by research.
- The belief that cause and effect are distinguishable and analytically separable.
- The belief that results of inquiry can be quantified.
- The belief that theory can be used to predict and to control outcomes
- The belief that research should follow the Scientific Method of investigation
- Rests on formulation and testing of hypotheses
- Employs empirical or analytical approaches
- Pursues an objective search for facts
- Believes in ability to observe knowledge.
- The researcher's ultimate aim is to establish a comprehensive universal theory, to account for human and social behaviour.
- Application of the scientific method.

3.5.3.2. Interpretivist Paradigm/Constructivist Paradigm/Subjectivist Paradigm

Interpretivism (or constructivism, anti-positivism, phenomenology, relativism, hermeneutics, humanism). This is a social scientific perspective that opposes the positivist or scientific paradigm. Interpretivists maintain that there are many subjective realities that can be constructed by individual interpretations. They endeavour to find 'meanings' or constructed knowledge through qualitative data (i.e. texts, stories or images) rather than objective facts. Many interpretivists acquire value-laden knowledge mostly through inductive reasoning that commences on collecting data followed by forming a pattern and formulating a theory (Figure-3.4). Nevertheless, a significant proportion of interpretive research, e.g., in social anthropology, is also theory-based using deductive reasoning. In their view, generalisation is feasible through theory creation rather than direct hypothesis testing. For interpretivists, research is value-bound and in that they are directly involved in the study with their own interpretations.

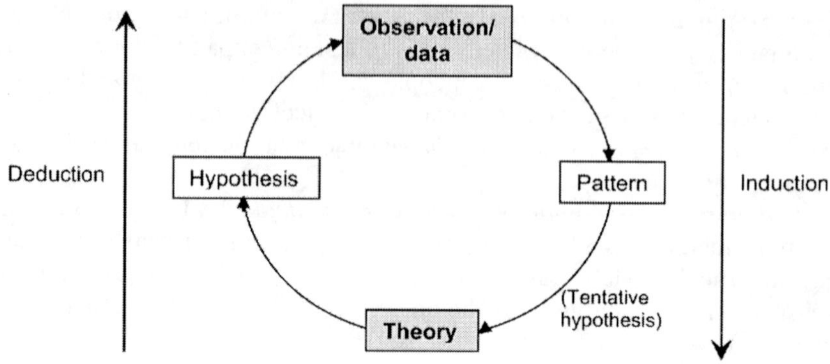

Figure 3.4 *Inductive and Deductive Reasoning*

The term interpretivism refers to the ways via which one can gain knowledge of the world, which loosely relies on interpreting or understanding the meanings that humans attach to their actions. It does not believe in a single relative but is based on the existence of multiple realities. Thus, it uses qualitative methods to reach those multiple realities. Interpretivism integrates human interest into a study and assumes that access to reality (or realities) is only through social constructions such as language, consciousness, shared meanings, and instruments. Thus, here data is collected through interviews and talking to people s that different perspectives (different realities) of people can be analyzed. So, it is important for the researcher as a social actor to appreciate differences between people thereby using qualitative analysis. Here the emphasis is laid on finding an answer to "WHY" and unlike positivism, it is not merely focused on establishing a relationship between existing variables. For example- why are the employees in an organization not able to adapt to the new training system. Further, interpretivism can be biased since it is based on individual believes and experiences.

Assumptions of Interpretivism: Here is how the four groups of assumptions look to an interpretivist (a social constructivist):

- *Ontological assumptions (nature of reality)*: There must be multiple realities, socially constructed by individuals together.
- *Relativist Ontology*: assumes that reality as we know it is constructed inter subjectively through the meanings and understandings developed socially and experientially.
- *Epistemological assumptions (knowledge)*: Knowledge is gained through an empathic understanding of participants' lived social realities; the goal of science is to describe people's subjective lived realities, experiences, and understandings.
- *Transactional or Subjectivist Epistemology*: assumes that we cannot separate ourselves from what we know. The investigator and the object of investigation are linked such that who we are and how we understand the world is a central part of how we understand ourselves, others and the world.

- *Axiological assumptions (role of values)*: The researcher's subjective values, intuition, and biases are important—they play a role in the dialog of social construction and inform his or her interpretation of the data.
- *Methodological assumptions (research strategies)*: Using qualitative research methods such as phenomenology, ethnography, case study, grounded theory, and ethnography provides access to participants inner, subjective experiences.

Characteristics of Research Located within the Interpretivist Paradigm: Research conducted under the Interpretivist paradigm usually exhibits the following characteristics:

- The admission that the social world cannot be understood from the standpoint of an individual.
- The belief that realities are multiple and socially constructed
- The acceptance that there is inevitable interaction between the researcher and his or her research participants
- The acceptance that context is vital for knowledge and knowing.
- The belief that knowledge is created by the findings, can be value laden and the values need to be made explicit
- The need to understand the individual rather than universal laws.
- The belief that causes and effects are mutually interdependent.
- The belief that contextual factors need to be taken into consideration in any systematic pursuit of understanding.

3.5.3.3. Critical Paradigm/Transformative Paradigm

The Critical paradigm situates its research in social justice issues and seeks to address the political, social and economic issues, which lead to social oppression, conflict, struggle, and power structures at whatever levels these might occur. Because it seeks to change the politics so as to confront social oppression and improve the social justice in the situation, it is sometimes called the *Transformative paradigm*.

Assumptions of Critical Paradigm/Transformative Paradigm

- This paradigm assumes a *transactional epistemology*, (in which the researcher interacts with the participants), an *ontology of historical realism*, especially as it relates to oppression; a *methodology that is dialogic*, and an axiology that respects *cultural norms*.
- *Historical ontology*: assumes that there is a 'reality' that is apprehendable. This is a reality created and shaped by social, political, cultural, economic, ethnic and gender-based forces that have been reified or crystallized over time into social structures that are taken to be natural or real. People, including researchers, function under the assumption that for all practical purposes these structures are real. Critical theorist believes this assumption is inappropriate.
- *Modified transactional or subjectivist epistemology*: we cannot separate ourselves from what we know and this inevitably influences inquiry. What can be known is inextricably tied to the interaction between a particular investigator and a particular object or group.

Characteristics of Research Located within the Critical Paradigm: We can attribute the following characteristics to research conducted within the Critical paradigm:

- The concern with power relationships set up within social structures.
- The conscious recognition of the consequences of privileging versions of reality
- The respect for cultural norms
- An examination of conditions and individuals in a situation, based on social positioning.
- The treatment of research as an act of construction rather than discovery.
- A central focus of the research effort on uncovering agency, which is hidden by social practices, leading to liberation and emancipation.
- And endeavour to expose conjunctions of politics, morality, and ethics.
- The deliberate efforts of the researcher to promote human rights, and increase social justice, and reciprocity.
- The deliberate efforts of the researcher to address issues of power, oppression and trust among research participants
- A high reliance on praxis.
- The use of ethno methodology, situating knowledge socially and historically
- An application of action research
- The utilisation of participatory research.

3.5.3.4. Pragmatist Paradigm

Pragmatism philosophy is dependent on the research question. It believes that the philosophy to be used in research is selected based on the research question. Pragmatics can combine both, positivism and interpretivism positions within the scope of single research according to the nature of the research question. It is a problem-oriented philosophy that takes the view that the best research methods are those that help to most effectively answer the research question. This then involves a mix of quantitative and qualitative methods used to evaluate different aspects of a research problem. To pragmatists, truth is what is really useful, albeit being influenced by the researchers. Both inductive and deductive approaches are employed to obtain practical knowledge, i.e., usually starting from data collection, through pattern formation, to theory creation. Additionally, research hypotheses can be formulated based on a theory and then tested. Pragmatist proponents see the linkage of facts and values, and carry out research with several quantitative or qualitative methods.

Assumptions of Pragmatist Paradigm: The paradigm advocates:

- *Relational epistemology* (i.e., relationships in research are best determined by what the researcher deems appropriate to that particular study),
- *Non-singular reality ontology* (that there is no single reality and all individuals have their own and unique interpretations of reality),
- *Mixed methods methodology* (a combination of quantitative and qualitative research methods), and
- *Value-laden axiology* (conducting research that benefits people).

Characteristics of Research Located within the Pragmatic Paradigm: Research located within this paradigm demonstrates the following characteristics:

- A rejection of the positivist notion that social science inquiry can uncover the 'truth' about the real world.
- An emphasis of 'workability' in research.
- The use of 'what works' so as to allow the researcher to address the questions being investigated without worrying as to whether the questions are wholly quantitative or qualitative in nature.
- Adoption of a worldview that allows for a research design and methodologies that are best suited to the purpose of the study.
- Utilising lines of action that are best suited to studying the phenomenon being investigated.
- A rejection of the need to locate your study either in a Positivist (post-positivist) paradigm or an Interpretivist (constructivist) paradigm.
- Seeking to utilise the best approaches to gaining knowledge using every methodology that helps that knowledge discovery.
- Choice of research methods depending on the purpose of the research.
- A search for useful points of connection within the research project that facilitate understanding of the situation.

3.6. General Characteristics of a Value-based Research: Axiological Approach

Axiology is a branch of philosophy that studies judgements about the value. Specifically, axiology is engaged with assessment of the role of researcher's own value on all stages of the research process. Axiology refers to the role of values and ethics within the research process, which incorporates questions about how we, as researchers, deal with our own values and also with those of our research participants.

Axiology primarily refers to the 'aims' of the research. This branch of the research philosophy attempts to clarify if you are trying to explain or predict the world, or are you only seeking to understand it. In simple terms, axiology focuses on what do you value in your research. This is important because your values affect how you conduct your research and what do you value in your research findings.

Axiology is the study of values. Axiology means what is good (or bad) in life and what do we find worthy. The bigger question in axiology is, what do I value in research? Axiology incorporates ethics (theory of morality) and aesthetics (theory of taste and of beauty), as well as other forms of value. Asking what 'ought to be' is axiological.

Our values affect how we do research and what we value in the results of our research.

Axiological concerns infuse research. Two general examples are:

- what makes a good researcher (eg., impartial, curious; caring; diligent, etc); and,
- what is worthwhile science (eg., co-relational, causal, problem-centred, hypothesis-centered, experimental, applied, private, public, etc).

Axiology refers to the ethical issues that need to be considered when planning a research proposal. It considers the philosophical approach to making decisions of value or the right decisions. It involves defining, evaluating and understanding concepts of right and wrong behaviour relating to the research. It considers what value we shall attribute to the different aspects of our research, the participants, the data and the audience to which we shall report the results of our research. Put simply, it addresses the question: What is the nature of ethics or ethical behaviour? In answer to this question, it is important to consider your regard for human values of everyone that will be involved with or participate in your research project. This consideration is facilitated by the following questions. What values will you live by or be guided by as you conduct your research? What ought to be done to respect all participants' rights? What are the moral issues and characteristics that need to be considered? Which cultural, intercultural and moral issues arise and how will I address them? How shall I secure the goodwill of participants? How shall I conduct the research in a socially just, respectful and peaceful manner? How shall I avoid or minimise risk or harm, whether it be physical, psychological, legal, social, economic or other?

Answers to these questions are best guided by four criteria of ethical conduct namely, teleology, deontology, morality and fairness.

- *Teleology*: Teleology is the theory of morality which postulates that doing what is intrinsically good or desirable, is a moral obligation that should be pursued in every human endeavour. And so, teleology refers to attempts made in research to make sure that the research results in a meaningful outcome that will satisfy as many people as possible. An application of this criterion is facilitated by questions such as, are the methods used in this research pragmatic and do they make common sense? Will the actions undertaken in the research produce more benefits than harm? Am I convinced that the actions that will be taken during the research will be the right ones? Have I considered all possible consequences of this research?
- *Deontology*: Deontology is the understanding that every action that will be undertaken during the research will have its own consequence, intended to benefit participants, the researcher, the scholastic community or the public at large. It also allows for flexibility to deal with individual participants or observations.
- *Morality*: Morality criterion refers to the intrinsic moral values that will be upheld during the research. For example, that the researcher will be truthful in their interpretation of the data.
- *Fairness*: The criterion of fairness draws the researcher's attention to the need to be fair to all research participants and to ensure that their rights are upheld. Implementation of this criterion is guided by questions such as, how fair will my research actions be? Will they treat all research participants in the same way? Will my actions show favouritism and/or discrimination towards any participants?

Researchers should demonstrate best ethical conduct by showing an understanding of what is right or wrong behaviour as you conduct the research. This consideration is founded on the understanding that all humans have dignity which must be respected, and they have a fundamental human right to make choices which you as a researcher must respect.

Principles of Ethical Consideration of Research

Implementation of ethical considerations focuses on four principles which you need to uphold when dealing with your participants and data. These principles have the acronym PAPA namely: Privacy, Accuracy, Property and Accessibility.

- *Privacy*: Under this principle, you need to consider what information participants will be required to reveal to you or to others about themselves, their associations or organisations? It considers the conditions and safeguards under which data will be gathered and analysed. What things, for example, can participants keep to themselves, and not be forced to reveal to you or any other people?
- *Accuracy*: This principle considers who is responsible for the authenticity, fidelity, and, accuracy of information? Similarly, it considers how you as the researcher will cross-check with participants so they know you have recorded the data accurately. It also makes it very clear who will be held accountable for any errors in data? And, if any party were to be injured, how would they be compensated?
- *Property*: Under this principle, you need to consider who will own the data? Will there be any payment for the data? If so, what will be the just and fair prices, for the exchange of data? Who will own the channels, such as publications and media through which information will be disseminated?
- *Accessibility*: This principle considers who will have access to the data? How will the data be kept safe and secure? Under what conditions and with what safeguards will researchers and participants have access to the data? How will access to the data be gained?

4

Introduction to Ethics

We know that *Axiology* is the branch of philosophy that considers the study of principles and values. *Axiology* is the philosophical investigation of value. *Axiology* can be divides into two major fields of investigation (or sub-branches): *Aesthetics* and *Ethics*. Ethics is the questioning of morals and personal values. Aesthetics is the examination of what is beautiful, enjoyable, or tasteful. In axiology education is more than just about knowledge but also quality of life.

Ethics is crucially important because it is devoted to answering questions like these:

- What is the best?
- What is the good life?
- How should I live?
- How should I behave towards other people?
- What is the purpose of life?

4.1. Meaning of Ethics

Etymologically the term *"ethics"* correspond to the Greek word *"ethos"* which means character, habit, customs, ways of behaviour, etc. Ethics is also called *"moral philosophy"*. The word *"moral"* comes from Latin word *"mores"* which signifies customs, character, behaviour, etc. Thus, ethics may be defined as the systematic study of human actions from the point of view of their rightfulness or wrongfulness, as means for the attainment of the ultimate happiness. It is the reflective study of what is good or bad in that part of human conduct for which human has some personal responsibility. In simple words ethics refers to what is good and the way to get it, and what is bad and how to avoid it. It refers to what ought to be done to achieve what is good and what ought not to be done to avoid what is evil.

4.1.1. Ethics as a Philosophical Discipline

As a philosophical discipline, ethics is the study of the values and guidelines by which we live. It also involves the justification of these values and guidelines. It is not merely following a tradition or custom. Instead, it requires analysis and evaluation of these guidelines in light of universal principles. As moral philosophy, ethics is the philosophical thinking about morality, moral problems, and moral judgments.

4.1.2. Ethics as a Science

Ethics is a science in as much as it is a set or body of reasoned truths organised in a logical order and having its specific material and formal objects. It is the science of what human ought to be by reason of what one is. It is a rational science in so far as its principles are deduced by human's reason from the objects that concern the freewill. Besides it has for its ulterior end the art by which human may live uprightly or comfortably to right reason. It is a normative/regulative science in as much as it regulates and directs human's life and gives the right orientation to one's existence.

4.1.3. Ethics as a Theoretical and Practical

Ethics is also theoretical and practical. It is theoretical in as much as it provides the fundamental principles on the basis of which moral judgments are arrived at. It is practical in as much as it is concerned about an end to be gained, and the means of attaining it.

4.2. Definitions of Ethics

- According to Thomas Garret, *"Ethics is the science of judging specifically human ends and the relationship of means to those ends. In some way it is also the art of controlling means so that they will serve human ends."*
- Manuel G. Velasquez, *"'Ethics' is the discipline that examines one's moral standard or moral standards of society. It asks how those standards apply to our life and whether these standards are reasonable or unreasonable — that is, whether these are supported by good reason or poor one."*
- Dale S. Beach, *"Ethics refer to a set of moral principles which should play a very significant role in guiding the conduct of managers and employees in the operation of any enterprise."*
- Carol Buchholtz, *"Ethics is that discipline which deals with what is good and bad and also deal with moral duty and obligation. Ethics are set of moral principles or values."*
- Post, Frederick, and Lawlrence, *"Ethics is a conception of right and wrong conduct. Ethics tell us when our behaviour is moral and when it is moral. Ethics deal with fundamental human relationship how we think and behave towards others and how we want them to think and behave towards us."*
- Webster's Directory, *"Ethics are formalised principles derived from social value. These are moral principle which originate from social value and represent rules for moral behaviour and conduct of individuals or groups thereof carrying on business."*

4.3. Why is Ethics Important?

Ethics is the branch of study dealing with what is the proper course of action for man. It answers the question, "What do I do?" It is the study of right and wrong in human endeavors. At a more fundamental level, it is the method by which we categorize our values and pursue them. Do we pursue our own happiness, or do we sacrifice ourselves to a greater cause? Is that foundation of ethics based on the Bible, or on the very nature of man himself, or neither?

Ethics is a requirement for human life. It is our means of deciding a course of action. Without it, our actions would be random and aimless. There would be no way to work towards a goal because there would be no way to pick between a limitless number of goals. Even with an ethical standard, we may be unable to pursue our goals with the possibility of success. To the degree which a rational ethical standard is taken, we are able to correctly organize our goals and actions to accomplish our most important values. Any flaw in our ethics will reduce our ability to be successful in our endeavors.

4.4. Difference between Ethics and Values

Ethics are the set of rules that govern the behaviour of a person, established by a group or culture. Values refer to the beliefs for which a person has an enduring preference. Ethics and values are important in every aspect of life, when we have to make a choice between two things, wherein ethics determine what is right, values determine what is important.

The fundamental differences between ethics and value are described in the given below points:

Table 4.1 *Differences between Ethics and Values*

Basis for Comparison	*Ethics*	*Values*
Meaning	Ethics refers to the guidelines for conduct, that address question about morality.	Value is defined as the principles and ideals that helps them in making judgment of what is more important.
What are they?	Ethics is a system of moral principles.	Values are the stimuli of our thinking.
Consistency	Ethics are consistent	Values are different for different persons, i.e. what is important for one person, may not be important for another person.
Tells	Ethics helps us in deciding what is morally correct or incorrect, in the given situation.	Values tell us what we want to do or achieve in our life,
Determines	Ethics determines to what extent our options are right or wrong.	Values define our priorities for life.
What it does?	Ethics compels to follow a particular course of action.	Values strongly influence the emotional state of mind. Therefore it acts as a motivator.

4.5. Difference between Morals and Ethics

The word Morals is derived from a Greek word *"Mos"* which means *'custom'*. On the other hand, if we talk about Ethics, it is also derived from a Greek word *"Ethikos"* which means *'character'*. Morals are the customs established by group of individuals whereas ethics defines the character of an individual. While morals are concerned with principles of right and wrong, ethics are related to right and wrong conduct of an individual in a particular situation.

The major differences between Morals and Ethics are as under:

Table 4.2 *Differences between Morals and Ethics*

Basis for Comparison	*Morals*	*Ethics*
Meaning	Morals are the beliefs of the individual or group as to what is right or wrong.	Ethics are the guiding principles which help the individual or group to decide what is good or bad.
What is it?	Morals are general guidelines framed by the society E.g. We should speak truth.	Ethics are a response to a particular situation, E.g. Is it ethical to state the truth in a particular situation?
Root word	The term morals is derived from a Greek word 'mos' which refers to custom and the customs are determined by group of individuals or some authority.	The term ethics is originated from Greek word 'ethikos' which refers to character and character is an attribute.
Governed By	Morals are dictated by society, culture or religion.	Ethics are chosen by the person himself which governs his life.
Deals with	Morals are concerned with principles of right and wrong.	Ethics stresses on right and wrong conduct.
Consistency	Morals may differ from society to society and culture to culture.	Ethics are generally uniform.
Expression	Morals are expressed in the form of general rules and statements.	Ethics are abstract.
Freedom to think and choose	As morals are framed and designed by the group, there is no option to think and choose; the individual can either accept or reject.	The people are free to think and choose the principles of his life in ethics.

4.6. Difference between Law and Ethics

In simple terms, the law may be understood as the systematic set of universally accepted rules and regulation created by an appropriate authority such as government, which may be regional, national, international, etc. It is used to govern the action and behavior of the members and can be enforced, by imposing penalties. Ethics are the principles that guide a person or society, created to decide what is good or bad, right or wrong, in a given situation. It regulates a person's behavior or conduct and helps an individual in living a good life, by applying the moral rules and guidelines.

The major differences between law and ethics are mentioned below:

Table 4.3 *Differences between Law and Ethics*

Basis for Comparison	*Law*	*Ethics*
Meaning	The law refers to a systematic body of rules that governs the whole society and the actions of its individual members.	Ethics is a branch of moral philosophy that guides people about the basic human conduct.
What is it?	The law consists of a set of rules and regulations	Ethics comprises of guidelines and principles that inform people about how to live or how to behave in a particular situation.

Basis for Comparison	*Law*	*Ethics*
Governed By	The law is created by the Government, which may be local, regional, national or international.	Ethics are governed by individual, legal or professional norms, i.e. workplace ethics, environmental ethics and so on.
Expression	The law is expressed in the constitution in a written form. They are expressed and published in writing.	As opposed to ethics, it cannot be found in writing form. They are abstract.
Violation	Violation of law is not permissible which may result in punishment like imprisonment or fine or both.	There is no punishment for violation of ethics.
Objective	Law is created with an intent to maintain social order and peace in the society and provide protection to all the citizens.	Ethics are made to help people to decide what is right or wrong and how to act.
Binding	Law has a legal binding.	Ethics do not have a binding nature.

4.7. Types of Ethics

Basically, there are four types of ethics, including normative ethics, personal ethics, social ethics and professional ethics.

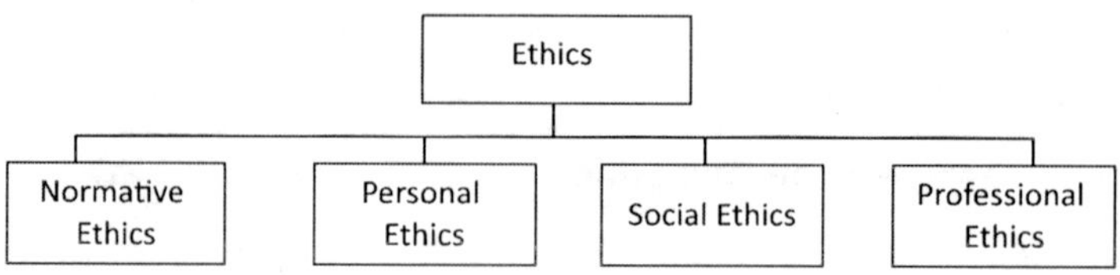

Figure 4.1 *Types of Ethics*

- *Normative Ethics*: It is the branch of moral philosophy, ethics or moral rules that have direct implications upon the human actions and institutions. It includes decision making abilities on moral principles that direct good and bad lead.
- *Personal Ethics*: This refers to a person's own code of ethics, with regard to scenarios involving other people and circumstances that they encounter in everyday life. It is an individual's own moral guide.
- *Social Ethics*: It governs the rightness of an action that is based on fairness, justice, poverty and the rights of an individual from a particular society or community. In short, it determines how the society itself, regulates the values that operate moral law within that society.
- *Professional Ethics*: These refer to a code of conduct, rules and regulations which are to be followed by individuals within a professional space or business environment. It guides people on how to behave or conduct themselves when in contact with other people or institutions in such an environment.

4.8. Making Ethical Decisions: Core Ethical Values

Figure 4.2 *Core Ethical Values*

The six key ethical values that can help to build character are given below:

Trustworthiness: A person who is trustworthy exhibits the following behaviors:

- Acts with integrity
- Is honest and does not deceive
- Keeps his/ her promises
- Is consistent
- Is loyal to those that are not present
- Is reliable
- Is credible
- Has a good reputation

Respect: A person who is respectful exhibits the following behaviors:

- Is open and tolerant of differences
- Is considerate and courteous
- Deals peacefully with anger, disagreements, and/or insults
- Uses good manners
- Treats others the way they want to be treated

Responsibility: A person who is responsible exhibits the following behaviors:

- Acts with self-discipline
- Thinks before acting
- Understands that actions create certain consequences
- Is consistent
- Is accountable for actions

Fairness: A person who is fair exhibits the following behaviors:

- Is open-minded and listens to others
- Takes turns and shares
- Does not lay the blame on others needlessly
- Is equitable and impartial

Caring: A person who is caring exhibits the following behaviors:

- Expresses gratitude to others
- Forgives others
- Helps people in need
- Is compassionate

Citizenship: A person who is a good citizen exhibits the following behaviors:

- Cooperates
- Shares information
- Stays informed
- Is a good neighbor
- Protects the environment
- Obeys the law
- Exhibits civic duty
- Seeks the common good for the most people

4.9. Scope of Ethics

Ethics deals with voluntary actions. We can distinguish between human actions and actions of human: human actions are those actions that are done by human consciously, deliberately and in view of an end. Actions of human may not be wilfully, voluntarily, consciously and deliberately done but all the same they are done by human (e.g. sleeping, walking, etc.). It is the intention which makes the difference between human action and action of human. In ethics we deal only with human actions

4.10. Branches of Ethics

Now, let us make a map of Ethics, so, we can see in more detail exactly what it, as an academic enterprise, entails. First, Ethics divides into two main branches:

- Ethical Theory and
- Ethical Application.

4.10.1. Ethical Theory

Ethical Theory is the investigation of the competing moral theories that have been proposed by philosophers. Ethical theory deals with the content of various moral theories and ethical application explores how those theories can be applied in the context of human existence.

4.10.1.1. Branches of Ethical Theory

It divides into two main sub-branches:

- Normative Ethics and
- Metaethics

Normative Ethics: Normative Ethics is concerned with the criteria of what is right or wrong. It includes the formulation of moral rules that have direct implications for what human actions, institutions and ways of life should be like. It deals with questions like: How should people act? What is the correct action? Normative ethics is the branch of ethics that studies ethical action. Basically, normative ethics attempts to determine which actions are right and wrong, or which character traits are good and bad.

Normative Theories: There are four major normative theories:

- *Utilitarianism*: According to this theory, the right action is the action that produces the greatest balance of overall happiness.
- *Kantianism*: Derived from the work of the German philosopher Immanuel Kant, this theory focuses on categorical imperative, which is a moral principle that acts as the fundamental principle of morality, and from which all our duties may originate from.
- *Ethical Intuitionism*: According to this theory, our intuitive awareness of value, or intuitive knowledge of evaluative facts, forms the foundation of our ethical knowledge.
- *Virtue Ethics*: This theory focuses on the inherent character of a person rather than on specific actions. In other words, it focuses on the role of character and virtue rather than doing one's duty or acting in order to bring about good consequences.

Metaethics: The second major branch of ethical theory is Metaethics. As the name implies, Metaethics investigates a series of questions about the normative theories. For example, all Teleological theories define 'the good' in terms of some end or consequence of our actions (e.g., happiness for me, pleasure for me, happiness/ pleasure for the greatest number of people, etc.). But, what is the nature of this end? Are the consequences we use to define what is good objective features of the world, or are they relative to individuals, cultures, historical epochs, or even species?

Meta-ethics is the branch of ethics that seeks to understand the nature of ethical properties, statements, attitudes, and judgments. While normative ethics

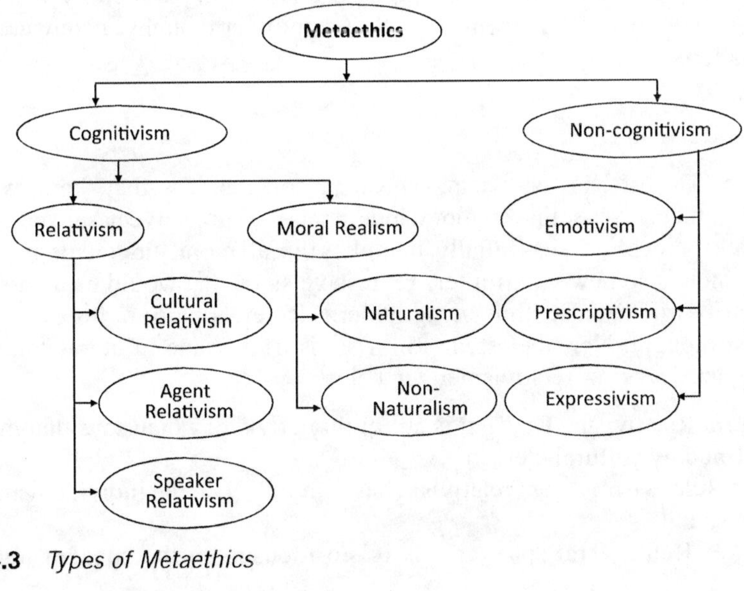

Figure 4.3 *Types of Metaethics*

addresses such questions as *"What should I do?"* evaluating specific practices and principles of action, meta-ethics addresses questions such as *"What is goodness?"* and *"How can we tell what is good from what is bad?"*, seeking to understand the nature of ethical properties and evaluations.

Metaethics is the study of moral thought and moral language. Rather than addressing questions about what practices are right and wrong, and what our obligations to other people or future generations are – questions of so-called 'normative' ethics – metaethics asks what morality actually is. The metaethicist is interested in whether there can be knowledge of moral truths, or only moral feelings and attitudes, and asks how we understand moral discourse as compared with other forms of speech and writing.

Meta-ethical Questions: According to Richard Garner and Bernard Rosen, there are three kinds of meta-ethical problems, or three general questions:

1. What is the meaning of moral terms or judgments? (moral semantics)
2. What is the nature of moral judgments? (moral ontology)
3. How may moral judgments be supported or defended? (moral epistemology

Types of Metaethics: There are two main sub-categories subsumed under the broader idea of metaethics.

i. Cognitivism
ii. Non-cognitivism

i. Cognitivism: The first is cognitivism, which holds that moral statements express propositions, meaning that they are truth-apt. Thus, moral statements have the capability of being objectively true of false since they are descriptive of some external reality in the world. For example, if I say killing is morally wrong, that is making a cognitivist statement of truth. Cognitivist thought encompasses two primary beliefs.

a. Relativism
b. Moral Realism

Relativism: The first is relativism, whose central thesis is that there exists no universal truth, but rather that all moral judgments are subjective based on differing contexts and perceptions. Essentially, it implies that all moral judgments are equally correct, which is somewhat infinitely regressive since that would mean no theory is necessarily true or false, thus being rather self-defeating in terms of following cognitivist thought. Nonetheless, it still assigns truth value to moral statements. There are three types of relativism given below:

- Cultural Relativism: The first is cultural relativism, which says that morality is defined by cultural elements.
- Agent Relativism: Agent relativism bases morality on the individual and their actions, and
- Speaker Relativism: speaker relativism focuses on the speaker and their claims.

b. Moral Realism: The second primary view of cognitivism is moral realism, which is statistically the most popular form of metaethics among philosophers. Contrary to relativism, it claims that there are such things as moral facts and values that are objective and independent of individual orientations towards them. Moral realism has two types:

- Naturalism: Naturalism lies under this theory, arguing that morality is derived from the natural world and thus can be reduced down into natural properties that constitute a posteriori (empirical) knowledge.
- Non-Naturalism: On the other hand, non-naturalism believes that moral values are independent of nature, rather characterizing natural actions or behaviors as good or bad.

Non-cognitivism: On the other hand, non-cognitivism rejects the notion of moral declarations being truth-apt. Rather, it views moral discourse as a way to express attitudes towards certain actions. The umbrella of non-cognitivism also lies several different varieties given below:

- Emotivism: It is popularized by A.J. Ayer and C.L. Stevenson, holds that ethical declarations express solely emotions, specifically those of approval or disapproval. Another type,
- Prescriptivism: prescriptivism claims that moral statements serve as universalizable imperatives or commands meant to influence the behaviors of all others. For example, the proposition "murder is wrong" actually means "Do not kill!"
- Expressivism: Expressivism, rather similarly, argues that moral statements do not assert any objective fact, but rather express an attitude. Another interesting term beneath this umbrella is Quasi-Realism, originally defended by Simon Blackburn, which states that ethical statements behave as factual claims that can reasonably be assigned some sort of truth value. Nonetheless, they cannot be called realist since there exist no ethical facts for them to associate with or correspond to.

4.11. Moral Philosophy

Moral philosophy is the branch of philosophy that contemplates what is right and wrong. It explores the nature of morality and examines how people should live their lives in relation to others. Moral Philosophy is the rational study of the meaning and justification of moral claims. A moral claim evaluates the rightness or wrongness of an action or a person's character. For example, "Lying is wrong" claims the act of lying is wrong, while "One shouldn't be lazy" claims a character trait (i.e., laziness) is wrong.

4.11.1. Origin of Morality

There are two ways to look at the source of morality:

- *Heteronomous theory of morality*: the man receives morality from elsewhere that of himself (God, moral law, society). This is the position of St. Thomas, Kant (Critique of Practical Reason), Schopenhauer, Bergson or Durkheim.

- *Autonomous theory of morality*: man creates, invents himself the principles of his action (Nietzsche, Sartre, Camus)

4.11.2. Schools of Moral Philosophy

Here is a brief overview of the main branches of moral philosophy, from ancient times to the present day:

- *Formalism or Deontology*: Kant's practical philosophy is related to this current. Formalism asserts that the morality of an act depends on the form of the act, and not on its content.
- *Individualism*: Individualism, in morality, posits the primacy of the individual over the social totality: values emanate from the individual. Nietzsche or Dumont are representatives of moral individualism.
- *Eudemonism*: According to eudemonism, the goal of action is the search for happiness.
- *Pessimism*: Pessimism, in morality, consists in thinking evil prevails over good, so man is condemned to act badly.
- *Utilitarianism*: Utility must be the criterion of action. According to the utilitarians, the principle of utility supposes a calculated search for pleasures (arithmetic of pleasures). In both quantitative and qualitative terms.
- *Hedonism*: Happiness is immediate pleasure. Happiness is enjoyment.
- *Stoicism*: It is the concept of destiny (fatum) that governs the morality of the Stoics. The actions of man must be guided by the acceptance of destiny. The man only mastering his view of things, not the things themselves.
- *Epicureanism*: Epicurean morality consists in satisfying only the natural and necessary pleasures.
- *Consequentialism*: Only the consequences of an act make it possible to qualify it in terms of moral or immoral.
- *Cynicism*: Cynicism consists of despising morals, conventions or even traditions.
- *Ethical Relativism*: The relativists consider that no morality can claim to the universal, that the cultures have a proper morality, equivalent to each other.
- *Altruism*: Altruism affirms that only moral acts guided by disinterestedness and the love of others.
- *Nihilism*: Nihilism defends a conception according to which there is no absolute, transcendent morality.
- *Existentialism*: Man invents his way and his morality freely. The bastard, on the contrary, guided by the spirit of seriousness, hides behind a legacy morality.

4.11.3. Major Philosophers of Morality and their Main Moral Work

- *Plato*: It is in Gorgias that his moral philosophy is best illustrated, even if the Republic also presents the main concepts of Platonic moral philosophy.
- *Aristotle*: Nicomachean Ethics
- *Jean-Jacques Rousseau*: The origin of inequalities among men
- *Immanuel Kant*: Metaphysics of Morals

- *David Hume*: Treatise on Human Nature
- *Friedrich Nietzsche*: The Genealogy of Morals
- *Arthur Schopenhauer*: Aphorisms on wisdom (very easy to read)
- *Baruch Spinoza*: Ethics
- *Jean-Paul Sartre*: Existentialism is a humanism (very easy to read)
- *Emmanuel Levinas*: Totality and Infinity (difficult work for neophytes)

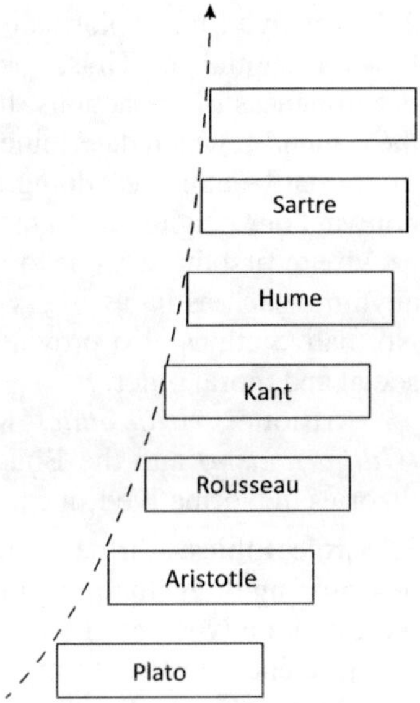

Figure 4.4 *Major Philosophers of Morality*

4.11.4. Importance of Moral Philosophy in Philosophy

Moral Philosophy is one of the major schools of philosophy. Moral philosophy relates to practical philosophy, while metaphysics refers to theoretical philosophy. Morality thus speaks of action (and answers questions such as "May war be fair? Is the death penalty moral?), some focusing on intentions that preside over actions, others on the consequences of our actions. Moral philosophy ultimately attempts to answer the following question: *What should I do?*

4.11.5. Moral Philosophy or Ethics?

We must distinguish moral philosophy from ethics. If the first refers to inter subjectivity (the relation to others), the second refers to personal actions, to the relation of the subject to himself. We often use one for the other in a wrong way. In some thinkers, ethics is a philosophy derived from ontology (Plato, Sartre), in others derived from politics (Aristotle). Some even reverse the theoretical/practical relationship: moral philosophy is the first philosophy (Levinas), it is from it that the other branches of philosophy must flow.

4.12. Branches of Moral Philosophy

The four main branches of moral philosophy are discussed below:

1. Descriptive Ethics: Descriptive ethics deals with what people actually believe (or made to believe) to be right or wrong, and accordingly holds up the human actions acceptable or not acceptable or punishable under a custom or law. However, customs and laws keep changing from time to time and from society to society. The societies have structured their moral principles as per changing time and have expected people to behave accordingly. Due to this, descriptive ethics is also called comparative ethics because it compares the ethics or past and present; ethics of one society and other. It also takes inputs from other disciplines such as anthropology, psychology, sociology and history to explain the moral right or wrong.

2. Normative Ethics: Normative Ethics deals with "norms" or set of considerations how one should act. Thus, it is a study of "ethical action" and sets out the rightness or wrongness of the actions. It is also called prescriptive ethics because it rests on the principles which determine whether an action is right or wrong. The Golden rule of normative ethics is "doing to other as we want them to do to us". Since, we do not want our neighbours to throw stones through our glass window, then it will not be wise to first throw stone through a neighbour's window. Based on this reasoning, anything such as harassing, victimising, abusing or assaulting someone is wrong. Normative ethics also provides justification for punishing a person who disturbs social and moral order.

Aristotle's *virtue ethics*, Kant's *deontological ethics*, Mill's *consequentialism (Utilitarianism)* and the Bhagwad Gita's *Nishkam Karmayoga* are some of the theories in Normative Ethics.

3. Virtue Ethics: Virtue ethics focuses on one's character and the virtues for determining or evaluating ethical behaviour. Plato, Aristotle and Thomas Aquinas were major advocates of Virtue ethics. Plato gave a scheme of four cardinal virtues viz. prudence, justice, temperance and fortitude (courage). His disciple Aristotle categorized the virtues as moral and intellectual. He identified some of the moral virtues including "wisdom".

4. Deontological Ethics: Deontological ethics or duty ethics focuses on the rightness and wrongness of the actions rather than the consequences of those actions. There are different deontological theories such as categorical imperative, moral absolutism, divine command theory etc.

- *Categorical Imperative*: First famous deontological theory is Immanuel Kant's Categorical Imperative or Kantianism. Kant said that the human beings occupy special place in creation and there is an ultimate commandment from which all duties and obligations derive. The moral rules, as per Kant, should follow two principles viz. universality and principle of reciprocity. By universality, he meant that a moral action must be possible to apply it to all people. By principle of reciprocity, he meant said "do as you would be done by. Such premise of morality is found in all religious systems, including Hinduism, Islam, Christianity, Judaism, Buddhism etc.
- *Moral absolutism*: Second famous deontological theory is Moral absolutism. It believes that there are absolute standards against which moral questions can be judged. Against these standards, certain actions are right while others are wrong regardless of the context of the act. For example, theft is wrong, regardless of context in which theft was carried out. It ignores that sometimes wrong act is done to reach out to right consequence.
- *Divine command theory*: Third deontological theory is Divine command theory. It says that an action is right if God has decreed it to be right. As per this theory, the rightness of any action depends upon that action being performed because it is a duty, not because of any good consequences arising from that action.

5. Consequentialism (Teleology): Consequentialism or teleological ethics says that the morality of an action is contingent with the outcome of that action. So, the morally right action would produce good outcome while morally wrong action would produce bad outcome. Based on the outcome, there are several theories such as:

- *Utilitarianism*(right action leads to most happiness of greatest number of people);
- *Hedonism*(anything that maximizes pleasure is right);
- *Egoism*(anything that maximizes the good for self is right);
- *Asceticism*(abstinence from egoistic pleasures to achieve spiritual goals is right action);
- *Altruism*(to live for others and not caring for self is right action).

The core idea of consequentialism is that *"the ends justify the means"*. An action that might not be right in the light of moral absolutism may be a right action under teleology.

6. Meta Ethics: The Meta-ethics has been discussed earlier in detail.

7. Applied Ethics: Applied ethics deals with the philosophical examination, from a moral standpoint, of particular issues in private and public life which are matters of moral judgment. This branch of ethics is most important for professionals in different walks of life including doctors, teachers, administrators, rulers and so on. There are six key domains of applied ethics:

- *Decision Ethics* (ethical decision-making process);
- *Professional Ethics* (for good professionalism);
- *Clinical Ethics* (good clinical practices);
- *Business Ethics* (good business practices);
- *Organizational Ethics* (ethics within and among organizations) and
- *Social Ethics* (It deals with the rightness or wrongness of social, economical, cultural, religious issues also. For example, euthanasia, child labour, abortion etc.)

4.13. Moral Reasoning

Moral reasoning is the process in which an individual tries to determine what is right and what is wrong. Moral reasoning is the process in which an individual tries to determine the difference between what is right and what is wrong in a personal situation by using logic. To make such an assessment, one must first know what an action is intended to accomplish and what its possible consequences will be on others. People use moral reasoning in an attempt to do the right thing. People are frequently faced with moral choices, such as whether to lie to avoid hurting someone's feelings, or whether to take an action that will benefit some while harming others. Such judgments are made by considering the objective and the likely consequences of an action. Moral reasoning is the consideration of the factors relevant to making these types of assessments.

According to consultant Lynn E. Swaner (2005), moral behavior has four components:

- *Moral sensitivity*, which is "the ability to see an ethical dilemma, including how our actions will affect others."
- *Moral judgment*, which is "the ability to reason correctly about what 'ought' to be done in a specific situation."
- *Moral motivation*, which is "a personal commitment to moral action, accepting responsibility for the outcome."
- *Moral character*, which is a "courageous persistence in spite of fatigue or temptations to take the easy way out."

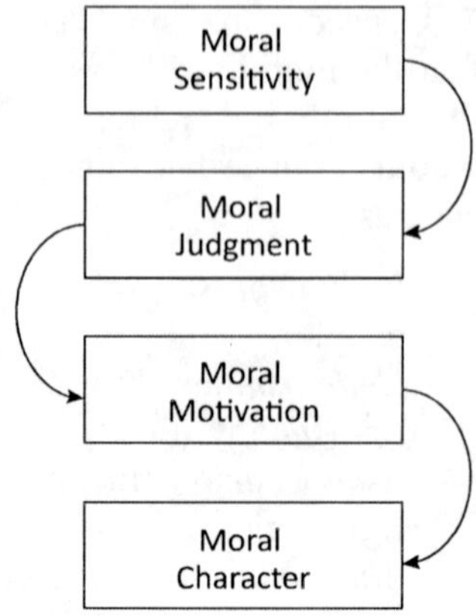

Figure 4.5 *Components of Moral Behaviour*

The ability to think through moral issues and dilemmas requires an awareness of a set of moral and ethical values; the capacity to think objectively and rationally about what may be an emotional issue; the willingness to take a stand for what is right, even in the face of opposition; and the fortitude and resilience to maintain one's ethical and moral standards.

4.14. Skills for Moral Expertise

Realizing good conduct, being an effective moral agent, and bringing values into one's work, all require skills in addition to a moral inclination. Studies have uncovered four skill sets that play a decisive role in the exercise of moral expertise.

- *Moral imagination*: The ability to see the situation through the eyes of others. Moral imagination achieves a balance between becoming lost in the perspectives of others and failing to leave one's own perspective. Adam Smith terms this balance "proportionality," which we can achieve in empathy.
- *Moral creativity*: Moral creativity is closely related to moral imagination, but it centers on the ability to frame a situation in different ways.
- *Reasonableness*: Reasonableness balances openness to the views of others with commitment to moral values and other important goals. That is, a reasonable person is open, but not to the extent where he is willing to believe just anything and/or fails to keep fundamental commitments.
- *Perseverance*: Perseverance is the ability to decide on a moral plan of action and then to adapt to any barriers that arise in order to continue working toward that goal.

4.15. Moral Consciousness

Ethics is a science of morality and it discusses the contents of moral consciousness and the various problems of moral consciousness. Moral consciousness is the consciousness of right and wrong. It involves three factors:

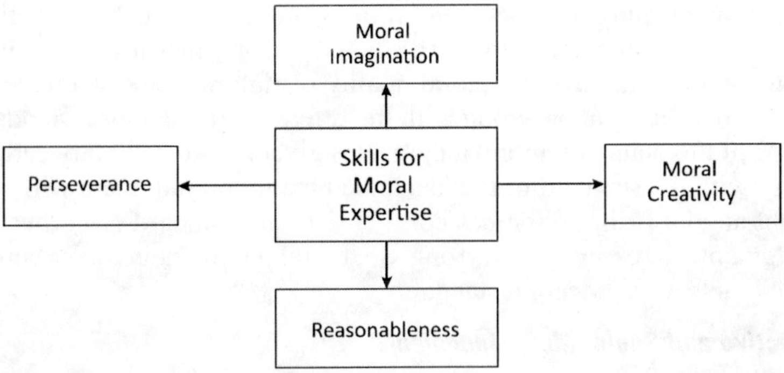

Figure 4.6 *Skills for Moral Expertise*

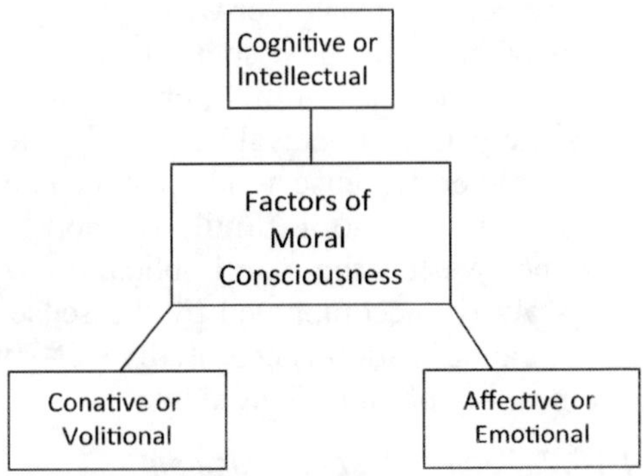

Figure 4.7 *Factors of Moral Consciousness*

i. *Cognitive or intellectual*: Moral judgement is the main cognitive factor in moral consciousness. It involves intuition of moral standard by reason and comparison of a voluntary action with it. It also involves evaluation of voluntary action of it as right and wrong.
ii. *Affective or emotional*: The emotional factors include the moral sentiments and moral judgements are followed by moral sentiments and not vice versa.
iii. *Conative or volitional*: Moral obligation is the main conative factor of moral consciousness and moral judgement involves moral obligation or the sense of duty or oughtness. It involves the moral impulse to do the right action. We feel we are under moral obligations to do what is right and avoid what is wrong.

4.16. Moral Judgment

The moral judgement is the judgement which deals with the moral value or quality of an action. It is a judgement of value and it evaluates the rightness or wrongness of our actions. When we analyse a moral judgement then we find that it contains:

- a subject which will judge;
- an object whose action will be judged;
- a standard in conformity to which the action of the subject will be judged and
- a power of judging the action as required. Moral judgment is the judgment of moral quality of voluntary habitual actions.

Generally, a moral judgment is given on the voluntary and habitual actions of a rational being. The voluntary actions of a rational person which involve deliberation, choice, and resolution, have the moral quality of rightness and wrongness. They are considered to be right or wrong with the reference to the moral standard. And on the basis of this standard, moral judgment is given. If the voluntary actions have conformity with the standard or the ideal, then the moral judgment will express it as the right action. If the action has conflict with the standard or norms, then the moral judgment will express it as wrong. So, moral judgment involves comparison of voluntary acts with the moral standard.

4.16.1. Active and Social Moral Judgment

- *Moral judgment is active in nature.* Because moral judgment is given upon voluntary and habitual acts of persons and not upon their passive experiences.
- *Moral judgment is social in character.* Because, as we know, voluntary acts of a person are right or wrong, because they more or less effect of the interest of others. Man is a social being. His rights and duties of actions rise out of his relation to other persons in society. So, moral judgment, apart from society is inconceivable. Moral judgment can be said to be obligatory in character. Because a judgment can be given as right, while we feel the moral obligation to do it. Similarly, moral judgment is given on an act as wrong, when we feel the moral obligation to refrain from it. Thus, moral judgment is always accompanied by the sense of duty or moral obligation. And this moral obligation is essentially self-imposed. In this way, we can find out the meaning of moral judgment.

4.16.2. Nature of Moral Judgment

Moral judgment is a judgment of values. It is distinct from the judgment of facts.

- A *Judgment of value* is a judgment of *"what ought to be"*. But, a judgment of fact is a judgment of *"what is"*.
- *Judgment of fact* is a descriptive judgment, while moral judgment is an appreciative or critical judgment.

So, moral judgment is a mental act of pronouncing a particular action to be right or wrong. According to Mackenzie, moral judgment is not merely to state the nature of some object, but to compare it with a standard and to pronounce it to be good or evil, right or wrong. So, it is normative. Muirhead says that moral judgment is concerned with the judgment upon conduct, the judgment that such and such conduct is right and wrong. The judgment upon conduct has a judicial sense and the judgment of fact has logical sense. Thus, when we perceive a voluntary action we compare it with the moral standard and thus judge whether the action is in conformity with it or not. So, it is clear that, moral judgment is inferential in nature, involving the application of a standard to a particular action. But, in the language of Bradley, ordinarily moral judgment is intuitive and immediate. Because, we intuitively brings an action under a moral rule recognized by the community and judge it to be right or wrong. It is only in difficult or doubtful cases that we consciously compare an action with the moral ideal and judge it as right or wrong.

Hence, we can find out that a moral judgment presupposes a subject, who judges an object that is judged, a standard according to which an action is judged.

Again, it is important to observe that moral judgment is distinguished from logical and aesthetical judgment. As we know Ethics, Logic and Aesthetics are normative science. And accordingly, they have three supreme norms and ideals of life:

i. ethics is concerned with the ideals of Highest Good,
ii. logic is concerned with the ideal of Truth and
iii. aesthetics is concerned with the ideal of Beauty.

It is true that all of them are appreciative or critical judgment. But, moral judgments are always accompanied by moral obligation and moral sentiments, which are not accompanied by logical and aesthetics judgments. When we judge an action to be right, we feel a moral obligation to perform it and have a feeling of approval. And we judge an action to be wrong, we feel that under moral obligation we are not to perform it and therefore, we have a feeling of disapproval. Feeling of approval, disapproval, rightness, wrongness etc. are called moral sentiments. Thus, moral judgments are obligatory in character and are accompanied by moral sentiments. So, they differ from logical and aesthetic judgments which are not accompanied by moral obligation and moral sentiments.

Moral judgements, whether something is good or bad in its own right are contained wholly in the field of ethics. In the process of reasoning also we find different classes of judgements and they are usually judgement of facts. But moral judgement as a judgement of value is concerned with what ought to be. It judges our actions ought to be. It has distinctive features. It is critical judgement and appreciative. It is the mental act of discerning and pronouncing a particular action to be right or wrong. After evaluation and deliberation actions are to be judged in conformity with a standard. 'To speak the truth is always right' is a moral judgement. Moral judgement differs from judgement of fact which is descriptive judgement and it describes what is. Judgements of facts are more objective because they depend on the real nature of the world. For example, 'Water is composed of oxygen and hydrogen'.

Moral judgement is inferential in character though the element of inference generally remains implicit. It involves the application of a standard to a particular action. When we perceive a voluntary action, we compare it with the moral standard and we judge whether the action is in conformity with it or not. Ordinarily moral judgements are intuitive and immediate. F.H. Bradley says that they are intuitive subsumptions. But, in complex and doubtful cases the whole process is becomes explicit and reflective. In complicated circumstances the moral standard is explicitly held before the mind and applied to the cases under consideration.

4.16.3. Difference between Moral Judgements and Logical Judgements

- Moral judgements are distinguished from logical judgements. Logical judgements refer to the ideal of Truth and it is merely a judgement about. But moral judgements refer to the ideal of supreme Good. The supreme Good or the highest Good is the ultimate standard of moral judgement.

- In moral judgement there is always moral obligation and moral sentiments. Moral obligation is the sense of duty or oughtness.
- Again, moral judgements are accompanied by a feeling of approval or disapproval, feeling of complacence or remorse etc. when we judge an action to be right, we feel under moral obligation to perform it and have a feeling of approval. When we judge an action to be wrong, we feel under moral obligation not to perform it and have a feeling of disapproval. But all are lacking in logical judgement.
- Moral judgement is a judgement upon action with reference to the moral ideal. For him moral judgement is not like a logical judgement which is a judgement about an action. He says that moral judgement does not consider the nature of an action, but it considers its moral value.
- Moral judgement is not a judgement in the logical sense of a 'proposition' but that it is a judgement in the judicial sense of a 'sentence'.

4.16.4. Difference between Moral Judgments and Aesthetics Judgments

- Moral judgements are also distinguished from Aesthetic judgements.
- Though moral judgements and aesthetic judgements are the matter of normative sciences, but their norms are different.
- Moral judgement deals with the ideal of Highest Good whereas aesthetic judgement deals with the ideal of Beauty.
- Again, aesthetic judgements are not accompanied by moral obligation and moral sentiments.
- On the other hand, moral judgements are obligatory in nature and accompanied by moral sentiments.
- Moral judgement has objective validity. An action is right in a particular situation from the standpoint of the universe. It is not determined by the subjective inclination and prejudices of the person who makes the judgement.

4.16.5. Object of Moral Judgment

Moral judgments are passed on the voluntary actions and habitual actions. Actually, habitual actions are voluntary actions turned into habit after constant repetitions. Hence, only voluntary actions are objects of moral judgement and they are judged to be right or wrong. Voluntary actions imply the freedom of will. Non voluntary actions are outside the scope of moral judgement.

Voluntary action has some internal factors:

- The mental stage of spring of action, motive, intention, desire, deliberation, choice and resolution.
- The organic stage of bodily action.
- The external stage of consequence

4.16.6. Subject of Moral Judgment

The subject of the moral judgement is the rational self or ideal self. Mackenzie holds that a person judges an action to be right or wrong from the standpoint of an ideal standard. For him, by the subject of the moral judgement we mean the point of view from which an action is judged to be good or bad. Shaftesbury maintains that conduct is judged to be good or bad by the moral connoisseur. Like Shaftesbury, Adam Smith holds that a person passes moral judgement on his own actions and actions of others from the stand point of an impartial spectator. The different interpretations of the subjects of the moral judgement bring out the fact that moral judgements involve a higher point of view of the ideal self. The ideal self passes moral judgements on the motives, intentions, on his own actions and actions of others.

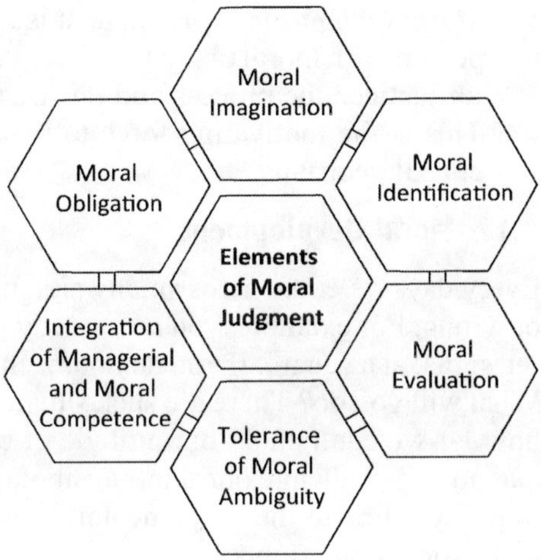

Figure 4.8 *Elements of Moral Judgment*

4.16.7. Elements of Moral Judgment

Moral judgments are evaluations or opinions formed as to whether some action or inaction, intention, motive, character trait, or a person as a whole is (more or less) good or bad as measured against some standard of good. Elements of Moral judgment are discussed below:

- *Moral Imagination*: It refers to the ability of a person to recognize that business and moral relationships do not exist independent of one another but instead are intertwined. Those with moral imagination see past the bottom-line mentality and recognize that everyday choices have moral and ethical implications.
- *Moral Identification and Ordering*: Once a person recognizes moral issues exist, it is necessary to identify and rank, or prioritize, the issues. A person who can order and identify these ethical problems can distinguish the valid and important from the rhetorical.
- *Moral Evaluation*: This is using analytical skills to reason out practical decisions. Those competent in moral evaluation use consistency and coherence in their ethical decision making. These people have foresight and make decisions based on a concern for others as well as the goals of the organization.
- *Tolerance of Moral Ambiguity*: If a person accepts that disagreement in a discussion of ethics, the person is more likely to make morals a part of the decision-making process. This element says that despite lack of clear-cut answers, people can make decisions that represent the best ethical choice as they understand it, knowing that others may disagree.
- *Integration of Managerial and Moral Competence*: Most ethical scandals that organizations have are created as the result of economic decisions. Leaders need to recognize that there are business and economic consequences of ethical decisions, and moral competence is an integral part of managerial or leadership competence.

- *Moral Obligation*: This element is foundational to all the other elements. The person with moral obligation feels a necessity or urgency to act with a concern for justice, due process and fairness to all peoples, groups and communities. This is the motivating force to making moral judgments and implementing ethical decisions.

4.17. Moral Development

Every day, we come across many situations which demand our reasoning of right or wrong. For example, you are already late for school and on your way you find a red signal at a square. If you do not reach on time half of your salary gets deducted. What will you do? There are such situations in our daily life which make us realize how far we can uphold our attitude of being self. In these situations, we need to extend and challenge our thinking about what is 'moral'. Actually, being moral or morality refers to the fundamental questions of right and wrong, justice, fairness and basic human rights.

Moral development focuses on the emergence, change and understanding of morality from infancy through adulthood. Morality develops across a lifetime and is influenced by an individual's experiences and their behavior when faced with moral issues through different periods' physical and cognitive development. In short, morality concerns an individual's growing sense of what is right and wrong; it is for this reason that young children have different moral judgement and character than that of a grown adult. Morality in itself is often a synonym for "rightness" or "goodness". It refers to a certain code of conduct that is derived from one's culture, religion or personal philosophy that guides one's actions, behaviors and thoughts.

4.18. Moral Development Theories

Below, we are describing the three moral development theories in detail:

4.18.1. Piaget's Theory of Moral Development

Before we try to understand Piaget's theory of moral development, let us consider two illustrations.

Case 1

Rajat is a very young boy. His younger brother is very hungry, but Rajat has no money left after buying medicine for his mother. His brother starts crying because of hunger. Rajat goes to a snack-stall and requests the shopkeeper to give kachori for his hungry brother. But he refuses. Finally, Rajat becomes desperate and steals two kachoris. He, then, runs out and gives that to his brother.

Case 2

Shivani goes to a shop. She sees a pretty piece of hair band hanging there in a shelf. She imagines that it would look very nice on her dress. So, while the sales girl turns back, she steals the hair band and runs away at once.

Are these children equally guilty? We will try to find the answer after studying Piaget's theory of moral reasoning. Here, Piaget called such situations as *moral dilemmas*, the problems that require individual judgments and moral reasoning based on our cognition. Therefore, Jean Piaget developed his theory of moral reasoning. He proposed two types of moral reasoning, which are closely related with cognitive development- *'heteronomous morality'* and *'autonomous morality'*.

Piaget conceptualizes moral development as a constructivist process, whereby the interplay of action and thought builds moral concepts. Piaget (1932) was principally interested not in what children do (i.e., in whether they break rules or not) but in what they think. In other words, he was interested in children's moral reasoning. Piaget was interested in three main aspects of children's understanding of moral issues. They were:

1. *Children's understanding of rules. This leads to questions like*:
   - Where do rules come from?
   - Can rules be changed?
   - Who makes rules?
2. *Children's understanding of moral responsibility. This leads to questions like*:
   - Who is to blame for "bad" things?
   - Is it the outcome of behavior that makes an action "bad"?
   - Is there a difference between accidental and deliberate wrongdoing?
3. *Children's understanding of justice. This leads to questions like*:
   - Should the punishment fit the crime?
   - Are the guilty always punished?

Piaget found that children's ideas regarding rules, moral judgements and punishment tended to change as they got older. In other words, just as there were stages to children's cognitive development so there were also universal stages to their moral development. Piaget (1932) suggested two main types of moral thinking:

1. *Heteronomous Moralities (Moral Realism)*: *Heteronomous Moralities* are those moral decisions which are based on the rules of people with supreme authority such as parents. Children who reason about moral issues using heteronomous morality hardly care about the motives or intentions behind actions. However, this type of moral reasoning may be found in some adults too.
2. *Autonomous Morality (Moral Relativism)*: Another type of moral reasoning is Autonomous morality, which is the ability to reason that appreciates the perspectives of others and the motives behind their words and actions. According to Piaget, autonomous morality develops parallel to the development of the stage of formal operations and abstract thinking.

Now, let us answer the question asked above on the moral dilemma regarding the subject of stealing, mentioned in above two short stories. The people of typical heteronomous morality, would respond that Rajat is guiltier than Shivani because two pieces of kachori costs more than a piece of hair band. While, people supporting autonomous morality would respond that Shivani is guiltier because she is being deceitful and Rajat has good intentions of sustaining his younger brother

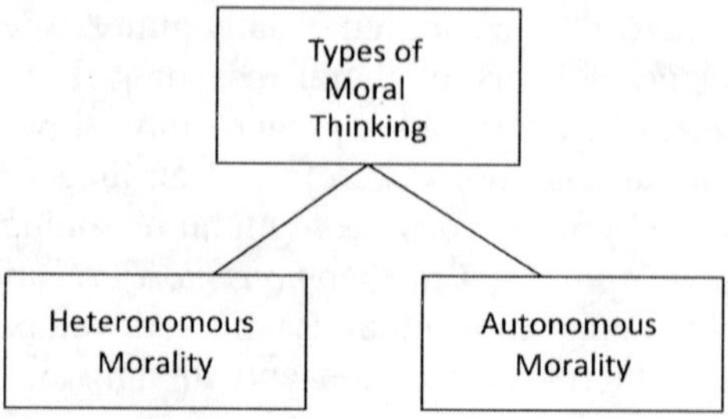

Figure 4.9 *Types of Moral Thinking according to Piaget*

4.18.2. Kohlberg's Theory of Moral Development

Before dealing with Kohlberg's theory of moral development, let's read the case below:

> Case 3
>
> *Atul was not prepared for his Physics Exam, so he wrote some important formulae on a slip of paper which he put in his pocket before the test. Just before the test began, the teacher informed the class that any student caught cheating would automatically fail the test. Even though Atul needed to use the information he wrote on the slip, he didn't use it because the teacher stood too close to his desk during the entire exam.*

What was the reason that stopped Atul from cheating in the examination? There are many such moral dilemmas systematized by Kohlberg under different stages in his theory of moral development. Lawrence Kohlberg (1927-1987) got inspired by Piaget's work and particularly his method of observing and interviewing children. Therefore, he also used a similar methodology of interviewing children and adolescents to collect his data on moral issues. Kohlberg's theory started from self-centeredness and moved towards others' centeredness.

American Psychologist, *Lawrence Kohlberg* (1927-1987), developed a comprehensive stage theory of moral development in 1958. Based on *Jean Piaget's* theory of moral judgment for children, Kohlberg's theory is cognitive in nature and focuses on the thinking process that occurs when one decides whether a behavior is *"right or wrong."* Emphasis is on how one decides to respond to a moral dilemma – not what one decides or how they proceed/act.

Kohlberg's schema or moral stage theory expands upon Piaget's work and hypothesizes that:

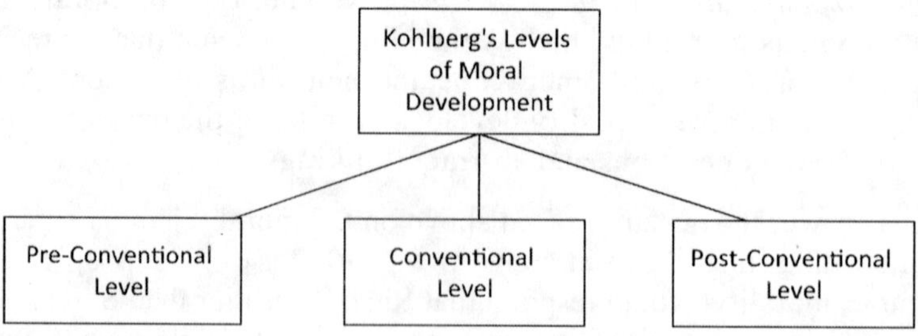

Figure 4.10 *Levels of Moral Development as proposed by Lawrence Kohlberg*

- all individuals in all cultures progress in moral reasoning through a sequence of six separate chronological stages,
- moral values and codes are developed from the interaction between the individual and the environment, and
- moral judgment is characterized in accordance with how a person reasons their delinquent behavior rather than what a person thinks about its content.

Kohlberg developed a six-stage theory of moral development and he grouped these six stages into three higher-order levels of development:

1. Pre-Conventional Level,
2. Conventional Level and
3. Post-Conventional Level.

Each level is then further sub-divided into two stages to make a total of six stages.

The Pre-Conventional Level includes:

- stage one, the punishment and obedience orientation, and
- stage two, the instrumental purpose orientation.

The Conventional Level includes:

- stage three, the morality of interpersonal cooperation, and
- stage four, the social-order-maintaining orientation.

The Post-Conventional Level includes:

- stage five, the social-contract orientation, and
- stage six, the universal ethical principle orientation.

Level 1: Pre-Conventional Level/Morality

At the pre-conventional level, morality is externally controlled. Rules imposed by authority figures are conformed to in order to avoid punishment or receive rewards. This perspective involves the idea that what is right is what one can get away with or what is personally satisfying.

At this level, judgment is based solely on a person's own needs and perceptions. Here, right and wrong is based primarily on external circumstances (punishments and rewards). The first two stages are included in this level:

Stage 1: Obedience or Punishment Orientation: Behavior is determined by consequences. An individual's right course of action involves blind compliance to authority to avoid punishment and keep away from trouble. The well-being of other people is not acknowledged at this stage.

At this stage, we try to avoid breaking rules for fear of punishment because a good or bad action is determined by its physical consequences. Here, the conscience that works is *'self-protection'*.

Example 1

I might be caught and punished
if I cheated!

Stage 2: Self-Interest Orientation or Personal Reward Orientation: Behavior is still determined by consequences, however this time the individual focuses on receiving rewards or satisfying personal needs. Moral decisions are predicated on concerns as the prevention of punishment and the furtherance of one's own self-interests. To do so, one must engage in interactions and agreements with other individuals. Consequently, others are important in an instrumental sense, in deal-making scenarios.

At this stage personal needs determine right and wrong and so; the conscience seems to be 'cunning'. Your behaviour is determined primarily by what will earn you a reward.

Example 2

Maybe he really had to pass because he might get a reward on scoring well. Nevertheless, maybe he should not cheat because the teacher would then fail him.

Level 2: Conventional Level

At the conventional level, conformity to social rules and norms remain important. However, the emphasis now shifts from self-interest to relationships with other people and social systems. In an effort to win approval or to maintain social order, one strives to follow guidelines set forth by socializing agents.

At this level, the judgment is based on other's approval, family expectations, traditional values, the laws of society, and loyalty to country.

Stage 3: Social Conformity Orientation: Moral reasoning is internally motivated by faithfulness to other individuals and by a desire to live up to what is expected by significant others. Behavior is determined by social approval as one desires to be viewed as a "good person."

This stage is the stage of social approval. Your behaviour is determined by what pleases and is approved by others. Here, mutual relations of trust and respect should be maintained provided they conform to your expected social role. The conscience at this stage is loyalty.

Example 3

He just wanted to pass the test and for this, he was taking help of that slip of paper. It doesn't mean he had no knowledge of Physics. It's all about the pressure of the examination! He just wanted to fulfil his parent's expectations.

Stage 4: Law and Order Orientation: Social rules and laws determine behavior. One begins to take into consideration a larger perspective: societal laws. Believing that the rules and laws maintaining social order are worth preserving, decisions become based in adherence of the norms and regulations of varied social institutions (such as the family, the community, and the country).

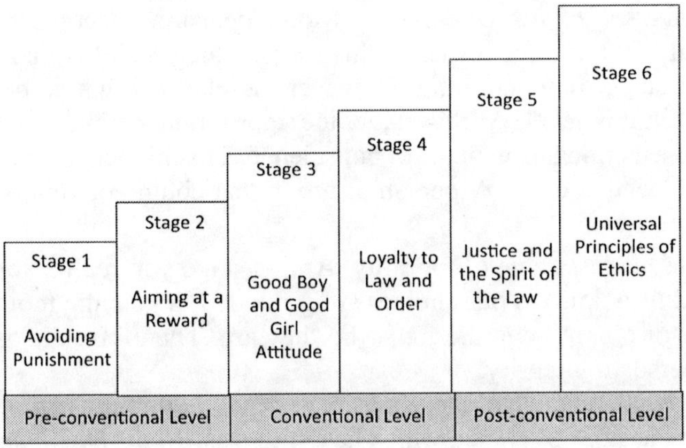

Figure 4.11 *Stages of Moral Development as proposed by Lawrence Kohlberg*

We are expected to respect the authority and maintain the social order. It is right to contribute to the society and fulfill social duties. Here, the conscience is good citizenship.

> *Example 4*
>
> It is wrong to cheat in exams because it is against rules of examination in school.

Level 3: Post-Conventional or Principled Level

At the post-conventional level, one moves beyond the perspective of his or her own society. Morality becomes defined in terms of abstract principles and values that apply to all situations and societies. The individual attempts to take the perspective of all individuals.

At this level, judgments are based on abstract, more personal principles that are not necessarily defined by society's laws.

Stage 5 Social Contract Orientation: Moral reasoning follows the utilitarian concept of a social contract: weighing certain rights, morals, and legal principles against the greatest good for the greatest number of individuals. Individual rights determine one's behavior as laws and rules become flexible tools (i.e., there are exceptions to rules.) When laws are not consistent with individual rights, interests of the majority, nor do they bring about good for people, then alternatives should be considered.

This stage is the stage of social utility and individual rights. Your loyalty is towards truth. At this stage, you are not only aware of the social contract between individuals, but also of the different moral perspectives of others. The conscience of this stage is reason.

> *Example 5*
>
> It is not right to cheat in examination because it is against moral values

Stage 6: Universal Ethics Orientation: Moral decisions become generated by several ethical ideologies of justice at this stage, which Kohlberg considered this is the highest stage of functioning. However, he claimed that some individuals will never reach this level. At this stage, the appropriate action is determined by one's self-chosen ethical principles of conscience. This higher-reasoning involves taking the perspective of every person or group that could potentially be affected by the decision.

This is the highest stage of morality. At this stage you realize to follow self-chosen ethical principles. Your choices are grounded in genuine moral interest in the wellbeing of others, regardless of who they are. Therefore, the conscience at this stage is personal integrity.

In order to understand Kohlberg's theory of moral dilemma in a better way, let us go through the story of Heinz, which he entitled as *'Heinz Dilemma'*.

Heinz Dilemma

A woman in Europe was diagnosed with a kind of cancer and was near her death. Only one medicine could save her as per doctors' opinion which was a kind of radium, discovered by one of the pharmacists in that town. But, that pharmacist was charging nearly ten times the cost of the radium, i.e., $2000 and that too for a small dose. Heinz, the sick woman's husband tried hard to collect money but could arrange for only half the amount. He requested the pharmacist to lend him the medicine because his wife really needed it but the latter didn't help. Heinz got so distressed that he broke into the pharmacist's shop to steal the medicine for his wife.

Let us study Heinz dilemma at all levels of morality by Kohlberg:

Stage 1: Heinz should not steal the medicine because he might be caught and punished or Heinz won't go to prison because he was not stealing something big and more importantly, he asked for it first and was ready to pay.

Stage 2: Heinz might steal the medicine to give happiness to his family at home by saving his wife. But he might get sentenced for a long term in prison which he could not stand.

Stage 3: Heinz was not doing wrong. He just wanted to save his beloved wife. It was the pharmacist who overcharged. He won't get a hard punishment because the judge would look at all sides of the situation.

Stage 4: Heinz should not have stolen because it was against the law or if he had to steal then he must be ready to take the punishment; otherwise, there would be a chaos if everybody sets up everybody's own beliefs.

Stage 5: Life is more important than property and Heinz should save his wife even if he had to steal. Let the moral and legal standpoints coincide or Heinz should not have stolen because even though his wife was sick, it couldn't make his action right.

Stage 6: Heinz should steal the medicine because human life has more value than the property rights of some person or Heinz should not have stolen because any other person might have needed the medicine more badly.

Source: Adapted from Kohlberg (1963, p. 19)

4.18.3. Gilligan's Theory of Moral Development

Carol Gilligan (1982) has proposed a different sequence of moral development in the form of *"ethics of care"*. She debated that Kohlberg's theory of stages are biased in favour of males, in a male dominant society and do not represent the way moral reasoning develops in women because he conducted a longitudinal study of men only. According to Gilligan, women are likely to think of right and wrong in terms of care and relationships, whereas men tend to think in terms of rules and justice. She describes three stages of moral reasoning:

Level 1: Pre-conventional Morality (Orientation to Individual Survival)

The goal of this stage is individual survival. Level 1, orientation to individual survival, shows the individual as self-centered and unable to distinguish between necessity and desire. The individual attempts to protect herself by not pursuing intimate relationships with others.

First Transition

The first transition is from selfishness to responsibility, in which there exists a new connection to others and a differentiation between needs and wants.

Level 2: Conventional Morality (Goodness as Self-sacrifice)

Goodness as self-sacrifice is the second level of development. In this stage, the individual places greater reliance on others and yearns for social acceptance. This

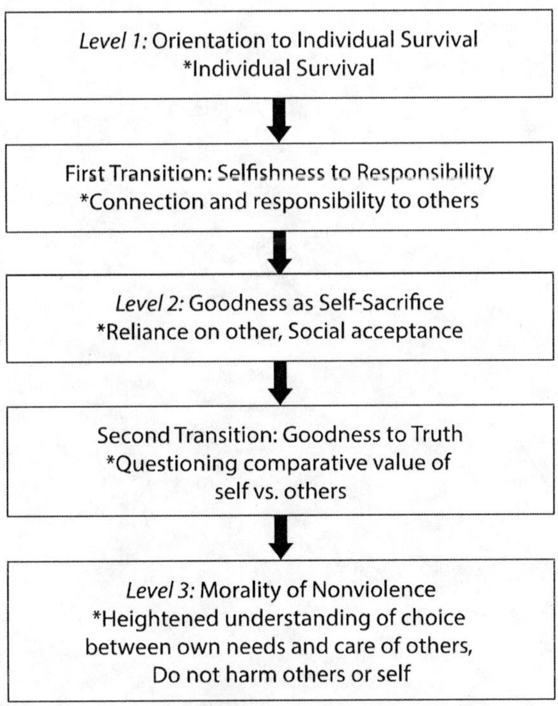

Figure 4.12 *Gilligan's Stages of the Ethics of Care [Levels and Characteristics (*)]*

level says that self-sacrifice is goodness. At this stage, transition is from goodness to the truth of the situation. We are motivated to perform actions which are based on what will care for and benefit others.

Second Transition

In the second transition, from goodness to truth, the individual questions why she places others' needs above her own.

Level 3: Post-conventional Morality (Morality of Nonviolence)

The third and last level, the morality of nonviolence, shows an individual with a transformed understanding of self. There is much respect for the self and individual needs, but the individual also recognizes responsibility and care for others and selects among competing choices. This stage favours the principle of nonviolence. It proposes not to hurt others or the self. We learn that it is just as wrong to ignore our own interests as it is to ignore the interests of others. We come to understand that a relation involves two people, and if either one is affronted, it troubles the relationship.

5

Research Ethics

The search for knowledge about ourselves and the world around us is a fundamental human endeavour. Research is a natural extension of this desire to understand and to improve the world in which we live. The results of this human nature to seek of knowledge enriched and improved human lives and human society in which we lived. In order to maximize the quality and benefits of research, a positive research environment is required. For researchers, this implies duties of honest and thoughtful inquiry, rigorous analysis, commitment to the dissemination of research results, and adherence to the use of professional standards.

It is important to note that a fundamental aspect of research is uncertainty, in relation to the outcome of the research, its potential benefits and the risks involved. Because, research aims at generating new knowledge, uncertainty is unavoidable. It is also important to recognise that research involving human subjects is carried out in a wide range of fields ranging from social sciences, to applied technology and design, and of course the biomedical sciences. All of these areas of research can raise significant and specific ethical challenges.

According to Committee on Publication Ethics (COPE), *"good research should be well adjusted, well-planned, appropriately designed, and ethically approved. To conduct research to a lower standard may constitute misconduct."* For this purpose, research ethics should be prepared and implemented. There should be specified ethically roles for each of the research community member e.g. researcher, scientist, publisher, reviewer, author etc. Research should seek to answer specific meaningful questions, rather than just collect meaningless data.

5.1. Meaning of Research Ethics

Research ethics govern the standards of conduct for scientific researchers. Research ethics refers to ethical conduct in process of research as well as the protection of research participants. Research ethics are the set of ethics that govern how scientific and other research is performed at research institutions such as universities and how it is disseminated. Research ethics provides guidelines for the responsible conduct of research. It educates and monitors researchers conducting research to ensure a high ethical standard.

Research ethics are the set of ethics that govern how scientific and other research is performed at research institutions such as universities, and how it is disseminated.

5.2. Need of Research Ethics

According to Resnick(2015) research ethics are important for a number of reasons:

- Research ethics encourage the aims of research, such as creating of new knowledge in terms of information, facts, concepts, theories, laws, procedures etc.
- Research ethics support the values required for collaborative research work, such as mutual respect and fairness. This is essential because scientific research depends on collaboration between researchers and groups.
- Research ethics make researchers responsible and accountable for their research activities and actions. Many researchers are supported by public money, and regulations on conflicts of interest, misconduct, and research involving humans or animals are necessary to ensure that money is spent appropriately.
- Research ethics ensure that the public can trust research. For people to support and fund research, they have to be confident in it.
- Research ethics support important social and moral values, such as the principle of doing no harm to others.

5.3. Why do Research Ethically

Following are the reasons that why we should include ethics in scientific research:

- *It ensures Scientific Progress*: Truth is the basis of science and the progress of ideas. The scientific community will be benefited only when each participant will publish the result of the research with integrity.
- *It protects Life and the Planet*: When we publish ethically then it ensures that we have genuine and trusted information and knowledge and this scientific knowledge will be helpful for scientific and technological processes and products. The unethical published work which is based on fraudulent data and results can form an inappropriate basis for follow up studies which leads to waste of resources and harmful effects to patients, communities, or habitats.
- *It promotes Ethical Behavior*: If we are the responsible member of the research society will work honestly and sincerely then surely it will set an example and will reinforce our peers and society.
- *It is good for our Reputation*: It is a very important question in front of us that we are researching and publishing for only getting job and increments or we are researching and publishing because we are the responsible members of the society and it is our moral and ethical duty to make researches for the betterment and development of our society and country.
- *It is the only Way*: A good reputation and acting with integrity opens the door to opportunity. Our work represents not only us but the research institution, the funding body, and other researchers.

5.4. Importance of Research Ethics

Research ethics are moral principles that guide researchers to conduct and report research without deception or intention to harm the participants of the study or members of the society as a whole, whether knowingly or unknowingly. Practising ethical guidelines while conducting and reporting research is essential to establish the validity of your research.

We must follow ethical guidelines issued by regulatory committees in order to ensure the safety of the participants of a study, the public at large, and that of the researcher himself/herself. Following ethical guidelines will ensure that our research is authentic and error-free, and will allow us to gain credibility and support from the public. We must adhere to ethical guidelines also while presenting our findings in our manuscript. This will ensure that our article is plagiarism-free and also no unverified data reaches the readers of our article. Apart from that, research ethics fill in a sense of responsibility among researchers and make it easy to fix responsibility in case of misconduct.

Research ethics are important for a number of reasons given below:

- They promote the aims of research, such as expanding knowledge.
- They support the values required for collaborative work, such as mutual respect and fairness. This is essential because scientific research depends on collaboration between researchers and groups.
- They mean that researchers can be held accountable for their actions. Many researchers are supported by public money, and regulations on conflicts of interest, misconduct, and research involving humans or animals are necessary to ensure that money is spent appropriately.
- They ensure that the public can trust research. For people to support and fund research, they have to be confident in it.
- They support important social and moral values, such as the principle of doing no harm to others.

5.5. Importance of Ethical Codes and Considerations in Research

Ethics is more of an innate quality for humans to develop further for a better life. It is the same for researches also. But, there are ethical codes by certain government agencies, who publish specific ethical codes to conduct research and report them. There are many reasons for adhering to certain basic ethical norms of scientific conduct during academic research like:

- To maintain the credibility of the scientific community
- For the proper perception of the people to judge and accept the new results
- To increase the authenticity of the published research results for its readers and scientific fraternity
- To be recognized in today's competitive nature of research
- To promote the essential values to collaborative work as researches are mostly teamwork and need mutual respect to conduct the research smoothly and successfully.
- To promote moral and social values along with the aims and results of the research
- To publish findings of the research transparently
- No to do or report faulty work or plagiarizing others' work

- To be accountable for the research being funded by public money, as many researchers are responsible for their actions during research. They are bound by regulations on conflict of interest, misconduct, and research involving humans or animals. They also have to ensure that public money has to be appropriately spent on the research.

5.5.1. Ethical Dos for Research

- Maintain a precise record of all research activities
- Report data in most cautiously and objectively possible
- During research on animals and trees, treat them with respect, care and empathy
- Respect all the intellectual property use in the research and give them their due credit in research for their contributions
- Maintain confidentiality wherever necessary during the research

5.5.2. Ethical Do Nots for Research

- During research never fabricate, manipulate or misrepresent data
- Do not have a bias in data interpretation, peer review, or in personal decisions
- Never try to deceive research sponsors, colleagues or ethical committees with malpractices
- Never use any existing external research data either published or unpublished without permission
- Strictly avoid Plagiarism and self-plagiarism
- Do not support irresponsible publication practices
- Do not duplicate publications, salami publication or redundant publications
- Without considering ethical issues, do not conduct research in humans, and or animals
- Do not ignore outliers, missing data, reporting post-hoc analysis without declaring them
- Do disclose a conflict of interest

5.6. Principles of Research Ethics

The following are the principles of research ethics:

- *Honesty*: It is the duty and responsibility of the researchers to honestly report the data, results, methods and procedures and publication status. It is very harmful and unethical to fabricate, falsify or misrepresent data.
- *Objectivity*: There should be objectivity in the whole process of the research and it is the ethical responsibility the researchers to avoid biasness in experimental design, data analysis, data interpretation, peer review, personnel decisions, grant writing, expert testimony and other aspects of research.
- *Integrity*: Researchers and scientists should keep their promises and agreements. They must act with sincerity.
- *Carefulness*: It is the ethical responsibility of the researchers to perform all their acts with very carefully and insightfully and should avoid careless

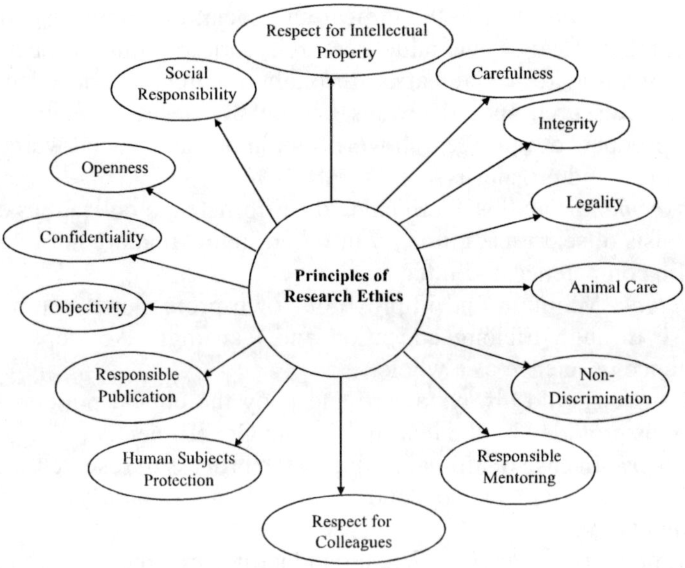

Figure 5.1 *Principles of Research Ethics*

errors and negligence. They should try to carefully and critically examine their research work and the work of their peers. Always try to keep good records of research activities.

- *Openness*: It is a very important principle of the research ethics that to share research data, results, ideas, tools, resources with other community members of research and always be open to criticism and new ideas.
- *Respect for Intellectual Property*: As a responsible member of the academic and research community member, we should always honor patents, copyrights and other forms of intellectual property. It is unethical to use the academic and research work of the other researchers without their permission. Always give credit where credit is due.
- *Confidentiality*: It is an important principle of research ethics that scientist and researchers should always protect confidential communications, such as papers or grants submitted for publication, personnel records, trade or military secrets and patient records.
- *Responsible Publication*: Always remember that we are a responsible member of the research community and our motive always should be publishing in order to advance research and scholarship and not to advance just our own career. Wasteful and duplicative publication is waste of money, time, energy and resources.
- *Responsible Mentoring*: Help to educate, mentor, and advise students. Promote their welfare and allow them to make their own decisions.
- *Respect for Colleagues*: We should always respect our colleagues and their research work and treat them fairly.

- *Social Responsibility*: It is the ethical and social duty and responsibility of the researchers to always conduct research work to promote social good and prevent or mitigate social harms through research, public education, and advocacy. Research should always be socially acceptable and the results and the products of the research work should promote social welfare, human development and prosperity.
- *Non-Discrimination*: It is unethical to discriminate our colleagues or students on the basis of sex, race, ethnicity or other factors that are not related to our scientific competence and integrity.
- *Competence*: Maintain and improve our own professional competence and expertise through lifelong education and learning; take steps to promote competence in science as a whole.
- *Legality*: We should always aware and obey the ethical policies, rules and regulations provided by the institutions and Government.
- *Animal Care*: In case of animals using in the process of research work always respect and care them. Do not conduct unnecessary or poorly designed animal experiments.
- *Human Subjects Protection*: When conducting research on human subjects, minimize harms and risks and maximize benefits; respect human dignity, privacy, and autonomy.

5.7. Ethical Conduct of Research

The grounds for the ethical conduct of research are the following:

- The researchers should strictly follow the rules and regulations that are approved by the research community for conducting research process;
- The researchers should give the due respect of other researchers' work and achievements and cites their work appropriately;
- The researchers should comply the norms and standards set for searching and creating scientific knowledge when planning, conducting and reporting the research;
- The researchers should acquire the necessary research permits and ensures that the preliminary ethical review is conducted (according to field- and research-specific requirements);
- The research group should define and documents the status, rights, obligations and responsibilities of researchers, as well as questions concerning the ownership of research results and the archiving of research materials;
- The researchers should announce his or her sources of financing and conflicts of interest to all the participants in the research and reports them when the research results are published;
- The researchers should apply ethically sustainable methods for data acquisition, research and evaluation and publish the results in an open and responsible fashion.

The research organisation should take the responsibility to apply good administrative practices in human resources and financial management and take into account regulations on disqualification as well as legislation on data protection.

5.8. Ethical Codes for Conduct of Researchers

Apart from the above important considerations for research, there are specific ethical codes prescribed by many Government agencies who fund for the research. Most of them publish their ethical codes, which are mostly advisable and some may have legal implications. The following ethical codes should be considered:

- Reporting researches honestly without any manipulation of data and others;
- Avoiding all kind of bias in research including design, data, analysis, interpretation and also peer review;
- Avoiding mistakes by reviewing the research thoroughly and carefully;
- Safekeeping of all the information regarding the research for future reference;
- Having an openness to share data and any new tools and techniques developed during the research;
- Being aware of the legalities concerned with the research area.

5.9. Codes and Policies for Research Ethics

Given the importance of ethics for the conduct of research, many different professional associations, government agencies and universities have adopted specific codes, rules, and policies relating to research ethics. Many government agencies have ethics rules for funded researchers. These agencies are:

- United Nations Educational, Scientific and Cultural Organization (UNESCO);
- National Institutes of Health (NIH);
- National Science Foundation (NSF);
- Food and Drug Administration (FDA);
- Environmental Protection Agency (EPA);
- US Department of Agriculture (USDA);
- World Health Organization (WHO);
- International Committee of Medical Journal Editors (ICMJE);
- National Science Foundation (NSF);
- Committee on Publication Ethics (COPE).

Other influential research ethics policies include:

- Nuremberg Code,
- Singapore Statement on Research Integrity,
- American Chemical Society,
- Chemist Professional's Code of Conduct,
- Code of Ethics (American Society for Clinical Laboratory Science),
- American Psychological Association,

- Ethical Principles of Psychologists and Code of Conduct,
- Statements on Ethics and Professional Responsibility (American Anthropological Association),
- Statement on Professional Ethics (American Association of University Professors),
- World Medical Association's Declaration of Helsinki.

5.9.1. Nuremberg Codes (1947): Ethical Guidelines for Research

The Nuremberg Code aimed to protect human subjects from enduring the kind of cruelty and exploitation the prisoners endured at concentration camps. The 10 elements of the code are:

1. Voluntary consent is essential.
2. The results of any experiment must be for the greater good of society.
3. Human experiments should be based on previous animal experimentation.
4. Experiments should be conducted by avoiding physical/mental suffering and injury.
5. No experiments should be conducted if it is believed to cause death/disability.
6. The risks should never exceed the benefits.
7. Adequate facilities should be used to protect subjects.
8. Experiments should be conducted only by qualified scientists.
9. Subjects should be able to end their participation at any time.
10. The scientist in charge must be prepared to terminate the experiment when injury, disability, or death is likely to occur.

5.9.2. United Nations Educational, Scientific and Cultural Organization (UNESCO) Code of Conduct and Ethical Guidelines for Social Science Research

UNESCO attaches the highest priority to the maintenance of high standards of integrity, responsibility and accountability in the research it supports. This applies to all aspects of that research from collection, recording, citing and reporting to the retention of scientific material.

The ethical guidelines developed by UNESCO provides a framework to guide research practice. Researchers should be fully aware of the ethical issues involved in their work and adhere to the following basic principles:

1. Responsibility for all procedures and ethical issues related to the project rests with the principal investigators.
2. Research should be conducted in such a way that the integrity of the research enterprise is maintained, and negative after-effects which might diminish the potential for future research should be avoided.
3. The choice of research issues should be based on the best scientific judgement and on an assessment of the potential benefit to the participants and society in relation to the risk to be borne by the participants. Studies should relate to an important intellectual issue.

4. The researcher should consider the effects of his/her work, including the consequences or misuse, both for the individuals and groups among whom they do their fieldwork, and for their colleagues and for the wider society.
5. The researcher should be aware of any potential harmful effects; in such circumstances, the chosen method should be used only if no alternative methods can be found after consultation with colleagues and other experts. Full justification for the method chosen should be given.
6. The research should be conducted in a competent fashion, as an objective scientific project and without bias. All research personnel should be qualified to use all of the procedures employed by them.
7. The research should be carried out in full compliance with, and awareness of, local customs, standards, laws and regulations.
8. All researchers should be familiar with, and respect, the host culture. Researchers undertaking research on cultures, countries and ethnic groups other than their own should make their research objectives particularly clear and remain aware of the concerns and welfare of the individuals or communities to be studied.
9. The principal investigators' own ethical principles should be made clear to all those involved in the research to allow informed collaboration with other researchers. Potential conflicts should be resolved before the research begins.
10. The research should avoid undue intrusion into the lives of the individuals or communities they study. The welfare of the informants should have the highest priority; their dignity, privacy and interests should be protected at all times.
11. Freely given informed consent should be obtained from all human subjects. Potential participants should be informed, in a manner and in language they can understand, of the context, purpose, nature, methods, procedures, and sponsors of the research. Research teams should be identified and contactable during and after the research activity.
12. There should be no coercion. Participants should be fully informed of their right to refuse, and to withdraw at any time during the research.
13. Potential participants should be protected against any and all potentially harmful effects and should be informed of any potential consequences of their participation.
14. Full confidentiality of all information and the anonymity of participants should be maintained. Participants should be informed of any potential limitations to the confidentiality of any information supplied. Procedures should be put in place to protect the confidentiality of information and the anonymity of the participants in all research materials.
15. Participants should be offered access to research results, presented in a manner and language they can understand.
16. All research should be reported widely, with objectivity and integrity.
17. Researchers should provide adequate information in all publications and to colleagues to permit their methods and findings to be properly assessed. Limits of reliability and applicability should be made clear.

18. Researchers are responsible for properly acknowledging the unpublished as well as published work of other scholars.
19. All research materials should be preserved in a manner that respects the agreements made with participants.

5.10. Moral Principles and Professional Standards in Research

Moral principles and professional standards play different roles in research. A moral obligation to *"be truthful,"* even when backed by a professional code, does not function in professional life the same way as a professional responsibility or institutional requirement *"to record and report data accurately in a bound, dated, and signed notebook."* Moral principles bring moral reasoning and ethics into consideration, particularly when different moral principles apply to a situation or when the moral principles themselves are the subject of debate.

By implication, moral principles raise questions about what researchers should do. Professional standards, supplemented by institutional and government rules and regulations, provide more or less clear guidance on what researchers should do. The different role moral principles and professional standards play in research is important enough to justify dividing the study of professional research behavior into two subfields: research behavior measured in terms of and guided by moral principles versus research behavior measured in terms of and guided by professional standards. The former reasonably falls under research ethics (RE) and can be defined as the critical study of the moral problems associated with or that arise in the course of pursuing research. The latter falls under research integrity (RI) and can be defined as possessing and steadfastly adhering to professional standards, as outlined by professional organizations, research institutions and, when relevant, the government and public.

- **Research Ethics:** Research behavior viewed from the perspective of moral principles
- **Research Integrity:** Research behavior viewed from the perspective of professional standards.

5.11. Meaning of Research Integrity

The term *"research integrity"* refers to a characterization or presents an evaluation of research behavior. *"Integrity"* stems from the Latin word *"integrita,"* which means wholeness or completeness. When applied to behavior, integrity describes a person who wholly or completely possesses *"soundness of moral principle; the character of uncorrupted virtue, especially in relation to truth and fair dealing; uprightness, honesty, sincerity."* If the context for discussing integrity is directed specifically to professional behavior, then professional integrity can be defined as *"the quality of possessing and steadfastly adhering to high moral principles or professional standards."* Further, research integrity is the quality of possessing and steadfastly adhering to high moral principles and professional standards, as outlined by professional organizations, research institutions and, when relevant, the government and public.

Research integrity relates to the performance of research to the highest standards of professionalism and rigour, and to the accuracy and truth of the research record in publications and elsewhere. Good research practice includes research ethics in the proposal and experimentation phase, as well as publication ethics in its analysis and dissemination. Research integrity means that research is trustworthy and is honestly, ethically and responsibly conducted, described and reported. Supporting research integrity enhances the excellence of research and ability to generate impact of research. Research integrity is about *"the performance of research to the highest standards of professionalism and rigour, in an ethically robust manner"*. Research integrity is vital because it creates trust and trust is at the heart of the research process. Researchers must be able to trust each other's work, and *"they must also be trusted by society since they provide scientific expertise that may impact people's lives"*.

5.12. Definitions of Research Integrity

1. According to Council of the European Union Irish Universities Association (2016), *"Research integrity relates to the performance of research to the highest standards of professionalism and rigour, and to the accuracy and truth of the research record in publications and elsewhere. Good research practice includes research ethics in the proposal and experimentation phase, as well as publication ethics in its analysis and dissemination"*.
2. *Research integrity can be defined as the coherent and consistent adherence to a set of principles underpinning the excellence and impact of research.*
3. *Research integrity is related to the performance of research to the highest standards of professionalism and rigour, in an ethically robust manner. The behaviours espoused by ethics and research integrity should ultimately ensure the accuracy and truth of the*
4. *research record in publications and elsewhere.*
5. *Research integrity can be defined as commitment of all research performing and financing parties (researchers, research performing organizations and research financing organizations) to the ethical principles and high professional standards essential for the responsible conduct of research.*
6. *Research integrity refers to high quality and robust practice across the full research process i.e. the planning and conduct of research, the recording*

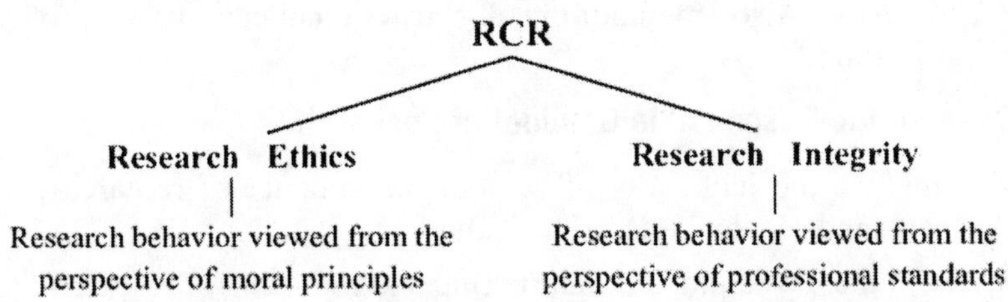

Figure 5.2 *Difference between Research Ethics and Research Integrity*

and reporting of results and the dissemination, application and exploitation of findings.

7. *Integrity in research means conducting and producing research that is honest, rigorous, transparent and open and undertaken with care and respect.*
8. *Research integrity may be defined as active adherence to the ethical principles and professional standards essential for the responsible practice of research.*

5.13. Fundamental Principles of Research Integrity

Good research practices are based on fundamental principles of research integrity. These are the following:

- *Reliability*: Reliability in ensuring the quality of research, reflected in the design, the methodology, the analysis and the use of resources.
- *Honesty*: in developing, undertaking, reviewing, reporting and communicating research in a transparent, fair, full and unbiased way. Respecting the essential value of truth and trustworthiness in research by reporting clearly, fully, and accurately all relevant aspects of one's research.
- *Respect*: Respect for colleagues, research participants, society, ecosystems, cultural heritage and the environment.
- *Accountability*: Accountability for the research from idea to publication, for its management and organisation, for training, supervision and mentoring, and for its wider impacts. Duty to answer truthfully about the motivations and conduct of one's activities as well as the duty to accept praise or blame for one's choices
- *Fairness*: Non-discrimination of others in the research environment, whether on the basis of age, gender, race, ethnicity, sexual orientation, nationality, and/or religion
- *Diligence*: Conducting research tasks—including performance of experiments, literature reviews, research compositions, and research presentations—with attention to detail and accuracy sufficient to permit verification and replication of the work.
- *Equity*: Treating members of the research group as equals according to their roles
- *Professionalism*: Adhering to the standards and practices normative for a "good professional" in the appropriate discipline and as a member of the University. Also, maintaining a spirit of collegiality in professional communication.

5.14. Code for the Responsible Conduct of Research

The following are the hallmarks of responsible conduct of research given by National Health and Medical Research Council of Australian:

P1: *Honesty* in the development, undertaking and reporting of research

- Present information truthfully and accurately in proposing, conducting and reporting research.

P2: *Rigour* in the development, undertaking and reporting of research
- Underpin research by attention to detail and robust methodology, avoiding or acknowledging biases.

P3: *Transparency* in declaring interests and reporting research methodology, data and findings
- Share and communicate research methodology, data and findings openly, responsibly and accurately.
- Disclose and manage conflicts of interest.

P4: *Fairness* in the treatment of others
- Treat fellow researchers and others involved in the research fairly and with respect.
- Appropriately reference and cite the work of others.
- Give credit, including authorship where appropriate, to those who have contributed to the research.

P5: *Respect* for research participants, the wider community, animals and the environment
- Treat human participants and communities that are affected by the research with care and respect, giving appropriate consideration to the needs of minority groups or vulnerable people.
- Ensure that respect underpins all decisions and actions related to the care and use of animals in research.
- Minimise adverse effects of the research on the environment.

P6: *Recognition* of the right of peoples to be engaged in research that affects or is of particular significance to them
- Recognise, value and respect the diversity, heritage, knowledge, cultural property and connection to land of peoples.
- Engage with peoples prior to research being undertaken, so that they freely make decisions about their involvement.
- Report to peoples the outcomes of research in which they have engaged.

P7: *Accountability* for the development, undertaking and reporting of research
- Comply with relevant legislation, policies and guidelines.
- Ensure good stewardship of public resources used to conduct research.
- Consider the consequences and outcomes of research prior to its communication.

P8: *Promotion* of responsible research practices
- Promote and foster a research culture and environment that supports the responsible conduct of research.

5.15. Integrity in Research

Integrity characterizes both individual researchers and the institutions in which they work. For a scientist, integrity embodies above all the individual's commitment to intellectual honesty and personal responsibility. It is an aspect of moral character and experience. For an institution, it is a commitment to creating an environment that promotes responsible conduct by embracing standards of excellence, trustworthiness,

Integrity in Research

Individual Level

For the individual scientist, integrity embodies above all a commitment to intellectual honesty and personal responsibility for one's actions and to a range of practices that characterize the responsible conduct of research, including:

- intellectual honesty in proposing, performing, and reporting research;
- accuracy in representing contributions to research proposals and reports;
- fairness in peer review;
- collegiality in scientific interactions, including communications and sharing of resources;
- transparency in conflicts of interest or potential conflicts of interest;
- protection of human subjects in the conduct of research;
- humane care of animals in the conduct of research; and
- adherence to the mutual responsibilities between investigators and their research teams.

Institutional Level

Institutions seeking to create an environment that promotes responsible conduct by individual scientists and that fosters integrity must establish and continuously monitor structures, processes, policies, and procedures that:

- provide leadership in support of responsible conduct of research;
- encourage respect for everyone involved in the research enterprise;
- promote productive interactions between trainees and mentors;
- advocate adherence to the rules regarding all aspects of the conduct of research, especially research involving human participants and animals;
- anticipate, reveal, and manage individual and institutional conflicts of interest;
- arrange timely and thorough inquiries and investigations of allegations of scientific misconduct and apply appropriate administrative sanctions;
- offer educational opportunities pertaining to integrity in the conduct of research; and
- monitor and evaluate the institutional environment supporting integrity in the conduct of research and use this knowledge for continuous quality improvement.

and lawfulness and then assessing whether researchers and administrators perceive that an environment with high levels of integrity has been created. Adherence to professional values and practices by individuals and institutions when conducting, reporting, and applying the results of scientific activities ensures objectivity, clarity, and reproducibility, and that provides insulation from bias, fabrication, falsification, plagiarism, inappropriate influence, political interference, censorship, and inadequate procedural and information security.

5.16. Intellectual Honesty

Intellectual property (IP) refers to creations of the mind – everything from works of art to inventions, computer programs to trademarks and other commercial signs. Intellectual honesty is a philosophy that demands that you acknowledge the contribution of others in scholarly writing and research. To claim contributions and ideas of another as your own, is cheating and deprives you and others of the opportunity and challenge to learn. Intellectual honesty is the cornerstone of modern ethical discourse. It is the thinking that, whether you agree or disagree with someone's ideology, you will not allow your beliefs regarding their opinions to alter your pursuit of the truth. The essential aspect of intellectual honesty is that you will pursue the truth even if it goes against your own previously held beliefs or narratives, and will hold principles over politics. According to Louis M. Guenin (2005), "Intellectual honesty is a virtuous disposition to eschew deception when given an incentive for deception"

We have a moral duty to be honest. This duty is especially important when we share ideas that can inform or persuade others. Intellectual honesty is honesty in the acquisition, analysis, and transmission of ideas. A person is being intellectually honest when he or she, knowing the truth, states that truth. Intellectual honesty pertains to any communication intended to inform or persuade. This includes all forms of scholarship, consequential conversations such as dialogue, debate, negotiations, product and service descriptions, various forms of persuasion and public communications such as announcements, speeches, lectures, instruction, presentations, publications, declarations, briefings, news releases, policy statements, reports, religious instructions, social media posts, and journalism including not only prose and speech, but graphs, photographs, and other means of expression.

Intellectual honesty combines good faith with a primary motivation toward seeking true beliefs. Intellectual honesty is an applied method of problem solving, characterized by an unbiased, honest attitude, which can be demonstrated in a number of different ways including:

- Ensuring support for chosen ideologies does not interfere with the pursuit of truth;
- Relevant facts and information are not purposefully omitted even when such things may contradict one's hypothesis;
- Facts are presented in an unbiased manner, and not twisted to give misleading impressions or to support one view over another;
- References, or earlier work, are acknowledged where possible, and plagiarism is avoided.

Intentionally committed fallacies and deception in debates and reasoning are called intellectual dishonesty. We have a moral duty to be honest. This duty is especially important when we share ideas that can inform or persuade others.

5.17. Importance of Intellectual Honesty

Intellectual honesty is the cornerstone of the development and acquisition of knowledge. Knowledge is cumulative and advances are predicated on the contributions of others. In the normal course of scholarship, these contributions are apprehended, critically evaluated, and form a foundation for further inquiry. Intellectual honesty demands that the contribution of others be acknowledged. To do less is to cheat. To pass off contributions and ideas of another as one's own is to deprive oneself of the opportunity and challenge to learn and to participate in the scholarly process of acquisition and development of knowledge. Not only will the cheater or intellectually dishonest individual be ultimately his/her own victim but also the general quality of scholarly activity will be seriously undermined.

It is for these reasons that the Universities insists on intellectual honesty in scholarship. The control of intellectual dishonesty begins with the individual's recognition of standards of honesty expected generally and compliance with those expectations.

5.18. Philosophical Basis of Intellectual Honesty

Some philosophers conceptualize intellectual honesty as a virtue, as an "intellectual virtue" concerning one's own thoughts and inner actions, as an ethical stance towards one's thoughts and beliefs. Again, this involves moral integrity. It means that, as often as possible, one's actions should be in accordance with the values one has adopted as one's own—and it concerns the question of what one should believe in the first place.

Let us look at four stages in the Western history of ideas in order to see this inner connection more clearly.

John Locke

For the British philosopher John Locke, the desire for knowledge itself was a religious duty towards God: *"He that believes, without having any reason for believing, may be in love with his own fancies; but neither seeks truth as he ought, nor pays the obedience due to his maker, who would have him use those discerning faculties he has given him, to keep him out of mistake and error..."* At the very beginning, philosophical honesty involves modesty. This is what Immanuel Kant would have said about honesty in general: The strict duty of honest comportment is "reason translated into social practice," because it first creates the preconditions for mutual trust between the members of a society and thereby forms the basis of public order.

Figure 5.3 *Locke*

Immanuel Kant

Kant tells us that this form of intellectual honesty is the innermost core of morality in general. It is the essence of the desire for ethical integrity. Here is how one put this in 1793: it is "the idea of the moral good in its absolute purity." In the Metaphysics of Morals (1797), he put this point concisely and clearly: *"... man's duty to himself regarded merely as a moral being ... is ... truthfulness."* At this point, Kant can also explain what intellectual dishonesty is, namely a kind of "inner lie." For Kant, dishonesty is simply a lack

Figure 5.4 *Immanuel Kant*

of conscientiousness. Lacking conscientiousness in the ethical sense of inner action is nothing other than a form of unconsciousness, a lack of awareness—a further, interesting connection not only to the spiritual stance, but also to the history of the concept of "consciousness" in the occidental tradition.

Friedrich Nietzche

For Friedrich Nietzsche, intellectual honesty is the *"conscience behind the conscience."* In 1883, he wrote in Zarathustra: *"Where my honesty ceases I am blind and also want to be blind. But where I want to know, I also want to be honest, namely venomous, rigorous, vigorous, cruel and inexorable."* Nietzsche was one of the first philosophers to really write about intellectual honesty, about *"conscientiousness of the mind"* as an ethics of cognitive action more narrowly conceived. For Nietzsche, intellectual honesty is the *"culmination and 'last virtue'"* of the Greco-Christian history of ideas, because it leads to the self-annihilation of the religious-moral interpretation of the will to truth. What exactly does this mean? In its highest form, the desire for truthfulness allows one to admit to oneself that there is no empirical evidence of God's existence whatsoever, and that in more than four thousand years of the history of philosophy, no convincing argument for the existence of God has emerged. It allows us to relinquish our search for emotional security and pleasant feelings, which has been hard-wired into our minds and bodies in the course of evolution, and admit that we are radically mortal beings with a tendency towards systematic forms of self-deception. Truthfulness towards ourselves allows us to discover the delusional and systematic denial of finitude, as expressed in our own conscious self-model.

Figure 5.5 *Friedrich Nietzche*

Figure 5.6 *William Kingdon Clifford*

William Kingdon Clifford

The British philosopher and mathematician William Kingdon Clifford was one of the first thinkers to ask the question "The Ethics of Belief", and subsequently became the founding father of this discussion, which is central to the distinction between religion and spirituality. His two main principles are:

- It is wrong always, everywhere, and for anyone, to believe anything upon insufficient evidence.
- At any time, at any place, and for every person it is wrong to ignore or carelessly reject the relevant evidence for one's own beliefs.

In academic philosophy, this position is simply called "evidentialism." This means only believing things for which one actually has arguments and evidence.

5.19. Intellectual Honesty in Proposing, Performing, and Reporting Research

Intellectual honesty in proposing, performing, and reporting research refers to honesty with respect to the meaning of one's research. It is expected that researchers present proposals and data honestly and communicate their best understanding of the work in writing and verbally. The descriptions of an individual's work found in such communications frequently present selected data from the work organized into frameworks that emphasize conceptual understanding rather than the chronology of the discovery process. Clear and accurate research records must underlie these descriptions, however. Researchers must be advocates for their research conclusions in the face of collegial skepticism and must acknowledge errors.

5.20. Unethical Publication

The concept of ethical writing entails an implicit contract between reader and writer whereby the reader assumes that the material written by the author, is new, is original and is accurate to the best of the author's abilities. However, authors used to increase the number of publications from a single study. In this essence, Elm, Poglia, Walder and Tramer (2004) identified six duplication patterns:

- identical samples and identical outcomes,
- identical samples and different outcomes,
- increasing sample and identical outcomes (new data added),
- decreasing sample and identical outcomes (reporting only part of a larger trial), and
- different sample and different outcomes.

However, Roig (2001) distinguished between four types of self-plagiarism:

- Duplicate (Dual) Publication;
- Data Fragmentation (Salami-Slicing);
- Text Recycling; and
- Copyright Infringement

5.20.1. Duplicate (Dual) Publication

Duplicate Publication is publication of a paper that overlaps substantially with one already published in print or electronic media. One of the foundations of science is that published work be an original contribution by the named author or authors. The standard practice for authors of scientific or scholarly papers is to submit their paper for publication to a single journal. Authors submitting their manuscripts to most journals must confirm that their work has not been published elsewhere. This is known as Duplicate publication, which is simply republication of papers that are identical to or similar to the original paper reporting the same body of research.

Duplicate Publication refers to the practice of publishing what is essentially the same paper in two or more journals. Duplicate Publication refers to the practice of submitting a paper with the same data to more than one journal, without alerting the editors or readers to the existence of other identical published versions, which may differ only slightly from the original by, for example, changes to the title, abstract, and/or order of the authors.

5.21.1.1. Definitions of Duplicate Publication

- According to Ibe, *'in duplicate publication, the papers usually differ only slightly in changes to the title, abstract (summary) and/or order of authors. In redundant publication, there is usually a somewhat different textual slant in the body of the paper from the original paper but the data are same. The differences often come in the forms of different interpretation of data or an introduction from a slightly different angle.'*
- According to Benos (2005), *"Duplicate publication is defined as "the publication of an article that is identical or overlaps substantially with an article already published elsewhere, with or without acknowledgment."*

5.20.2. Redundant Publication

Redundant or repetitive publication is defined as "the publication of copyrighted material with additional new or unpublished data". Redundant Publication occurs when an author reuses some portion of previously published data in a new publication. Redundant publication is a related and more frequent practice which occurs when researchers publish the same data, with a somewhat different textual slant within the body of the paper. For example, redundant publication papers may contain a slightly different interpretation of the data or the introduction to the paper may be described in a somewhat different theoretical or empirical context.

The issue is not with the paper being published twice, but with the author's intention to deceive (the Editor, reviewers, readers, and perhaps in the longer term, other stakeholders such as supervisors, funding bodies, grant committees) that each paper is an original work. This is what constitutes self-plagiarism.

For the Duplicate or redundant publication to be acceptable, the author would need to indicate that the paper had been submitted elsewhere, and for the published version of the paper to have a statement that it also appears in another journal. Following are some instances in which dual publication may be acceptable:

- Some authors who submit the same article to more than one journal do so with the rationale that their paper would be of interest to each set of readers who would probably not otherwise be aware of the other publication. However, the editors of both journals would have to agree to this arrangement and the existence of each version of the published paper would have to be made clear to each set of readers.
- Duplication of text from a non-peer-reviewed source (e.g., most conference preprints, project progress reports, personal or project websites, dissertations) will not constitute plagiarism in general. Summaries or abstracts of papers that are published in conference proceedings are often subsequently published

in expanded form as a journal article. This is mainly because, in theory, the journal submission would be a substantially revised version of the conference presentation, having benefitted from extensive peer review and feedback at the conference.

- Another instance when an article published in one language is translated into a different language and published in a different journal.
- Furthermore, submitting a significantly revised version of a previously published paper to a new journal would be acceptable, only if there is some clear acknowledgement of the previously published work.
- Only where a conference paper has been orally presented but never published in any format, would be legitimate academic practice to then publish it as a journal article with no reference to the former presentation.

In these and other cases where redundant or duplicate publication is being considered by the author, the editors and the readers of each paper must be made aware that a second published version exists. Similarly, where authors neglect to mention the original conference paper and therefore implies that the journal article is original, this could arguably be described asself-plagiarism. The same argument applies to conference papers already published electronically. In both cases, in addition to acknowledging the original conference paper, the author may need to seek permission from the Editor of the conference proceedings to ensure that no copyright has been infringed.

5.20.2.1. Definitions of Redundant Publication

Committee on Publication Ethics (COPE), describes redundant publication as follows: *'When a published work (or substantial sections from a published work) is/are published more than once (in the same or another language) without adequate acknowledgment of the source/cross-referencing/justification, OR, When the same (or substantially overlapping) data is presented in more than one publication without adequate cross-referencing/justification, particularly when this is done in such a way that reviewers/readers are unlikely to realise that most or all the findings have been published before.'*

5.20.3. Multiple Submission

Multiple submission means sending your manuscript to more than one journal at a time in the hope that it will be published by one of them. Never submit your work to more than one journal at a time. It might seem like a good idea to submit your manuscript to more than one publication to save time and increase your chances of acceptance. Do not do this. You must only submit your work to only one journal at a time. It is considered unethical to submit a manuscript to multiple journals at the same time because doing so can potentially lead to copyright problems and waste journals' time and resources. Another reason is that repeated evidence in the literature will bias the overall evidence, because a study may be counted more than once in meta-analyses that pool all available data to calculate an overall effect.

5.20.4. Salami Publication (Salami Slicing/Fragmented Publication/ Piecemeal Publication/Divided Publication)

Salami Science means 'slicing of a data set in to several pieces called least publishable units (LPU).' When there are multiple small publications from a single study/project, it is called salami publication or salami slicing. It is a form of self-plagiarism. The *"slicing"* of research that would form one meaningful paper into several different papers is called *"salami publication"* or *"salami slicing"*. Unlike duplicate publication, which involves reporting the exact same data in two or more publications, salami slicing involves breaking up or segmenting a large study into two or more publications. These segments are referred to as *"slices"* of a study.

"Salami" publication or salami slicing is the practice of dividing the findings of one study into a series of shorter articles. The technical term is publishing the "least publishable unit", "smallest publishable unit", "minimum publishable unit", or "publon".

Authors may feel pressured to publish salami to increase their number of publications. However, these separate papers will share methodologies, study populations, or hypotheses. Publishing findings in parts, and not in one place in full, means the reader is not provided with all the information necessary for critical evaluation. The chance for duplication of text or data (and hence self-plagiarism) is also very high.

This practice is very different from sequential publishing, which is publishing several articles in chronological order, building on and developing previous research. As a general principle, if the results of several papers all come from the same study population, and results are dependent on one another, they should be published in the same study.

5.20.5. Text Recycling (Reuse)

As well as reusing the same data, authors might recycle ideas or reuse text that they have used before in another article. Actually, an author might recycle some introductory background material, literature review text and, where appropriate, study methods descriptions. It is possible to have two or more papers describing legitimately different observations that contain almost identical methodology, literature reviews, discussions, and other very similar or even identical textual material. There are those who would argue that not citing your own work when you have used large sections of text from one or more previously published

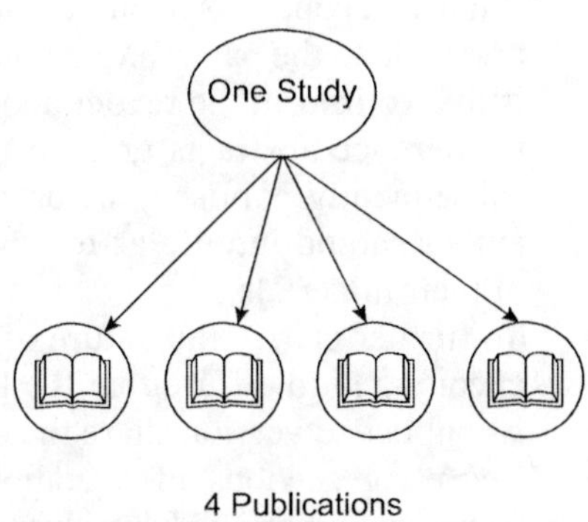

Figure 5.7 *Example of Salami Publication*

papers in a paper presented as 'original' is almost fraudulent. Their perspective represents what is known as Text Recycling. Text recycling is the copying of portions of one's own previously published work, especially when studies include "almost identical methodology, literature reviews, discussions and other similar or identical textual material". It can be defined simply as a writer's reuse of portions of text that have appeared previously in other works.

Collberg and Kobourov(2005) addressed Different forms of text recycling given below:

- *Textual reuse*: incorporating text/images/etc. from previously published work, which is articles published in refereed conferences and journals where copyright is assigned to someone different from the author.
- *Semantic reuse*: incorporating ideas from previously published work.
- *Blatant reuse*: incorporating texts or ideas from previously published work such that the two works are virtually indistinguishable.
- *Selective reuse*: incorporating bits-and-pieces from previously published work.
- *Incidental reuse*: incorporating texts or ideas not directly related to the new ideas presented in the paper (such as related work sections, motivating examples, etc.).
- *Reuse by cryptomnesia*: incorporating texts or ideas from previously published work while unaware of the existence of that work.
- *Opaque reuse*: incorporating texts or ideas from previously published work without acknowledging the existence of this work.
- *Advocacy reuse*: incorporating texts or ideas from previously published work when writing to a community different from that in which the original work was published.

Roig (2001) identified forms of acceptable text recycling:

- Recycling text from types of proposals reviewed within academic institutions is generally considered an acceptable practice.
- Published paper based on a conference presentation where some modifications are made to the paper based on the audience's feedback: the standard practice is to also inform the reader about its prior version.
- Conference abstracts or even the preliminary papers themselves which are subsequently published as proceedings by the sponsoring organization, the author should inquire as to whether that organization permits republication of their materials.
- To further clarify the nature of these two products, authors are also strongly encouraged to ensure that the both, the paper presented at a conference and its published version share the same or similar title.
- Recycling sections of a complex method section (which are often highly technical and can be laborious to write) from a previously published paper.

5.21. Selective Reporting or Reporting Biases

Research can only contribute to knowledge if it is communicated from investigators to the community. The generally accepted primary means of communication is "full" publication of the study methods and results in an article published in a scientific journal. Sometimes, investigators choose to present their findings at a scientific meeting as well, either through an oral or poster presentation. These presentations are included as part of the scientific record as brief "abstracts" which may or may not be recorded in publicly accessible documents typically found in libraries or the World Wide Web.

Complete, accurate and timely reporting of all outcomes is essential for syntheses of research to be valid and as precise as possible. Complete or unselective reporting refers to both unselective publication of all results of a study as well as unselective or complete reporting within publications on all planned outcomes. In other words, all planned outcomes should be reported on within a reasonable time frame.

5.21.1. Meaning of Selective Reporting Bias?

Selective reporting bias is when results from scientific research are deliberately not fully or accurately reported, in order to suppress negative or undesirable findings. The end result is that the findings are not reproducible, because they have been skewed by bias during the analysis or writing stages. Selective reporting bias can incorporate a number of other types of bias, such as:

- *Publication bias* – where the results of negative clinical trials are not published or under-published
- *Outcome reporting bias* – where the results of negative clinical trials are cherry-picked or distorted to improve the overall findings
- *Spin* – communicating results in a way which amplifies positive findings or tones down negative findings
- *Citation bias* – positive studies are more likely to be cited than negative studies

Selective reporting bias, FFP (Falsification, Fabrication, and Plagiarism), and other examples of research misconduct, all contribute to a culture of mistrust in science and academia. However, journal editors can play a role in helping change this perception, by upholding a culture of research integrity on their journals. Selective reporting is one type of bias which undermines the integrity of academic research. It is a large contributor to the current 'reproducibility crisis' facing scientific publishing.

Selective reporting leads to bias if specific results remain unpublished because the decision to report depends on the nature of the results (e.g., direction or magnitude of the target association). Reporting bias is an important threat to the validity of systematic reviews which clinicians, researchers, policy makers and citizens rely on. Reporting bias is wasteful, distorts the aggregate body of scientific evidence, threatens the credibility of science, but it may also result in suboptimal treatment or even in avoidable harm to, e.g., patients' health. Therefore, in addition to validity and efficiency reasons, there is an ethical imperative to report all results including those of clinical trials.

Selective reporting is wasteful, leads to bias in the published record and harms the credibility of science. Reporting bias occurs when the dissemination of research findings is influenced by the nature and direction of the results, for instance in systematic reviews. Positive results are a commonly used term to describe a study finding that one intervention is better than another.

Various attempts have been made to overcome the effects of the reporting biases, including statistical adjustments to the results of published studies. None of these approaches has proved satisfactory, however, and there is increasing acceptance that reporting biases must be tackled by establishing registers of controlled trials and by promoting good publication practice. Until these problems have been addressed, estimates of the effects of treatments based on published evidence may be biased.

Reporting biases arise when the dissemination of research findings is influenced by the nature and direction of the results and can arise from processes acting within a study or at the level of the whole study. Within studies, researchers may report their findings selectively—choosing to report selected outcomes and analyses based on the results. Reporting bias can thus result from selective outcome reporting (SOR), wherein only a subset of the original outcomes measured and analyzed in a study are fully reported based on the magnitude of the treatment effect or the statistical significance of selected outcomes.

Kirkham and colleagues describe three main types of SOR:

- selective reporting of an entire study outcome (i.e., analyzed outcomes are not reported);
- selective reporting of a specific outcome (e.g., selected follow-up intervals), and
- incomplete reporting of a specific outcome (e.g., incomplete reporting of non-significant p values, such as $p>0.05$).

SOR can result in outcome reporting bias (ORB), which is the bias produced from choosing which outcomes to publish based on the results.

Reporting bias arising from within-study processes can also result from the selection of analyses for reporting (SAR), which can lead to analysis reporting bias (ARB). Examples of SAR include selective reporting of data on subgroups, presentation of adjusted rather than unadjusted analyses, selection of as-treated rather than intention-to-treat analyses, selective approaches to the handling of missing data, choosing to analyze continuously measured variables categorically (outcomes or predictors in adjusted models), and choice of cut-point values to define categorical variables.

5.21.2. Types of Reporting Bias

The main types of reporting bias are discussed below:

1. *Publication Bias*: The publication or non-publication of research findings, depending on the nature and direction of the results. Although medical writers have acknowledged the problem of reporting biases for over a century, it was not until the second half of the 20th century that researchers began to investigate the sources and size of the problem of reporting biases.

   Over the past two decades, evidence has accumulated that failure to publish research studies, including clinical trials testing intervention effectiveness, is pervasive. Almost all failure to publish is due to failure of the investigator to submit; only a small proportion of studies are not published because of rejection by journals.

The most direct evidence of publication bias in the medical field comes from follow-up studies of research projects identified at the time of funding or ethics approval. These studies have shown that "positive findings" is the principal factor associated with subsequent publication: researchers say that the reason they don't write up and submit reports of their research for publication is usually because they are "not interested" in the results (editorial rejection by journals is a rare cause of failure to publish).

The main factor associated with failure to publish is negative or null findings. Controlled trials that are eventually reported in full are published more rapidly if their results are positive. Publication bias leads to overestimates of treatment effect in meta-analyses, which in turn can lead doctors and decision makers to believe a treatment is more useful than it is. It is now well-established that publication bias with more favorable efficacy results is associated with the source of funding for studies that would not otherwise be explained through usual risk of bias assessments.

2. *Time Lag Bias*: The rapid or delayed publication of research findings, depending on the nature and direction of the results. In a systematic review of the literature, Hopewell and her colleagues found that overall, trials with "positive results" (statistically significant in favor of the experimental arm) were published about a year sooner than trials with "null or negative results" (not statistically significant or statistically significant in favor of the control arm).
3. *Multiple (duplicate) Publication Bias*: The multiple or singular publication of research findings, depending on the nature and direction of the results. Investigators may also publish the same findings multiple times using a variety of patterns of "duplicate" publication. Many duplicates are published in journal supplements, potentially difficult to access literature. Positive results appear to be published more often in duplicate, which can lead to overestimates of a treatment effect.
4. *Location Bias*: The publication of research findings in journals with different ease of access or levels of indexing in standard databases, depending on the nature and direction of results. There is also evidence that, compared to negative or null results, statistically significant results are on average published in journals with greater impact factors, and that publication in the mainstream (non-grey) literature is associated with an overall greater treatment effect compared to the grey literature.
5. *Citation Bias*: The citation or non-citation of research findings, depending on the nature and direction of the results. Authors tend to cite positive results over negative or null results, and this has been established over a broad cross section of topics. Differential citation may lead to a perception in the community that an intervention is effective when it is not, and it may lead to over-representation of positive findings in systematic reviews if those left uncited are difficult to locate.

Selective pooling of results in a meta-analysis is a form of citation bias that is particularly insidious in its potential to influence knowledge. To minimize bias, pooling of results from similar but separate studies requires an exhaustive search for all relevant studies. That is, a meta-analysis (or pooling of data from multiple studies) must always have emerged from a systematic review (not a selective review of the literature), even though a systematic review does not always have an associated meta-analysis.

6. *Language Bias*: The publication of research findings in a particular language, depending on the nature and direction of the results. There is longstanding question about whether there is a language bias such that investigators choose to publish their negative findings in non-English language journals and reserve their positive findings for English language journals. Some research has shown that language restrictions in systematic reviews can change the results of the review and in other cases, authors have not found that such a bias exists.
7. *Knowledge Reporting Bias*: The frequency with which people write about actions, outcomes, or properties is not a reflection of real-world frequencies or the degree to which a property is characteristic of a class of individuals. People write about only some parts of the world around them; much of the information is left unsaid.
8. *Outcome Reporting Bias*: The selective reporting of some outcomes but not others, depending on the nature and direction of the results. A study may be published in full, but pre-specified outcomes omitted or misrepresented. Efficacy outcomes that are statistically significant have a higher chance of being fully published compared to those that are not statistically significant.

5.22. Taxonomy of Putative Determinants of Selective Reporting

The taxonomy of putative determinants of selective reporting given by Jenny, T.; Cornelis, A. et. al. (2018) is given below:

Table 5.1 *Taxonomy of Putative Determinants of Selective Reporting*

Determinant classification, category	*Description*	*Examples*
1. Focus on preferred findings	A focus on finding results that match preferences, mostly statistically significant or otherwise positive findings, wishful thinking and acting.	Significance chasing, finding significant results, larger effect size, suppressing publication of unfavorable results, not being intrigued by null findings.
2. Poor or flexible research design	Attributes of study design relating to power and level of evidence provide much leeway in how studies are performed and in interpretation of their results.	Not a controlled or blinded study, study protocol unavailable, small sample size.

Determinant classification, category	Description	Examples
3. High-risk area and its development	Area of research or discipline or specialty including its historical development and competitiveness, the currently dominant paradigms and designs, and career opportunities.	Ideological biases in a research field, area with much epidemiological research versus clinical or laboratory research ("hard sciences"), humanities, experimental analytic methods, "hot" fields, publication pressure in the specific field.
4. Dependence upon sponsors	Financial conflict of interest resulting in lack of academic freedom.	Requirements and influence of funding source with financial interests in study results.
5. Prejudice	A conscious or unconscious belief that may be unfound-ed, and of which one may or may not be aware.	Prior belief about efficacy of treatment, author reputation or gender bias in the phase of review.
6. Lack of resources, including time	Insufficient manpower or finances.	Lack of time resulting from excessive workload, or lack of personnel due to life events.
7. Doubts about reporting being worth the effort	Weighing investment of time and means versus likelihood of gain through publication.	Anticipating disappointment of yet another rejection or low chances of acceptance of a manuscript, belief that findings are not worth the trouble.
8. Limitations in reporting and editorial practices	Constraints and barriers to the practice of reporting relevant detail.	Journal space restrictions, author writing Skills.
9. Academic publication system hurdles	Various hurdles to full reporting related to submission and processing of manuscripts (other than reporting) including those that represent an intellectual conflict of interest.	Solicited manuscripts, authors indicating non-preferred reviewers, editor's rejection rate.
10. Unfavorable geographical or regulatory environment	Geographical or regulatory environment that affects how research is being performed.	Continents under study included North America, Europe and Asia; few international collaborations; no governmental regulation of commercially sponsored research.

Determinant classification, category	Description	Examples
11. Relationship and collaboration issues	Intellectual conflict of interest between reporting and maintaining good relationships.	Disagreement among co-authors and between authors and sponsors, sponsors prefer to work with investigators who share the sponsor's position.
12. Potential harm	Publishing data can harm individuals.	Risk of bioterrorism, or confidentiality restriction.
13. Not specified	Referring to a stakeholder only.	Selective publication not caused by editors.

5.23. Misrepresentation of Data

Research data is presently a publicly-funded resource that passes into private hands without explicit permission, or remuneration to the public purse. The overwhelming volume of research across the disciplines are funded by government via research councils and institutions of higher education and by non-profit-making institutions set up for the public good. Organisations wish to maximise value in their investment and there are growing opinion from funders that access to data is part of that value.

The concept of *'misrepresentation,'* unlike *'fabrication'* and *'falsification,'* is neither clear nor uncontroversial. Most scientists will agree that fabrication is making up data and falsification is changing data. But, what does it mean to misrepresent data? As a minimal answer to this question, one can define *'misrepresentation of data'* as 'communicating honestly reported data in a deceptive manner.' But what is deceptive communication? The use of statistics presents researchers with numerous opportunities to misrepresent data. For example, one might use a statistical technique, such as multiple regression or the analysis of variance, to make one's results appear more significant or convincing than they really are. Or one might eliminate (or trim) outliers when 'cleaning up' raw data. Other ways of misrepresenting data include drawing unwarranted inference from data, creating deceptive graphs of figures, and using suggestive language for rhetorical effect.

However, since researchers often disagree about the proper use of statistical techniques and other means of representing data, the line between misrepresentation of data and 'disagreement about research methods' is often blurry. Since *'misrepresentation'* is difficult to define, many organizations have refused to characterize misrepresenting data as a form of scientific misconduct. On the other hand, it is important to call attention to the problem of misrepresenting data, if one is concerned about promoting objectivity in research, since many of science's errors and biases result from the misrepresentation of data.

5.24. Mis-representation and Distortion of Research

Publication in peer-reviewed journals is an essential step in the scientific process. It generates knowledge, influences future experiments and may impact clinical practice and public health. Ethically, research results must be reported completely, transparently, and accurately. However, publication is not simply the reporting of facts arising from a straightforward and objective analysis of those facts. When writing a manuscript reporting the results of an experiment, investigators usually have broad latitude in the choice, representation, and interpretation of the data. They may be tempted consciously or unconsciously to shape the impression that the results will have on readers and consequently "spin" their study results.

5.24.1. What is Spin?

Spin has become a standard concept in public relations and politics in recent decades. It is *"a form of propaganda, achieved by providing a biased interpretation of an event or campaigning to persuade public opinion in favor of or against some organization or public figure"*. The concept of spin can also be applied to scientific communications. Spin can also be defined as a specific reporting that fails to faithfully reflect the nature and range of findings and that could affect the impression that the results produce in readers, away to distort science reporting without actually lying. Spin could be unconscious and unintentional. Reporting results in a manuscript implies some choices about which data analyses are reported, how data are reported, how they should be interpreted, and what rhetoric is used. These choices, which can be legitimate in some contexts, in another context can create an inaccurate impression of the study results.

5.24.2. Practices of Spin

There are several ways to spin a report. These different practices are usually interrelated, and the amount of spin in published reports varies.

5.24.2.1. Misreporting the Methods

Authors could intentionally or unintentionally misrepresent the methods they used. This type of spin will alter the readers' critical appraisal of the study and could impact the interpretation of evidence synthesis. It could consist of changing objectives, reporting post hoc hypotheses as if they were pre-specified, switching outcomes and analysis, or masking protocol deviations. Scientists could also engage in what we characterize as "beautification" of the methods, when they report the methods as if they were complying with the highest standards when in fact they were not.

5.24.2.2. Misreporting the Results

Misreporting of results is defined as an incomplete or inadequate reporting of results in a way that could mislead the reader. This type of spin particularly involves selective reporting of statistically significant results, ignoring results that contradict or counterbalance the initial hypothesis and misleading display of results through choice of metrics and figures. Undesirable consequences include wasted time and resources on misdirected research and ill-founded actions by health providers misled by partial results.

- *Selective reporting of outcomes and analysis*: Selective reporting of outcomes and analysis is defined as the reporting of some outcomes or analysis but not others, depending on the nature and direction of the results. The literature contains evidence of researchers favoring statistically significant results.

- *Ignoring or understating results that contradict or counterbalance the initial hypothesis*: Authors may be tempted to consciously or unconsciously mask or understate some troublesome results, such as non-statistically significant outcomes or statistically significant harm.
- *Misreporting results and figures*: The presentation of results can affect their interpretation. For example, choosing to report the results as either relative risk reduction or absolute risk reduction can substantially impact readers' interpretation and understanding, particularly when the baseline risk is low. Similarly, reporting odds ratios (ORs) instead of risk ratios (RRs) when the baseline risk is high can easily be misinterpreted.
- *Misinterpretation*: Misinterpretation refers to an interpretation of the results that is not consistent with the actual results of the study. In the Discussion section of a paper, authors may take a strong position that relies more on their opinion than on the study results. Interpretation of results is misleading when researchers focus on a within-group comparison; when they ignore regression to the mean and confounding; when they inappropriately posit causality; when they draw an inappropriate inference from a composite outcome; or report P values as a measure of an effect whereas, in reality, it is only a measure of how likely it is that a result occurs by chance.

5.24.2.3. Impact of Spin

One important question is whether spin matters and can actually impact readers' interpretations of study results. Spin can affect researchers, physicians, and even journalists who are disseminating the results, but also the general public, who might be more vulnerable because they are less likely to disentangle the truth.

5.24.2.4. Why Researchers Add Spin to their Reports

- *Competitive Environment and Importance of Positive Findings*: Scientists are under pressure to publish, particularly in high-impact factor journals. Publication metrics, such as the number of publications, number of citations, journal impact factor, and h-index are used to measure academic productivity and scientists' influence. However, we have some evidence that editors, peer-reviewers, and researchers are more interested in statistically significant effects. The highly competitive "publish or perish" environment may favor detrimental research practices; thus, spinning the study results and a "spun" interpretation could be an easy way to confer a more positive result and increase the interest of reviewers and editors.
- *Lack of Guidelines to Interpret Results and Avoid Spin*: To improve transparency, authors are encouraged to report their studies according to reporting guidelines.

5.24.2.5. How Can We Reduce the Use of Spin?

- *Change the Perception of Spin from "Commonly Accepted Practice" to "Seriously Detrimental Research Practice."*: Editors, funders, institutions, and researchers take very seriously such research misconduct as data falsification or fabrication and plagiarism. Researchers should be specifically trained to detect and avoid spin in published reports.

- *Require and Enforce Protocol Registration*: To detect spin, essential information in the protocol and statistical analysis plan, such as the pre-specified primary outcome and pre-specified analysis, must be accessible.
- *Reporting Guidelines and New Processes of Reporting*: The development of reporting guidelines was a very important step toward achieving complete, accurate, and transparent reporting. These guidelines are endorsed by editors who require adherence to the guidelines in their instructions to authors. These guidelines indicate the minimum set of information that should be systematically reported by authors for specific studies.
- *Editors, Peer-Review, and Post-publication Monitoring/Feedback*. In theory, peer-reviewers and editors should determine whether the conclusions match the results. Regular monitoring of the content of research publications, which has been successfully-implemented for the detection of selective reporting of outcomes, could be an effective method to change the practices of researchers and editors alike.
- *Changing the Reward System and Developing Collaborative Research*: The current reward system for scientists, based mainly on the number of publications and the journal impact factor, could be aiding and abetting the misleading behavior.

6

Publication Ethics

Publication ethics is a crucial- part of scholars' efforts to pursue their scholarly practices in accordance with fundamental principles of research integrity. Research and publication ethics are closely connected as each new study leads to new finding, which on publication enter the public domain. By ensuring research is conducted ethically, the participants of any study are protected from direct harm during research. Also, these policies protect patients indirectly from poor application of research concepts. In recent years, both research and publication ethics are considered together and researchers are expected to portray research integrity and good research practices.

The publication of an article in a peer-reviewed journal is an essential building block in the development of a coherent and respected network of knowledge. It is a direct reflection of the quality of the work of the authors and the institutions that support them. Peer-reviewed articles support and embody the scientific method. It is therefore important to agree upon standards of expected ethical behavior for all parties involved in the act of publishing: the author, the journal editor, the peer reviewer, the publisher and the society of society-owned or sponsored journals.

6.1. Meaning of Publication Ethics

Publication ethics are rules of conduct generally agreed upon when publishing results of scientific research or other scholarly work. Generally, it is a standard that protects intellectual property and forbids the re-publication of another's work without proper credit. It also forbids the use of plagiarism of another's efforts. Data and information published as original must, in fact, be original.

Publication is the final stage of research and therefore a responsibility for all researchers. Scholarly publications are expected to provide a detailed and permanent record of research. Because publications form the basis for both new research and the application of findings, they can affect not only the research community but also, indirectly, society at large. Researchers therefore have a responsibility to ensure that their publications are honest, clear, accurate, complete and balanced, and should avoid misleading, selective or ambiguous reporting. Journal editors also have responsibilities for ensuring the integrity of the research literature and these are set out in companion guidelines. The topic of research ethics is important not only when conducting research but also when publishing it. It is one of the crucial pillars for maintaining scientific integrity and credibility. The onus to implement fair practices lies with researchers, universities/institutions, and publishers.

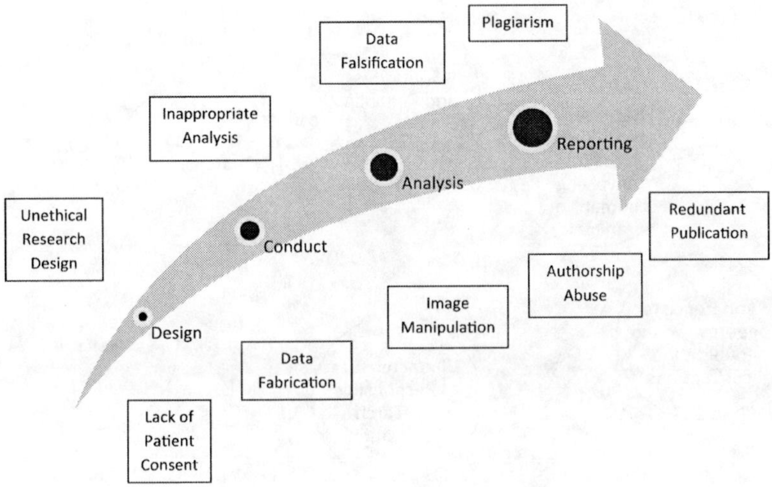

Figure 6.1 *Relationship between Research Ethics and Publication Ethics*

6.2. Importance of Scientific Publication

Assumption, interpretation and experimentation are the basic pillars of science. In the past, thousands of scientists worked in several fields without any social boundaries. Every person should have the authority to utilize scientific innovations for a favorable life style. A shared understanding between the government policies, scientists and industries is required for research upgrading. Innovative ideas should be largely shared among the scientific community to benefit the entire mankind. Publication is the best way for sharing ideas, innovations and views to the scientific world. It is last and most crucial phase of a successful research project. It is the outcome of long-term efforts on careful preparations and experimental analysis. As most of the research projects are directly or indirectly supported through public investment, it should be developed for the benefits of entire society. A detailed description of the performed procedures should be universally accessible and easily acceptable. As a particular objective is responsible for raising so many scientific aims consequently affecting the entire world, publications should be comprehensive, truthful, correct, and fair and should not give deceptive information

6.3. Characteristics of Responsible Research Publication

Soundness and Reliability

- The research being reported should have been conducted in an ethical and responsible manner and follow all relevant legislation.
- The research being reported should be sound and carefully executed.
- Researchers should use appropriate methods of data analysis and display (and, if needed, seek and follow specialist advice on this).

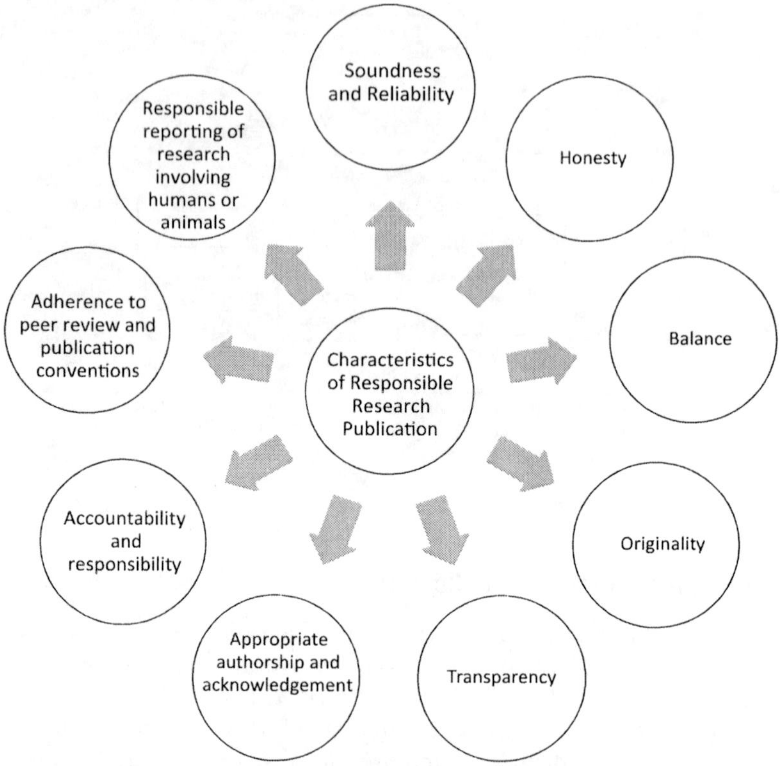

Figure 6.2 *Characteristics of Responsible Research Publication*

- Authors should take collective responsibility for their work and for the content of their publications. Researchers should check their publications carefully at all stages to ensure methods and findings are reported accurately. Authors should carefully check calculations, data presentations, typescripts/ submissions and proofs.

6.3.1. Honesty

- Researchers should present their results honestly and without fabrication, falsification or inappropriate data manipulation. Research images (e.g. micrographs, X-rays, pictures of electrophoresis gels) should not be modified in a misleading way.
- Researchers should strive to describe their methods and to present their findings clearly and unambiguously. Researchers should follow applicable reporting guidelines. Publications should provide sufficient detail to permit experiments to be repeated by other researchers.
- Reports of research should be complete. They should not omit inconvenient, inconsistent or inexplicable findings or results that do not support the authors' or sponsors' hypothesis or interpretation.

- Research funders and sponsors should not be able to veto publication of findings that do not favour their product or position. Researchers should not enter agreements that permit the research sponsor to veto or control the publication of the findings (unless there are exceptional circumstances, such as research classified by governments because of security implications).
- Authors should alert the editor promptly if they discover an error in any submitted, accepted or published work. Authors should cooperate with editors in issuing corrections or retractions when required.
- Authors should represent the work of others accurately in citations and quotations.
- Authors should not copy references from other publications if they have not read the cited work.

6.3.2. Balance

- New findings should be presented in the context of previous research. The work of others should be fairly represented. Scholarly reviews and syntheses of existing research should be complete, balanced, and should include findings regardless of whether they support the hypothesis or interpretation being proposed. Editorials or opinion pieces presenting a single viewpoint or argument should be clearly distinguished from scholarly reviews.
- Study limitations should be addressed in publications.

6.3.3. Originality

- Authors should adhere to publication requirements that submitted work is original and has not been published elsewhere in any language. Work should not be submitted concurrently to more than one publication unless the editors have agreed to co-publication. If articles are co-published this fact should be made clear to readers.
- Applicable copyright laws and conventions should be followed. Copyright material (e.g., tables, figures or extensive quotations) should be reproduced only with appropriate permission and acknowledgement.
- Relevant previous work and publications, both by other researchers and the authors' own, should be properly acknowledged and referenced. The primary literature should be cited where possible.
- Data, text, figures or ideas originated by other researchers should be properly acknowledged and should not be presented as if they were the authors' own. Original wording taken directly from publications by other researchers should appear in quotation marks with the appropriate citations.
- Authors should inform editors if findings have been published previously or if multiple reports or multiple analyses of a single data set are under consideration for publication elsewhere. Authors should provide copies of related publications or work submitted to other journals.
- Multiple publications arising from a single research project should be clearly identified as such and the primary publication should be referenced.

Translations and adaptations for different audiences should be clearly identified as such, should acknowledge the original source, and should respect relevant copyright conventions and permission requirements. If in doubt, authors should seek permission from the original publisher before republishing any work.

6.3.4. Transparency

- All sources of research funding, including direct and indirect financial support, supply of equipment or materials, and other support (such as specialist statistical or writing assistance) should be disclosed.
- Authors should disclose the role of the research funder(s) or sponsor (if any) in the research design, execution, analysis, interpretation and reporting.
- Authors should disclose relevant financial and non-financial interests and relationships that might be considered likely to affect the interpretation of their findings or which editors, reviewers or readers might reasonably wish to know. This includes any relationship to the journal, for example if editors publish their own research in their own journal. In addition, authors should follow journal and institutional requirements for disclosing competing interests.

6.3.5. Appropriate Authorship and Acknowledgement

- The research literature serves as a record not only of what has been discovered but also of who made the discovery. The authorship of research publications should therefore accurately reflect individuals' contributions to the work and its reporting.
- In cases where major contributors are listed as authors while those who made less substantial, or purely technical, contributions to the research or to the publication are listed in an acknowledgement section, the criteria for authorship and acknowledgement should be agreed at the start of the project. Ideally, authorship criteria within a particular field should be agreed, published and consistently applied by research institutions, professional and academic societies, and funders. While journal editors should publish and promote accepted authorship criteria appropriate to their field, they cannot be expected to adjudicate in authorship disputes. Responsibility for the correct attribution of authorship lies with authors themselves working under the guidance of their institution. Research institutions should promote and uphold fair and accepted standards of authorship and acknowledgement. When required, institutions should adjudicate in authorship disputes and should ensure that due process is followed.
- Researchers should ensure that only those individuals who meet authorship criteria (i.e., made a substantial contribution to the work) are rewarded with authorship and that deserving authors are not omitted. Institutions and journal editors should encourage practices that prevent guest, gift, and ghost authorship.
- All authors should agree to be listed and should approve the submitted and accepted versions of the publication. Any change to the author list should be approved by all authors including any who have been removed from the list. The

corresponding author should act as a point of contact between the editor and the other authors and should keep co-authors informed and involve them in major decisions about the publication (e.g., responding to reviewers' comments).

- Authors should not use acknowledgements misleadingly to imply a contribution or endorsement by individuals who have not, in fact, been involved with the work or given an endorsement.

6.3.6. Accountability and Responsibility

- All authors should have read and be familiar with the reported work and should ensure that publications follow the principles set out in these guidelines. In most cases, authors will be expected to take joint responsibility for the integrity of the research and its reporting. However, if authors take responsibility only for certain aspects of the research and its reporting, this should be specified in the publication.
- Authors should work with the editor or publisher to correct their work promptly if errors or omissions are discovered after publication.
- Authors should abide by relevant conventions, requirements, and regulations to make materials, reagents, software or datasets available to other researchers who request them. Researchers, institutions, and funders should have clear policies for handling such requests. Authors must also follow relevant journal standards. While proper acknowledgement is expected, researchers should not demand authorship as a condition for sharing materials.
- Authors should respond appropriately to post-publication comments and published correspondence. They should attempt to answer correspondents' questions and supply clarification or additional details where needed.

6.3.7. Adherence to Peer Review and Publication Conventions

- Authors should follow publishers' requirements that work is not submitted to more than one publication for consideration at the same time.
- Authors should inform the editor if they withdraw their work from review, or choose not to respond to reviewer comments after receiving a conditional acceptance.
- Authors should respond to reviewers' comments in a professional and timely manner.
- Authors should respect publishers' requests for press embargos and should not generally allow their findings to be reported in the press if they have been accepted for publication (but not yet published) in a scholarly publication. Authors and their institutions should liaise and cooperate with publishers to coordinate media activity (e.g., press releases and press conferences) around publication. Press releases should accurately reflect the work and should not include statements that go further than the research findings.

6.3.8. Responsible Reporting of Research Involving Humans or Animals

- Appropriate approval, licensing or registration should be obtained before the research begins and details should be provided in the report (e.g., Institutional

Review Board, Research Ethics Committee approval, national licensing authorities for the use of animals).

- If requested by editors, authors should supply evidence that reported research received the appropriate approval and was carried out ethically (e.g., copies of approvals, licenses, participant consent forms).
- Researchers should not generally publish or share identifiable individual data collected in the course of research without specific consent from the individual (or their representative). Researchers should remember that many scholarly journals are now freely available on the internet, and should therefore be mindful of the risk of causing danger or upset to unintended readers (e.g., research participants or their families who recognise themselves from case studies, descriptions, images or pedigrees).
- The appropriate statistical analyses should be determined at the start of the study and a data analysis plan for the pre specified outcomes should be prepared and followed. Secondary or post hoc analyses should be distinguished from primary analyses and those set out in the data analysis plan.
- Researchers should publish all meaningful research results that might contribute to understanding. In particular, there is an ethical responsibility to publish the findings of all clinical trials. The publication of unsuccessful studies or experiments that reject a hypothesis may help prevent others from wasting time and resources on similar projects. If findings from small studies and those that fail to reach statistically significant results can be combined to produce more useful information (e.g., by meta-analysis) then such findings should be published.
- Authors should supply research protocols to journal editors if requested (e.g., for clinical trials) so that reviewers and editors can compare the research report to the protocol to check that it was carried out as planned and that no relevant details have been omitted. Researchers should follow relevant requirements for clinical trial registration and should include the trial registration number in all publications arising from the trial.

6.4. Role and Responsibilities of Authors

6.4.1. Authorship

The first step in creating transparency for readers is accurate identification of those who participated in the research and the reporting. Authors are generally defined as persons who have contributed sufficiently to a scientific report to be listed on the by-line of the published report. Principles on authorship include the following:

- It is the prerogative of journal editors to define authorship and contributorship criteria; journals are encouraged to use one of the widely accepted sets of criteria for authorship, but the editor of the journal may vary the criteria if appropriate for the scientific discipline. It is key that the criteria be clearly defined to the authors.
- Identification of authors and other contributors is the responsibility of the researchers who performed the work based on the criteria of the journal

to which the work is submitted. Researchers should determine which individuals have contributed sufficiently, according to the authorship criteria, to warrant authorship. Individuals who contributed to the work but whose contributions were not of sufficient magnitude to warrant authorship should be identified by name in a contributor's appendix, a co-investigators appendix, or an acknowledgments section; Authors should also ensure they have notified/obtained permission from those they have named within the Acknowledgements section.

- All individuals who qualify for authorship or acknowledgment should be identified. Every person identified as an author or acknowledged contributor should qualify for these roles.
- Individuals listed as authors should review and approve the final manuscript before publication.
- In addition to being accountable for the parts of the work he or she has done, an author should be able to identify which of their co-authors are responsible for specific other parts of the work.
- Editors should require authors and those acknowledged to identify their contributions to the work and make this information available to readers.
- The ultimate reason for identification of authors and other contributors is to establish accountability for and transparency surrounding the reported work.

Authorship should be limited to those who have made a significant contribution to the conception, design, execution, or interpretation of the reported study. All those who have made significant contributions should be listed as co-authors. Where there are others who have participated in certain substantive aspects of the research project, they should be acknowledged or listed as contributors. The corresponding author should ensure that all appropriate co-authors and no inappropriate co authors are included on the paper and that all co-authors have seen and approved the final version of the paper and have agreed to its submission for publication.

6.4.2. Authorship Issues

Inappropriate types of authorship are given below:

- *Guest Authorship*: Guest authorship has been defined as authorship based solely on an expectation that inclusion of a particular name will improve the chances that the study will be published or increase the perceived status of the publication. The "guest" author makes no discernible contributions to the study, so this person meets none of the criteria for authorship.
- *Honorary or Gift Authorship*: Honorary or gift authorship has been defined as authorship based solely on a tenuous affiliation with a study. A salient example would be "authorship" based on one's position as the head of a department in which the study took place.
- *Ghost Authorship*: Ghost authors participate in the research, data analysis, and/or writing of a manuscript but are not named or disclosed in the author by-line or Acknowledgments.

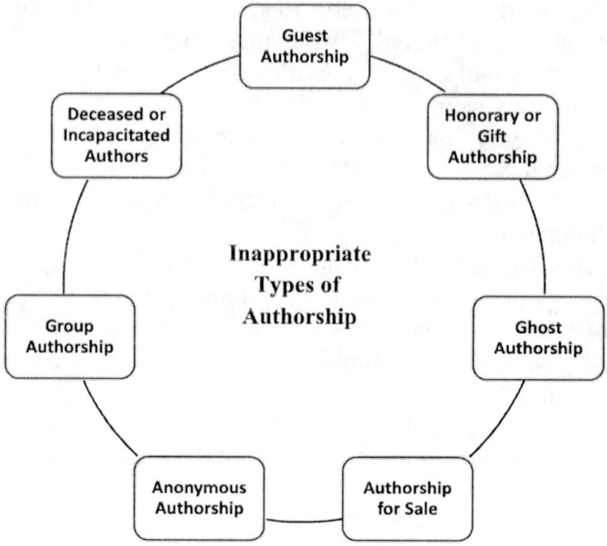

Figure 6.3 *Inappropriate Types of Authorship*

- *Authorship for Sale*: Some instances have been reported in which non-authors have attempted to buy authorship from an author of a paper, often after the paper has been invited for revision or provisionally accepted. Editors should be aware of changes made in the author by-line during the review process. If a change is requested, the corresponding author of the paper should provide an explanation for the request, and all authors on a paper should approve any author changes.
- *Anonymous Authorship*: Because authorship should be transparent and requires public accountability, it is not appropriate to use pseudonyms or to publish scientific reports anonymously. In extremely rare cases, when the author can make a credible claim that attaching his or her name to the document could cause serious hardship (e.g., threat to personal safety or loss of employment), a journal editor may decide to publish anonymous content.

Other categories of authorship that may be acceptable in certain circumstances include group authorship and the inclusion of deceased or incapacitated authors.

- *Group Authorship*: Group authorship may be appropriate when a group of researchers has collaborated on a project, such as a multicenter trial, a consensus document, or an expert panel. Because it can be inaccurate and impossible to list all collaborators (some would not meet a journal's authorship criteria, and by-line space may preclude such a listing), authors need to think about how to communicate credit and responsibility for content. Editors have outlined 2 group authorship models:
    - Authorship in which each person in the group meets authorship criteria, in which case the group is listed as the author, with at least 1 co-author assuming the role of content guarantor.

- Authorship in which a select subgroup of the whole is listed in the by-line on behalf of the whole.

- *Deceased or Incapacitated Authors*: For cases in which a co-author dies or is incapacitated during the writing, submission, or peer-review process, co-authors should obtain disclosure and copyright documentation from a familial or legal proxy.

6.4.3. Order of Authors

The order of authors in the by-line is a collective decision of the authors or study group. Disagreements about author order should be resolved by the authors before the article is submitted for publication. Disputes that arise after submission could delay or prevent publication. Authors should not expect editors to become embroiled in disputes among authors over name placement in the by-line.

6.4.4. Changes to the Author By-line

Any changes the authors wish to make to the author by-line after the initial submission of a manuscript should be made in writing and the document should be

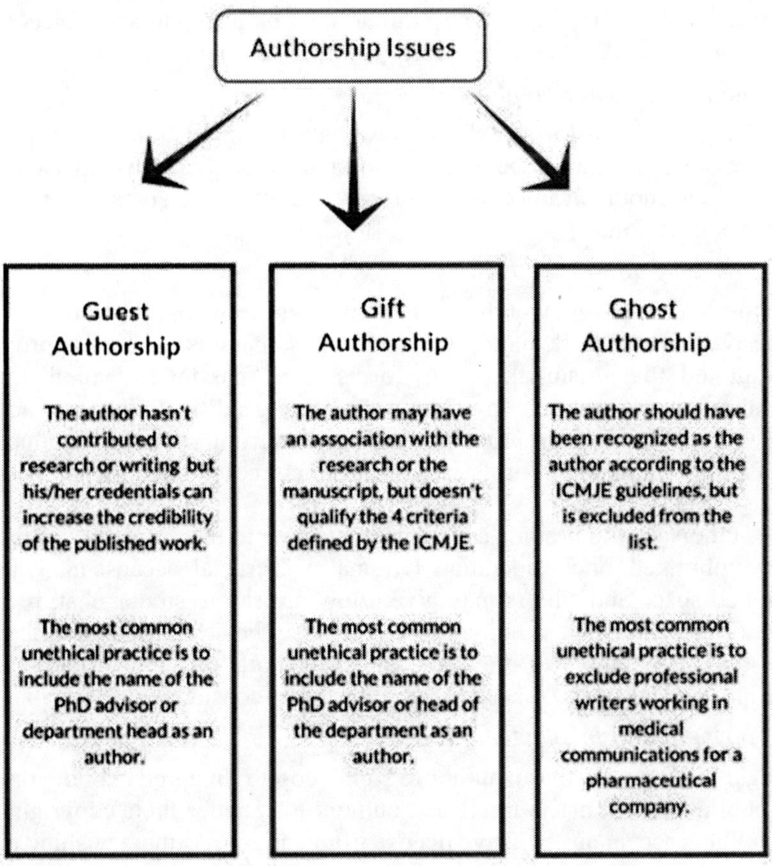

Figure 6.4 *Authorship issues*

signed by all authors, including those being added or removed. The new author list should be stated directly along with a justification for the change.

6.4.5. Confidentiality

The author-editor relationship is founded on confidentiality. Authors should hold all communication between themselves and the journal in confidence. Authors should designate a specific contact for all communication about the manuscript throughout peer review and (if accepted) the publication process. Authors should observe journal policy on communication with external peer reviewers (the policy may vary depending on whether a journal uses masked or non-masked peer review) and should observe journal policy on prepublication embargoes.

6.4.6. Reporting Standards

Authors of papers should present an accurate account of the work performed as well as an objective discussion of its significance. Underlying data should be represented accurately in the paper. A paper should contain sufficient detail and references to permit others to replicate the work. Fraudulent or knowingly inaccurate statements constitute unethical behavior and are unacceptable. Review and professional publication articles should also be accurate and objective, and editorial opinion works should be clearly identified as such.

6.4.7. Data Access and Retention

Authors may be asked to provide the raw data in connection with a paper for editorial review, and should be prepared to provide public access to such data, if practicable, and should in any event be prepared to retain such data for a reasonable time after publication.

6.4.8. Originality and Plagiarism

The authors should ensure that they have written entirely original works, and if the authors have used the work and/or words of others, that this has been appropriately cited or quoted. Plagiarism takes many forms, from "passing off" another's paper as the author's own paper, to copying or paraphrasing substantial parts of another's paper (without attribution), to claiming results from research conducted by others. Plagiarism in all its forms constitutes unethical publishing behaviour and is unacceptable.

The authors should provide a statement attesting to the originality of the study they have submitted for consideration. Originality is crucial, because many journals have limited space and editors may give a low priority to studies that, regardless of scientific accuracy and validity, do not advance the scientific enterprise. Some journals may ask authors to provide copies of reports on other studies (articles, manuscripts, and abstracts) related to the study under consideration.

6.4.9. Copyright and Intellectual Property

It is a legal requirement for an author to sign a copyright agreement of some kind before publication. Some journals ask authors to transfer their copyright to the journal. Others accept an exclusive license from authors. Authors wishing to make their article open access must sign an Open Access Agreement. Publishers are legally required to have explicit authority from an author to publish any article. A brief and abridged description of three types copyright is given below:

- *Copyright Transfer Agreement (CTA)*: Under this form of agreement, the author retains certain re-use rights in their article, but transfers copyright to the society or publisher.
- *Exclusive License Agreement (ELA)*: This form of copyright agreement grants exclusive rights to the journal owner, but the authors retain copyright in their article.
- *Open Access Agreement*: Some journals require authors wishing to make their article open access to sign an Open Access Agreement providing for the article to be made available under one of the Creative Commons Licenses in order to meet the terms of open access publication and ensure the widest possible dissemination.

6.4.10. Citations

Citation and reference to appropriate and relevant literature is an essential part of scholarly publishing and is a shared responsibility among all involved (authors, editors, peer reviewers). Authors should not engage in excessive self-citation of their own work. Editors and peer reviewers should not ask authors to add citations to their papers when there is no strong scholarly rationale for doing so.

6.4.11. Permissions

Authors frequently wish to reuse previously published images and other copyrighted material. It is the author's responsibility to follow journal or publisher guidelines to reuse any copyrighted material and provide proper attribution. This includes the author's own work if the copyright was ever transferred to a publisher or journal. Authors should contact the journal or publisher of the source material or consult the "permissions" information that can be found on many of their web sites. Permission should be granted in writing and the authors should retain this documentation. The editor may request a copy of this notification as well.

6.4.12. Data Sharing

Data sharing is the practice of making data used for scholarly research available to other investigators. Authors should be aware of their data sharing responsibilities imposed by their funding agencies. The goal of this policy is to promote reproducibility and availability of underlying data sets. At the beginning of a study the authors should consider where they will submit their data and should consider the journals, they may want to submit their study and review the data sharing policies for each journal.

6.4.13. Registration of Clinical Trials

Some journals e.g., medical journals require that to be considered for publication, any prospective, interventional clinical research study must have been appropriately recorded in an approved trial registry before enrolment of the first subject. The goal of this policy is to promote the public availability of a comprehensive database of clinical trials.

6.4.14. Human Subjects Research

All journals should require formal affirmation that human subject's research on which a submission is based was approved by an institutional review board (IRB) or complied with the Declaration of Helsinki and/or relevant forms. The researchers must have conducted the study according to the approved protocol and acceptable research standards, including having obtained informed consent of study subjects.

6.4.15. Animal Research

All journals should require formal affirmation that any research involving animals was approved by an animal care and use committee and was conducted according to the approved protocol and acceptable research standards for animal experimentation.

6.4.16. Multiple, Redundant or Concurrent Publication

An author should not in general publish manuscripts describing essentially the same research in more than one journal or primary publication. Submitting the same manuscript to more than one journal concurrently constitutes unethical publishing behaviour. In general, an author should not submit for consideration in another journal a previously published paper.

6.4.17. Text Recycling (sometimes known as self-plagiarism)

Authors are expected to submit original content to publications. It is only acceptable for research to be repeated if it leads to different or new conclusions or for comparisons with new data. In all cases, it is important to reference the previously published work. If any element of the work has been published previously, authors must ensure that this work is fully referenced and state it at the point of submission so that the Editor may make a fully-informed decision.

6.4.18. Acknowledgement of Sources

Proper acknowledgment of the work of others must always be given. Authors should cite publications that have been influential in determining the nature of the reported work. Information obtained privately, as in conversation, correspondence, or discussion with third parties, must not be used or reported without explicit, written permission from the source. Information obtained in the course of confidential services, such as refereeing manuscripts or grant applications, must not be used without the explicit written permission of the author of the work involved in these services.

6.4.19. Disclosure and Conflicts of Interest

All authors should disclose in their manuscript any financial or other substantive conflict of interest that might be construed to influence the results or interpretation of their manuscript. All sources of financial support for the project should be disclosed. Examples of potential conflicts of interest which should be disclosed include employment, consultancies, stock ownership, honoraria, paid expert testimony, patent applications/registrations, and grants or other funding. Potential conflicts of interest should be disclosed at the earliest stage possible. Readers should be informed about who has funded research and on the role of the funders in the research.

6.4.20. Fundamental Errors in Published Works

When an author discovers a significant error or inaccuracy in his/her own published work, it is the author's obligation to promptly notify the journal editor or publisher and cooperate with the editor to retract or correct the paper. If the editor or the publisher learns from a third party that a published work contains a significant error, it is the obligation of the author to promptly retract or correct the paper or provide evidence to the editor of the correctness of the original paper.

6.4.21. Hazards and Human or Animal Subjects

If the work involves chemicals, procedures or equipment that have any unusual hazards inherent in their use, the author must clearly identify these in the manuscript.

To summarize the above, the responsibilities of the authors are given below:

6.4.22. Responsibilities of Authors

1. The author should not submit concurrent manuscripts (or manuscripts essentially describing the same subject matter) to multiple journals. Likewise, an author should not submit any paper previously published anywhere to the journals for consideration. The publication of articles on specific subject matter, such as clinical guidelines and translations, in more than one journal is acceptable if certain conditions are met.
2. The author should present a precise and brief report of his or her research and an impartial description of its significance.
3. The author should honestly gather and interpret his or her research data. Publishers, editors, reviewers, and readers are entitled to request the author to provide the raw data for his or her research for convenience of editorial review and public access. If practicable, the author should retain such data for any possible use after publication.
4. The author should guarantee that the works he or she has submitted are original. If the author has used work and/or words by others, appropriate citations are required. Plagiarism in all its forms constitutes unethical publishing behavior and is unacceptable.
5. The author should indicate explicitly all sources that have supported the research and also declare any conflict(s) of interest.
6. The author should give due acknowledgement to all of those who have made contributions to the research. Those who have contributed significantly to the research should be listed as co-authors. The author should ensure that all co-authors have affirmed the final version of the paper and have agreed on its final publication.
7. The author should promptly inform the journal editor of any obvious error(s) in his or her published paper and cooperate earnestly with the editor in retraction or correction of the paper. If the editor is notified by any party other than the author that the published paper contains an obvious error, the author should write a retraction or make the correction based on the medium of publication.

6.5. Role and Responsibilities of Editor

6.5.1. Editorial Freedom

An editor essentially is responsible for what appears in his or her journal. The editor's right to editorial freedom may be supported by the following and should be agreed on by both the editor and the journal owner/publisher:

- A journal mission statement
- Written editorial priorities, objectives, and measures of success
- Written editorial policies
- A written job description, specifically detailing components of editorial freedom, including the degree of control regarding editorial content, acceptance and publication, and advertising content (a sample job description can be found in the Appendix to this section)
- An editorial board, including associate, assistant, and topic editors, that is nominated or appointed by and reports to the editor
- Sufficient support from the parent society, publisher, owner, or other journal sponsors in both funding and staff to carry out the journal's stated mission
- A mechanism for regular and objective evaluation of editor performance by the publisher or sponsoring organization based on predetermined and agreed-upon measures of success
- Direct lines of communication with the publisher, owner, and any publication oversight body
- A mechanism to prevent inappropriate influence on the editor by others and to handle conflicts in an objective and transparent manner with the goal of conflict resolution and maintenance of trust

6.5.2. Confidentiality

Editor and any editorial staff must not disclose any information about a submitted manuscript to anyone other than the corresponding author and the reviewer(s). Editors will ensure that material submitted remains confidential while under review. Editors and the publication staff should keep all information about a submitted manuscript confidential, sharing it only with those involved in the evaluation, review, and publication processes. Editors should consider adding a confidentiality notice to all correspondence, including reviewer forms, to serve as a reminder to authors, editors, and reviewers.

6.5.3. Fair Play

Editor should evaluate manuscripts for their intellectual content without regard to race, gender, sexual orientation, religious belief, ethnic origin, citizenship, or political philosophy of the authors. Editors' decision to accept or reject a paper for publication should be based only on the paper's importance, originality and clarity, and the study´s relevance to the aim of journal.

6.5.4. Publication Decisions

The editor board journal is responsible for deciding which of the articles submitted to the journal should be published. The validation of the work in question and its importance to researchers and readers must always drive such decisions. The editors may be guided by the policies of the journal's editorial board and constrained by such legal requirements as shall then be in force regarding libel, copyright infringement and plagiarism. The editors may confer with other editors or reviewers in making this decision.

6.5.5. Review of Manuscripts

The editor must ensure that each manuscript is initially evaluated by the editor for originality. The editor should organize and use peer review fairly and wisely. Editors should explain their peer review processes in the information for authors and also indicate which parts of the journal are peer reviewed. The editor should use appropriate peer reviewers for papers that are considered for publication by selecting people with sufficient expertise and avoiding those with conflicts of interest.

6.5.6. Research Ethics

It is essential practice for journals to adopt publication policies to ensure that ethical and responsible research is published and that all necessary consents and approvals have been obtained from authors to publish their work.

6.5.7. Animals in Research

Research involving animals should be conducted with the same rigor as research in humans. Journals should encourage authors to implement the 3Rs principles of replacement.

Journals should encourage authors to adhere to animal research reporting standards, for example the ARRIVE guidelines (Animal Research: Reporting of In Vivo Experiments) reporting guidelines, which describe the details journals should require from authors regarding:

- Study design and statistical analysis.
- Experimental procedures.

3 Rs Principles

- ***Replacement:*** Replacement refers to technologies or approaches which directly replace or avoid the use of animals in experiments where they would otherwise have been used.
- ***Reduction:*** Reduction refers to methods that minimise the number of animals used per experiment or study consistent with the scientific aims. It is essential for reduction that studies with animals are Refinement
- ***Refinement:*** Refinement refers to methods that minimise the pain, suffering, distress or lasting harm that may be experienced by research animals, and which improve their welfare. Refinement applies to all aspects of animal use, from their housing and husbandry to the scientific procedures performed on them. Examples of refinement include ensuring the animals are provided with housing that allows the expression of species-specific behaviours, using appropriate an aesthesia and analgesia to minimise pain, and training animals to cooperate with procedures to minimise any distress.

- Experimental animals.
- Housing and husbandry.

Journals should ask authors to confirm that ethical and legal approval was obtained prior to the start of the study and state the name of the body giving the approval. Authors also should state whether experiments were performed in accordance with relevant institutional and national guidelines and regulations.

6.5.8. Bias-free Language

For research which includes, or refers to, human participants, it is necessary to detail the study population which requires the use of descriptors. It is important that the language and descriptors used to describe research populations are bias-free. The sixth edition of the Publication Manual of the American Psychological Association (APA, 2009) provides recommendations for eliminating bias in language in relation to gender, age, racial and ethnic background, sexual orientation, disability status, and socioeconomic status.

6.5.9. Borders and Territories

Potential disputes over borders and territories may have direct relevance for authors when describing their research in a submitted manuscript, or in the address they use for correspondence. The choices made by authors should be respected, but should a perceived dispute or complaint be raised, then editorial teams should attempt to find a resolution that works for all parties. Ultimately, the final decision on content is an editorial matter and will rest with the journal editors which, where necessary, will be in consultation with the relevant society and publisher.

6.5.10. Cultures and Heritage

There is recognition of increasing innovation in the management of joint copyright in relation to intercultural research, to enable appropriate legal acknowledgment of intellectual property in attribution and acknowledgment. Editors should consider any sensitivities when publishing images of objects that might have cultural significance or cause offence (for example, religious texts or historical events).

6.5.11. Ethnicity and Race

When detailing demographic information about a study population, it is advisable to use terms to designate ethnicity (e.g., African American and South Asian) rather than race.

6.5.12. Human Studies and Subjects

Journals should only consider publishing research which includes individual participants' information and images where the authors' have obtained the prior informed consent to publish from all participants. For manuscripts reporting studies involving human participants, including but extending beyond medical research, journals should require a statement from authors to confirm that the appropriate ethical approval has been received, along with details of the approving ethics committee, and that the study conforms to recognized standards, see for example, Declaration of Helsinki; US Federal Policy for the Protection of Human

Subjects; European Medicines Agency Guidelines for Good Clinical Practice or the Ethical Review Methods for Biomedical Research involving Humans adopted by the National Health and Family Planning Commission of the People's Republic of China.

6.5.13. Procedures for dealing with Unethical Behaviour

Unethical behaviour may be identified and brought to the attention of the editor and publisher at any time, by anyone. Whoever informs the editor or publisher of such conduct should provide sufficient information and evidence in order for an investigation to be initiated. Every reported act of unethical publishing behavior must be looked into, even if it is discovered years after publication.

The editor will take reasonably responsive measures when ethical complaints have been presented concerning a submitted manuscript or published paper. Such measures will generally include contacting the author of the manuscript or paper and giving due consideration of the respective complaint or claims made, but may also include further communications to the relevant institutions and research bodies, depending on the misconduct seriousness. Minor misconduct might be dealt with without the need to consult more widely. In any event, the author should be given the opportunity to respond to any allegations.

Serious misconduct might require application of one or more following measures:

- Informing or educating the author or reviewer where there appears to be a misunderstanding or misapplication of acceptable standards.
- Publication of a formal notice detailing the misconduct.
- A formal letter to the head of the author's or reviewer's department or funding agency.
- Formal retraction or withdrawal of a publication from the journal, in conjunction with informing the head of the author or reviewer's department
- Imposition of a formal embargo on contributions from an individual for a defined period.

6.5.14. Plagiarism, Duplicate/Redundant Publication, Duplicate Submission, Text Recycling and Translations

1. Plagiarism: Plagiarism includes both the theft or misappropriation of intellectual property and the substantial unattributed textual copying of another's work. Editors can help educate about and prevent plagiarism by screening submitted manuscripts for duplicated text. Journals should explain in their instructions to authors how submitted manuscripts are screened for duplicated text and possible plagiarism.

2. Duplicate or Redundant Publication:

- *Duplicate publication*: This refers to the practice of submitting the same study to two journals or publishing more or less the same study in two journals. These submissions/publications can be nearly simultaneous or years later.
- *Redundant publication (also described as 'salami publishing')*: this refers to the situation that one study is split into several parts and submitted to two or more journals. Or the findings have previously been published elsewhere without

proper cross-referencing, permission or justification. "Self-plagiarism" is considered a form of redundant publication. It concerns recycling or borrowing content from previous work without citation. This practice is widespread and might be unintentional. Transparency by the author on the use of previously published work usually provides the necessary information to make an assessment on whether it is deliberate or unintentional.

Authors must avoid duplicate publication, which is reproducing verbatim content from their other publications. Journals should establish processes to avoid duplicate and redundant publication, including:

- Screening submitted manuscripts for duplicated text.
- Reminding authors in the journal's guidelines that duplicate publication is not acceptable.
- Requiring that any previously published results, including numerical information and figures or images, are labeled to make it clear where they were previously reported.
- Papers, particularly medical research papers, that present new analyses of results that have already been published (for example, subgroup analyses) should identify the primary data source, and include a full reference to the related primary publications.
- Ensuring that the Copyright Transfer Agreement, Exclusive License Agreement or Open Access Agreement – one of which must be signed the corresponding author before publication– includes a warranty that the manuscript is an original work, has not been published before, and is not being considered for publication elsewhere in its final form.

The following types of *"prior publication"* do not present cause for concerns about duplicate or redundant publication:

- Abstracts and posters presented as part of conference proceedings.
- Results presented at meetings (for example, to inform investigators or participants about findings).
- Results in databases and clinical trials registries (data without interpretation, discussion, context or conclusions in the form of tables and text to describe data/information).
- Dissertations and theses in university archives.

3. Duplicate Submission: Journals should consider how they might detect concurrent or multiple submissions. For example, in cases where journals are part of an editorial group or portfolio with legitimate access to internal information for the whole journal family, detection aids or mechanisms should be put in place for editors to use as part of their editorial office system.

4. Text Recycling: The Text Recycling Research Project (TRRP, http://textrecycling.org/) has defined text recycling as follows (2020):

"Text recycling is the reuse of textual material (prose, visuals, or equations) in a new document where (1) the material in the new document is identical to that of the source (or substantively equivalent in both form and content), (2) the material

is not presented in the new document as a quotation (via quotation marks or block indentation), and (3) at least one author of the new document is also an author of the prior document."

Journals may find it useful to establish a policy about how much, if any, and under what circumstances, they consider it acceptable to recycle text and results between manuscripts. This may be important, for example, for authors who wish to communicate results from a research project to multiple audiences. In this instance, full or partial results – with appropriate citation of prior publication(s) – might be recycled for legitimate reasons, although the discussion and conclusions would be different.

6.5.15. Translations

Journals may choose to publish materials that have been accurately translated from an original publication in a different language. Journals that translate and publish material that has been published elsewhere should ensure that they have appropriate permission. They should indicate clearly that the material has been translated and re-published and should identify the original source of the material.

6.5.16. Disclosure and Conflicts of Interest

Conflicts of interest in publishing can be defined as conditions in which an individual holds conflicting or competing interests that could bias editorial decisions. Conflicts of interest may be only potential or perceived, or they may be factual. Personal, political, financial, academic, or religious considerations can affect objectivity in numerous ways.

One challenge for editors is to recognize the potential for biases arising from conflicts of interest in the publishing process and to take appropriate action when biases are likely. Some specific types of conflict of interest are mentioned below:

- *Personal conflicts*: Editors should avoid making decisions on manuscripts that conflict with their own interest, such as those submitted from their department or by research collaborators, co-authors, competitors, or those addressing an issue in which they stand to gain financially. If they may have a perceived or actual conflict of interest, editors should delegate handling of any decision to other editors with decision-making responsibility. Also, editors should submit their own manuscripts to the journal only if full masking of the process can be ensured (e.g., anonymity of the peer reviewers and lack of access to records of their own manuscript). Journals should have a procedure in place to guide the handling of submissions by editors, associate editors, editorial board members, and colleagues/students of any of these to allow for peer review and decision making that avoids any conflict of interest. Editorials and/or opinion pieces are an exception to this rule.
- *Financial Conflicts*: The most evident type of potential conflict of financial interest arises when an individual or organization may benefit financially from a decision to publish or to reject a manuscript. Financial conflicts may include salary, grants from a company with an interest in the results, honoraria, stock or equity interests, and intellectual property rights (patents, royalties, and copyrights).

- *Nonfinancial Conflicts*: Other nonfinancial conflicts of interest should also be avoided or disclosed. Some of these include personal, political, academic, and religious conflicts.

6.5.17. Conflict of Interest Disclosure

It is the editors' responsibility to establish the authorship criteria guidelines for their journals. Journals should require disclosure of all conflicts of interest from everyone involved in the publication process: editors, reviewers, editorial board members, editorial staff, and authors. The intent of disclosure is to allow others to make an informed decision about the existence and impact of potential conflicts of interest or bias, including the necessity for recusal or disqualification under extraordinary circumstances.

- *Author Disclosures*: Some editors and journals require authors to identify the organizations that provided support for their research and describe the role played by these organizations in the study and in the analysis of the results. Authors may also be required to disclose all personal, financial, and other relationships they may have with the manufacturer of any product mentioned in the manuscript or with the manufacturers of competing products.
- *Reviewer Disclosures*: Some journals have established policies that require reviewers to reveal any potential personal or financial conflicts of interest with respect to the authors or content of manuscripts they are asked to review, or to affirm that they have no conflicts. In most instances when such conflicts exist, editors request that reviewers decline to comment on the manuscript.

6.5.18. Citation Manipulation

Most metrics of scholarly performance, including the Journal Impact Factor (JIF), are based on citations to published articles. This may generate strong temptation to inappropriately increase citations, something that is referred to as citation manipulation or citation gaming. Citation manipulation refers to any systematic practice that inappropriately pressures authors to cite material with the primary goal of boosting citation rates. The following forms of citation manipulation (for the purpose of increasing citation rates) have been reported:

- *Coercion*: At some point during the peer-review process, editors (or anyone else involved in the process) request that authors add citations from their own journal (or a journal from the same publisher).
- *Editorials*: Editors write editorials in which a disproportionate number of articles from their own journal are cited.
- *Reviewers*: Suggesting citations of their own work. Reviewers may suggest that authors cite their articles.
- *Self-citation*: Authors cite disproportionately large numbers of their own articles in all or most of their publications.
- *Citation Swapping*: A group of colleagues (perhaps students or research associates of a particular researcher) agrees to preferentially and regularly cite each other's articles in all or most of their publications.

It should be stressed that some of the practices described above are only inappropriate if the additional citations requested do not add significantly to the scholarly content of the manuscript. Anybody involved in the peer-review process can become a party to citation manipulation. Therefore, it is every participant's responsibility to judge how reasonable such requests are. Stakeholders in the peer-review and editorial process should be alerted to citation manipulation and bring concerns to the attention of the editor, publisher, or other accountable party. Journals may also decide to publish a policy statement condemning citation manipulation practices. It should be noted that most impact factor formulas monitor when self-citation by a journal reaches an unacceptable level. Although such behavior may result in a short-term gain, the strategy may not work in the long-term.

6.5.19. Editorial Board Participation

The editor-in-chief or principal editor should define the terms and roles of the editors and editorial board that are appointed by and report to him or her. As mentioned above, the editor-in-chief should require disclosure of any conflicts of interest.

6.5.20. Timeliness of the Publication Process

Editors are responsible for monitoring the turnaround time for every publishing stage from manuscript receipt to publication or rejection. Processing data and evaluating trends can help editors scrutinize acceptance and rejection rates of specific types of manuscripts, manage the inventory/backlog of accepted manuscripts, track reviewers' and editors' performance, and assess staffing needs.

6.5.21. Errata, Correction, Retractions and Expressions of Concern

- *Errata*: Errata provide a means of correcting errors that occurred during the writing, typing, editing, or publication (e.g., a misspelling, a dropped word or line, or mislabeling in a figure) of a published article. Sometimes listed as a "corrigendum" instead of "erratum," these terms indicate when the mistake originates from the author. An erratum is used to simply correct a small but important mistake or omission that does not alter the conclusion of the paper. The erratum is a result of honest error, but it does not excuse or invite post-publication corrections because not all corrections will be considered if they are not of sufficient importance. For example, the misspelling of an insignificant word or correcting an error in a reference list does not count.
- *Corrections*: Author Corrections provide a means of correcting errors of omission (e.g., author names or citations) and errors of a scientific nature that do not alter the overall basic results or conclusions of a published article (e.g., an incorrect unit of measurement or order of magnitude used throughout, contamination of one of numerous cultures, or misidentification of a mutant strain, causing erroneous data for only a [noncritical] portion of the study).
- *Retraction*: Retractions are reserved for major errors or breaches of ethics that, for example, may call into question the source of the data or the validity of the results and conclusions of an article. Articles are retracted because the results of a study are unreliable as a result of misconduct, fraudulent research, or honest error, which means the conclusions of the paper are invalidated.

It is also appropriate action for redundant articles that have been published before without permission and acknowledgement of prior or simultaneous publication, and research that is subsequently deemed to be unethical. The retraction will give the reason why an article has been retracted. There has to be a reason for a retraction and it is not an author-instigated action, although the author may request it.

- *Expression of Concern*: This is used to raise awareness to readers that an article may be unreliable. It may be a precursor to a full retraction, but not always. An expression of concern should only be published if an unresolved, ongoing investigation is occurring or if the evidence is inconclusive. An editor does not want to raise doubts about the integrity of an article needlessly and will weigh the impact of the concern (e.g., if it had clinical implications), confidentiality, and the need of journal readers to know. This note will give brief details of the area of concern.

Editors have a responsibility to maintain the integrity of the literature by publishing *errata* or corrections identifying anything of significance, *retractions* and *expressions of concern* as quickly as possible. When appropriate, they should provide a forum (e.g., letters to the editors) for offering responsible alternative opinions.

Errors in published articles require a published correction or erratum. These corrections should be made in such a way that secondary publication services, such as PubMed, will identify them and associate them with the original publication. Many online journals provide a direct link between the original article and the correction published later.

Editors should monitor the number and types of errors that appear in their journals. This review can be done simultaneously with the evaluation of other journal statistics. Editors should take corrective measures when there is evidence of an increase in preventable errors.

6.5.22. Addressing Authorship Disputes

Editors are responsible for promoting the integrity of the literature and fostering good publication practices. Journals should develop and define authorship or contributorship criteria to minimize confusion about expectations. Authorship disputes persist despite the current common efforts to make authorship or contributorship transparent.

6.5.23. Considering Appeals for Reconsideration of Rejected Manuscripts

Despite editors' best efforts to solicit fair and unbiased reviews to evaluate manuscripts fairly, and to make decisions that are in the best interest of the journal and its readers, authors may still want to challenge editorial decisions. Editors should have a policy in place to address complaints and help resolve these issues, although it is not easy to explain to an author that the research reported in his or her manuscript does not warrant publication in comparison with the many others under consideration.

- Determine whether the decision was clearly explained to the author and whether it may have been based on wrong or questionable information, for example, on an incorrect reading of the manuscript or on bad advice from a reviewer.

- Reconsider rejected manuscripts if the author provides good reasons why the decision may have been wrong and is willing to revise the manuscript in response to the valid comments of the reviewers and editors. Many journals allow authors to write a rebuttal letter explaining why their manuscript should be re-evaluated.
- Encourage resubmission of manuscripts that are potentially acceptable but were rejected because major revision or additional data were required, explaining precisely what is needed to make the manuscript potentially acceptable, and the process and procedures that will be followed in handling the resubmitted manuscript.

6.5.24. Addressing Allegations or Findings of Misconduct

Concerns of possible scientific misconduct are usually expressed first to the editors of a journal about a manuscript that is under consideration or has already been published. Journals should develop a consistent policy to encourage the reporting of indications of misconduct, for evaluating the allegations, and for handling the findings. Journals should include a general statement in their Instructions for Authors that allegations of misconduct will be pursued.

6.5.25. Corrections, Expressions of Concern, Retractions and Withdrawals

- *Corrections*

  Journals should encourage readers and authors to notify them if they find errors, especially errors that could affect the interpretation of data or information presented in an article. When an error is identified:
  - Journals should work with authors and their publisher to correct important published errors.
  - Journals should consider retraction when errors are so fundamental that they invalidate the findings.
  - Corrections arising from errors within an article should be distinguishable from retractions and statements of concern relating to questionable research practices.
  - Corrections should be included in indexing systems and linked to the original article.
  - Corrections should be free to access.

For those articles which have been published in an issue, a corresponding correction statement should be published and linked to the original article. In these cases, the changes should usually not be made directly to the article.

- *Expressions of Concern*

  Expressions of Concern may be published if editors have well-founded concerns or suspicions and feel that readers should be made aware of potentially misleading information. The title of an Expression of Concern should include the words *"Expression of Concern"* as well as information to identify the article that it refers to. It should be published on a numbered page and should be listed in the journal's table of contents. It should cite the original article and link electronically with the original electronic publication wherever possible. It should explain the editor's concerns about the contents of the article. It should be in a form that enables indexing and abstracting services to identify and link to original publications and be free to access.

- *Retractions*
  Journals should be committed to playing their part in maintaining the integrity of the scholarly record, therefore on occasion, it may be necessary to retract articles. COPE has published guidelines for retracting articles which suggest that journals should consider publishing retractions for articles when:
  - They have clear evidence that the findings are unreliable, either as a result of major error (e.g., miscalculation or experimental error), or as a result of fabrication (e.g., of data) or falsification (e.g., image manipulation);
  - It constitutes plagiarism;
  - The findings have previously been published elsewhere without proper attribution to previous sources or disclosure to the editor, permission to republish, or justification (i.e., cases of redundant publication);
  - It contains material or data without authorization for use;
  - Copyright has been infringed or there is some other serious legal issue (e.g., libel, privacy);
  - It reports unethical research;
  - It has been published solely on the basis of a compromised or manipulated peer review process;
  - The author(s) failed to disclose a major competing interest or conflict of interest that, in the view of the editor, would have unduly affected interpretations of the work or recommendations by editors and peer reviewers.

The title of a Retraction should include the words "Retraction" as well as information to identify the article that it refers to. It should be published on a numbered page and should be listed in the journal's table of contents. It should cite the original article and link electronically with the original electronic publication wherever possible. It should enable the reader to identify and understand why the article is being retracted. It should be in a form that enables indexing and abstracting services to identify and link to original publications and be free to access.

- *Withdrawals*
  There may be circumstances under which an article may be withdrawn. Where an accepted article is to be retracted because, for example, it contains errors, has been accidentally submitted twice or infringes a professional ethical code of some type, it may be deleted and replaced with a withdrawal statement.
- *Appeals*
  Journals/editors should consider establishing and publishing a mechanism for authors to appeal editorial decisions, to facilitate genuine appeals, and to discourage repeated or unfounded appeals.

- Editors should allow appeals to override earlier decisions following appropriate reconsideration of the editorial process and decision making (for example, additional factual input by the authors, revisions, extra material in the manuscript, or appeals about conflicts of interest and concerns about biased peer review). Author protest alone should not affect decisions.
- Editors should mediate all exchanges between authors and peer reviewers during the peer-review process. Editors may seek comments from additional peer reviewers to help them make their final decision.
- Journals should state in their guidelines that the editor's decision following an appeal is final.
- Journals should consider establishing a mechanism for authors and others to comment on aspects of the journal's editorial management, perhaps via the publisher or a third-party.

6.5.26. Preprint Servers

In scientific publishing, a preprint server is an online repository where research findings and data can be deposited before, during, or after the peer review process. Editors have a responsibility to present clear guidelines to authors regarding their policy on preprint servers, including what content can be shared on preprint servers before, during, and after the review process.

6.5.27. Academic Debate

Journals should facilitate post-publication academic debate either on their site, through letters to the editor or on an external moderated site. They must have mechanisms for correcting, revising and retracting articles after publication. Journals should encourage correspondence and constructive criticism of the work they publish. If an item of correspondence discusses a specific article, the journal should invite the authors of the work to respond before the correspondence is published. When possible, the correspondence and the authors' response should be published at the same time. Authors may choose not to respond to this invitation. They do not have a right to veto comments about their work that the editor judges to be constructive. They may advise editors accordingly about unconstructive comments.

To summarize the above, the responsibilities of the editors are given below:

6.5.28. Responsibilities of Editors

Editors of scientific journals have responsibilities toward the authors who provide the content of the journals, the peer reviewers who comment on the suitability of manuscripts for publication, the journal's readers and the scientific community, the owners/publishers of the journals, and the public as a whole. Depending upon the relationship between the editor and publisher for particular journals, some of the roles and responsibilities between the two may overlap in some of the following:

1. Editor Responsibilities toward Authors

- Providing guidelines to authors for preparing and submitting manuscripts
- Providing a clear statement of the Journal's policies on authorship criteria

- Treating all authors with fairness, courtesy, objectivity, honesty, and transparency
- Establishing and defining policies on conflicts of interest for all involved in the publication process, including editors, staff (e.g., editorial and sales), authors, and reviewers
- Protecting the confidentiality of every author's work
- Establishing a system for effective and rapid peer review
- Making editorial decisions with reasonable speed and communicating them in a clear and constructive manner
- Being vigilant in avoiding the possibility of editors and/or referees delaying a manuscript for suspect reasons
- Establishing clear guidelines for authors regarding acceptable practices for sharing experimental materials and information, particularly those required to replicate the research, before and after publication
- Establishing a procedure for reconsidering editorial decisions
- Describing, implementing, and regularly reviewing policies for handling ethical issues and allegations or findings of misconduct by authors and anyone involved in the peer review process
- Informing authors of solicited manuscripts that the submission will be evaluated according to the journal's standard procedures or outlining the decision-making process if it differs from those procedures
- Developing mechanisms, in cooperation with the publisher, to ensure timely publication of accepted manuscripts
- Clearly communicating all other editorial policies and standards

2. Editor Responsibilities toward Reviewers

- Assigning papers for review appropriate to each reviewer's area of interest and expertise
- Establishing a process for reviewers to ensure that they treat the manuscript as a confidential document and complete the review promptly
- Informing reviewers that they are not allowed to make any use of the work described in the manuscript or to take advantage of the knowledge they gained by reviewing it before publication
- Providing reviewers with written, explicit instructions on the journal's expectations for the scope, content, quality, and timeliness of their reviews to promote thoughtful, fair, constructive, and informative critique of the submitted work
- Requesting that reviewers identify any potential conflicts of interest and asking that they recues themselves if they cannot provide an unbiased review
- Allowing reviewers appropriate time to complete their reviews
- Requesting reviews at a reasonable frequency that does not overtax any one reviewer
- Finding ways to recognize the contributions of reviewers, for example, by publicly thanking them in the journal; providing letters that might be used in applications for academic promotion; offering professional education credits; or inviting them to serve on the editorial board of the journal

3. Editor Responsibilities toward Readers and the Scientific Community

- Evaluating all manuscripts considered for publication to make certain that each provides the evidence readers need to evaluate the authors' conclusions and that authors' conclusions reflect the evidence provided in the manuscript
- Providing literature references and author contact information so interested readers may pursue further discourse
- Identifying individual and group authorship clearly and developing processes to ensure that authorship criteria are met to the best of the editor's knowledge
- Requiring all authors to review and accept responsibility for the content of the final draft of each paper or for those areas to which they have contributed; this may involve signatures of all authors or of only the corresponding author on behalf of all authors. Some journals ask that one author be the guarantor and take responsibility for the work as a whole
- Maintaining the journal's internal integrity (e.g., correcting errors; clearly identifying and differentiating types of content, such as reports of original data, opinion pieces [e.g., editorials and letters to the editor], corrections/errata, retractions, supplemental data, and promotional material or advertising; and identifying published material with proper references)
- Ensuring that all involved in the publication process understand that it is inappropriate to manipulate citations by, for example, demanding that authors cite papers in the journal
- Disclosing sources (e.g., authorship, journal ownership, and funding)
- Creating mechanisms to determine if the journal is providing what readers need and want (e.g., reader surveys)
- Disclosing all relevant potential conflicts of interest of those involved in considering a manuscript or affirming that none exist.
- Providing a mechanism for a further discussion on the scientific merits of a paper, such as by publishing letters to the editor, inviting commentaries, article blogs, or soliciting other forms of public discourse
- Explicitly stating journal policies regarding ethics, embargo, submission and publication fees, and accessibility of content (freely available versus subscriber only)
- Working with the publisher to attract the best manuscripts and research that will be of interest to readers
- In some instances, a publisher may put pressure on an editor to publish a review or article in an effort to increase reprint sales. The editor has a responsibility to readers and the scientific community to resist such pressure

4. Editor Responsibilities toward Journal Owners/Publishers

- Conducting peer review of submitted manuscripts
- Complying with the guidelines and procedures of the owner organization, including any terms specified in the contract with that organization
- Making recommendations about improved evaluation and dissemination of scientific material

- Adhering to the owner's and publisher's fiscal policies towards the Journal, at least in so much as they do not encroach upon editorial independence
- Adhering to the agreed-upon mission, publication practices, and schedule

6.6. Role and Responsibilities of Reviewers

Peer review is the principal mechanism by which the quality of research is judged. Most funding decisions in science and the academic advancement of scientists are based on peer-reviewed publications. Because the number of scientific articles published each year continues to grow, the quality of the peer-review process and the quality of the editorial board are cited as primary influences on a journal's reputation, Journal Impact Factor (JIF), and standing in the field. Scientific journals publishing peer-reviewed articles depend heavily on the scientific referees or reviewers who typically volunteer their time and expertise. In most circumstances, at least two reviewers are solicited to evaluate a manuscript; some journals request three or more reviews. This may be required in situations where review by a statistician is needed. In cases of controversy or strong disagreement regarding the merits of the work, an additional review may also be solicited or one of the journal's editors might give an evaluation. More than three reviewers are sometimes used if reviewers from several fields are needed to obtain a thorough evaluation of a paper. In addition to fairness in judgment and expertise in the field, reviewers have significant responsibilities toward authors, editors, and readers.

6.6.1. Confidentiality

Any manuscripts received for review must be treated as confidential documents. They must not be shown to or discussed with others except as authorized by the editor. Material under review should not be shared or discussed with anyone outside the review process unless necessary and approved by the editor. Material submitted for peer-review is a privileged communication that should be treated in confidence, taking care to guard the author's identity and work. Reviewers should not retain copies of submitted manuscripts and should not use the knowledge of their content for any purpose unrelated to the peer review process.

6.6.2. Constructive Critique

Reviewer comments should acknowledge the positive aspects of the material under review, identify negative aspects constructively and indicate the improvements needed. A reviewer should explain and support his or her judgment clearly enough that editors and authors can understand the basis of the comments. The reviewer should ensure that an observation or argument that has been previously reported be accompanied by a relevant citation and should immediately alert the editor when he or she becomes aware of duplicate publication. The purpose of peer review is not to demonstrate the reviewer's proficiency in identifying flaws. Reviewers have the responsibility to identify strengths and provide constructive comments to help the author resolve weaknesses in the work. A reviewer should respect the intellectual independence of the author.

6.6.3. Contribution to Editorial Decisions

Peer review assists the editor in making editorial decisions and through the editorial communications with the author may also assist the author in improving the paper. Peer review is an essential component of formal scholarly communication. Authors who wish to contribute to publications have an obligation to do a fair share of reviewing.

6.6.4. Promptness

Any selected referee who feels unqualified to review the research reported in a manuscript or knows that its prompt review will be impossible should notify the editor and excuse himself from the review process

6.6.5. Standards of Objectivity

Reviews should be conducted objectively. Personal criticism of the author is inappropriate. Referees should express their views clearly with supporting arguments.

6.6.6. Competence

Reviewers who realize that their expertise on the subject of the manuscript is limited have a responsibility to make their degree of competence clear to the editor. Reviewers need not be expert in every aspect of a manuscript's content, but they should accept an assignment only if they have adequate expertise to provide an authoritative assessment. A reviewer without the requisite expertise is at risk of recommending acceptance of a submission with substantial deficiencies or rejection of a meritorious paper. In such cases, the reviewer should decline the review.

6.6.7. Impartiality and Integrity

Reviewer comments and conclusions should be based on an objective and impartial consideration of the facts, exclusive of personal or professional bias. All comments by reviewers should be based solely on the paper's scientific merit, originality, and quality of writing as well as on the relevance to the journal's scope and mission, without regard to race, ethnic origin, sex, religion, or citizenship of the authors.

6.6.8. Disclosure and Conflict of Interest

Unpublished materials disclosed in a submitted manuscript must not be used in a reviewer's own research without the written consent of the author. Privileged information or ideas obtained through peer review must be kept confidential and not used for personal advantage. Reviewers should not consider manuscripts in which they have conflicts of interest resulting from competitive, collaborative, or other relationships or connections with any of the authors, companies, or institutions connected to the papers.

To the extent possible, the review system should be designed to minimize actual or perceived bias on the reviewer's part. If reviewers have any interest that might interfere with an objective review, they should either decline the role of reviewer or disclose their conflict of interest to the editor and ask how best to address it. Some journals require reviewers to sign disclosure forms that are similar to those signed by authors.

6.6.9. Timeliness and Responsiveness

Reviewers are responsible for acting promptly, adhering to the instructions for completing a review, and submitting it in a timely manner. Failure to do so undermines the review process. Every effort should be made to complete the review within the time requested. If it is not possible to meet the deadline for the review, then the reviewer should promptly decline to perform the review or should inquire whether some accommodation can be made with respect to the deadline.

6.6.10. Acknowledgement of Sources

Reviewers should identify relevant published work that has not been cited by the authors. Any statement that an observation, derivation, or argument had been previously reported should be accompanied by the relevant citation. A reviewer should also call to the editor's attention any substantial similarity or overlap between the manuscript under consideration and any other published paper of which they have personal knowledge.

To summarize the above, the responsibilities of the reviewers are given below:

6.6.11. Responsibilities of Reviewers

1. Reviewer Responsibilities toward Authors

- Providing written, unbiased, constructive feedback in a timely manner on the scholarly merits and the scientific value of the work, together with the documented basis for the reviewer's opinion
- Indicating whether the writing is clear, concise, and relevant and rating the work's composition, scientific accuracy, originality, and interest to the journal's readers
- Avoiding personal comments or criticism
- Maintaining the confidentiality of the review process: not sharing, discussing with third parties, or disclosing information from the reviewed paper

2. Reviewer Responsibilities toward Editors

- Notifying the editor immediately if unable to review in a timely manner and, if able, providing the names of alternative reviewers
- Alerting the editor about any potential personal, finance
- al or perceived conflict of interest and declining to review when a conflict exists
- Complying with the editor's written instructions on the journal's expectations for the scope, content, and quality of the review
- Providing a thoughtful, fair, constructive, and informative critique of the submitted work, which may include supplementary material provided to the journal by the author
- Determining scientific merit, originality, and scope of the work; indicating ways to improve it; and, if requested, recommending acceptance or rejection using whatever rating scale the editor deems most useful
- Noting any ethical concerns, such as any violation of accepted norms of ethical treatment of animal or human subjects or substantial similarity between the reviewed manuscript and any published paper or any

manuscript concurrently submitted to another journal that may be known to the reviewer

- Refraining from direct author contact

3. Reviewer Responsibilities toward Readers

- Ensuring that the methods and analysis are adequately detailed to allow the reader to judge the scientific merit of the study design and be able to replicate the study
- Ensuring that the article cites all relevant work by other scientists

6.7. Publication Ethics-related Organizations and their Role in Providing Best Practices/Standard Setting for Scholarly Publication

A good research involves many coordinated steps. It starts from hypothesis, selection of appropriate study design, study execution, data collection, analysis and finally publication. Not only the conduct of the study requires ethics to be adhered to but also the process of publication comes under the purview of ethics. Any publication that reports the results and draws the conclusion from the data which have been manipulated is considered research fraud or scientific misconduct.

There are organizations which give recommendations and develop guidelines to assist authors, editors and reviewers. The purpose is to create and disseminate accurate, clear, reproducible, unbiased research papers. The organizations involved with publication ethics are:

- Committee on Publication Ethics (COPE)
- World Association of Medical Editors (WAME)
- Open Access Scholarly Publishers Association (OASPA)
- International Committee of Medical Journals Editors (ICMJE)

6.7.1. The Committee on Publication Ethics (COPE)

COPE was founded in 1997 by a group of medical journal editors concerned about publication misconduct, e.g., plagiarism, attempted or actual redundant publication, attempts to pass off fraudulent data, unethical research, breaches

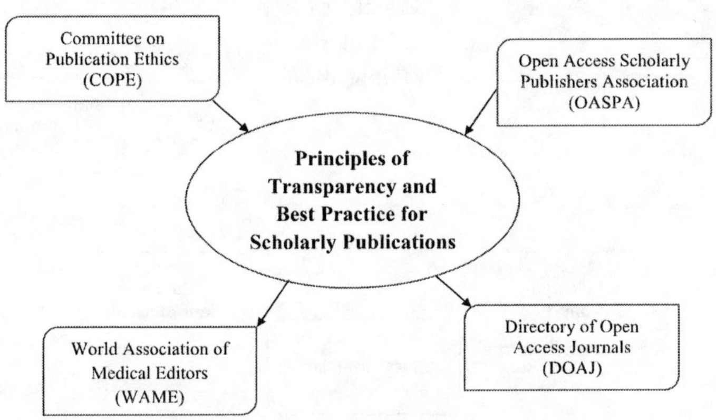

Figure 6.5 *Publication Ethics-related Organizations*

of confidentiality, and so on. The Committee on Publication Ethics (COPE) is a forum for editors of peer-reviewed journals to discuss issues related to the integrity of the scientific record. It supports and encourages editors to report, catalogue and instigate investigations into ethical problems in the publication process. COPE (Committee on Publication Ethics) is committed to educating and supporting editors, publishers and those involved in publication ethics with the aim of moving the culture of publishing towards one where ethical practices become a normal part of the publishing culture.

6.7. 1.1. COPE's Ethical Core Practices for Scholarly Publication

The Core Practices were developed in 2017. They are applicable to all involved in publishing scholarly literature: editors and their journals, publishers, and institutions. The Core Practices should be considered alongside specific national and international codes of conduct for research and are not intended to replace these. Journals and publishers should have robust and well described, publicly documented practices in all of the following areas for their journals:

1. *Allegations of Misconduct*: Journals should have a clearly described process for handling allegations, however they are brought to the journal's or publisher's attention. Journals must take seriously allegations of misconduct

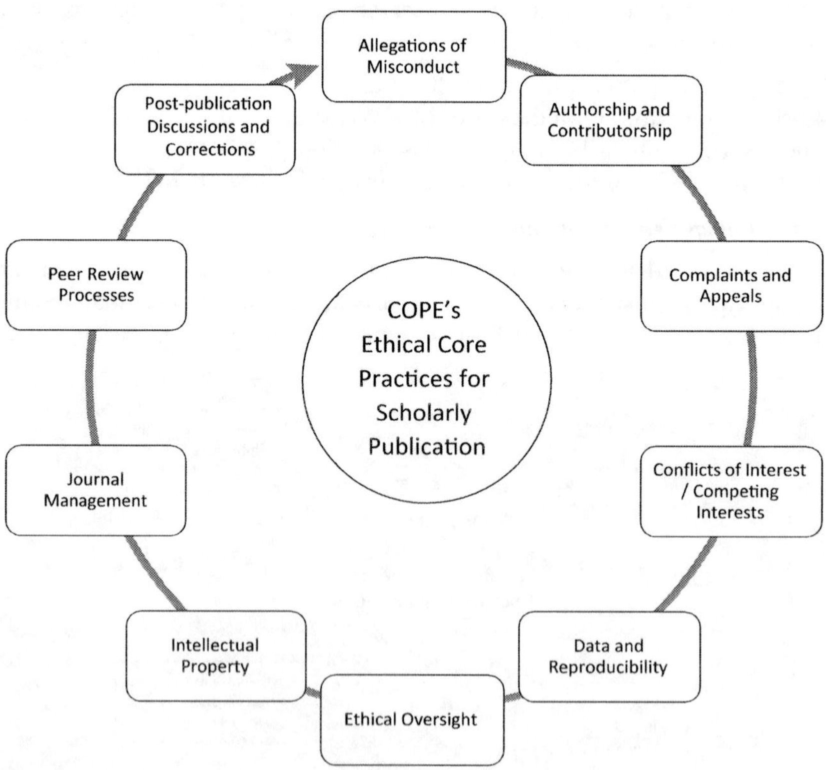

Figure 6.6 *COPE's Ethical Core Practices for Scholarly Publication*

pre-publication and post-publication. Policies should include how to handle allegations from whistleblowers.

2. *Authorship and Contributorship*: Clear policies (that allow for transparency around who contributed to the work and in what capacity) should be in place for requirements for authorship and contributorship as well as processes for managing potential disputes
3. *Complaints and Appeals*: Journals should have a clearly described process for handling complaints against the journal, its staff, editorial board or publisher
4. *Conflicts of Interest / Competing Interests*: There must be clear definitions of conflicts of interest and processes for handling conflicts of interest of authors, reviewers, editors, journals and publishers, whether identified before or after publication
5. *Data and Reproducibility*: Journals should include policies on data availability and encourage the use of reporting guidelines and registration of clinical trials and other study designs according to standard practice in their discipline
6. *Ethical Oversight*: Ethical oversight should include, but is not limited to, policies on consent to publication, publication on vulnerable populations, ethical conduct of research using animals, ethical conduct of research using human subjects, handling confidential data and ethical business/marketing practices.
7. *Intellectual Property*: All policies on intellectual property, including copyright and publishing licenses, should be clearly described. In addition, any costs associated with publishing should be obvious to authors and readers. Policies should be clear on what counts as prepublication that will preclude consideration. What constitutes plagiarism and redundant/overlapping publication should be specified?
8. *Journal Management*: A well-described and implemented infrastructure is essential, including the business model, policies, processes and software for efficient running of an editorially independent journal, as well as the efficient management and training of editorial boards and editorial and publishing staff.
9. *Peer Review Processes*: All peer review processes must be transparently described and well managed. Journals should provide training for editors and reviewers and have policies on diverse aspects of peer review, especially with respect to adoption of appropriate models of review and processes for handling conflicts of interest, appeals and disputes that may arise in peer review.
10. *Post-publication Discussions and Corrections*: Journals must allow debate post publication either on their site, through letters to the editor, or on an external moderated site, such as Pub-Peer. They must have mechanisms for correcting, revising or retracting articles after publication.

6.7.2. World Association of Medical Editors (WAME)

Established in 1995, WAME (pronounced "whammy") is a 501(c)(3) nonprofit voluntary association of editors of peer-reviewed medical journals from countries throughout the world who seek to foster international cooperation among and education of medical journal editors. WAME is a global association of editors of peer-reviewed medical journals who seek to foster cooperation and communication among editors; improve editorial standards; promote professionalism in medical editing through education, self-criticism, and self-regulation; and encourage research on the principles and practice of medical editing. Membership in WAME is free and all decision-making editors of peer-reviewed medical journals are eligible to join. Membership is also available to selected scholars in journal editorial policy and peer review. WAME has more than 1830 members representing more than 1000 journals from 92 countries.

WAME is dedicated to high ethical and scientific principles in the pursuit of the following common goals:

- to facilitate worldwide cooperation and communication among editors of peer-reviewed medical journals;
- to improve editorial standards, to promote professionalism in medical editing through education, self-criticism and self-regulation;
- to encourage research on the principles and practice of medical editing.
- to publish original, important, well-documented peer-reviewed articles on clinical and laboratory research;
- to provide continuing education in basic and clinical sciences to support informed clinical decision making;
- to enable physicians to remain informed in one or more areas of medicine;
- to improve public health internationally by improving the quality of medical care, disease prevention and medical research;
- to foster responsible and balanced debate on controversial issues and policies affecting medicine and health care;
- to promote peer review as a vehicle for scientific discourse and quality assurance in medicine and to support efforts to improve peer review;
- to achieve the highest level of ethical medical journalism;
- to promote self-audit and scientifically supported improvement in the editing process;
- to produce publications that are timely, credible and enjoyable to read;
- to forecast important issues, problems and trends in medicine and health care;
- to inform readers about non-clinical aspects of medicine and public health, including political, philosophic, ethical, environmental, economic, historical and cultural issues;
- to recognize that, in addition to these specific objectives, a medical journal has a social responsibility to improve the human condition and safeguard the integrity of sciences.

6.7.2.1. WAME Recommendations on Publication Ethics Policies for Medical Journals

WAME's comprehensive policy on publication ethics is summarized here, which addresses all the major areas of ethics:

1. *Study Design and Ethics*: Good research should be well justified, well planned, and appropriately designed, so that it can properly address the

research question. Research should be conducted to high standards of quality control and data analysis. Data and records must be retained and produced for review upon request. Fabrication, falsification, concealment, deceptive reporting, or misrepresentation of data constitutes scientific misconduct.

Documented review and approval from a formally constituted review board (Institutional Review Board or Ethics committee) should be required for all studies involving people, medical records, and human tissues. For those investigators who do not have access to formal ethics review committees, the principles outlined in the Declaration of Helsinki should be followed. If the study is judged exempt from review, a statement from the committee should be required. Informed consent by participants should always be sought. If not possible, an institutional review board must decide if this is ethically acceptable. Journals should have explicit policies as to whether these review board approvals must be documented by the authors, or simply attested to in their cover letter, and how they should be described in the manuscript itself. Animal experiments should require full compliance with local, national, ethical, and regulatory principles, and local licensing arrangements.

Journal recommendations for preferred presentation and analysis of data should be described in the Information for Contributors or Authors. Wherever possible, recommendations should be based on evidence about methods of data presentation that are readable and most likely to be interpreted correctly by readers. Editors should keep themselves informed of this research and adapt their recommendations as it evolves.

2. *Authorship*: Journals should publish guidance about what constitutes authorship. While there is no universally agreed definition of authorship, contributors should be made aware of the guidelines developed by the International Committee of Medical Journal Editors. Authorship implies a significant intellectual contribution to the work, some role in writing the manuscript and reviewing the final draft of the manuscript, but authorship roles can vary. Who will be an author, and in what sequence, should be determined by the participants early in the research process, to avoid disputes and misunderstandings which can delay or prevent publication of a paper.

   For all manuscripts, the corresponding author should be required to provide information on the specific contributions each author has made to the article. (Alternatively, since authors may differ on the nature and magnitude of contributions, each author may be asked to describe their own.) All authors are responsible for the quality, accuracy, and ethics of the work, but one author must be identified who will reply if questions arise or more information is needed, and who will take responsibility for the work as a whole. This description of author contributions should be printed with the article. The authors are responsible for creating all components of the manuscript. If writers are provided by the sponsoring or funding institution or corporation to draft or revise the article, the name of the writer and their sponsoring organization must be provided. Their names and contributions will be provided with the acknowledgments. Journals should discourage

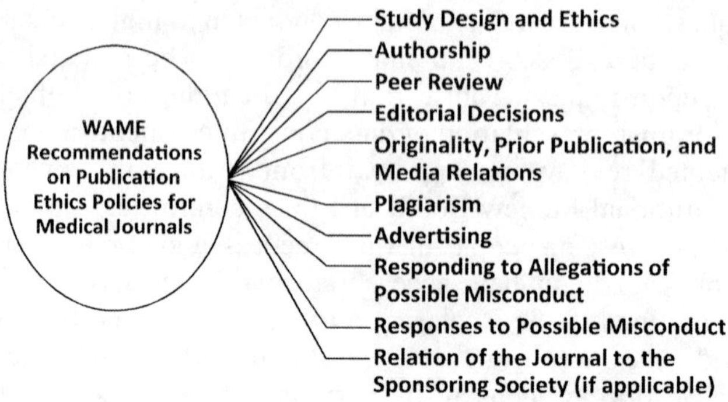

Figure 6.7 *WAME Recommendations on Publication Ethics Policies for Medical Journals*

"honorary" authorship (when authorship is granted as a favor to someone powerful or prestigious who would not have qualified for it otherwise) and should also try to ensure that all those who qualify as authors are listed.

All authors must take responsibility in writing for the accuracy of the manuscript, and one author must be the guarantor and take responsibility for the work as a whole. A growing trend among journals is to also require that for reports containing original data, at least one author (e.g., the principal investigator) should indicate that she or he had full access to all the data in the study and takes responsibility for the integrity of the data and the accuracy of the data analysis. This helps assure that authors, and not funding sources, have final say over the analysis and reporting of their results.

3. *Peer Review*: Peer review is fundamental to the scientific publication process and the dissemination of sound science. Peer reviewers are experts chosen by editors to provide written assessment of the strengths and weaknesses of written research, with the aim of improving the reporting of research and identifying the most appropriate and highest quality material for the journal. Regular reviewers selected for the journal should be required to meet minimum standards (as determined and promulgated by each journal) regarding their background in original research, publication of articles, formal training, and previous critical appraisal of manuscripts.

Peer reviewers should be experts in the scientific topic addressed in the articles they review, and should be selected for their objectivity and scientific knowledge. Individuals who do not have such expertise should not be reviewers, and there is no role for review of articles by individuals who have a major competing interest in the subject of the article (e.g., those working for a company whose product was tested, its competitors, those with special political or ideological agendas, etc.).

Reviews will be expected to be professional, honest, courteous, prompt, and constructive. The desired major elements of a high-quality review should be as follows:

- The reviewer should have identified and commented on major strengths and weaknesses of study design and methodology

- The reviewer should comment accurately and constructively upon the quality of the author's interpretation of the data, including acknowledgment of its limitations.
- The reviewer should comment on major strengths and weaknesses of the manuscript as a written communication, independent of the design, methodology, results, and interpretation of the study.
- The reviewer should comment on any ethical concerns raised by the study, or any possible evidence of low standards of scientific conduct.
- The reviewer should provide the author with useful suggestions for improvement of the manuscript.
- The reviewer's comments to the author should be constructive and professional
- The review should provide the editor the proper context and perspective to make a decision on acceptance (and/or revision) of the manuscript. (Some journals may wish a recommendation on whether the article should be published; others will not, as such decisions are usually made on priorities different than the reviewer's).

4. *Editorial Decisions*: Decisions about a manuscript should be based only on its importance, originality, clarity, and relevance to the journal's scope and content. Studies with negative results despite adequate power, or those challenging previously published work, should receive equal consideration. There should be an explicit written policy on the procedure that will be followed if an author appeals a decision. If a published paper is subsequently found to have errors or major flaws, the Editor should take responsibility for promptly correcting the written record in the journal. The specific content of the correction may address whether the errors originated with the author or the journal. The correction should be listed in the table of contents to ensure that it is linked to the article to which it pertains in public databases such as PubMed.

   Ratings of review quality and other performance characteristics of editors should be periodically assessed to assure optimal journal performance, and must contribute to decisions on reappointment. Individual performance data must be confidential. These performance measures should also be used to assess changes in process that might improve journal performance.

   The handling of manuscripts that may represent a conflict of interest for editors is described under the section on conflict of interest. The process by which candidates are nominated to the Editorial Board, and the qualities sought in candidates, should be explicitly described.

5. *Originality, Prior Publication, and Media Relations*: Journals should state their policies on what type of content they accept for publication. Journals should generally seek original work that has not been previously published. Web and other electronic publication should be considered the same as print publication for this purpose. Redundant publication occurs when multiple papers, without full cross reference in the text, share the same data, or results. Republication of a paper in another language, or simultaneously in multiple

journals with different audiences may be acceptable, provided that there is full and prominent disclosure of its original source at the time of submission of the manuscript. At the time of submission, authors should disclose details of related papers they have authored, even if in a different language, similar papers in press, and any closely related papers previously published or currently under review at another journal.

Because medical research findings are of increasing interest to the lay media, journalists attend scientific meetings at which preliminary research findings are presented, which can lead to their premature publication in the mass media. Publication of details not included in the abstract or meeting presentation is not advised until the article has appeared in a peer-reviewed journal, as this means that enough detailed evidence has been provided to satisfy peer reviewers and editors. Where this is not possible, authors should help journalists to produce accurate reports, but refrain from supplying additional data, if they wish their material to be of sufficient original interest to warrant publication in peer-reviewed journals. Authors should be discouraged from holding press conferences to publicize their abstract results, as these results are preliminary and generally the complete report has not yet undergone peer review. Journals should address these concerns in their formal policies on originality of submitted materials.

Previous publication of an abstract during the proceedings of meetings (in print or electronically) does not preclude subsequent submission for publication, but full disclosure should be made at the time of submission. The journal's embargo policy (on release of information to the press about upcoming contents) should be made available.

6. *Plagiarism*: Plagiarism is the use of others published and unpublished ideas or words (or other intellectual property) without attribution or permission, and presenting them as new and original rather than derived from an existing source. The intent and effect of plagiarism is to mislead the reader as to the contributions of the plagiarizer. This applies whether the ideas or words are taken from abstracts, research grant applications, Institutional Review Board applications, or unpublished or published manuscripts in any publication format (print or electronic).

   Plagiarism is scientific misconduct and should be addressed as such. Self-plagiarism refers to the practice of an author using portions of their previous writings on the same topic in another of their publications, without specifically citing it formally in quotes. This practice is widespread and sometimes unintentional, as there are only so many ways to say the same thing on many occasions, particularly when writing the Methods section of an article. Although this usually violates the copyright that has been assigned to the publisher, there is no consensus as to whether this is a form of scientific misconduct, or how many of one's own words one can use before it is truly "plagiarism." Probably for this reason self-plagiarism is not regarded in the same light as plagiarism of the ideas and words of other individuals. If journals have developed a policy on this matter, it should be clearly stated for authors.

7. *Advertising*: Many scientific journals derive a substantial income from advertising or reprints, creating a potential conflict of interest. Editorial decisions should not be influenced by advertising revenue or reprint potential. Editorial and advertising functions at the journal should be independent. Advertisers and donors should have no control over editorial material under any circumstances.

   Reprinted articles must be published as they originally appeared in the journal (including subsequent corrections); that is, there is no alteration or revision of articles for a supplement or reprint other than corrections. The content of special supplementary issues (if any) should be determined only by the usual editorial process and not be influenced in any way by the funding source or advertisers. Limitations on how reprinted articles may be combined with advertisements or endorsements of a product or company should be explicitly addressed in journal policy. If supplements do not undergo peer review or undergo a peer review process different from the rest of the journal that should be explicitly stated.

   Journals should have a formal advertising policy and this should be made available to all constituents of the journal. Briefly, journals should require all advertisements to clearly identify the advertiser and the product or service being offered. In the case of drug advertisements, the full generic name of each active ingredient should appear. Commercial advertisements should not be placed adjacent to any editorial matter that discusses the product being advertised, nor adjacent to any article reporting research on the advertised product, nor should they refer to an article in the same issue in which they appear. Limitations on how reprinted articles may be combined with advertisements or endorsements of a product or company should be explicitly addressed in journal policy. Ads should have a different appearance from editorial material so there is no confusion between the two. Similar limitations (for the regular journal as well as supplements) may include placement of ads for related products on the front, rear, or inside cover pages of an issue that carries an editorial or original article on that topic. Policies on these issues should be explicit, and published in print or on the Web.

   Products or services being advertised should be germane to (a) the practice of medicine, (b) medical education, or (c) health care delivery. Advertisements may not be deceptive or misleading. Exaggerated or extravagantly worded copy should not be allowed. Advertisements should not be accepted if they appear to be indecent or offensive in either text or artwork, or contain negative content of a personal, racial, ethnic, sexual orientation, or religious character.

   Journals must have the right to RECUSE any advertisement for any reason. The decision as to acceptance (and any questions about eligibility raised by readers or others) should be made in consultation with the journal's editorial content team and the editorial team should be regularly informed about the evaluation of advertising, especially those that are refused due to non-compliance with the journal's guidelines.

8. *Responding to Allegations of Possible Misconduct*: Journals should have a clear policy on handling concerns or allegations about misconduct, which can arise regarding authors, reviewers, editors, and others. Journals do not have the resources or authority to conduct a formal judicial inquiry or arrive at a formal conclusion regarding misconduct. That process is the role of the individual's employer, university, granting agency, or regulatory body. However, journals do have a responsibility to help protect the integrity of the public scientific record by sharing reasonable concerns with authorities who can conduct such an investigation.

   Deception may be deliberate, by reckless disregard of possible consequences, or by ignorance. Since the underlying goal of misconduct is to deliberately deceive others as to the truth, the journal's preliminary investigation of potential misconduct must take into account not only the particular act or omission, but also the apparent intention (as best it can be determined) of the person involved. Misconduct does not include unintentional error. The most common forms of scientific misconduct include:

   - *Falsification of data*: ranges from fabrication to deceptive selective reporting of findings and omission of conflicting data, or willful suppression and/or distortion of data.
   - *Plagiarism*: The appropriation of the language, ideas, or thoughts of another without crediting their true source, and representation of them as one's own original work.
   - *Improprieties of authorship*: Improper assignment of credit, such as excluding others, misrepresentation of the same material as original in more than one publication, inclusion of individuals as authors who have not made a definite contribution to the work published; or submission of multi-authored publications without the concurrence of all authors.
   - *Misappropriation of the ideas of others*: an important aspect of scholarly activity is the exchange of ideas among colleagues. Scholars can acquire novel ideas from others during the process of reviewing grant applications and manuscripts. However, improper use of such information can constitute fraud. Wholesale appropriation of such material constitutes misconduct.
   - *Violation of generally accepted research practices*: Serious deviation from accepted practices in proposing or carrying out research, improper manipulation of experiments to obtain biased results, deceptive statistical or analytical manipulations, or improper reporting of results.
   - *Material failure to comply with legislative and regulatory requirements affecting research*: Including but not limited to serious or substantial, repeated, willful violations of applicable local regulations and law involving the use of funds, care of animals, human subjects, investigational drugs, recombinant products, new devices, or radioactive, biologic, or chemical materials.
   - *Inappropriate behavior in relation to misconduct*: this includes unfounded or knowingly false accusations of misconduct, failure to

report known or suspected misconduct, withholding or destruction of information relevant to a claim of misconduct and retaliation against persons involved in the allegation or investigation.

Deliberate misrepresentation of qualifications, experience, or research accomplishments to advance the research program, to obtain external funding, or for other professional advancement.

9. *Responses to Possible Misconduct*: Journals should have an explicit policy describing the process by which they will respond to allegations of misconduct. All such allegations should be kept confidential; the number of inquiries and those involved should be kept to the minimum necessary to achieve this end. Whenever possible, references to the case in writing should be kept anonymous.

Journals have an obligation to readers and patients to ensure that their published research is both accurate and adheres to the highest ethical standard. Therefore, if the inquiry concludes there is a reasonable possibility of misconduct, responses should be undertaken, chosen in accordance with the apparent magnitude of the misconduct. Responses may be applied separately or combined, and their implementation should depend on the circumstances of the case as well as the responses of the participating parties and institutions. The following options are ranked in approximate order of severity:

- A letter of explanation (and education) sent only to the person against whom the complaint is made, where there appears to be a genuine and innocent misunderstanding of principles or procedure.
- A letter of reprimand to the same party, warning of the consequences of future such instances, where the misunderstanding appears to be not entirely innocent.
- A formal letter as above, including a written request to the supervising institution that a investigation be carried out and the findings of that inquiry reported in writing to the journal.
- Publication of a notice of redundant or duplicate publication or plagiarism, if appropriate (and unequivocally documented). Such publication will not require approval of authors, and should be reported to their institution.
- Formal withdrawal or retraction of the paper from the scientific literature, published in the journal, informing readers and the indexing authorities (National Library of Medicine, etc.), if there is a formal finding of misconduct by an institution. Such publication will not require approval of authors, should be reported to their institution, and should be readily visible and identifiable in the journal. It is recommended that editors inform readers and authors of their reservation of the right to publish a retraction if it meets these conditions, thereby helping decrease arguments with authors.

Editors or reviewers who are found to have engaged in scientific misconduct should be removed from further association with the journal, and this fact reported to their institution.

10. *Relation of the Journal to the Sponsoring Society (if applicable)*: The journal should have an explicit policy describing its governance and relationship to the sponsoring society. Editors-in-chief and the owners of their journals both want the journals to succeed, but they have different roles. The primary responsibilities of the editors-in-chief are to inform and educate readers, with attention to the accuracy and importance of journal articles, and to protect and strengthen the integrity and quality of the journal and its processes. Owners are ultimately responsible for all aspects of publishing the journal, including its staff, budget, and business policies. The relationship between owners and editors-in-chief should be based on mutual respect and trust, and recognition of each other's authority and responsibilities, because conflicts can damage the intellectual integrity and reputation of the journal and its financial success.

    The following are guidelines for protecting the responsibility and authority of editors-in-chief and owners:

    - The conditions of the editors-in-chief's employment, including authority, responsibilities, term of appointment, and mechanisms for resolving conflict, should be explicitly stated and approved by both editor and owners before the editor is appointed.
    - Editors-in-chief should have full authority over the editorial content of the journal, generally referred to as "editorial independence." Owners should not interfere in the evaluation, selection, or editing of individual articles, either directly or by creating an environment in which editorial decisions are strongly influenced.
    - Editorial decisions should be based mainly on the validity of the work and its importance to readers, not the commercial success of the journal. Editors should be free to express critical but responsible views about all aspects of medicine without fear of retribution, even if these views might conflict with the commercial goals of the publisher. To maintain this position, editors should seek input from a broad array of advisors, such as reviewers, editorial staff, an editorial board, and readers.
    - Editors-in-chief should establish procedures that guard against the influence of commercial and personal self-interest on editorial decisions.
    - Owners have the right to hire and fire editors-in-chief, but they should dismiss them only for substantial reasons, such as a pattern of irresponsible editorial decisions, scientific misconduct, disagreement with the long-term editorial direction of the journal, or personal behavior (such as criminal acts), that are incompatible with a position of trust. Furthermore, it is preferable that any evaluation on which hiring or firing is based should be performed by a panel of independent experts, rather than a small number of executives of the owning organization.
    - Editors-in-chief should report to the highest governing body of the owning organization, not its administrative officers. Major decisions regarding the editor's employment should be made by this body with open discussion and time to hear from all interested parties. Some owners

have found it useful to appoint an independent board to advise them on major decisions regarding their editor and journal.

- Editors should resist any actions that might compromise these principles in their journals, even if it places their own position at stake. If major transgressions do occur, editors should participate in drawing them to the attention of the international medical community.

6.7.3. Open Access Scholarly Publishing Association (OASPA)

The Open Access Scholarly Publishing Association (OASPA) is a membership organization that was established in 2008 in order to represent the interests of Open Access (OA) globally in all scientific, technical and scholarly disciplines. This mission is carried out through exchanging information, setting standards, advancing models, advocacy, education, and the promotion of innovation. OASPA develop and disseminate solutions that advance open access and ensure a diverse, vibrant, and healthy open access community, through:

- *Leadership and Development*: Create awareness of the benefits of OA publishing and highlight policies that enhance and support OA publications.
- *Collaboration and Convening*: Convene community stakeholders to share experiences, discuss problems and identify opportunities in the advancement of open access.
- *Setting Standards*: Promote best practice and ethical standards in open access, applying rigorous criteria and in-depth review to membership and actively collaborating on important standard-raising scholarly communication initiatives.
- *Promoting Innovation*: Contribute to the development and dissemination of the innovative approaches to scholarly publishing and the related opportunities that OA content allows.
- *Supporting the OA Ecosystem*: Promote the development of diverse systems, business models and policies that support OA publishing and encourage a vibrant and competitive market for pure OA publishing in the longer term.

6.7.3.1. Principles of Transparency and Best Practice in Scholarly Publishing

The Principles of Transparency and Best Practice in Scholarly Publishing is a statement drafted in collaboration between the World Association of Medical Editors (WAME), the Committee on Publication Ethics (COPE), the Directory of Open Access Journals (DOAJ) and the Open Access Scholarly Publishers Association (OASPA). These organisations strongly encourage journal editors and publishers to review the principles and criteria and consider whether their journals meet the criteria.

6.7.3.2. OASPA Principles of Transparency

The Open Access Scholarly Publishing Association (OASPA) has identified the following principles for scholarly publications:

- *Website*: A journal's website, including the text that it contains, shall demonstrate that care has been taken to ensure high ethical and professional

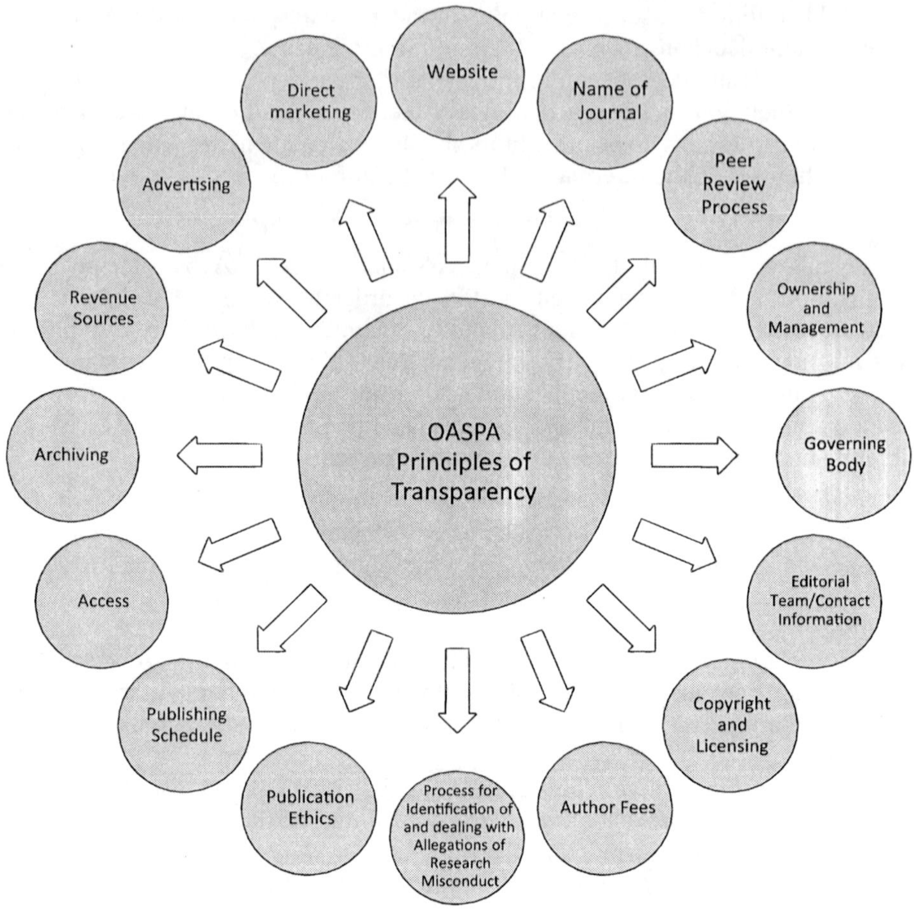

Figure 6.8 *OASPA Principles of Transparency*

standards. It must not contain information that might mislead readers or authors, including any attempt to mimic another journal/publisher's site. An 'Aims & Scope' statement should be included on the website and the readership clearly defined. There should be a statement on what a journal will consider for publication including authorship criteria (e.g., not considering multiple submissions, redundant publications) to be included. ISSNs should be clearly displayed (separate for print and electronic).

- *Name of journal*: The Journal name shall be unique and not be one that is easily confused with another journal or that might mislead potential authors and readers about the Journal's origin or association with other journals.
- *Peer review process*: Journal content must be clearly marked as whether peer reviewed or not. Peer review is defined as obtaining advice on individual manuscripts from reviewers expert in the field who are not part of the

journal's editorial staff. This process, as well as any policies related to the journal's peer review procedures, shall be clearly described on the journal website, including the method of peer review used. Journal websites should not guarantee manuscript acceptance or very short peer review times.

- *Ownership and management*: Information about the ownership and/or management of a journal shall be clearly indicated on the journal's website. Publishers shall not use organizational or journal names that would mislead potential authors and editors about the nature of the journal's owner.
- *Governing body*: Journals shall have editorial boards or other governing bodies whose members are recognized experts in the subject areas included within the journal's scope. The full names and affiliations of the journal's editorial board or other governing body shall be provided on the journal's website.
- *Editorial team/contact information*: Journals shall provide the full names and affiliations of the journal's editors on the journal website as well as contact information for the editorial office, including a full address.
- *Copyright and Licensing*: The policy for copyright shall be clearly stated in the author guidelines and the copyright holder named on all published articles. Likewise, licensing information shall be clearly described in guidelines on the website, and licensing terms shall be indicated on all published articles, both HTML and PDFs. If authors are allowed to publish under a Creative Commons license then any specific license requirements shall be noted. Any policies on posting of final accepted versions or published articles on third party repositories shall be clearly stated.
- *Author fees*: Any fees or charges that are required for manuscript processing and/or publishing materials in the journal shall be clearly stated in a place that is easy for potential authors to find prior to submitting their manuscripts for review or explained to authors before they begin preparing their manuscript for submission. If no such fees are charged that should also be clearly stated.
- *Process for identification of and dealing with allegations of research misconduct*: Publishers and editors shall take reasonable steps to identify and prevent the publication of papers where research misconduct has occurred, including plagiarism, citation manipulation, and data falsification/fabrication, among others. In no case shall a journal or its editors encourage such misconduct, or knowingly allow such misconduct to take place. In the event that a journal's publisher or editors are made aware of any allegation of research misconduct relating to a published article in their journal, the publisher or editor shall follow COPE's guidelines (or equivalent) in dealing with allegations.
- *Publication Ethics*: A journal shall also have policies on publishing ethics. These should be clearly visible on its website, and should refer to: i) Journal policies on authorship and contributorship; ii) How the journal will handle complaints and appeals; iii) Journal policies on conflicts of interest / competing interests; iv) Journal policies on data sharing and reproducibility; v) Journal's

policy on ethical oversight; vi) Journal's policy on intellectual property; and vii) Journal's options for post-publication discussions and corrections.

- *Publishing schedule*: The periodicity at which a journal publishes shall be clearly indicated.
- *Access*: The way(s) in which the journal and individual articles are available to readers and whether there are associated subscription or pay per view fees shall be stated.
- *Archiving*: A journal's plan for electronic backup and preservation of access to the journal content (for example, access to main articles via CLOCKSS or PubMed Central) in the event a journal is no longer published shall be clearly indicated.
- *Revenue sources*: Business models or revenue sources (e.g., author fees, subscriptions, advertising, reprints, institutional support, and organizational support) shall be clearly stated or otherwise evident on the journal's website. Publishing fees or waiver status should not influence editorial decision making.
- *Advertising*: Journals shall state their advertising policy if relevant, including what types of adverts will be considered, who makes decisions regarding accepting adverts and whether they are linked to content or reader behaviour (online only) or are displayed at random. Advertisements should not be related in any way to editorial decision making and shall be kept separate from the published content.
- *Direct marketing*: Any direct marketing activities, including solicitation of manuscripts that are conducted on behalf of the journal, shall be appropriate, well targeted, and unobtrusive. Information provided about the publisher or journal is expected to be truthful and not misleading for readers or authors.

6.7.4. ICMJE's Recommendations for the Conduct, Reporting, Editing and Publication of Scholarly Work in Medical Journals

The ICMJE (International Committee of Medical Journal Editors) was established in 1978, in Vancouver, British Columbia, Canada, by a group of medical journal editors. ICMJE developed these recommendations to review best practice and ethical standards in the conduct and reporting of research and other material published in medical journals, and to help authors, editors, and others involved in peer review and biomedical publishing create and distribute accurate, clear, reproducible, unbiased medical journal articles. The recommendations may also provide useful insights into the medical editing and publishing process for the media, patients and their families, and general readers.

Purpose of the Recommendations: ICMJE developed these recommendations to review best practice and ethical standards in the conduct and reporting of research and other material published in medical journals, and to help authors, editors, and others involved in peer review and biomedical publishing create and distribute accurate, clear, reproducible, unbiased medical journal articles. The recommendations may also provide useful insights into the medical editing and publishing process for the media, patients and their families, and general readers.

Who should use the Recommendations?: These recommendations are intended primarily for use by authors who might submit their work for publication to ICMJE member journals. Many non-ICMJE journals voluntarily use these recommendations (see www.icmje.org/journals-following-the-icmje-recommendations/). The ICMJE encourages that use but has no authority to monitor or enforce it. In all cases, authors should use these recommendations along with individual journals' instructions to authors.

Journals that follow these recommendations are encouraged to incorporate them into their instructions to authors and to make explicit in those instructions that they follow ICMJE recommendations. Journals that wish to be identified on the ICMJE website as following these recommendations should notify the ICMJE secretariat at www.icmje.org/journals-following-the-icmje-recommendations/journal-listing-request-form/.

6.8. Conflicts of Interest (CoI) and Conflicts of Commitment (CoC)

Trust is essential in scientific pursuit of knowledge. Objectivity is fundamental to this trust. In order to maintain that trust it is important to understand the policies regarding identification and management of conflicts of interest. In the research environment, a Conflict of Interest (COI) exists when a researcher's personal interests, such as career, reputation, or finances, may or do conflict with his/her professional obligations to conduct honest, objective research activities. COIs that go unmanaged may lead to a loss of confidence in the integrity of the researcher, data, and research institution. They can also lead to injury or harm to study participants or the patients who may use a product wrongly approved. COIs reduce the trust and confidence that people generally have in the pursuit of research.

6.8.1. Definition of Conflict of Interest

The University of Southern California defines Conflict of Interest as *"a situation in which financial or other personal considerations compromise, or have the appearance of compromising an individual's professional judgment in proposing, conducting, supervising or reporting research"*. The appearance of a conflict of interest exists when a reasonable person would think that the professional's judgment is likely to be compromised. A conflict of interest only implies the potential for bias. It is important to note that a conflict of interest exists whether or not decisions are affected by personal interest. While conflicts of interest apply to a wide range of behaviors, they all involve the use of a person's authority for personal/financial gain.

6.8.2. Types of Conflict of Interest (CoI)

Types of COIs are given below:

6.8.2.1. Tangible Conflicts of Interest

Conflicts of Interest can be tangible (i.e., able to be seen and measured, and typically involving financial relationships – also known as material)

Definition: A tangible conflict of interest is one that can be quantified or measured; as such, it usually involves a financial connection or arrangement between two or more parties involved in the research

Examples:

- A researcher has a financial interest in the company sponsoring their research (tangible)
- A researcher conducts a clinical trial that is sponsored by an individual or organisation with a financial interest in the results of the trial (tangible)
- A researcher takes part in the negotiation of an agreement between the University and a company where they or their family or close personal friend/s have a financial or nonfinancial interest in that company (tangible)

6.8.2.2. Intangible Conflicts of Interest

Intangible conflict of interest typically involves academic activity that can lead to gain of a non-financial nature.

Definition: Intangible conflicts of interest involve scholarly or academic, professional, or social concerns

Examples:

- A researcher has an affiliation that may benefit directly or indirectly from the dissemination of research outcomes in a particular way (intangible)
- A researcher undertakes peer review of a research output or grant application submitted by a close personal friend, family member or affiliate or, conversely, by an adversary (intangible)
- A researcher with a close personal or familial relationship with a student or a student's family is involved in decisions about that student's admission, supervision, or award of prizes or scholarships (intangible and tangible)

6.8.2.3. Individual Conflict of Interest

The term individual conflict of interest refers to situations in which financial or other personal considerations may conflict, or have the appearance of conflicting, with an employee's professional judgment in exercising any university duty or responsibility in administration, management, instruction, research and other professional activities. The term individual conflict of commitment refers to situations in which outside relationships or activities (such as professional consulting for a fee) conflict, or have the appearance of conflicting, with an employee's commitment to his/her university duties or responsibilities.

6.8.2.4. Institutional Conflict of Interest

The term Institutional conflict of interest refer to situations in which the teaching, research, outreach, administrative, financial, operational or other activities of the university could be compromised because of external financial interests and/or business relationships held by the university as a body corporate or by a university or campus official acting within his/her authority on behalf of the university or campus, that could bring financial gain to the university, campus, any of its units, and the individuals covered by this policy.

6.8.2.5. Actual Conflict of Interest

An actual conflict of interest is a situation where a researcher's ability to perform her/his responsibilities to the University are compromised by financial, personal or professional interests.

6.1.1.6. Perceived Conflict of Interest

A perceived conflict of interest is one in which an independent observer might reasonably think that the researcher's responsibilities may be or be seen to be unduly influenced by their own interests.

6.1.1.7. Potential Conflict of Interest

A potential conflict of interest involves a situation that may develop into an actual conflict of interest.

6.8.3. Identification of Conflicts of Interest (CoI)

The following list provides examples of activities or actions that have the potential of creating a conflict of interest:

- Consulting activities.
- The purchase of goods or services from businesses in which an employee or his/her family has a financial interest or, as the result of such purchase, may directly benefit.
- Receipt of gifts, gratuities, loans, or special favors from research sponsors or vendors.
- Holding of an equity, royalty, or debt instrument by the employee or the employee's family in an entity that provides financial support to the employee's institute/organization, including research or other support or services, if this support will benefit the employee or persons who are supervised, either directly or indirectly, by the employee.
- Receipt, directly to the employee from non-institutional/organizational sources of cash, services, or equipment provided in support of the employee's institutional/organizational activities.
- Use of information received as an employee (that is not otherwise publicly available) for personal purposes and financial gain.

1.1.3. Conflicts of Interest (CoI) in Sponsored Funding

Example-1

Situation

A research institute employee serves as PI or Co-PI on a grant that includes a subcontract to a member of the employee's immediate family.

Why could this be perceived to be a conflict of interest?

Subcontracting to a member of one's family gives the perception of use of Federal or state resources for personal gain. Note that when funds are given to the university/research institution from any source, they become university/institute funds.

What should the employee do?

The employee should disclose the conflict. The situation will be reviewed by the Compliance Office and the President to determine if there is a way to reduce or eliminate the conflict. If needed, a management plan will be established to prevent the institute employee from using, or appearing to use, his/her position to benefit his/herself or the family member. This is generally done by transferring the responsibility for the grant to a third party.

Example-2

Situation

An employee gets a grant from an engineering company to conduct research on the efficiency of energy conservation in various engine designs, one of which is sold by the engineering company. The employee's spouse owns more than 5 percent of the company stock.

Why could this be perceived to be a conflict of interest?

The employee's spouse, and therefore the employee, stands to gain financially depending on the outcome of the research, which raises questions about the integrity of the research.

What should the employee do?

To protect research integrity, institute policy prohibits investigators from receiving grants from entities in which they or their family members have a management role or a significant financial interest. Therefore, the employee should disclose the situation. A management plan will be needed and it will likely either: 1) transfer the grant to a third party to provide oversight, or 2) establish an oversight committee to monitor the integrity of the research.

6.9. Conflicts of Commitment

Conflicts of commitment arise from situations that place competing demands on researchers' time and loyalties. At any time, a researcher might be:

- working on one or more funded projects
- preparing to submit a request for a new project
- teaching and advising students
- attending professional meetings and giving lectures
- serving as a peer reviewer
- sitting on advisory boards
- working as a paid consultant, officer, or employee in a private company

Each of these activities requires time and makes demands on a researcher's institutional commitments. Care needs to be taken to assure that these commitments do not inappropriately interfere with one another.

6.10. Handling Complaints and Appeals

The policy of the journal should be primarily aimed at protecting the authors, reviewers, editors and the publisher of the journal. Authors have the right to appeal an Editor's decision on their article. There should be a system that the editor or publisher need to develop that if an author wants to appeal an editor's decision, he can write an email to the journal explaining why he think the decision should be overturned. All appeals should be sent to the journal's Editor-in-Chief, who should assess the article and the details of the peer review process before the final decision. Editors should try to manage appeals as quickly as possible as with any complaint, editors should acknowledge the receipt and keep the authors informed during the appeals process.

Post-Publication Issues

Journals make their efforts for accurate publishing and want to strive to ensure that every article may published with accuracy, but there are instances where problems are raised after publication. These fall into different categories and result in different responses:

- *Erratum*: Where the production process has introduced an error in the article, journal should publish an *Erratum*.
- *Corrigendum*: Where the authors notice a mistake that has not been introduced by editor, journal should publish a *Corrigendum*.
- *Expression of Concern*: Where there are issues which may affect the validity of the scientific record, such as suspected image manipulation, but the authors are not willing to publish a Corrigendum, journal should publish an *Expression of Concern*.
- *Retraction*: Where major issues are affecting the validity of the scientific record, such as duplicates publication or proven plagiarism, journal should publish a *Retraction*.

In all such cases, journals should work in collaboration with the authors as well as the Editor who managed the article's peer review and the Editor-in-Chief, to determine the best option from our available responses. If the issue was raised by a third party, they are also kept informed. All *Errata, Corrigenda, Expressions of Concern*, and *Retractions* should be free to view and digitally linked to the original published article both on journal's site and on third-party websites that collect journal's metadata (e.g., PubMed, ASCI Database, Index ONE, ADL, and Google Scholar).

6.10.1. Who complains or makes an appeal?

Submitters, authors, reviewers, and readers may register complaints and appeals in a variety of cases as follows: falsification, fabrication, plagiarism, duplicate publication, authorship dispute, conflict of interest, ethical treatment of animals, informed consent, bias or unfair inappropriate competitive acts, copyright, stolen data, defamation, and legal problem. If any individuals or institutions want to inform the cases, they can send a letter to editor. For the complaints or appeals, concrete data with answers to all factual questions (who, when, where, what, how, why) should be provided.

6.10.2 Who is responsible to resolve and handle complaints and appeals?

The Editor, Editorial Board, or Editorial Office is responsible for them.

6.10.3 What may be the consequence of remedy?

It depends on the type or degree of misconduct. The consequence of resolution will follow the guidelines of the Committee of Publication Ethics.

6.11. How to Handle Complaints

One of the responsibilities of a journal editor is to ensure, as far as is possible, that articles accepted for publication adhere to ethical standards in terms of the research conducted and the reporting of the research within the written article.

6.11.1. Author Complaints

Authors can make a complaint about a retraction or related issue regarding the article or paper.

6.11.1.1. Retractions

Circumstances under which journal/editor should retract an article
Journals should be committed to play its part in maintaining the integrity of the scholarly record, therefore on occasion, it is necessary to retract articles. Articles may be retracted if:

- There is major scientific error which would invalidate the conclusions of the article, for example where there is clear evidence that findings are unreliable, either as a result of misconduct (e.g. data fabrication) or honest error (e.g. miscalculation or experimental error).
- Where the findings have previously been published elsewhere without proper cross-referencing, permission or justification (i.e., cases of redundant publication).
- Where there are ethical issues such as plagiarism (appropriation of another person's ideas, processes, results, or words without giving appropriate credit including those obtained through confidential review of others' manuscripts) or inappropriate authorship (e.g., "guest" authorship).
- Where unethical research has been reported.

Retraction Process

In order to ensure that retractions are handled according to industry best practice, and in accordance with COPE guidelines, journals should adopt the following retraction process:

- An article requiring potential retraction is brought to the attention of the journal editor.
- The journal editor should follow the step-by-step guidelines according to the COPE flowcharts (including evaluating a response from the author of the article in question).
- Before any action is taken, the editor's findings should be review. The purpose of this step is to ensure a consistent approach in accordance with industry best practice.
- The final decision as to whether to retract is then communicated to the author and, if necessary, any other relevant bodies, such as the author's institution on occasion.

- The retraction statement is then posted online and published in the next available issue of the journal.

Complaints Procedure

To challenge to a retraction or a related issue, the procedure should be as follows:

- The complaint may be submitted via the journal editor or directly to publisher.
- An independent investigation should be carried out by at least two representatives from journal, one of whom must be legally qualified.
- The investigation should involve reviewing all correspondence relating to the case in question and, if necessary, obtaining further written responses to queries from the parties involved.
- The purpose of the investigation should establish that correct procedures have been followed, that decisions have been reached based on academic criteria, that personal prejudice or bias of some kind has not influenced the outcome, and that appropriate sanctions have been applied where relevant.
- The investigatory panel will then submit its findings to journal for further review before any onward communications to the appropriate parties.

Process for Issuing a Retraction Statement

Where the decision is taken to retract and the article to be retracted is the Version of Record (i.e., it has been published in Early View or within an issue of a journal), journal should recommend to issue a retraction statement which should be published separately but should be linked to the article being retracted. A *"retracted"* watermark should also be added to the article; however, the article as first published should be retained online in order to maintain the scientific record. Issuing a retraction statement will mean the following:

- The retraction will appear on a numbered page in a prominent section of the journal;
- The retraction will be listed in the contents page and the title of the original article will be included in its heading;
- The text of the retraction should explain why the article is being retracted; and
- The statement of retraction and the original article must be clearly linked in the electronic database so that the retraction will always be apparent to anyone who comes across the original article.

Circumstances under which an Article may be Deleted

It should be journal's policy to strongly discourage withdrawal of the Version of Record in line with the International Association of Scientific, Technical and Medical Publishers guidelines on retractions and preservation of the objective record of science. Therefore, deletion of the Version of Record should be rare and journal will only consider it in the following limited circumstances:

- Where there has been a violation of the privacy of a research subject;
- Where there are errors to which a member of the general public might be exposed and if followed or adopted, would pose a significant risk to health; or

- Where a clearly defamatory comment has been made about others in the relevant field or about their work.
- Where an Accepted Article (which represents an early version of an article) is to be retracted, because for example it contains errors, has been accidentally submitted twice or infringes a professional ethical code of some type, it may be deleted.

Even in the above circumstances, bibliographic information about the deleted article should be retained for the scientific record, and an explanation given, however brief, about the circumstances of its removal.

6.11.1.2. Withdrawals

Circumstances under which an article may be withdrawn.

Accepted Articles
An Accepted Article is the uncorrected, unedited, non-typeset version of an article published in journal. Where an Accepted Article is to be retracted because, for example, it contains errors, has been accidentally submitted twice or infringes a professional ethical code of some type, it may be deleted and replaced with a withdrawal statement. Even in the above circumstances, bibliographic information about the deleted article should be retained for the scientific record, and an explanation given, however brief, about the circumstances of its removal.

Version of Record
It is should be journal's policy to strongly discourage withdrawal of the Version of Record in line with the International Association of Scientific, Technical and Medical Publishers guidelines on retractions and preservation of the objective record of science. Therefore, deletion of the Version of Record is rare and journal should only consider it in limited circumstances, such as the following:

- Where there has been a violation of the privacy of a research subject;
- Where there are errors to which a member of the general public might be exposed and if followed or adopted, would pose a significant risk to health; or
- Where a clearly defamatory comment has been made about others in the relevant field or about their work.

6.11.1.3. Expressions of Concern

Journal editors may consider issuing an Expression of Concern if they have well-founded concerns and feel that readers should be made aware of potentially misleading information contained in an article. However, Expressions of Concern should only be issued if an investigation into the problems relating to the article has proved inconclusive, and if there remain strong indicators that the concerns are valid. On very rare occasions, an Expression of Concern may be issued while an investigation is underway but a judgement will not be available for a considerable time. However, in such cases there must be well-founded grounds to suggest that the concerns are valid. In all cases, editors should be aware that an Expression of Concern carries the same risks to a researcher's reputation as a retraction, and it is often preferable to wait to publish a retraction until a definitive judgement has been achieved by an independent investigation.

6.12. Appeals

Journals should consider establishing and publishing a mechanism for authors to appeal editorial decisions, to facilitate genuine appeals and to discourage repeated or unfounded appeals. Editors should allow appeals to override earlier decisions following appropriate reconsideration of the editorial process and decision making (for example, additional factual input by the authors, revisions, extra material in the manuscript, or appeals about conflicts of interest and concerns about biased peer review). Author protest alone should not affect decisions.

- Editors should mediate all exchanges between authors and peer reviewers during the peer-review process. Editors may seek comments from additional peer reviewers to help them make their final decision.
- Journals should state in their guidelines that the editor's decision following an appeal is final.
- Journals should consider establishing a mechanism for authors and others to comment on aspects of the journal's editorial management, perhaps via the publisher or a third-party.

6.13. How to Handle Author Misconduct

Complaints should be made in confidence to the editor or editorial office, rather than directly to the author or in the public domain, and should be managed in confidence until they are resolved.

6.13.1. Prior to Publication

Review may raise a concern about a submitted manuscript during the course of the review process:

- Where appropriate, the reviewer should be asked for information to substantiate their concern (e.g., suspicious data in the paper).
- Contact the author should to raise the concern and, if appropriate, ask for clarification. Avoid accusatory or defamatory language; stick to factual statements, presenting any available evidence.
- The review process should be put on hold until the matter is resolved.
- *If the author provides a satisfactory explanation*, then the review process can proceed, perhaps following changes by the author.
- *If the author acknowledges misconduct* or is unable to provide a satisfactory explanation then the submission should be rejected.
- The reviewer who raised the complaint should be told of the outcome once the matter is resolved.

6.13.2. After Publication

A reader may raise a concern about a published manuscript. As above, the reader should be asked for substantiating information and then the author should be contacted to raise the concern. If the complaint proves to be unfounded no further action may be required. If action is required, there are three main options.

Author can publish a *correction statement* to include information that was missing from the published version (e.g., undisclosed conflict of interests).

- *Publish an expression of concern*, alongside the article, if there are well-founded suspicions of misconduct, though this is a halfway house and it is usually preferable to fully resolve the issue.
- One can *retract the published article*. This may be appropriate for more serious concerns, such as fabricated data or plagiarized material.

As before, we should inform the reader who raised the complaint of the outcome once the matter is resolved.

6.13.3. Further Action and Retraction

- If you have concerns contact your publisher, who can provide legal support if necessary. Resources for editors, including guidelines and training materials, are also available from the Committee on Publication Ethics.
- In instances of severe misconduct, one should consider whether to raise the issue with the author's institution, either to their superior and/or to the person responsible for research governance.
- In cases of plagiarism, one may also wish to inform the editor of other journal(s) involved and the victim.
- Bear in mind that accusations of misconduct, and subsequent actions such as a retraction, can have serious repercussions for someone's career. Therefore, complaints of author misconduct should always be handled with sensitivity, tact, and in confidence.
- If authors are considering issuing a retraction, they may contact their editorial representative/publisher in order to obtain support from Publisher. This will ensure that there is a legal review of the proposed statements in order to protect all parties from potential litigation.

6.14. How to Handle Reviewer Misconduct

Reviewer misconduct can range from minor issues, such as rude or unconstructive reviews, to major issues, such as the appropriation of author's ideas or data. As an editor, you entrust reviewers with a high level of responsibility. They are given access to privileged information (i.e., unpublished research) and their recommendations can sway the publication outcome. Unfortunately, there are rare occasions when that trust is misplaced.

Minor problems are relatively easy to respond to. Delete rude comments, and don't invite reviewers again if they supply poor quality, late, or unconstructive reviews. There may be other instances where editors receive complaints from authors about reviewer misconduct. We outline approaches to these instances below.

6.14.1. Appeals

Following the rejection of a paper, the author may appeal to the editor. Your Journal should have a clear appeals policy stating under what circumstances an appeal will be considered and how the appeal process will be handled.

6.14.2. Conflicts of Interest

One issue author might raise during an appeal for reviewer misconduct is bias due to conflict of interests. If journal operates open peer review, the author will know the identity of the reviewer and can specify the potential conflict of interests. For journals operating single- or double-blind peer review, accusations of bias are likely to be suppositional rather than substantiated, but should still be given careful consideration.

Appeals can often be resolved by getting a second opinion. Engaging a new reviewer will eliminate the potential alleged bias. It is difficult in these cases to evidence malicious intent on behalf of a reviewer, but you retain the right not to use reviewers who you feel are unable to give an objective assessment.

6.14.3. Appropriated Data

Another possible complaint of reviewer misconduct concerns the alleged appropriation of data during the review process. An author may raise a complaint if they discover their ideas or data are used in a published paper. They may conclude that these can only have been appropriated during the review process. These issues can be complicated because there is likely to be some time lag between the review process conducted at your journal and the publication of the appropriated data. Because complaints may involve another journal and another editorial team, it's best to make sure you keep them informed.

7

Citation Indexing and Databases

Bibliometrics is the application of quantitative methods to analyse and identify patterns in the usage of materials or the historical development of a specific body of literature, in particular its authorship, publication and use. Bibliometric techniques are often adopted for the assessment of authors, departments and higher education institutions. For example, *'Web of Science'* database can be used for bibliometric assessment and evaluative purposes by many groups and organisations. The term 'citation' refers to a paper being cited by another author. A cited work is a paper that has been mentioned in another paper, while a citing work refers to other cited papers that it references.

Citation indexing is the process of building an index of citations to cited items. A citation index is a database connecting citing articles to cited articles. While in a given paper its reference list points to earlier work as influences, only a citation index can provide a list of the later papers that cited the given paper. Citation indexes are used for citation analysis.

With the growth of online capabilities, citation indexes and analysis have become more sophisticated. More full-text content is now available online, providing connections between documents in the form of citations and hyperlinks. With the rise in Open Access (OA) journals and repositories there is potential for a greater number of journals and articles to be included in online citation indexes.

7.1. What is Indexing?

Indexing is the quality parameter and reflection of the higher quality of the journal. Indexing is a process in which indexes are created in order to maintain the records so that the researchers can reach the requisite particular record easily. Scopus, Web of Science, Google Scholar and Indian Citation Index are some indexing agencies.

Indexing is the process of creating indexes for record collections. Having indexes allows researchers to more quickly find records for specific individuals; without them, researchers might have to look through hundreds or thousands of records to locate an individual record. It also represents a number referring to a list of terms, definitions, topics etc. arranged in alphabetical order in order to efficiently guide the readers to the desired information within the content. Indexing facilitates in the organization of literature in such a manner that makes the document of interest easily identifiable by the readers.

7.2. Meaning of Citation Indexing

A citation index is an ordered list of cited articles along with a list of citing articles. The cited article is identified as the reference and the citing article as the source.

The index is prepared utilizing the association of ideas existing between the cited and the citing articles, as the fact is that whenever a recent paper cites a previous paper there always exists a relation of ideas, between the two papers.

7.3. History of Citation Indexing

A citation index is a kind of bibliographic index, an index of citations between publications, allowing the user to easily establish which later documents cite which earlier documents. A form of citation index is first found in 12th-century Hebrew religious literature. Legal citation indexes are found in the 18th century and were made popular by citators such as Shepard's Citations (1873). In 1960, Eugene Garfield's Institute for Scientific Information (ISI) introduced the first citation index for papers published in academic journals, first the Science Citation Index (SCI), and later the Social Sciences Citation Index (SSCI) and the Arts and Humanities Citation Index (AHCI). The first automated citation indexing was done by CiteSeer in 1997 and was patented. Other sources for such data include Google Scholar, Elsevier's Scopus, and the National Institutes of Health's iCite.

7.4. Principles of Citation Indexing

The concept of citation indexing relies on three principles given below:

- All knowledge from whatever discipline is always dependent on or related to tenets already accepted and established.
- The core literature on a given subject is contained in only a selection of journals relevant to that subject and identification of these core periodicals will save research time.
- The product of research is knowledge which is recorded and published and a possible measure of its significance is the frequency of citation in subsequent research.

7.5. Definitions of Citation Index

Some important definitions of Citation Index are given below:

1. Eugene Garfield, the inventor of citation indexing, defined a citation index as *"an ordered list of cited articles each of which is accompanied by a list of citing articles. The citing article is identified by a source index, the cited article by a reference citation. The reference is arranged by reference citations."*
2. According to Wikipedia- *"A citation index is a kind of bibliographic database, an index of citations between publications, allowing the user to easily establish which later documents cite which earlier documents."*
3. A Citation Index is a reference tool that presents bibliographic data on published journal articles. What distinguishes it from other indexes is that it includes all the cited references (footnotes or bibliographies) published with each article it covers.
4. Citation Index/databases compile the citations in the reference lists (bibliographies) of scholarly publications. Citation database records also

include bibliographic content that identify a publication: article title, journal name, author, abstract, etc.

5. A Citation Index is a reference tool that presents bibliographic data on published journal articles.
6. Citation indexes track references that authors put in the bibliographies of published papers. They provide a way to search for and analyze the literature in a way not possible through simple keyword/topical searching. It also enables users to gather data on the "impact" of journals, as well as assessing particular areas of research activity and publication. This field is called bibliometrics.
7. A citation index is simply a database or a table keeping the record of all publications (mainly journal articles).
8. Citation indexes or databases enable you to identify and search for references to previously published works cited by authors in their bibliographies. The ability to search for cited references makes these databases unique and especially valuable to scholars.
9. Citation databases compile the citations in the reference lists (bibliographies) of scholarly publications. Citation database records also include bibliographic content that identify a publication: article title, journal name, author, abstract, etc.

Citation indexes can be used to:

- build up a more extensive bibliography on a particular subject
- identify researchers currently active in particular areas
- establish whether there has been a review of the subject, whether a concept has been applied
- a theory confirmed, or a method improved.

7.7. Meaning of Citation Indexes

Searching for cited and citing references has its own special output requirements which help the users to find the most cited papers by an author, journal or on a subject. As citation searching gains acceptance, there will be a growing demand to display information prominently about the absolute and relative citedness of the papers, and to sort the search results by citedness score.

Citation indexes allow researchers to trace the impact of an article upon later publications. Besides including the bibliographic information about an article (author, article title, journal title, date, etc.), citation indexes also provide each article's references or bibliography (the list of sources cited). The database then links papers together using these citations, allowing the researcher to see both the references an author has used as well as other authors who later cited this article in their own papers

7.8. Terminology Used in Citation Index

- *Citation*: It is a entry in a bibliography or footnote that refers to an earlier work of some kind. It is also frequently called a "reference".

- *Cited Reference*: It is same as a citation. It is an entry in a bibliography or footnote describing an earlier work.
- *Citing Reference*: The work in which a cited reference appears. This is what you're really searching for when you use a citation index to look forward in the literature.

7.9. Mechanism of Citation Index

The concept of citation indexes is simple. Many of the papers, notes, reviews, corrections and correspondence published in the serials literature contain citations. These cite - generally by author, title and where/when published - documents that support, provide a precedent for, illustrate or elaborate what the author has to say. Citations are thus the formal, explicit linkages between papers that have particular points in common. A citation index is built around these linkages. A citation index lists the publications that have been cited and identifies the sources of the citations. Anyone conducting a literature search can find from one to many additional papers on a subject just by knowing one that has been cited. And every paper that is found provides a list of new citations with which to continue the search.

7.10. Why is Citation Indexing Essential?

- *Accessibility*: Since the main purpose of a journal is to be accessible to a wide audience, once it is indexed by a database, it is immediately made available to all users of a database that has indexed that journal
- *Reputation*: Being accessible has a direct impact on a journal's reputation; if a journal is available for a large number of academic population, it will be considered a reliable source of high-quality information in a certain field.
- *Readership*: Every researcher will look to established, well-known databases as the first activity in his/her studies; if a journal is indexed in a known database in that researcher's field, he/she will find that easily and read it. This increases that journal's readership.

7.11. Advantages of Citation Indexing

- Citation indexing eliminates the need, for intellectual indexing; it has the potential of being automated to a large degree.
- Citation indexing overcomes the problems of vocabulary and semantic difficulties.
- It overcomes the language barrier, because citation patterns, especially in scientific disciplines, are similar across languages.
- Literature searches using citation indexing are highly effective in gathering a large number of relevant documents quickly.
- Objective factors such as the number of citations and frequency of being cited can be used in introducing various weighting and other procedures to improve the quality and effectiveness of retrieval.

7.12. Uses of Citation Index

Citation index can be used to:

- Find papers that cite earlier papers. Citation indexing is a way to look forward in the literature from the starting point of a particular paper or group of papers. For example, if you have an excellent paper on a particular topic that was published in 1992, you can use Science Citation Index (via Web of Science) to find papers published after 1992 that cited that paper. Citation implies a direct subject relationship between the papers. So, by searching for later papers citing your known paper, you can find more documents on the same or similar topic without using any keywords or subject terms.
- Find out how many times my papers have been cited. Determine h-Index. With the help of different citation indexes, you can find out that how many times your papers have been cited. You can also calculate h-index and other important calculations.
- Determine the Best Journals of Your Field. Citation data have long been used to rank journals within particular subject areas, usually based on the ISI Impact Factor. The impact factor is simply a numerical ratio of the total number of citations a journal receives in ISI Source Journals in one year to the total number of "citable" articles it published in the previous two years. It is a useful way to see how journals perform in relation to others in the same subject area.
- Identify and map research fronts.
- Define disciplines and emerging specialties through journal relationships.
- Determine the interdisciplinary or multidisciplinary character and impact of research programs and projects.
- Literature based mapping can provide valuable insights for policy makers.
- It can reveal a nation's strength in publishing research articles in journals.
- It can bring to light core authors, journals, institutions, etc., in a discipline.
- Build up a more extensive bibliography on a particular subject.
- Identify researchers currently active in particular areas.
- Establish whether there has been a review of the subject, whether a concept has been applied.

7.13. Major Citation Indexing Services

"Counting citations" sounds simple; however, citation analysis tools count citations from different sets of publications. At the time of performing a citation analysis, one may wish to use several resources to count citations in order to fully capture an article's impact. Several citation indexing services/tools can help us to find out how many times a specific article, author or journal has been cited. There are several citation indexing services which is used to citation analysis. Major citation indexing services are as follows:

- Scopus
- Google Scholar (GS)
- Indian Citation Index (ICI)
- Publish or Perish (PoP)

- CiteSeerX
- Crossref
- PubMed
- Web of Science (WoS)
- Journal Citation Reports (JCR)
- SCImago Journal and Country Rank
- MathSciNet
- ScienceDirect
- Amazon.com
- PsychINFO
- Sociological Abstracts
- Worldwide Political Science Abstracts
- Business Source Premier, Communication and Mass Media Complete
- SciFinder Scholar
- INSPEC

Below, we are discussing the features of some citation indexing services:

7.13.1. Scopus

Owned by Elsevier, Scopus is a multidisciplinary database that covers peer-reviewed journals, books, conference proceedings, and patents across the fields of science, technology, medicine, social sciences, and arts and humanities. Scopus launched in November 2004. Scopus is the world's largest scientific abstract and citation database. In addition to the search options found in most scholarly databases, Scopus also provides several smart tools that allow you to track, visualize, and assess a number of bibliographic categories available within the database's metadata. It is the largest abstract and citation database of peer-reviewed literature, featuring smart tools to track, analyze and visualize research. With 22,800 titles from more than 5,000 international publishers, Scopus delivers the most comprehensive view of the world's research output in the fields of science, technology, medicine, social science and arts and humanities.

7.13.1.1. Why to Use Scopus

Scopus is a source-neutral abstract and citation database, curated by independent subject matter experts. It places powerful discovery and analytics tools in the hands of researchers, librarians, institutional research managers, and funders. Scopus generates precise citation search results and automatically updated researcher profiles, creating richer connections between people, published ideas, and institutions. In addition to protecting the integrity of the scholarly record, Scopus helps bolster institutional research performance, rank, and reputation. Scopus can help a researcher, author and librarian to achieve:

- Combat predatory publishing to protect the integrity of scholars and the scholarly record
- Make research and analytics workflows more efficient and effective
- Bolster research performance, rank and reputation
- Identify research gaps for further exploration and discovery

- Optimize research funding and investments
- Support educational goals of instructors and students at institutions of any size and focus

7.13.1.2. Publishers Indexed in Scopus

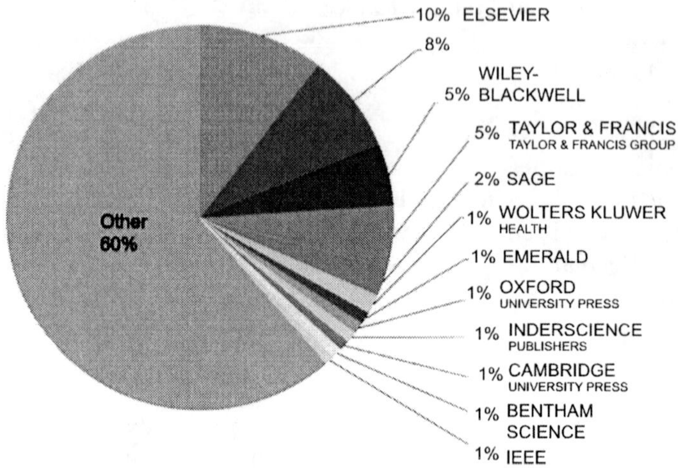

Figure 7.1 *Publishers Indexed in Scopus*

7.13.1.3. Scopus at a Glance (Updated May 2021)

75+ million records

- 68 million post-1970 records, including references
- 6.5+ million pre-1970 records going back as far as 1788
- 8.5+ million Open Access articles
- 9+ million Conference papers

24,600+ active titles

- 23,500+ peer-reviewed journals, of which more than 4,000 are Gold Open Access
- 740+ book series
- 300+ trade publications
- Articles-in-press (i.e., articles that have been accepted for publication) from over 8,000 titles from international publishers, including Cambridge University Press, the Institute of Electrical and Electronics Engineers (IEEE)

194,000+ books

- Including monographs, edited volumes, major reference works and graduate level text books
- Focuses on social sciences and arts & humanities, but also includes science, technology & medicine (STM).

7.13.1.4. Scopus Content Coverage by Subject Area

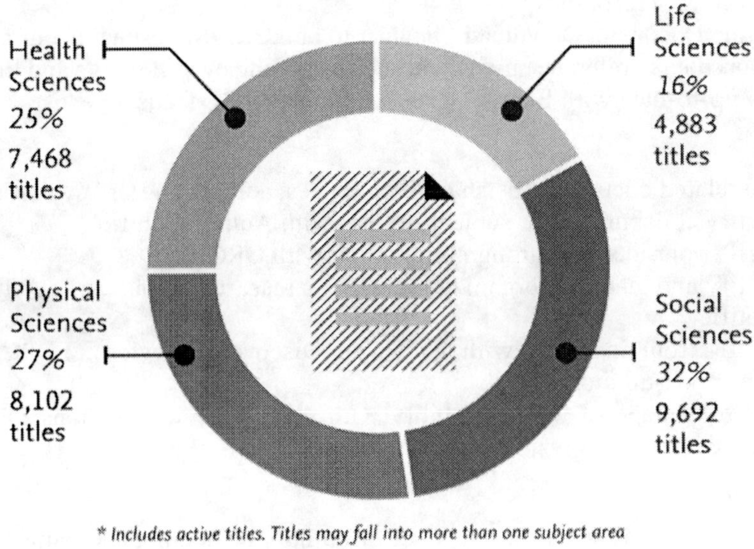

Figure 7.2 *Scopus Content Coverage by Subject Area*

7.13.1.5. Scopus Content Growth

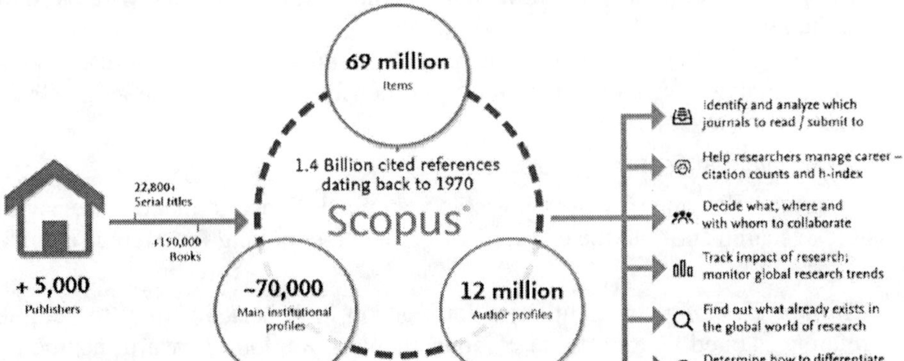

Figure 7.3 *Scopus Content Growth*

7.13.1.6. Scopus supports researchers and librarians in three key areas:

A. Search

- Search by document, author or affiliation, or use Advanced Search
- Refine results by access type, source type, year, language, author, affiliation, funding sponsor and more

- Link to full-text articles your institution already subscribes to, along with other library resources
- Use the Document Download Manager to bulk retrieve results in .pdf format
- Export data to reference managers such as Mendeley, RefWorks and EndNote
- Stay up-to-date with Email Alerts, RSS and HTML feeds

B. Discover

- Find related documents by shared references, authors and/or keywords
- Identify collaborators or subject experts with Author Identifier
- Clarify your identity through integration with ORCID
- Identify and match an organization with its research output using Affiliation Identifier
- Benefit from indexing with Universal Discovery Services: EBSCOHost, Primo and Summon
- Take advantage of interoperability with other Elsevier solutions including ScienceDirect, Reaxys, Engineering Village and SciVal

C. Analyze

- Track citations over time for a set of authors or documents using Citation Overview
- Assess trends in search results with Analyze Results
- View h-index for specific authors
- Analyze an author's publishing output and research impact with Author Evaluator
- Gain insight into journal performance with Compare Journals, a tool allowing you to analyze journals across multiple metrics, including CiteScore, SNIP and SJR

7.13.1.7. Searching Features of Scopus

Scopus comes with an array of impressive features designed to make it as easy as possible to search and find the citation researchers are looking for. Here is a quick overview:

- *Citation Tracking*: In addition to letting you look back in time (to see the references cited by an article), Scopus also lets you look forward in time by linking to more recent papers that cite the article being examined.
- *Flexible Search*: Using Scopus' assortment of helpful and comprehensive search features, you can:
  - Sort results by date, relevance, author, source, title, or number of citations received ('Cited by').
  - Conduct a new search within results.
  - Search for 'Related documents' to see the number of articles with shared references—and refine the search by selecting specific search criteria.
  - Browse references that are not indexed in the Scopus database by clicking the 'View secondary documents' link above your search results.
  - Set alerts or RSS feeds (from within Search History) to be notified when a new article matching your criteria is listed.

- *Graph Results*: Click the 'Analyze search results' link (located at the top of the results page) to see how the results break down by year, source, author, affiliation, country/territory, document type, and subject area.
- *Compare Sources*: To compare groups of up to 10 journals, click the 'Compare sources' link (located on the main search page). You can choose table or graph format to see how journals compare in the following categories:
    - Impact metrics (CiteScore, SJR, and SNIP)
    - Number of times cited in a year
    - Number of published articles in a year
    - Percentage of articles that are review articles
    - Percentage of documents published in a year that have never been cited
- Bibliographic Management: Citations can be exported into your preferred reference manager (e.g., Mendeley, RefWorks and EndNote).

7.13.1.8. Features/Characteristics of Scopus

Scopus is designed to serve the information needs of researchers, educators, administrators, students and librarians across the entire academic community. Whether searching for specific information or browsing topics, authors, journals or books, Scopus provides precise entry points to peer-reviewed literature in the fields of science, technology, medicine, social sciences and the arts and humanities.

Scopus uniquely combines a comprehensive, expertly curated abstract and citation database with enriched data and linked scholarly literature across a wide variety of disciplines. Scopus quickly finds relevant and authoritative research, identifies experts and provides access to reliable data, metrics and analytical tools. Be confident in progressing research, teaching or research direction and priorities — all from one database and with one subscription.

1. Academic Institutions: Empower Research Productivity and Scholarship: Scopus is designed to serve the information needs of researchers, educators, administrators, students and librarians across the entire academic community. Whether searching for specific information or browsing topics, authors, journals or books, Scopus provides precise entry points to peer-reviewed literature in the fields of science, technology, medicine, social sciences and the arts and humanities.

Researchers and Authors: The demands on researchers to stay productive and increase research output are considerable, so tools that can simplify processes and inform decision-making are crucial. Scopus supports researchers and authors with:

- Searching for relevant topics/articles during the literature review phase
- Deciding where to publish – analyze the top journals and authors in your discipline
- Finding information to support your grant or other applications
- Exploring how many citations an article or author has received, and identifying potential collaborators
- Discovering who is citing you
- Using APIs to showcase citation counts for your work.

Editors and Reviewers: With the explosion of published content, the strain on editors and reviewers is increasing. Tools that provide insights into publishing trends and authorship, while easing the review process, are essential. Scopus supports editors and reviewers with:

- Identifying and contact potential editorial board members
- Evaluating an author's previously published work
- Finding and evaluating referees and authors for review papers and thematic issues
- Quickly reviewing performance and coverage of other journals
- Monitoring journal trends: for example, comparing the current scope of a journal with citation patterns to see if a shift has occurred

Educators and Students: Educators and students need access to the latest research and data to inform and enhance classroom learning and support writing assignments. Scopus supports educators and students with:

- Finding resources to complement course materials, such as locating new articles and images to enhance lectures, and engage students' interest
- Identifying articles to inform the literature review process and support development of research papers and theses
- Uncover literature in adjacent disciplines to foster interdisciplinary exploration
- Help students understand the scholarly conversation of a topic through reference lists and cited articles

Librarians: Librarians are a driving force in information literacy and discovery, guiding researchers, students and instructors toward relevant resources, information and data more efficiently. Scopus supports librarians with:

- Providing users with a global, comprehensive abstract and citation database of peer-reviewed publications
- Linking quickly and accurately to full-text articles, optimizing the institution's investments
- Increasing the visibility of and access to other library resources
- Informing collection management decisions through analysis of highly-cited articles and journals

Research Administrators: Administrators are charged with ensuring the requisite return on research investment, and allocating the appropriate resources where necessary. Scopus supports administrators with:

- Assessing the scientific output of individual researchers or of your institution
- Allocating financial resources to researchers or departments by tracking impact
- Checking a researcher and tenure candidate's production, citations and h-index, and comparing them to others in the same subject area

2. Government and Funding Agencies: Empowering Research Performance Analysis: Agencies and government bodies can rely on Scopus to inform their overall strategic direction, identify funding resources, measure researcher performance and more.

3. Research and Development: Improving R&D productivity is a priority within industry. To improve productivity R&D teams need access to the latest R&D innovations found in Scopus. Scopus is a research database that indexes and connects the work of millions of researchers, institutions and companies around the world. Using its built-in tools on high-quality content, one can:

- *Save time in R&D*
  - Be productive fast with an easy-to-use interface
  - Get the latest research delivered via alerts
  - Find the most relevant results using filters
- *Gain competitive intelligence*
  - Benchmark the competition via rich profiles
  - Track research trends with smart analytics
  - Learn from other industries with interdisciplinary content

4. Ranking Organizations: Around the world, individuals and institutions look to prominent ranking organizations to guide application, funding and research decisions and those organizations look to Scopus to supply the reliable and comprehensive research performance data and analytics that their rankings are based on. Over the past 10 years, Elsevier has emerged as the partner of choice in the fast-developing field of rankings. Scopus data is used to calculate the influential rankings for the following organizations:

- Times Higher Education - (THE) World University Rankings
- QS World University Rankings
- US News & World Report's Best Arab Region Universities Rankings
- Shanghai Ranking Consultancy

7.13.2. Google Scholar (GS)

Google Scholar (GS) is a freely accessible web search engine that indexes the full text or metadata of scholarly literature across an array of publishing formats and disciplines. Released in November 2004, the Google Scholar index includes most peer-reviewed online academic journals and books, conference papers, theses and dissertations, preprints, abstracts, technical reports, and other scholarly literature,

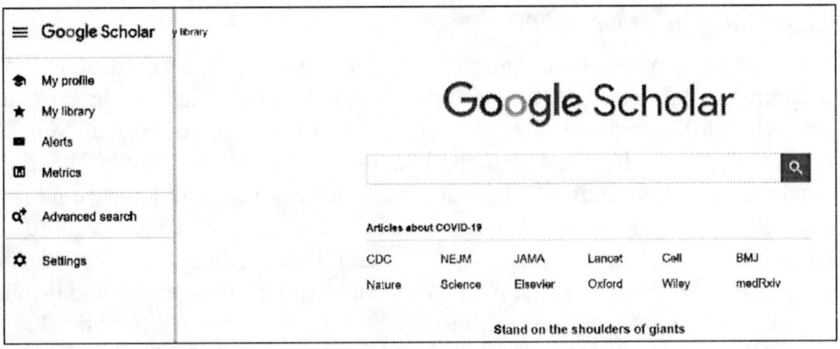

Figure 7.4 *Home Page of Google Scholar*

including court opinions and patents. While Google does not publish the size of Google Scholar's database, scientometric researchers estimated it to contain roughly 389 million documents including articles, citations and patents making it the world's largest academic search engine in January 2018.

Google Scholar provides a simple way to broadly search for scholarly literature. From one place, researchers can search across many disciplines and sources: articles, theses, books, abstracts and court opinions, from academic publishers, professional societies, online repositories, universities and other web sites. Google Scholar helps researchers find relevant work across the world of scholarly research.

7.13.2.1. Features of Google Scholar

- Search all scholarly literature from one convenient place
- Explore related works, citations, authors, and publications
- Locate the complete document through your library or on the web
- Keep up with recent developments in any area of research
- Check who's citing your publications, create a public author profile

7.13.2.2. Scope and Limitations of Google Scholar

There is no official statement about how big the Scholar search index is, but unofficial estimates are in the range of about 160 million and it is supposed to continue to grow by several millions each year. Google Scholar has the following publication types:

- *Journal articles*: articles published in journals. It's a mixture of articles from peer reviewed journals, predatory journals and pre-print archives.
- *Books*: Links to the Google limited version of the text, when possible.
- *Book chapters*: Chapters within a book, sometimes they are also electronically available.
- *Book reviews*: Reviews of books, but it is not always apparent that it is a review from the search result.
- *Conference proceedings*: Papers written as part of a conference, typically used as part of presentation at the conference.
- *Patents*: Google Scholar only searches patents if the option is selected in the search settings described above.

7.13.3. Indian Citation Index (ICI)

Indian Citation Index (ICI) is a comprehensive multidisciplinary citation index for the research journals published from India. Indian Citation Index is developed by The Knowledge Foundation (a registered society) with the support of M/s Diva Enterprises Pvt. Ltd. ICI was launched in India in October, 2009. The Indian Citation Index (ICI) is a multidisciplinary online bibliographic database containing abstracts and citations from academic journals. Currently ICI covers more than 1100 journals from India covering scientific, technical, medical and social sciences that includes arts and humanities. ICI covers data from 2004 onwards and provides full text of the title for Open Access journals, at present there are more than 300 OA journals. ICI provides search and analytical features.

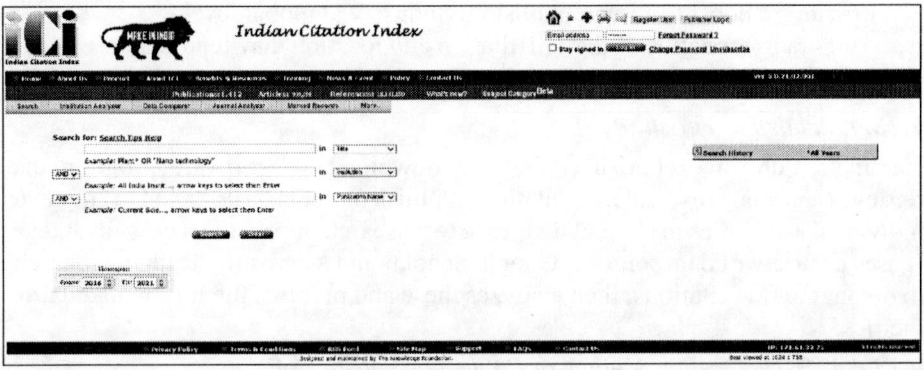

Figure 7.5 *Home Page of Indian Citation Index (ICI)*

The ICI database also produces other useful by products like Indian Science Citation Index (ISCI), Indian Social Science and Humanities Citation Index (ISSHCI), Indian Journals Citation Reports (IJCR), Indian Science and Technology Abstracts (ISTA), and Directory of Indian Journals (DOIJ).

7.13.3.1. Benefits of Indian Citation Index

Indian Citation Index (ICI) empowers scholarly community to map the knowledge published in local national journals/periodicals etc. Whether researchers are just starting their scholarly work, academic research as an experienced researcher or teacher, or a librarian or administrator, ICI delivers objective content and the tools to support researcher's role in the research workflow.

Researchers can use ICI to learn more about how to discover and analyze data, track and measure trends and performance, and collaborate, author, and publish research. Using ICI, one can take crucial decisions on accurate, objective information and sound metrics; track research performance; establish benchmarks; make funding decisions; look for transfer opportunities; formulate strategies etc. Additionally, following are the major benefits of having ICI in place for scholarly community:

- A comprehensive research and evaluation tool for Indian literature
- Facilitates comprehensive scientometric and bibliometric studies on Indian literature
- Helps to measure and analyze individual, institutional, regional, and national R&D output for strategic planning
- An authentic tool to generate complete and comprehensive analytic reports on the health of Indian R&D
- ICI can generate national R&D indicators like, Indian Journals Citation Reports, etc.
- Catalyze the image & visibility of Indian knowledge contents and publications
- Helps decision makers to arrive at some conclusive point to decide the superiority of competitor (s), for some awards, fellowships, recruitments etc.

- Provides a boost to Indian publishing industry at global level
- Authors irrespective of their affiliation and location may tend to publish their R&D findings in local national Journals of India

7.13.4. Publish or Perish (PoP)

Harzing's Publish or Perish (PoP) is a downloadable software program that retrieves and analyzes academic citations. Publish or Perish is designed to empower individual academics to present their case for research impact to its best advantage. It uses a variety of data sources (Google Scholar and Microsoft Academic Search) to obtain the raw citations, then analyzes these and presents the following citation metrics:

7.13.4.1. Basic Citation Metrics of Publish or Perish (PoP)

The basic metrics are quite straightforward and are calculated as follows in Publish or Perish:

- *Total number of papers*: This is simply the number of papers returned by Google Scholar or Microsoft Academic Search in reply to a query.
- *Total number of citations*: The sum of the citation counts across all papers.
- *Average number of citations per paper*: The sum of the citation counts across all papers, divided by the total number of papers. The median and mode are also calculated.
- *Number of citations per author*: For each paper, its citation count is divided by the number of authors for that paper to give the normalized per-author citation count for the paper. The normalized citation counts are then summed across all papers to give the number of citations per author over the result set.
- *Number of citations per author per year*: This is the number of citations per author as above, divided by the number of years covered by the result set.
- *Number of papers per author*: For each paper, 1/author count is calculated to give the normalized author count for the paper. The normalized author counts are then summed across all papers to give the number of papers per author.

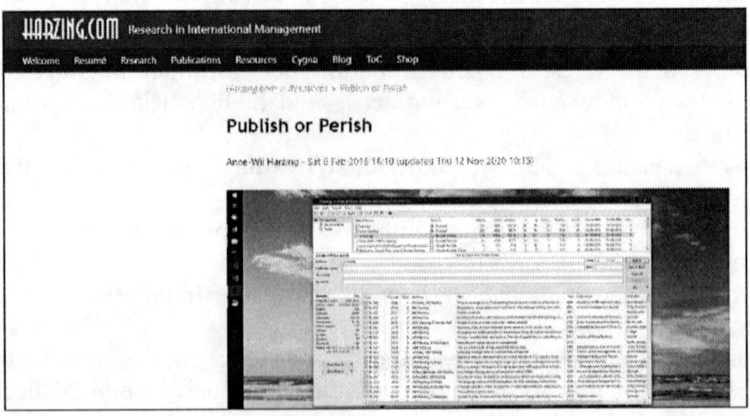

Figure 7.6 *Home Page of Publish or Perish (PoP)*

- *Average number of authors per paper*: The sum of the author counts across all papers, divided by the total number of papers. The median and mode are also calculated.

7.13.4.2. Advanced Citation Metrics of Publish or Perish (PoP)

In addition to the various simple statistics (number of papers, number of citations, and others), Publish or Perish calculates the following citation metrics:

- *Hirsch's h-index*: It was proposed by 'J.E. Hirsch' in his paper *"An index to quantify an individual's scientific research output"*. It aims to provide a robust single-number metric of an academic's impact, combining quality with quantity.
- *Egghe's g-index*: It was proposed by 'Leo Egghe' in his paper *"Theory and practice of the g-index"*. It aims to improve on the h-index by giving more weight to highly-cited articles'.
- *Zhang's e-index*: Publish or Perish also calculates the e-index as proposed by 'Chun-Ting Zhang' in his paper "The e-index, complementing the h-index for excess citations". The e-index is the (square root) of the surplus of citations in the h-set beyond h2, i.e., beyond the theoretical minimum required to obtain a h-index of 'h'. The aim of the e-index is to differentiate between scientists with similar h-indices but different citation patterns.
- *Contemporary h-index*: Proposed by 'Antonis Sidiropoulos, Dimitrios Katsaros, and Yannis Manolopoulos' in their paper *"Generalized h-index for disclosing latent facts in citation networks"*. It aims to improve on the h-index by giving more weight to recent articles, thus rewarding academics who maintain a steady level of activity.
- *Age-weighted citation rate (AWCR) and AW-index*: The AWCR measures the average number of citations to an entire body of work, adjusted for the age of each individual paper. It was inspired by 'Bihui Jin's' note *"The AR-index: complementing the h-index"*. The Publish or Perish implementation differs from Jin's definition in that we sum over all papers instead of only the h-core papers.
- *Individual h-index (original)*: The Individual h-index was proposed by 'Pablo D. Batista, Monica G. Campiteli, Osame Kinouchi, and Alexandre S. Martinez' in their paper *"Is it possible to compare researchers with different scientific interests?"* It divides the standard h-index by the average number of authors in the articles that contribute to the h-index, in order to reduce the effects of co-authorship.
- *Individual h-index (PoP variation)*: Publish or Perish also implements an alternative individual h-index called *hI, norm* that takes a different approach: instead of dividing the total h-index, it first normalizes the number of citations for each paper by dividing the number of citations by the number of authors for that paper, then calculates the h-index of the normalized citation counts.
- *Multi-authored h-index*: A further h-like index is due to 'Michael Schreiber' and first described in his paper *"To share the fame in a fair way, hm modifies*

h for multi-authored manuscripts". Schreiber's method uses fractional paper counts instead of reduced citation counts to account for shared authorship of papers, and then determines the multi-authored hm index based on the resulting effective rank of the papers using undiluted citation counts.

- *Average annual increase in the individual h-index*: As of release 4.3 Publish or Perish also calculates the average annual increase in *hI, norm*, called *hI, annual.* This average annual increase in the individual h-index is useful for the following reasons:
  - In common with the *hI, norm* index, it removes to a considerable extent any discipline-specific publication and citation patterns that otherwise distort the h-index.
  - It also reduces the effect of career length and provides a fairer comparison between junior and senior researchers.

The *hI, annual* is meant as an indicator of an individual's average annual research impact, as opposed to the lifetime score that is given by the h-index or hI, norm.

7.13.5. Citeseerx

Citeseerx is a scientific literature digital library and search engine that focuses primarily on the literature in computer and information science. Citeseerx aims to improve the dissemination of scientific literature and to provide improvements in functionality, usability, availability, cost, comprehensiveness, efficiency, and timeliness in the access of scientific and scholarly knowledge. Rather than creating just another digital library, Citeseerx attempts to provide resources such as algorithms, data, metadata, services, techniques, and software that can be used to promote other digital libraries. Citeseerx has developed new methods and algorithms to index PostScript and PDF research articles on the Web. Citeseerx provides the following features:

7.13.5.1. Features of Citeseerx

- *Autonomous Citation Indexing (ACI)*: CiteSeer uses ACI to automatically create a citation index that can be used for literature search and evaluation. Compared to traditional citation indices, ACI provides improvements in cost, availability, comprehensiveness, efficiency, and timeliness.

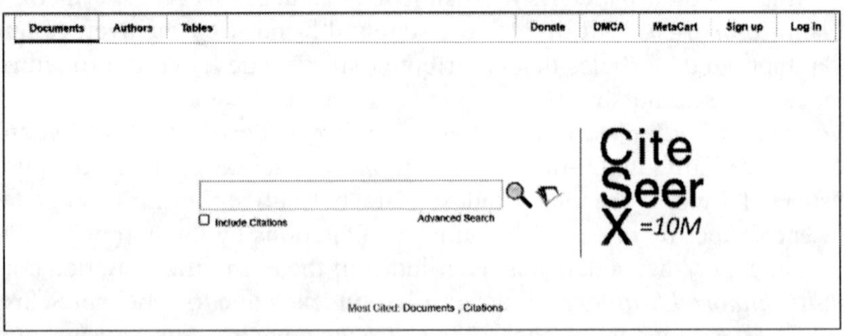

Figure 7.7 *Home Page of CiteSeerX*

- *Citation Statistics*: CiteSeer computes citation statistics and related documents for all articles cited in the database, not just the indexed articles.
- *Reference Linking*: As with many online publishers, CiteSeer allows browsing the database using citation links. However, CiteSeer performs this automatically.
- *Citation context*: CiteSeer can show the context of citations to a given paper, allowing a researcher to quickly and easily see what other researchers have to say about an article of interest.
- *Awareness and Tracking*: CiteSeer provides automatic notification of new citations to given papers, and new papers matching a user profile.
- *Related documents*: CiteSeer locates related documents using citation and word-based measures and displays an active and continuously updated bibliography for each document.
- *Full-Text Indexing*: CiteSeer indexes the full-text of the entire articles and citations. Full boolean, phrase and proximity search is supported.
- *Query-Sensitive Summaries*: CiteSeer provides the context of how query terms are used in articles instead of a generic summary, improving the efficiency of search.
- *Up-To-Date*: CiteSeer is regularly updated based on user submissions and regular crawls.
- *Powerful Search*: CiteSeer uses fielded search to all complex queries over content, and allows the use of author initials to provide more flexible name search.
- *Harvesting of Articles*: CiteSeer automatically harvests research papers from the Web.
- *Metadata of Articles*: CiteSeer automatically extracts and provides metadata from all indexed articles.
- *Personal Content Portal*: Personal collections, RSS-like notifications, social bookmarking, social network facilities. Personalized search settings. Institutional data tracking possible. Transparent document submission system.

7.13.6. Crossref

Crossref is a not-for-profit membership organization for scholarly publishing. Crossref makes research outputs easy to find, cite, link, assess, and reuse. Unlike PubMed, it is not discipline-specific. Publishers of electronic scholarly content join as members of Crossref and are assigned a unique Digital Object Identifier (DOI) prefix. For each content item a publisher wishes to register in the system, it creates a unique DOI (incorporating the assigned prefix) and tags it to the article's metadata and the URL where the article resides. The publisher submits the record to the Crossref metadata database. Crossref then registers each article DOI and URL in a central DOI directory. This allows for permanent inbound links to the publisher's content, because other publishers, librarians, and affiliates (such as subscription agents and secondary publishers) can retrieve from Crossref the DOIs that link to that content.

7.13.6.1. Features of Crossref

Crossref Metadata Search allows researchers to search across the almost 50 million Crossref Metadata records for journal articles and conference proceedings. It supports the following features:

- ORCID Support
- A completely new UI
- Faceted searches (Faceted search is a technique which involves augmenting traditional search techniques with a faceted navigation system, allowing users to narrow down search results by applying multiple filters based on faceted classification of the items)
- Copying of search results as formatted citations using CSL (The Citation Style Language (CSL) is an open XML-based language to describe the formatting of citations and bibliographies.)
- COinS (Context Objects in Spans (COinS) is a method to embed bibliographic metadata in the HTML code of web pages.), so that you can easily import results into Zotero and other document management tools
- An API, so that you can integrate Crossref Metadata Search into your own applications, plugins, etc.
- Basic Open Search support- so that you can integrate Crossref Metadata Search into your browser's search bar.
- Searching for a particular Crossref DOI
- Searching for a particular Crossref ShortDOI
- Searching for articles in a particular journal via the journal's ISSN
- Links to any patents that cite a particular Crossref DOI

7.13.7. PubMed

PubMed is the freely accessible search interface for over 30 million citations and abstracts of biomedical literature. PubMed is a free web-based interface for searching MEDLINE.

- PubMed is created by the National Library of Medicine and contains the MEDLINE database.
- It covers journal articles in medicine, nursing, dentistry, veterinary medicine, and the health care system.
- PubMed has information about journal articles (currently over 24 million) published in 5,600 journals in 30 languages dating back to 1946.
- It does not include information about meeting abstracts, conference proceedings, dissertations, patents, or websites.
- NLM indexers add words called Medical Subject Headings (MeSH) to the information about each article. Searching with MeSH words helps you find more relevant articles.

PubMed provides access to:

- Citations from journals indexed in MEDLINE (MEDLINE is the largest component of PubMed.) and selected non-MEDLINE biomedical journals.

- Very new citations for articles that have not yet been indexed for MEDLINE (in-process citations)
- Citations from international biomedical journals from 1946-1965 (OLDMEDLINE)
- Citations to *PubMed Central* articles, a full-text archive of manuscripts deposited in accordance with the NIH Public Access Policy.
- Open access e-books that are available through the *NCBI Bookshelf.*

7.13.7.1. Searching Features of PubMed

Citations in PubMed primarily stem from the biomedicine and health fields, and related disciplines such as life sciences, behavioral sciences, chemical sciences, and bioengineering. PubMed facilitates searching across several NLM literature resources:

- *MEDLINE*: MEDLINE is the largest component of PubMed and consists primarily of citations from journals selected for MEDLINE; articles indexed with MeSH (Medical Subject Headings) and curated with funding, genetic, chemical and other metadata.
- *PubMed Central (PMC)*: Citations for PubMed Central (PMC) articles make up the second largest component of PubMed. PMC is a full text archive that includes articles from journals reviewed and selected by NLM for archiving (current and historical), as well as individual articles collected for archiving in compliance with funder policies.
- *Bookshelf*: The final component of PubMed is citations for books and some individual chapters available on Bookshelf. Bookshelf is a full text archive of books, reports, databases, and other documents related to biomedical, health, and life sciences.

7.13.8. Web of Science (WoS)

Web of Science is a platform consisting of several literature search databases designed to support scientific and scholarly research.

There are databases with a subject focus like Medline, BIOSIS Citation Index, and Zoological Record; databases with a document type focus like Derwent Innovations Index (patents) and Data Citation Index (datasets and data studies); and databases highlighting content from regions around the world. Web of Science Core Collection is a premier resource on the platform and includes over 21,000 peer-reviewed, high-quality scholarly journals published worldwide (including Open Access journals); over 205,000 conference proceedings; and over 104,000 editorially selected books.

7.13.8.1. Cross-disciplinary Research and Comprehensive Citation Search

Web of Science (previously known as Web of Knowledge) is an online subscription-based scientific citation indexing service originally produced by the Institute for Scientific Information (ISI), now maintained by Clarivate Analytics (previously the Intellectual Property and Science business of Thomson Reuters), that provides a comprehensive citation search. Web of Science is a platform consisting of several

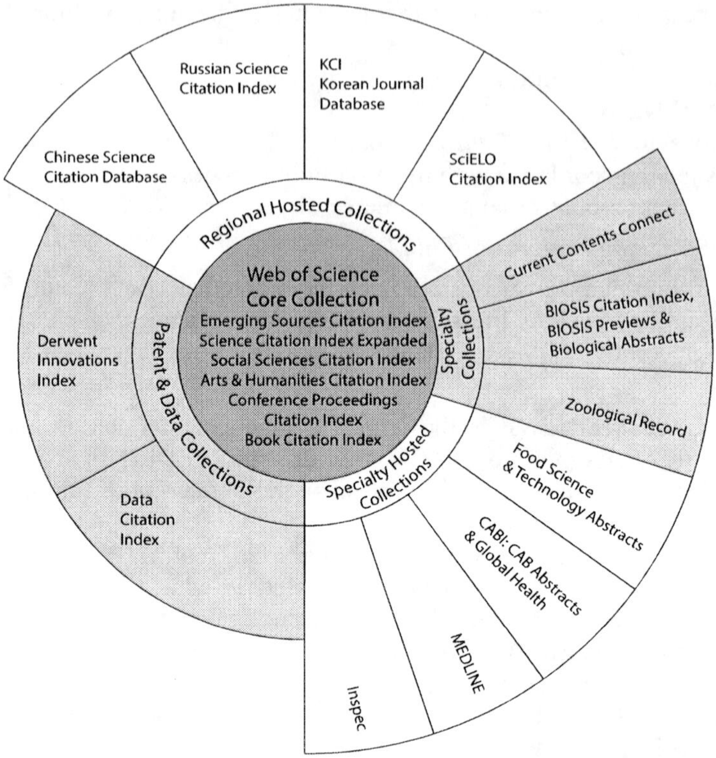

Figure 7.8 *Web of Science Platform*

literature search databases designed to support scientific and scholarly research. It gives access to multiple databases that reference cross-disciplinary research, which allows for in-depth exploration of specialized sub-fields within an academic or scientific discipline.

Web of Science (ISI) is an online subscription-based scientific service maintained by Thomson Reuters that provides a *comprehensive citation search*. It gives access to multiple databases that reference *cross-disciplinary research*, which allows for in-depth exploration of specialized sub-fields within an academic or scientific discipline. Whether looking at data, books, journals, proceedings or patents, Web of Science provides a single destination to access the most reliable, integrated, *multidisciplinary research*. Quality, curated content delivered alongside information on emerging trends, subject specific content and analysis tools make it easy for students, faculty, researchers, analysts, and program managers to pinpoint the most relevant research to inform their work.

A citation index is built on the fact that citations in science serve as linkages between similar research items, and lead to matching or related scientific literature, such as journal articles, conference proceedings, abstracts, etc. In addition, literature which shows the greatest impact in a particular field, or more than one discipline, can be easily located through a citation index. For example, a paper's influence can be determined by linking to all the papers that have cited it. In this way, current trends, patterns, and emerging fields of research can be assessed. Citations are the formal, explicit linkages between papers that have particular points in common. A citation index is built around these linkages. It lists publications that have been cited and identifies the sources of the citations. Anyone conducting a literature search can find from one to dozens of additional papers on a subject just by knowing one that has been cited. And every paper that is found provides a list of new citations with which to continue the search.

The simplicity of citation indexing is one of its main strengths. Web of Science is described as a unifying research tool which enables the user to acquire, analyze, and disseminate database information in a timely manner. This is accomplished because of the creation of a common vocabulary, called ontology, for varied search terms and varied data. Moreover, search terms generate related information across categories. Acceptable content for Web of Knowledge is determined by an evaluation and selection process based on the following criteria: impact, influence, timeliness, peer review, and geographic representation.

Web of Science employs various search and analysis capabilities. Citation indexing is employed, which is enhanced by the capability to search for results across disciplines. The influence, impact, history, and methodology of an idea can be followed from its first instance, notice, or referral to the present day. This technology points to a deficiency with the keyword-only method of searching. Subtle trends and patterns relevant to the literature or research of interest, become apparent. Broad trends indicate significant topics of the day, as well as the history relevant to both the work at hand, and particular areas of study.

7.13.8.2. Features of Web of Science (WoS)

- High quality, curated, multidisciplinary, subject-specific and regional research.
- Powerful search and navigation options.
- Seamless, integrated search across all content.

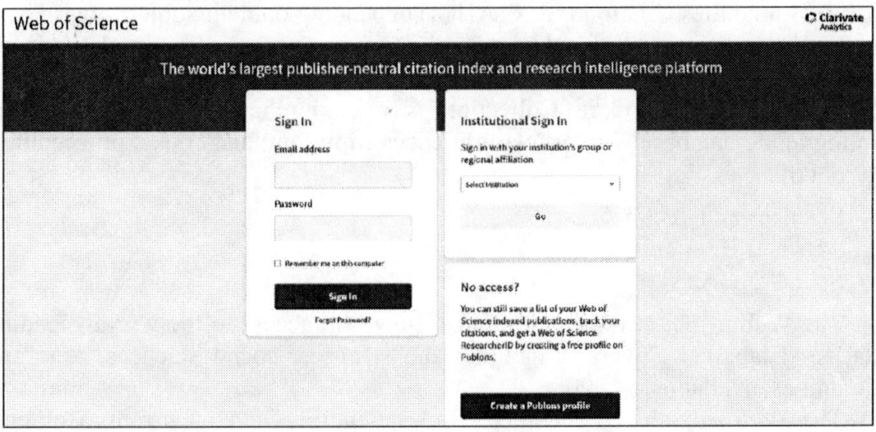

Figure 7.9 *Home Page of Web of Science*

- Analysis tools to discover trends and patterns.
- Cited Reference Searching to find articles cited a previously published work.
- Visual and graphical representations of citation activity.

7.13.8.3. Benefits of Web of Science (WoS)

- Access the highest quality, curated, multidisciplinary content.
- Pinpoint subject-specific and regional research.
- Identify emerging trends.
- Discover the most relevant research to inform your work.
- Identify qualified collaborators.

7.13.8.4. Web of Science Core Collection

The Web of Science Core Collection is a curated collection of over 20,000 peer-reviewed, high-quality scholarly journals published worldwide in over 250 science, social sciences, and humanities disciplines. Curated with care by an expert team of in-house Web of Science™ Editors, the Web of Science Core Collection™ allows researchers to search with confidence and explore the deep citation connections in the sciences, social sciences, arts, and humanities. Web of Science Core Collection is a premier resource on the Web of Science platform and the world's original citation index for scientific and scholarly research. A curated collection, Web of Science Core Collection contains over 21,100 peer-reviewed, high-quality scholarly journals published worldwide (including Open Access journals) in over 250 sciences, social sciences, and arts & humanities disciplines. Conference proceedings and book data are also available.

Journals are selected for inclusion in the Web of Science Core Collection using a single set of twenty-eight evaluation criteria journals: Twenty-four quality criteria (designed to select for editorial rigour and best practice at the journal level) and four impact criteria designed to select the most influential journals in their respective fields. Journals that meet the quality criteria enter Emerging Sources Citation Index (ESCI). Journals that meet the additional impact criteria enter Science Citation Index Expanded (SCIE), Social Sciences Citation Index (SSCI) or Arts & Humanities Citation Index (AHCI) depending on their subject area. These are dynamic collections subject to continuous curation to ensure journals are in the appropriate collection.

Web of Science Core Collection is a comprehensive interdisciplinary, bibliographic database with article references from journals, books, proceedings, i.e., out of:

- Sciences and Technology
- Arts and Humanities
- Social Sciences

The Web of Science provides quick, powerful access to the world's leading citation databases. Coverage includes the sciences, social sciences, arts, and humanities, available to 1900.

The Web of Science Includes: Biosis Citation Index, Currents Contents Connect, Data Citation Index, Derwent Innovations Index, MEDLINE, SciELO

Citation Index, Zoological Record, and the Web of Science Core Collection: Arts & Humanities Citation Index, Book Citation Index, Conference Proceedings Citation Index, Current Chemical Reactions, Index Chemicus, Science Citation Index Expanded, and Social Sciences Citation Index.)

Powered by Clarivate, the Web of Science Core Collection database is a collection of several cross-searchable databases and you can search one or more of these databases from the Web of Science interface:

- Social Science Citation Index (SSCI), 1976 to present
- Science Citation Index Expanded (SCI-Expanded), 1976 to present
- Arts & Humanities Citation Index (A&HCI), 1976 to present
- Emerging Sources Citation Index (ESCI), 2015 to present
- Conference Proceedings Citation Index (CPCI-S and CPCI-SSH)
- Book Citation Index (BKCI)
- Current Chemical Reactions and Index Chemicus

1. Social Sciences Citation Index (SSCI) - Publication years: 1900 to present: Social Sciences Citation Index is a multidisciplinary index to the journal literature of the social sciences. The Social Sciences Citation Index is a multidisciplinary index. The Social Sciences Citation Index offers bibliographical access to a curated collection of over 3,400 journals across 58 social sciences disciplines, as well as selected items from 3,500 of the world's leading scientific and technical journals. Being a citation index, it allows searching for articles that cite a known author or

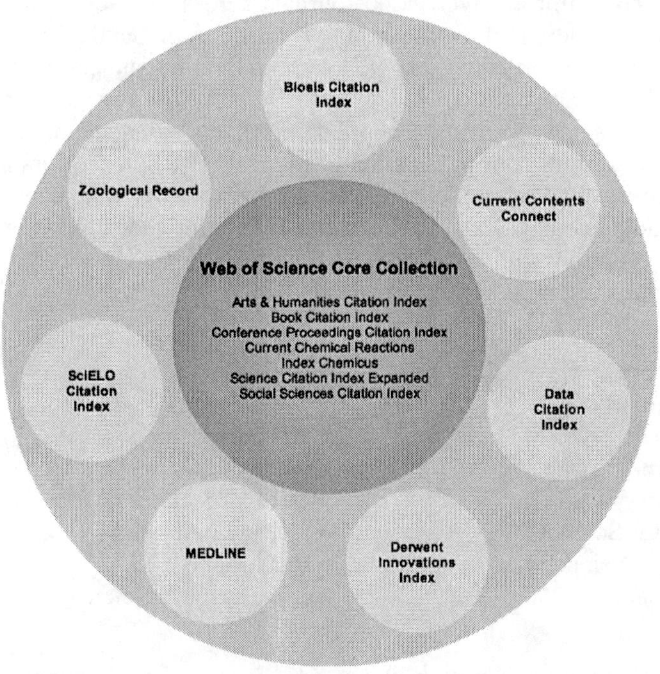

Figure 7.10 *Web of Science Core Collection*

work (Cited Reference Search), as well as searching by subject, author, journal, and author. *'Cited reference searching'* lets you track how any idea, innovation, or creative work has been confirmed, applied, improved, extended, or corrected, and discover who is citing your publication of interest. The Social Sciences Citation Index is accessed through the Web of Science platform, with which more databases can be searched simultaneously. To search the Social Sciences Citation Index individually use the More Settings option at the foot of the Web of Science search screen.

Some of the disciplines covered include:

- Anthropology
- History
- Industrial Relations
- Information Science & Library Science
- Law
- Linguistics
- Philosophy
- Political Science
- Psychiatry
- Psychology
- Public Health
- Social Issues
- Social Work
- Sociology
- Substance Abuse
- Urban Studies
- Women's Studies

2. Science Citation Index Expanded (SCIE) - Publication years: 1900 to present: Science Citation Index Expanded is a multidisciplinary index to the journal literature of the sciences. The Science Citation Index Expanded offers bibliographical access to a curated collection of over 9,200 journals across 178 scientific disciplines. Being a citation index, it allows searching for articles that cite a known author or work (Cited Reference Search), as well as searching by subject, author, journal, and author. *'Cited reference searching'* lets you track how any idea, innovation, or creative work has been confirmed, applied, improved, extended, or corrected, and discover who is citing your publication of interest. The Science Citation Index is accessed through the Web of Science platform, with which more databases can be searched simultaneously. To search the Science Citation Index individually use the More Settings option at the foot of the Web of Science search screen.

Some of the disciplines covered include:

- Agriculture
- Astronomy
- Biochemistry
- Biology
- Biotechnology
- Chemistry
- Computer Science
- Materials Science
- Mathematics
- Medicine
- Neuroscience
- Oncology
- Pediatrics
- Pharmacology
- Physics
- Plant Sciences
- Psychiatry
- Surgery
- Veterinary Science
- Zoology

3. Arts & Humanities Citation Index (AHCI): Arts & Humanities Citation Index is a multidisciplinary index. The Arts & Humanities Citation Index offers bibliographical access to a curated collection of over 1,800 journals across 28 arts & humanities disciplines and individually selected, relevant items from over 6,800 major science and social science journals. Being a citation index, it allows searching for articles that cite a known author or work, as well as searching by subject, author, journal, and author. *'Cited reference searching'* lets researchers track how any idea, innovation, or creative work has been confirmed, applied, improved, extended, or corrected, and discover who is citing your publication of interest. The Arts & Humanities Citation Index (1988-present) is accessed through the Web of Science platform, with which more databases can be searched simultaneously. To search the Arts & Humanities Citation index individually use the More Settings option at the foot of the Web of Science search screen.

Arts & Humanities Citation Index is a multidisciplinary index to the journal literature of the arts and humanities. It fully covers over 1,600 of the world's leading arts and humanities journals. It also indexes individually selected, relevant items from over 6,000 major science and social science journals.

Some of the disciplines covered include:

- Archaeology
- Architecture
- Art
- Asian Studies
- Classics
- Dance
- Folklore
- History
- Language
- Linguistics
- Literary Reviews
- Literature
- Music
- Philosophy
- Poetry
- Radio, Television, & Film
- Religion
- Theater

4. Emerging Sources Citation Index - Publication years: 2015 - present:
The Emerging Sources Citation Index (ESCI) was launched in late 2015 by Thomson Reuters as a new database in Web of Science. Around 3,000 journals were selected for coverage at launch, spanning the full range of subject areas. Since 2017 the index has been produced by Clarivate Analytics. The Emerging Sources Citation Index aims to extend the scope of publications in the Web of Science to include high-quality, peer reviewed publications. It ensures important research is visible in the Web of Science Core Collection even if it is not yet internationally recognized.

5. Conference Proceedings Citation Index (CPCI) – Science (CPCI-S) and Social Sciences & Humanities (CPCI-SSH) - Publication years: 1990 to present: The Conference Proceedings Citation Indexes – Science (CPCI-S) and Social Science & Humanities (CPCI-SSH) – offer bibliographical access to a curated collection of over 205,900 conference proceedings in the sciences, social sciences and the arts & humanities. The conference proceedings citation indexes allow searching for conference papers that cite a known author or work (Cited Reference Search), as well as searching by subject, author, journal, and author. *'Cited reference searching'* lets you track how any idea, innovation, or creative work has been confirmed, applied, improved, extended, or corrected, and discover who is citing your publication of interest. Conference proceedings represent the leading edge of research – revealing emerging trends and new ideas before they appear in journals. The Conference Proceedings Citation Indexes are accessed through the Web of Science platform, with which more databases can be searched simultaneously. To search the Conference Proceedings Citation Indexes individually use the More Settings option at the foot of the Web of Science search screen.

Conference Proceedings Citation Index - Science (CPCI-S): This citation index covers conference literature in all scientific and technical fields, including:

- Agriculture
- Biochemistry
- Biology
- Biotechnology
- Chemistry
- Computer Science
- Engineering
- Environmental Sciences
- Medicine
- Physics

Conference Proceedings Citation Index - Social Sciences & Humanities (CPCI-SSH): This citation index covers conference literature in all fields of social sciences, arts, and humanities, including:

- Art
- Economics
- History
- Literature
- Management
- Philosophy
- Psychology
- Public Health
- Sociology

6. Book Citation Index- Science (BKCI-S) and Social Sciences & Humanities (BKCI-SSH): The Book Citation Index allows researchers to search for books (series and non-series) and book chapters using all of the fields and features available in Web of Science Core Collection.

The Book Citation Index includes the published scholarly literature of books and book chapters. Book citations are seamlessly integrated with other citation indexes in the Web of Science platform to provide a complete citation count of an author's published work. These citations are included in the overall citation count of a published work. Use these indexes to track who is citing your published works and the published works of your peers. Textbooks, Encyclopedias, Reference Books are not included in the Book Citation Index.

Users must have a subscription to one or both indexes to search for books and book chapters. The citation indexes include:

- Book Citation Index– Science (BKCI-S) – 2005-present
- Book Citation Index– Social Sciences & Humanities (BKCI-SSH) – 2005-present

The Book Citation Index is a multidisciplinary index to the literature of the sciences, social sciences, and humanities.

Some of the disciplines covered include:

- Agriculture
- Biology
- Chemistry
- Clinical Medicine

- Computer Science
- Economics
- Education
- Engineering
- History
- Life Sciences
- Physics
- Psychology
- Social & Behavioral Sciences
- Technology

Features of Book Citation Index: The following features are available when searching for books and book chapters:

- View unified citation counts captured for books and book chapters for Citing Articles, Cited References, Related Records, and Shared Records for all available years.
- View unified citation counts provided to book sources from journal articles and conference-proceedings that cite books and book chapters and vice-versa.
- Search for records of journal articles, conference proceedings, books, and book chapters that have cited a previously published book by using Cited Reference Search.
- View complete bibliographic information captured and displayed from the Full Record page. Book records are indexed as Article and Book document types. Book chapters are indexed as Article and Book Chapter.
- Access full text links for books and book chapters from both the Results and Full Record pages based on your subscription coverage.
- Navigate between structured search results so that book chapters are linked to books (Book Chapter Count field) and books are linked to corresponding book chapters (Source field) from the Full Record.
- Create Citation Reports that provide aggregate citation statistics for a set of books and book chapters that include the total number of citations to a record and the average number of times a book or book chapter has been cited.
- Analyze your results by grouping and ranking book and book chapter records in a set of results by Book Series Titles.
- Search for records of books and book chapters by restricting your search to Book and Book Chapter document types by using Search and Advanced Search.
- Refine your results and rank book and book chapter records by Book, Book Chapter, or Book Series Titles.
- Create Citation Maps and view a graphical representation that shows the citation relationships (cited references and citing articles) between a book and other works (articles, conference proceedings, and books) using various visualization tools and techniques.
- Add book and book chapter records to your Marked List and later print, save, e-mail, order, or export them from the Marked List page. Create customized book and book chapter Citation Reports from your marked list.
- View complete source information captured and displayed from the Results page that includes book authors, editors, title, book series, publication date, and more.

7. Current Chemical Reactions (CCR) and Index Chemicus: Current Chemical Reactions and Index Chemicus provide deep chemical structure and reaction indexing. An integrated chemical drawing tool lets researchers draw compounds and structures to search with precision, while integration with Web of Science Core Collection provides seamless citation navigation and ensures resource quality.

7.13.8.5. Search Techniques in Web of Science

Researchers can search the top journals, conference proceedings and books in the sciences, social sciences and arts and humanities to find the high-quality research most relevant to their area of interest. Below we are providing the search techniques, search results and cited reference search in Web of Science Core Collection:

1. Basic Search Techniques

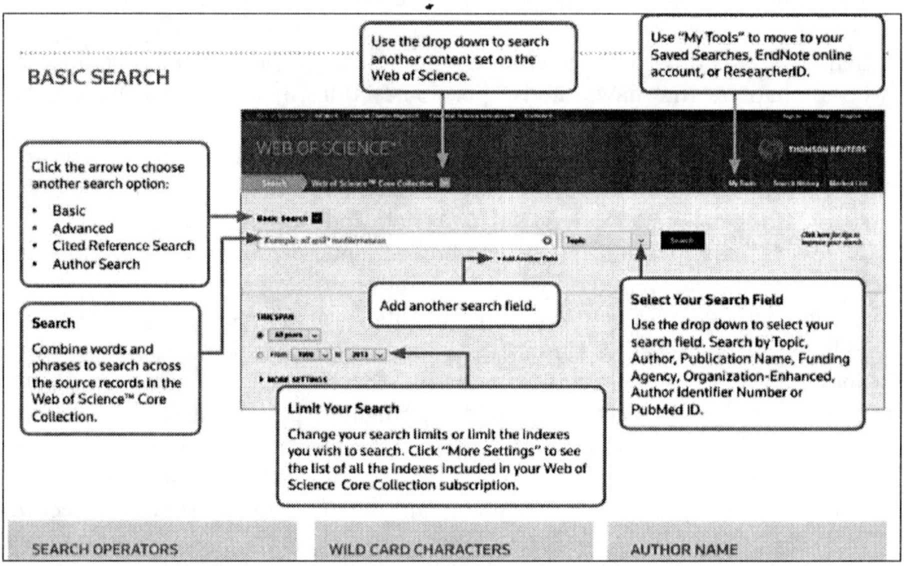

Figure 7.11 *Basic Search Techniques in Web of Science*

2. Search Results

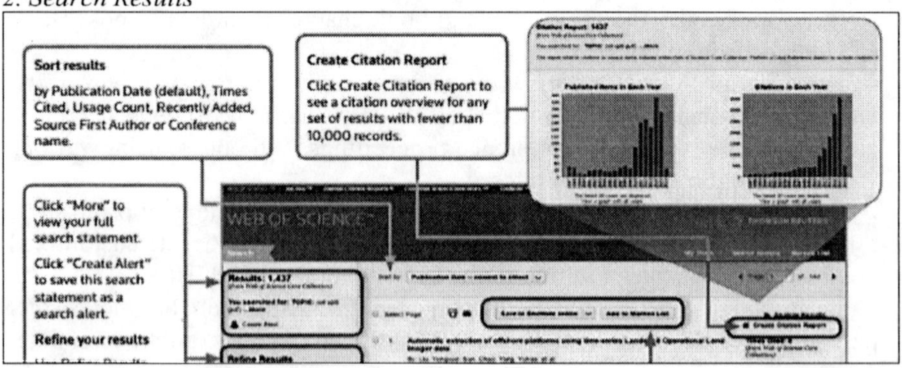

Figure 7.12a *Search Results in Web of Science*

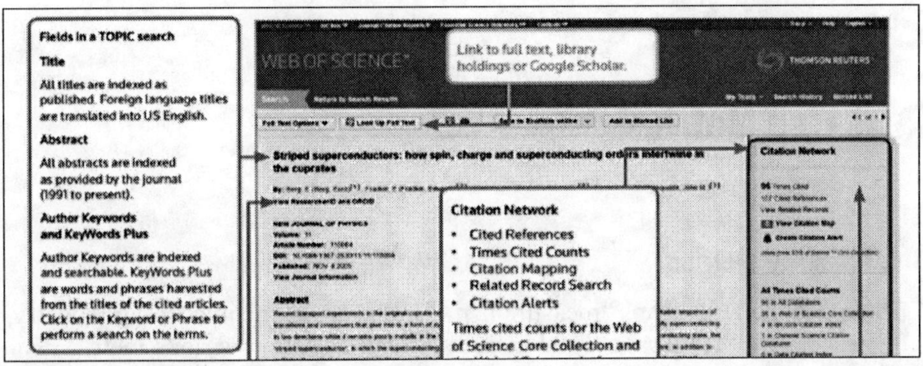

Figure 7.12b *Search Results in Web of Science*

3. Cited Reference Search

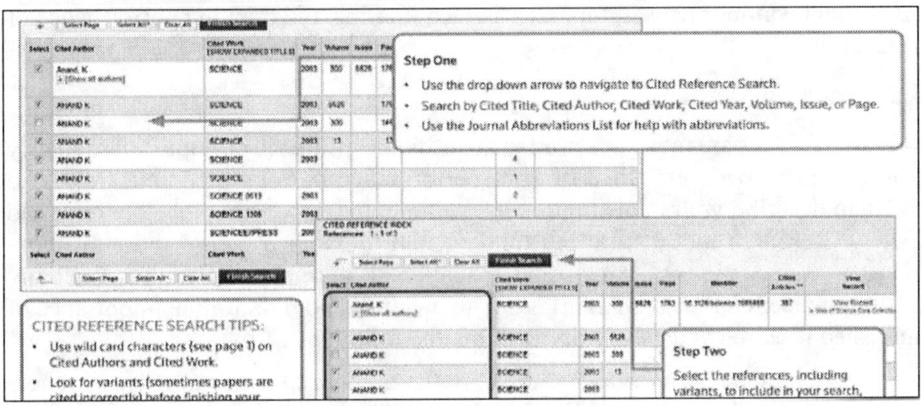

Figure 7.13 *Cited reference Search in Web of Science*

8

Research Metrics

8.1. What are Metrics?

The word metrics means "measurement." In the academic publishing industry, we measure the impact of published research based on various metrics. For example, we look at how many times a paper is cited by subject or author and how many times a specific article in a journal is cited to assess the importance of the journal and its impact on the field of study. Metrics are measures of quantitative assessment commonly used for assessing, comparing and tracking performance or production.

8.2. Research Metrics

Research metrics are measures used to quantify the influence or impact of scholarly work. They provide evidence of your performance in your academic field, and can help describe your contribution and value to the university, the economy and society. Research metrics are the fundamental tools used across the publishing industry to measure performance, at article level, journal level, author-level and institutional level. Research metrics aim to quantify and monitor the importance of published research and can be divided into the following:

- *Citation metrics (bibliometrics)* score the number of times other researchers refer to (cite) a given publication and can be a useful measure of the level of attention within scholarly publishing. They can be generated on *article, author, Journal (publication)* or *institutional level.*
- *Alternative metrics ("altmetrics")* summarise the level of attention received in social media and other platforms, offering useful information about impact outside of scholarly publishing, and also serving as early indicators of possible intentions to cite a publication.
- *Advanced metrics* are a broad category of advanced indicators that can be utilized for in-depth impact analysis. These are not *"ready-made"* metrics, and require some specialized knowledge to calculate.

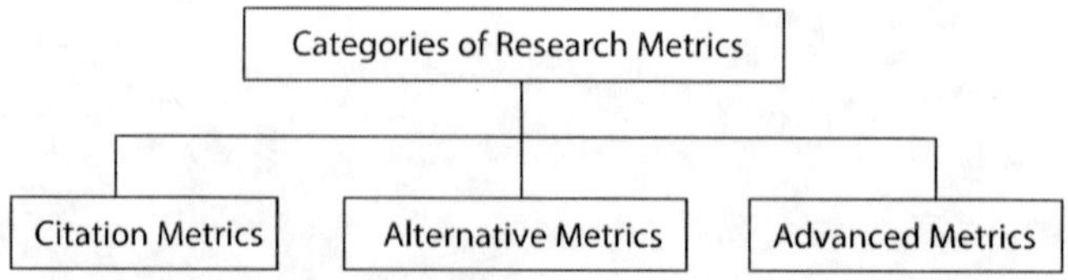

Figure 8.1 *Categories of Research Metrics*

8.2.1. Citation-based Research Metrics

These metrics focus on article citations as a gold standard for measuring the impact of research. Citation metrics can be used to evaluate individual researchers, departments/centres, institutions, disciplines, countries and other modes. Citation-based research metrics look at the number of times your publications have been cited by other researchers within a given article database.

☞ If your research is cited frequently in other academic literature, it is an indication that your research is making a significant impact.

8.2.1.1. Types of Citation-Based Research Metrics

1. *Citation Count*: The aggregate number of academic citations a given publication or group of publications has received.

2. *Citation Impact*: The average number of citations a given author receives per publication.

3. *Impact Factor*: The Impact Factor is probably the most well-known metric for assessing journal performance. Designed to help librarians with collection management in the 1960s, it has since become a common proxy for journal quality. The Impact Factor is a simple research metric: it's the average number of citations received by articles in a journal within a two-year window. The Web of Science Journal Citation Reports (JCR) publishes the official results annually, based on this calculation:

> Number of citations received in one year to content published in *Journal X* during the two previous years, divided by the total number of articles and reviews published in *Journal X* within the previous two years.

For example, the 2017 Impact Factors (released in 2018) used the following calculation:

> Number of citations received in 2017 to content published in *Journal X* during 2015 and 2016, divided by the total number of articles and reviews published in *Journal X* in 2015 and 2016.

4. *5-year Impact Factor*: The 5-year Impact Factor is a modified version of the Impact Factor, using five years' data rather than two. A journal must be covered by the JCR for five years or from Volume 1 before receiving a 5-year Impact Factor. The 5-year Impact Factor calculation is:

> Number of citations in one year to content published in *Journal X* during the previous five years, divided by the total number of articles and reviews published in *Journal X* within the previous five years.

The 5-year Impact Factor is more useful for subject areas where it takes longer for work to be cited, or where research has more longevity. It offers more stability for smaller titles as there are a larger number of articles and citations included in the calculation. However, it still suffers from many of the same issues as the traditional Impact Factor.

☞ Where can we see it? Available in JCR (Journal Citation Reports)

5. Eigenfactor: In 2007, the Web of Science JCR grew to include *Eigenfactors* and *Article Influence Scores*. Unlike the Impact Factor, these metrics do not follow a simple calculation. Instead, they borrow their methodology from network theory. The Eigenfactor measures the influence of a journal based on whether it is cited within other reputable journals over five years. A citation from a highly-cited journal is worth more than from a journal with few citations. The Eigenfactor is calculated using an algorithm to rank the influence of journals according to the citations they receive. A five-year window is used and journal self-citations are not included. This score does not take journal size into account. That means larger journals tend to have larger Eigenfactors as they receive more citations overall. The Eigenfactor calculation is:

> Number of citations in one year to content published in *Journal X* in the previous five years (weighted), divided by the total number of articles published in *Journal X* within the previous five years.

6. Article Influence Score: The Article Influence Score is a measure of the average influence of a journal's articles in the first five years after publication. A score greater than 1.00 shows above-average levels of influence. The Article Influence Score calculation is:

> (0.01 x Eigenfactor of *Journal X*) divided by (number of articles published in *Journal X* over five years, divided by the number of articles published in all journals over five years).

These are then normalized so that the average journal in the JCR has a score of 1. Like 5-year Impact Factors, journals do not receive an Article Influence Score unless they have been covered by the JCR for at least five years, or from Volume 1.

7. CiteScore: CiteScore is the ratio of citations to research published. It is currently available for journals and book series which are indexed in Scopus. CiteScore considers all content published in a journal, not just articles and reviews. CiteScore was produced by Scopus in December 2016 and you can easily replicate it via the Scopus database. In addition to CiteScore, Scopus also publish additional rankings, such as the CiteScore percentile based on subject categories and a monthly CiteScore tracker. The CiteScore calculation is:

> Number of all citations recorded in Scopus in one year to content published in *Journal X* in the last three years, divided by the total number of items published in *Journal X* in the previous three years.

Journals that publish a large amount of front matter (such as editorials or peer commentaries) will perform worse by CiteScore than by Impact Factor because this front matter is rarely cited.

Differences between CiteScore and Impact Factor

- CiteScore is based on the Scopus database rather than Web of Science. This means the number of citations and journal coverage in certain subject areas is notably higher.

- CiteScore uses a three-year citation window, whereas Impact Factor uses a two-year citation window.
- The CiteScore denominator includes all content published in the journal. The Impact Factor denominator includes only articles and reviews.
- CiteScore covers all subject areas, whereas the Impact Factor is only available for journals indexed in the SCIE and SSCI.

8. SNIP (Source Normalized Impact per Paper): SNIP was created by Professor Henk F. Moed at Centre for Science and Technology Studies (CWTS), University of Leiden. SNIP is a journal-level metric which attempts to correct subject-specific characteristics, simplifying cross-discipline comparisons between journals. It measures citations received against citations expected for the subject field, using Scopus data. SNIP is published twice a year and looks at a three-year period. The SNIP calculation is:

> Journal citation count per paper, divided by citation potential in the field.

SNIP normalizes its sources to allow for cross-disciplinary comparison. In practice, this means that a citation from a publication with a long reference list has a lower value. SNIP only considers citations to specific content types (articles, reviews, and conference papers), and does not count citations from publications that Scopus classifies as "non-citing sources". These include trade journals, and many Arts and Humanities titles.

> Where can we see it? Available in Scopus and from CWTS Journal Indicators

9. SJR (Scimago Journal Rank): The SJR aims to capture the effect of subject field, quality, and reputation of a journal on citations. It calculates the prestige of a journal by considering the value of the sources that cite it, rather than counting all citations equally. Each citation received by a journal is assigned a weight based on the SJR of the citing journal. So, a citation from a journal with a high SJR value is worth more than a citation from a journal with a low SJR value. The SJR calculation is:

> Average number of (weighted) citations in a given year to Journal X, divided by the number of articles published in Journal X in the previous three years.

As with SNIP and CiteScore, SJR is calculated using Scopus data.

10. h-index: The h-index is an author-level research metric, first introduced by Hirsch in 2005. The h-index attempts to measure the productivity of a researcher and the citation impact of their publications. The basic h-index calculation is:

> Number of articles published which have received the same number of citations.

For example, if you have published at least 10 papers that have each been cited 10 times or more, you will have a h-index of 10.

10 Index: The number of publications (in a given group of publications) that have been cited at least 10 times.

8.2.2. Altmetrics (Alternative Metrics)

Altmetrics measure and monitor the reach and impact of scholarship and research through online interactions. Altmetrics stands for *"alternative metrics."* The *"alternative"* part references traditional measurements of academic success such as citation counts, journal prestige (impact factor), and author H-index. Altmetrics are meant to compliment, not totally replace, these traditional measures. Supporters of the altmetrics movement believe that doing so will give a more complete picture of how research and scholarship is used.

Altmetrics consider how people interact with your research output in both traditional media (e.g., newspapers, tv news, journal websites) and social media (e.g., Twitter, Mendelay, Dataverse, Github, etc.). Alternative metrics (or "altmetrics") help researchers to measure the impact of a journal by looking at the social activity around it. They use quantitative and qualitative data alongside traditional citation and usage-based metrics to provide an insight into the attention, influence and impact of academic research.

☞ If your research is being widely read, discussed, and shared it is an indication that your research is making a significant impact.

By considering a range of indicators beyond citation counts, altmetrics can measure the impact of a diverse range of research outputs (e.g., articles, books, datasets, presentations, software, etc.).

8.2.2.1. How Altmetrics Work?

You probably already know that nearly everything on the internet is tracked. What you click can be used to inform website design, serve targeted adds, or as a simple measure of popularity. Altmetrics uses this ability to track interaction with online items as a way of measuring research impact and reach.

Altmetrics can answer questions such as:

- How many times was it downloaded?
- Who is reading my work? (on Mendeley, bookmarking sites, etc.)
- Was it covered by any news agencies?
- Are other researchers commenting on it?
- How many times was it shared? (on Facebook, Twitter, etc.)
- Which countries are looking at my research?

8.2.2.2. Benefits of Altmetrics

Capture Elements of Societal Impact: Altmetrics data can inform researchers of elements of the societal impact of their research. For example, altmetrics data can help researchers understand how their research is being interacted with by the public, government, policy makers, and other researchers.

Complement Traditional Metrics: Altmetrics provide a wider range of data, from a wider range of sources than traditional metrics. Altmetrics data is also highly nuanced and can be provided in high detail and in the context in which it originates.

Offer Speed and Discoverability: Altmetrics data accumulates at a faster speed compared to traditional metrics. In disciplines where citations grow slowly, or in the context of new researchers, this speed helps determine which outputs are gaining online attention.

Advantage of Open Access: Providers like Altmetric.com and ImpactStory provide access to their API and source code. Altmetrics providers also pull their data from open sources, who give access to their APIs or raw usage data, which makes altmetrics data more easily replicable than data in proprietary databases.

8.2.2.3. Why Use Altmetrics?

- Speed of feedback, they are nearly real-time metrics of scholarly impact.
- More complete picture of scholarly activities.
- To demonstrate public impact.
- View up-to-date trends in research.
- Demonstrate an impact through alternatives metrics.
- Improve your impact.
- A more nuanced understanding of impact, showing us which scholarly products are read, discussed, saved and recommended as well as cited.
- Often more timely data, showing evidence of impact in days instead of years.
- A window on the impact of web-native scholarly products like datasets, software, blog posts, videos and more.
- Indications of impacts on diverse audiences including scholars but also practitioners, clinicians, educators and the general public.
- Altmetrics rely on more than just citations; altmetrics include discussion by the media, mentions in the news, discussion by the public as well as importance to colleagues.
- They are often based on open data. The difference between altmetrics and traditional metrics is that altmetrics use mostly publicly available data, making the process and calculations completely transparent.

8.2.2.4. Altmetrics by Item Type

A. Articles

- *Citations*: Scopus, Web of Science, PubMed Central, and Google Scholar citations; citations in policy documents
- *Bookmarks*: scholarly bookmarks on Mendeley & CiteULike; bookmarks by the public on Delicious & Pinboard; Twitter favourites
- *Discussion*: peer reviews on F1000, Publons, and other post-publication peer review websites; Twitter mentions and Facebook wall posts; newspaper articles, videos, and podcasts; mentions on scholarly blog networks like ResearchBlogging
- *Shares*: Twitter mentions, Facebook shares
- *Views*: Pageview & download statistics from the journal website or repository where you've archived your paper

B. Book and Book Chapters

- *Citations*: Web of Science and Scopus citations; Google Book citations
- *WorldCat holdings*: the number of libraries worldwide that have purchased your book

- *Views*: Pageview & download statistics from your publisher's website or the repository where you've archived your book/chapter.
- *Ratings*: Amazon.com and Goodreads ratings
- *Discussion*: see "Articles" above
- *Bookmarks*: see "Articles" above

C. Data

- *Citations*: Data Citation Index and Google Scholar citations
- *Views*: views and downloads from Figshare, Zenodo, Dryad, ICPSR, or other subject or institutional repositories
- *Reuse*: GitHub forks
- *Discussion*: Figshare comments; also see "Articles" above
- *Bookmarks*: see "Articles" above

D. Software

- *Citations*: Google Scholar citations
- *Downloads*: download statistics from GitHub, Bitbucket, Sourceforge, or other institutional or subject repository
- *Adaptations*: GitHub forks, Bitbucket clones
- *Collaborators*: GitHub collaborators
- *Discussion*: GitHub gists, mentions on Twitter, Figshare comments
- *Bookmarks, Shares*: see "Articles" above

E. Posters

- *Views*: views and downloads on Figshare, Zenodo, or other institutional or subject repository
- *Discussion*: Figshare comments; see also "Articles" above
- *Bookmarks, Shares*: see "Articles" above

F. Slides

- *Views*: views and downloads on Slideshare, Speakerdeck, and Figshare
- *Discussion*: Slideshare and Figshare comments; see also "Articles" above
- *Shares*: Slideshare embeds on other websites; mentions on Twitter, Facebook shares, LinkedIn shares
- *Likes*: Slideshare and Speakerdeck likes
- *Bookmarks*: see "Articles" above

G. Videos

- *Views*: Youtube, Vimeo, and Figshare views
- *Likes/Dislikes*: Youtube likes and dislikes; Vimeo likes
- *Discussion*: Youtube, Vimeo, and Figshare comments; see also "Articles" above
- *Shares, Bookmarks*: see "Articles" above

8.2.2.5. Types of Altmetrics

There are two types of Altmetrics:

1. Standalone Altmetrics

- *Mentions/ Shares*: The number of times your research has been mentioned in media or social media contexts

- *Views/ Downloads*: The number of times your article, dataset, presentation, etc. has been accessed from a given website or database
- *Ratings/ Reviews*: Personal or professional evaluations of a researcher's output reported through traditional or social media (e.g., book reviews in journals; product ratings on Amazon, etc.)

2. Aggregate Altmetrics

- *Altmetric Attention Score*: Indicates the amount of attention a given research output has received based on a weighted count of various standalone indicators tracked by the Altmetric tool. More information can be found here.
- *Attention Score In-Context*: Normalizes the attention score of a given research output to see how it compares to other outputs from similar publication dates and publications

8.2.2.6. How to Calculate Altmetrics

A number of advanced altmetrics tools are available for researchers (with both free and subscription-based options).

1. Altmetric: Altmetric is a commercial organisation that monitors social media sites, science blogs, news sites and referencing tools for mentions of academic papers. Altmetric can provide a single score for a paper as a quantitative measure of the paper's impact. The Altmetric Score is a weighted count of the different sources that mention the paper. It is weighted to reflect the relative importance of each type of source. The Altmetric score is based on three factors:

- The number of times a paper has been mentioned
- Where the paper has been mentioned
- How often the author of each mention discusses scholarly articles

The Altmetric site includes a free bookmarklet and the code that is used by Altmetric is freely available for academic and non-commercial use, otherwise a commercial licence needs to be purchased.

Services using Altmetric to provide article-level metrics: A number of service providers automatically embed data from Altmetric for individual publication outputs. These providers include:

- Scopus
- Science Direct
- The Cochrane Library
- Wiley Online Library
- Highwire Press Journal
- Springerlink Journals
- Nature Journals
- Science Open
- BMJ Journals
- Royal Society of Chemistry scientific journals
- Biomed Central

2. Impactstory: Impactstory is a free service that tracks the buzz surrounding your research output on Twitter, blogs, and news outlets and generates a wide variety of altmetrics and statistics based on this data. Accounts can be synchronized with ORCiD to update automatically when new content is published.

3. Plum Analytics: PlumX Metrics provide insights into the ways people interact with individual pieces of research output (articles, conference proceedings, book

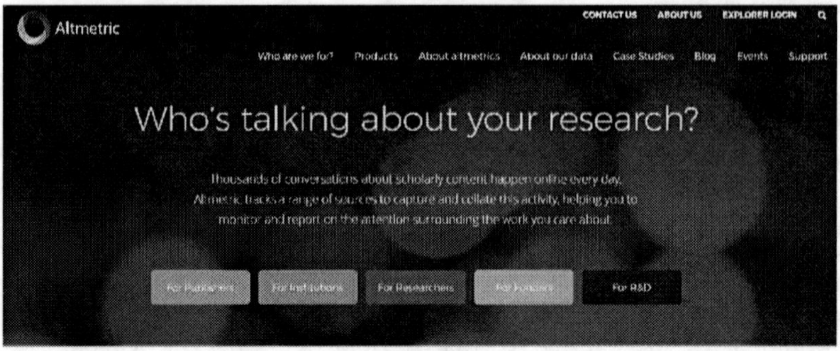

Figure 8.2 *Home Page of Altmetric*

Figure 8.3 *Home Page of Impactstory*

chapters, and many more) in the online environment. Examples include, when research is mentioned in the news or is tweeted about. Collectively known as PlumX Metrics, these metrics are divided into five categories to help make sense of the huge amounts of data involved and to enable analysis by comparing like with like. PlumX gathers and brings together appropriate research metrics for all types of scholarly research output.

Plum Analytics categorize metrics into 5 separate categories given below:

Citations: This is a category that contains both traditional citation indexes such as Scopus, as well as citations that help indicate societal impact such as Clinical or Policy Citations.

Examples: citation indexes, patent citations, clinical citations, policy citations Learn more

Usage: A way to signal if anyone is reading the articles or otherwise using the research. Usage is the number one statistic researchers want to know after citations.

Examples: clicks, downloads, views, library holdings, video plays Learn more

Captures: Indicates that someone wants to come back to the work. Captures can be an leading indicator of future citations.

Examples: bookmarks, code forks, favorites, readers, watchers Learn more

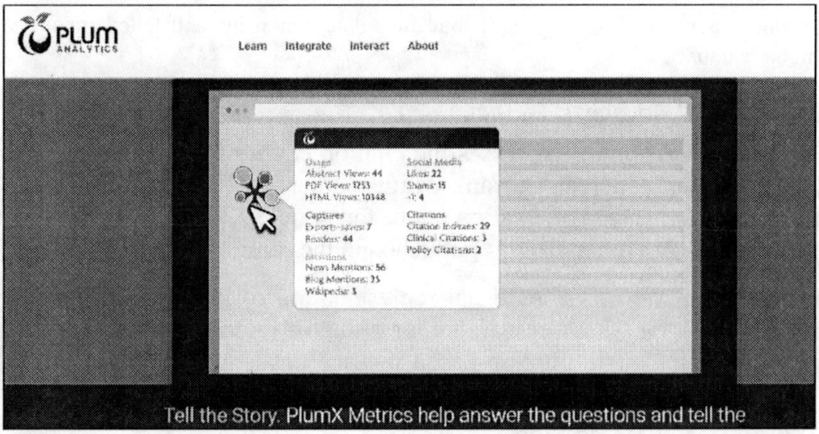

Figure 8.4 *Home Page of Plum Analytics*

Mentions: Measurement of activities such as news articles or blog posts about research. Mentions is a way to tell that people are truly engaging with the research.

Examples: blog posts, comments, reviews, Wikipedia references, news media Learn more

Social media: This category includes the tweets, Facebook likes, etc. that reference the research. Social Media can help measure "buzz" and attention. Social media can also be a good measure of how well a particular piece of research has been promoted.

Examples: shares, likes, comments, tweets

4. ResearchGate (RG) Score: The academic social networking site, ResearchGate, calculates a score based on peer evaluations of users' contributions. Contributions can include publications, data, etc. Your RG score is weighted by the RG score of whoever is evaluating your work.

As stated above, research metrics are the fundamental tools that can be used to measure performance at article level, journal level, author-level and institutional level. Now, we will see the research metrices in this point of view.

8.2.3. Advanced Metrics

Advanced metrics are a broad category of advanced indicators that can be utilized for in-depth impact analysis. These are not "ready-made" metrics, and require some specialized knowledge to calculate.

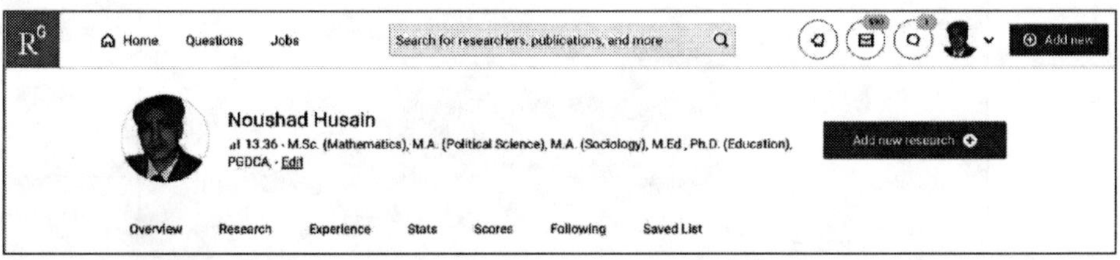

Figure 8.5 *Home Page of ResearchGate*

Analyzing patterns of citation and publication data can paint a detailed picture of a researcher's impact.

8.2.3.1. Types of Advanced Metrics

1. Normalized Percentile: Expresses the citation count of a publication or group of publications as a percentile rank against other publications from the same discipline and year (e.g. The citation count for Article X is in the 90th percentile when compared with other articles published in the same discipline and year).

2. Collaboration Networks: A visual representation of the authors, institutions, funding agencies, etc. that a researcher, or group of researchers. has collaborated with. Can be paired with citation-based metrics to identify the most successful collaborations.

8.2.3.2. Advanced Metrics Tools

InCites is a citation analysis tool that can be used to calculate advanced metrics. InCites, by Clarivate, is a benchmarking and analytics tool that uses publication information to analyze productivity, impact, and collaborations as reflected in the literature indexed in the Web of Science Databases. It includes all academic disciplines, but is stronger and provides more narrow sub-field data for STEM fields.

Of the biggest strengths of using InCites for analysis is that researchers can use and compare normalized metrics that take into account what is 'expected' for other items of the same year, subject area or journal, and publication type. Also, some metrics use percentages rather than absolute values so that researchers can compare publications across different subject research areas on an equal footing.

8.2.3.3. Metrics Used in InCites

1. Basic (Direct) Metrics: These metrics are essentially 'counting' metrics as indicators of publication productivity and impact. They form the basis for most of the other metrics used in InCites.

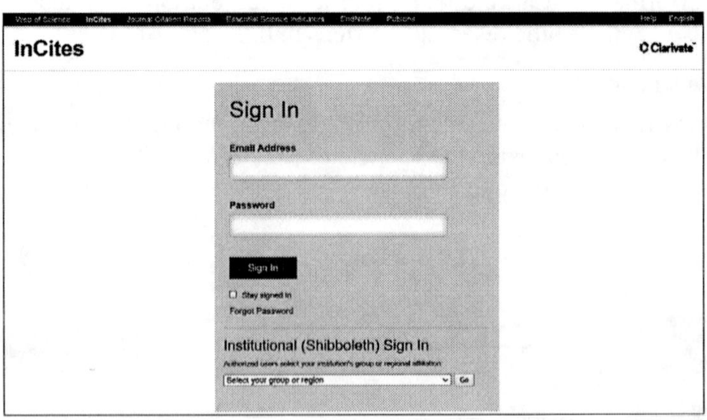

Figure 8.6 *Home Page of InCites*

- *Web of Science Documents*: The basic productivity measure. The total number of Web of Science Core Collection items for a given entity (researcher, organization, region, funder, etc.) published in the given time period, regardless of document type.
- *Times Cited*: The basic impact measure. The total number of times at least one item in a set of Web of Science Documents has been cited.
- *Percent Cited*: The percentage documents in the set that have received at least 1 citation
- *Citation Impact*: The ratio of Times Cited per Web of Science Document. This gives the average number of citations per item. This measure is more 'stable' for large sets of documents, otherwise small changes in the number of documents can result in large shifts in citation impact.
- *h-index (or hirsch index)*: A measure designed to combine productivity and impact into a single number. The h-index for a set of documents is the highest number for which the following is true: "There are h documents cited at least h times". This number is designed to correct for the influence of highly cited papers or highly prolific authors in a single measure.

Note: These metrics should only be used to directly rank or compare researchers or publications in the same research area and time period, since patterns of publication and citation practices can vary widely across disciplines.

2. Percentile and Normalized Metrics: Percentile and Normalized metrics make comparisons across journals, research areas, and organizations easier since they take into account research subject areas, publication year, and document type.

1. *Percentiles*: In percentile metrics, the percentile is the percent of items cited more often than the item of interest, and therefore smaller percentile indicates better relative performance.
   - *Average Percentile*: for a set of items, the average percentile is the mean of the percentiles of each individual item. If an item appears in more than one research area category, the best (lowest) percentile is used when calculating the mean.
   - *% of Documents in top 10%*: for a set of items, the proportion that is ranked in the top tenth percentile in its year, subject, and document type.
   - *% of Documents in top 1%*: for a set of items, the proportion that is ranked in the top 1 percentile in its year, subject, and document type.

   Related percentile metrics are based on the papers reaching certain percentile benchmarks in the 22 Essential Science Indicators (ESI) categories, rather than the narrower Web of Science Research Areas. Arts & Humanities journals are not included in the ESI categories.
   - *% of Highly Cited Papers*: for a set of items, the proportion that is ranked in the top 1% of one of the 22 ESI categories based on the most recent 10 years of citations.

- *% of Hot Papers*: for a set of items, the proportion that is ranked in the top 0.1% of one of the 22 ESI categories based on the most recent 2 months of citations to publications less than 2 years old.

Note: All metrics dealing with percentiles should take into consideration that analysis of small groups of records (such as a single researcher) may not have statistical significance; these metrics are more appropriately used for medium and large data sets.

2. *Normalized Metrics*: Normalized metrics for citation counts compare the times cited for an item to the expected (average) number of citations received by other items of the same publication type, year of publication, and subject area or journal. If the normalized citation impact is a ratio less than 1, the set of items is performing poorer than expected; if it is greater than 1, the set of items is performing better than its peers.
    - *Category Normalized Citation Impact*: calculated by dividing an actual citation count by an expected citation rate for documents with the same document type, year of publication, and subject area. When a document is assigned to more than one subject area, the harmonic average is used. The CNCI of a set of documents is the average of the CNCI values for all of the documents in the set.
    - *Journal Normalized Citation Impact*: is calculated by dividing an actual citation count by an expected citation rate for documents with the same document type, year of publication, and journal.

Note: All metrics of citation impact should take into consideration that citation counts for recent publications can be low and variable, so citation impacts may be influenced by the time period under analysis.

3. *Collaboration Metrics*: When analyzing collaborations, InCites provides certain metrics that can indicate what type of collaborations exist as evidenced by co-authored publications.
    - *International Collaborations*: the total number of publications in a set with at least two authors located in different countries
    - *% International Collaborations*: the percent of paper in a set that have at least two authors located in different countries
    - *% Industry Collaborations*: Industry collaborations are papers with at least one corporate author affiliation. This indicator shows the percentage of publications in a set that have a corporate co-author. All papers by individual at a corporation are considered industry collaborations, no matter what their co-authors' affiliation.
4. *Journal Quartile Metrics*: Journals are grouped into quartiles according to what percentage of journals rank lower than them when arranged by Journal Impact Factor, a measure of the average number of citations received in a two-year period. A Quartile 1 (Q1) journal ranks higher than 75% of the journals in its category, a Q2 journal ranks higher than 50% of journals, but lower than Q1 journals, etc.

$$75\% < Q1 < 100\%$$
$$50\% < Q2 < 75\%$$
$$25\% < Q3 < 50\%$$
$$0\% < Q4 < 25\%$$

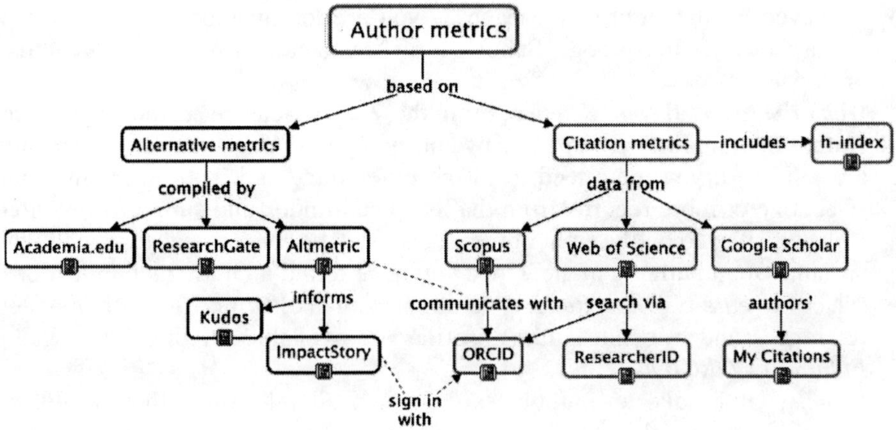

Figure 8.7 *Mind Map of Author Metrics*

InCites has several metrics that use this ranking.

- *Documents in Q1, etc.*: Number of documents that appear in a journal in a particular Journal Impact Factor Quartile in a given year.
- *Percentage of Documents in Q1, etc.*: Percentage of documents that appear in a journal in a particular Journal Impact Factor Quartile in a given year.

Note: InCites uses the best quartile for journals that appear in multiple Web of Science Research Areas. However, when a research area is specified in an analysis, the quartile for that particular journal and research area is used.

8.3. Author-Level Metrics

Author-level metrics provide an assessment of the impact that an author makes on the scientific community or field of the study. Author Level Metrics are the measurement of a scholar's impact by assessing the quality and quantity of publications. The most common is the *H-Index* but there are many variations of this measure including *Egghe's g-index* and *Age-Weighted Citation Rate (AWCR)*.

8.3.1. Author-Level Metrics and Databases

- *h-index*: A score that aims to summarize a researcher impact and productivity with a single number.
- *g-index*: For calculating g-index, articles are ranked in a decreasing order of the number of citations. It indicates the largest number such that the top g articles received at least g^2 citations.
- *Citation Count*: A simple measure of the number of citations for an article, researcher or publication.
- *Google Scholar*: Google Scholar is a good source for an author's h-index and citation counts. Scopus also provides charts and graphs of an author's h-factor and number of citations. Go to a (or create your own) Google Scholar profile page. You will see the h-index, number of citations and other metrics

displayed on the right of the page. If you are looking for the h-index of a researcher without a Google Scholar Profile, you could use Harzing's Publish or Perish.

- *Web of Science*: *Web of Science*: From the Web of Science search page, select Author Search. Find your papers by entering your name - if numerous results are retrieved, you may need to refine by country and institution, and then select one or more records from the list. The h-index and sum of times cited is then displayed on the right of the page. Use *"Author Finder"* to identify the variants of an author's name. Once you have found an author's publications, select *"Create Citation Report"* to obtain a breakdown of the author's cited references and h-index. Author profiles are available for those that set up *Publons* or *ORCIDs*.
- *Scopus*: Undertake an author search, select all relevant author results by ticking the boxes, then click to "View Citation Overview" – the h-index will be displayed on the right of the page. Scroll down to see a table listing your publications and the number of citations for each, the top row gives totals for all of your publications. Use *"Author Search"* to identify the variants of an author's name. Click on *"View citation overview"* for the author's profile and h-index.
- *SciVal*: Includes individual Field-weighted Citation Impact (FWCI).
- *Google Scholar*: The h-index and other citation metrics are available for those authors that set up *Google Scholar* account.
- *Dimensions*: Includes publication citations, linked clinical trials and patents, as well as supporting grants.
- *ResearchGate*: Creating a profile on *ResearchGate* may help you stay connected to other researchers in your field but it also offers a score based on your contributions, interactions and reputation.
- *Academia.edu*: You can follow other researchers in your field and it also offers analytics on your profile and on your individual papers.
- *ImpactStory*: Create an *ImpactStory* profile to see how often you are cited, saved by scholars, or discussed by the public.

8.4. Article-Level Metrics

Article-level metrics (ALMs) are used to quantify the impact of published articles-how published papers are being discussed and shared. The ALM process uses various sources of information. Article Level Metrics are the measures of the impact of a specific article based upon citation analysis. Each article can be assessed for its *Relative Citation Ratio* (a field normalized metric that shows the influence of one or more articles in relation to the average paper in a discipline.)

8.4.1. Article-Level Metrics and Databases

There are several article level metrics and databases that you may find useful to consider for your portfolio.

- *Citation Counts*: Citation counts can be obtained from the three key platforms, *Web of Science, Scopus* and *Google Scholar*, and are usually displayed in your results list. The citation count will depend on the coverage of the database used. Whilst citation counts can be useful, they do have their limitations in that they do not give an idea of whether a citation count is high or low for that discipline, age of paper, or type of paper (e.g., review articles tend to generate more citations).

- *Field Weighted Citation Impact (FWCI)*: Field weighted citation impact (FWCI) is available from *Scopus*, and gives a score based on the number of citations received, compared to expected number of citations for similar documents. The FWCI normalizes to take into account the publication type, disciplinary differences in citation cultures, and the period it takes for citations to build up. A FWCI score of 1 indicates that a paper is receiving the expected number of citations for a paper of that age, discipline and type; higher than 1 means that your paper has a higher-than-average number of citations. FWCI is available in the Scopus Document Details page.
- *Percentile*: Percentile benchmark available from *Scopus*, complements the *FWCI* and compares items of the same age, subject area and document type over 18 months. The score shows how citations received by an article compare with the average for similar articles. 99th percentile is high, and indicates an article in the top 1% globally. Percentile benchmark is given on the *Scopus Document Details page*, under the *"Citations in Scopus"* score.
- *Highly Cited*: Highly Cited is a *Web of Science* indicator takes the form of a small golden trophy icon that displays in the results list and on the *Web of Science* article page. The Highly Cited trophy is given to papers in the top 1% in each of the 22 Web of Science subject categories, per year.
- *Hot Papers*: Hot papers is a *Web of Science* indicator takes the form of a small red flame that displays in the results list and on the *Web of Science* article page. Hot papers are in the top 0.1% of papers by citations for field and age.

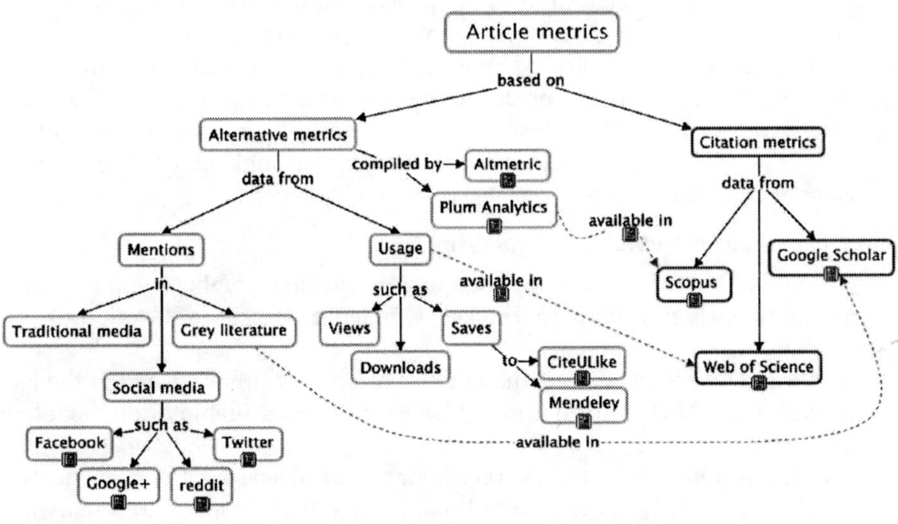

Figure 8.8 *Mind Map of Article Metrics*

- *Altmetric*: Alternative to citation-based metrics. Gives a score for individual articles based on the quantity and quality of attention received, such as tweets and readers in *Mendeley* and *CiteULike*. Add the Altmetric bookmarklet to your browser to get free metrics on individual articles.
- *Scopus*: Provides citation counts from publications in *Scopus* but alternative metrics are also included using *PlumX Metrics* (Plum Analytics) when available.
- *Web of Science*: Provides citation counts from publications in *Web of Knowledge* databases. Also provides usage counts from the last 180 days or since 2013. The counts are record exports (to *EndNote*, etc.) and clicks to full text.
- *Google Scholar*: Provides citation counts from items in *Google Scholar* and links to *Web of Science* citations for those with access to the database.
- *Dimensions*: Includes publication citations, linked clinical trials and patents, as well as supporting grants.
- *PatCite*: from *The Lens*. Find article citations in patents.
- *CiteSeerX*: Citation statistics for the literature in computer and information science.
- *Mendeley*: Crowd-sourced resource that provides information on readership (included in Scopus PlumX Metrics).
- *Individual Publishers*: Increasingly, publishers are providing metrics at the article level with information on the many ways that they are viewed, cited, saved, and discussed, such as *Public Library of Science (PLOS), BioMed Central, and Institute of Physics*. Citation counts, provided by *CrossRef*, are available for Springer articles and chapters.

8.5. Journal/Publication-Level Metrics

Journal-level metrics are used to determine the impact a journal has on the scientific community. Journal Level Metrics are the measure reflecting the yearly average number of citations to recent articles published in a journal. More sophisticated measures assess journal impact by enabling fair comparisons in fields (1) using more and less citations as measured by what is typical for a field of research or (2) using rankings based on longer or shorter periods of time. Common ones include *Journal Impact Factor (JIF), Eigenfactor* and *Source Normalization Impact per Paper (SNIP)*. JIF is the most widely used, and is increasingly being challenged as a measure of research quality

8.5.1. Journal-Level Metrics and Databases

- *CiteScore*: A new metric by Scopus, it includes eight complementary indicators such as CiteScore Tracker, CiteScore Percentile, Citation Count, and more.
- *h5 Index*: This metric counts the number of articles (h) published in the past five years that have a minimum of h citations. It is available through Google Scholar.
- *Immediacy Index*: It is the average number of article citations in the first of publication. It helps to assess how quickly these papers are cited. It is published annually in JCR. It also sources its data from Web of Science.

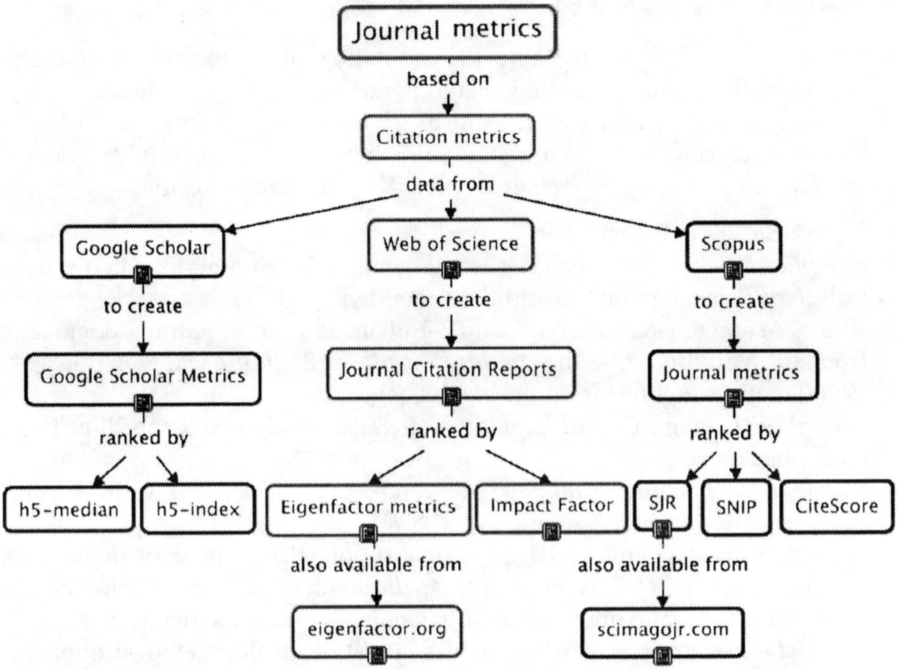

Figure 8.9 *Mind Map of Journal Metrics*

- *Impact Factor*: This metric has been used most frequently. It is the average number of citations of an article, a proceeding, or a review published in a journal in the last two years. It is published in Journal Citation Reports (JCR). This metric is published on an annual basis and can be often found on the websites of the journals. Similarly, 5-year IF is also measured to assess the journal metrics.
- *Eigenfactor*: Eigenfactor gives higher weightage citations from influential journals and does not consider self-citations. It is based on the average citations in a JCR year to papers published in the last 5 years. It is also published in JCR and sources its data from Web of Science.
- *SCImago Journal Rank (SJR)*: Similar to Eigenfactor, SJR gives greater weightage to citations from influential journals. It is based on the average number of weighted citations in a year to that published in the last 3 years. It uses information from Scopus to produce country and journal-specific indicators. SJR is published in SCImago journal and country rank reports.
- *Source Normalized Impact per Paper (SNIP)*: It is based on the weighted citations in a year to papers published in the last three years. Published in CWTS Journal Indicators, the data for this indicator is sourced from Scopus. It also corrects the differences in citation practices in different disciplines, making it easier to compare this metric across various fields.
- *Google Scholar Metrics*: Publications arranged by language and research area.

8.6. Institution-Level Metrics

Institutional Level Metrics measure the reputation of an institution of higher education as reflected in its (1) ranking and (2) influence. Metrics in this area range from rankings such as *Maclean's*, to measuring the productivity and influence of research occurring at a given institution using tools such as *InCites, SciVal, Essential Science Indicators, Web of Science, Scopus* and *Dimensions*.

- *SciVal*: Based on Scopus data.
- *Essential Science Indicators*: Uses citation counts from highly cited articles in *Web of Science* to rank institutions worldwide.
- *Web of Science*: Has an Organization-Enhanced field to pull out documents from an institution. Use the *Analyze Results* and *Citation Report* (for up to 10000 records) options from the results page.
- *ShanghaiRanking's Global Ranking of Academic Subjects*: Since 2009, based on Scopus data.
- *SCImago Institutions Rankings*: Research, innovation, and web visibility rankings based on *Scopus* data.
- *Scopus*: View the unique ID of an institution, the number of documents, authors, and patents by performing an *Affiliation search*. The citation overview is available for a maximum of 20,000 documents from the institution.
- *CWTS Leiden Ranking 2015*: Provides statistics on the scientific impact of universities and on universities' involvement in scientific collaboration, based on *Web of Science* indexed publications.
- *Mapping Scientific Excellence*: Estimated probabilities of institutions of (i) publishing highly cited papers (Best Paper Rate) or (ii) publishing in the most influential journals (Best Journal Rate) using data from Scopus.
- *Snowball Metrics*: Learn about these global standards for institutional benchmarking.

8.7. Measuring Journal Impact

With the help of knowing the impact and importance of a journal, the researchers can decide where to submit their articles. With bibliometric databases researchers can compare and evaluate journals, see the most productive research areas, download data, follow journals, and create robust data visualizations. Quantitative analysis of journals is a way traditional peer review may be augmented to gain a more complete picture of a scholar's impact in his chosen field. Three measures can be used:

- number of publications
- number of times an author's publications have been cited
- the importance of the journal where the article is published, or the Journal Ranking.

Publishing traditions vary between disciplines. Because of this, it is important to compare journals within the same or similar disciplines as much as possible. This will not always be easy as more research becomes interdisciplinary but in order for

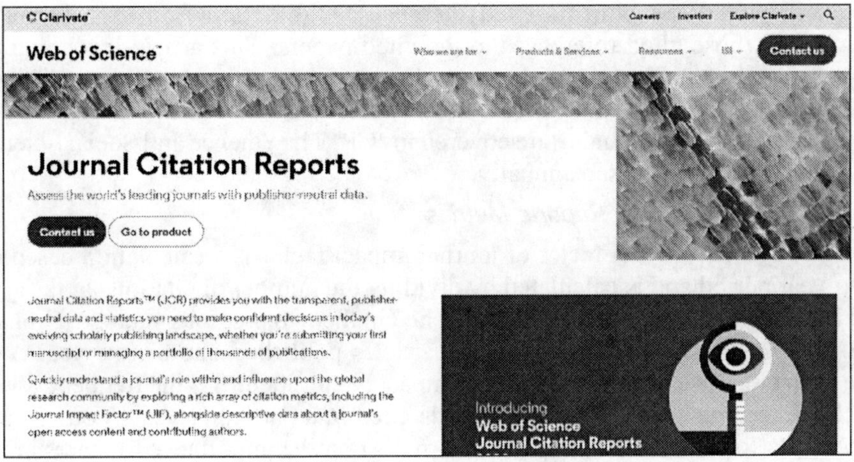

Figure 8.10 *Home Page of Journal Citation Reports (JCR)*

these journal ranking systems to have meaning the factors measured must compare journals in similar disciplines or subject areas.

8.8. Tools to Measure Journal Impact

Below, we are discussing some important databases and metrics for which researchers and scholars can measure the different scores and indices for comparing different journals.

- Journal Citation Report (JCR)
- Scopus for Journal Ranking
- Google Scholar Journal Metrics
- CWTS Journal Indicators (For SNIP)
- *SCIMago Journal and Country Rank (For SJR)*
- Eigenfactor

8.8.1. Journal Citation Reports (JCR)

Journal Citation Reports (JCR) is an annual publication by Clarivate Analytics (previously the intellectual property of Thomson Reuters). It has been integrated with the Web of Science and is accessed from the Web of Science-Core Collections. It provides information about academic journals in the natural sciences and social sciences, including impact factors. The JCR was originally published as a part of Science Citation Index. Currently, the JCR, as a distinct service, is based on citations compiled from the Science Citation Index Expanded and the Social Sciences Citation Index.

8.8.1.1. Journal Citation Reports Data

Journal Citation Reports is sourced from Web of Science Core Collection, the premier citation index on the Web of Science platform. Journals must undergo a rigorous evaluation by our editorial team in order to be covered in Web of Science

Core Collection. We capture the cited references for all content from these journals, and we link those cited references to the cited papers. This article-level citation data is aggregated to the journal-level at the end of the year to create the indicators available in JCR. Over 11,500 titles from the Science Citation Index-Expanded and Social Sciences Citation Index are covered in JCR. The Science and Social Science editions of JCR are released annually.

8.8.1.2. Journal Citation Reports Metrics

1. Impact Factor: Impact factor or journal impact factor is a calculation based on a two-year period and is calculated by dividing the number of citations in the JCR year by the total number of articles published in the two previous years. An impact factor of 2 means that, on average, the articles published one or two years ago have been cited two times. The Journal Impact Factor identifies the frequency with which an average article from a journal is cited in a particular year. You can use this number to evaluate or compare a journal's relative importance to others in the same field or see how frequently articles are cited to determine which journals may be better for your collection.

Example 2017 Impact Factor Calculation:

How is Journal Impact Factor Calculated?

$$\text{JIF} = \frac{\text{Citations in 2017 to items published in } \mathbf{2015\ (3485) + 2016\ (2516)}}{\text{Number of citable items in } \mathbf{2015\ (356) + 2016\ (311)}} = \frac{6001}{667}$$

- *Impact Factor Numerator: Cites to recent items*: The numerator looks at citations in a particular JCR year to a journal's previous two years of content. For example, the 2017 Journal Impact Factor for a journal would take into account 2017 items that cited that journal's 2015 or 2016 content. The numerator includes citations to anything published by the journal in that 2015-2016 timeframe.
- *Impact Factor Denominator: Number of recent items*: The denominator takes into account the number of citable items published in the journal in 2015 and 2016. Citable items include articles and reviews. Document types that aren't typically cited, e.g., letters or editorial materials, are not included in the Impact Factor denominator.

2. 5-Year Impact Factor: The 5-year journal impact factor is the average number of times articles from a journal published in the past five years have been cited in the chosen JCR year.

3. Immediacy Index: The immediacy index is the average number of times an article is cited in the year it is published. It is a way of determining the "hot topics" in a discipline. The Immediacy Index measures how frequently the average article

from a journal is cited within the same year as publication. This number is useful for evaluating journals that publish cutting-edge research.
Example 2015 Immediacy Index Calculation:

Cites in 2015 to items published in 2015 = 991
Number of items published in 2015 = 113

$$\text{Calculation: } \frac{\text{Cites to recent items}}{\text{Number of recent items}} \quad \frac{991}{113} = 8.77$$

- *Immediacy Index Numerator - Cites to recent items*: The numerator looks at citations in a particular JCR year to a journal's content from the same year. For example, the 2015 Immediacy Index for a journal would take into account 2015 citations to the journal's 2015 papers. The numerator includes citations to anything published by the journal in that year.
- *Immediacy Index Denominator - Number of recent items*: The denominator takes into account the number of citable items published in the journal in 2015. Citable items include articles and reviews.

4. EigenFactor: The Eigenfactor Score calculation is based on the number of times articles from the journal published in the past five years have been cited in the JCR year, but it also considers which journals have contributed these citations so that highly cited journals will influence the network more than lesser cited journals. References from one article in a journal to another article from the same journal are removed, so that Eigenfactor Scores are not influenced by journal self-citation.

5. Article Influence Score: This score is a means of measuring the influence of a journal's articles over the first five years since publication. It is calculated by multiplying the Eigenfactor Score by 0.01 and dividing that by the number of articles in the journal.

6. JIF Quartile: A journal's quartile ranking is determined by comparing a journal to others in its JCR category based on Impact Factor score. If a journal falls in Q1, it means that the journal performs better than at least 75% of journals in that category, based on its Impact Factor score.

7. JIF Percentile: The journal's rank in category, determined by Impact Factor, expressed as a percentile. For example, a journal with a JIF percentile of 89 performs better than 89% of journals in that category, based on its Impact Factor score. JIF percentiles give you a more granular view than quartiles do.

8. Cited Half-Life: The citing half-life is the average age of articles cited by the journal in the JCR year. For example, in JCR 2014, the journal International Social Work has a citing half-life of 7.1. That means that 50% of all articles cited by articles in International Social Work in 2014 were published between 1995 and 2014 (inclusive). This helps to evaluate the currency of the research cited.

8.8.2. Scopus for Journal Ranking

Scopus is Elsevier's abstract and citation database launched in 2004. Scopus covers nearly 36,377 titles (22,794 active titles and 13,583 inactive titles) from approximately 11,678 publishers, of which 34,346 are peer-reviewed journals in top-level subject fields: life sciences, social sciences, physical sciences and health sciences. It covers three types of sources: book series, journals, and trade journals. All journals covered in the Scopus database are reviewed for sufficiently high quality each year according to four types of numerical quality measure for each title; those are h-Index, CiteScore, SJR (SCImago Journal Rank) and SNIP (Source Normalized Impact per Paper). Searches in Scopus also incorporate searches of patent databases.

Scopus is the largest abstract and citation database of peer-reviewed literature: scientific journals, books and conference proceedings. Delivering a comprehensive overview of the world's research output in the fields of science, technology, medicine, social sciences, and arts and humanities, Scopus features smart tools to track, analyse and visualise research. Scopus uniquely combines a comprehensive, expertly curated abstract and citation database with enriched data and linked scholarly literature across a wide variety of disciplines.

Scopus quickly finds relevant and authoritative research, identifies experts and provides access to reliable data, metrics and analytical tools. Scopus brings together the superior quality and coverage of Scopus data, as well as advanced analytics and technology in one solution. Scopus helps:

- Combat predatory publishing and protect the integrity of the scholarly record
- Make the research workflow more efficient and effective
- Empower institutions to bolster performance, rank, and reputation
- Enable funders to optimize their investments

Each journal overview Scopus page contains these details:

- Scopus coverage
- Publisher information
- Subject areas
- CiteScore
- CiteScore Tracker (monthly update)
- SNIP
- SJR
- CiteScore Rank and Trend

Journal Comparison

- Compare up to 10 sources and review results on a chart or in table format
- Search for sources to compare by title, ISSN, publisher, subject area
- Compare CiteScore for each publication by year

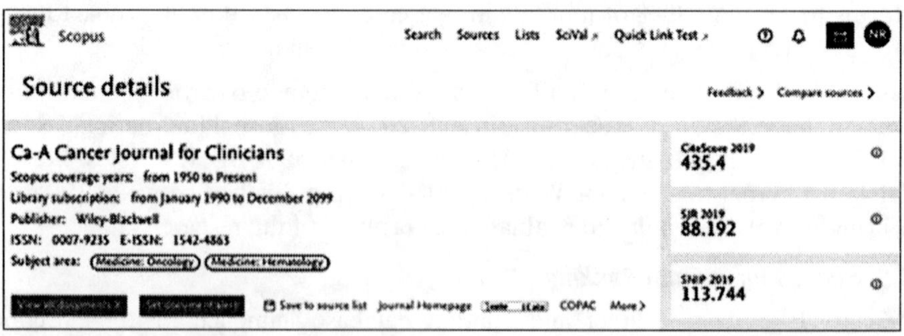

Figure 8.11 *Journal Page on Scopus*

- Compare SNIP for each publication by year
- Compare SJR for each publication by year
- Compare number of documents for each publication by year
- Compare percent of articles cited for each publication by year
- Compare percent of review articles published in each publication by year

8.8.2.1. Metrics of Scopus Journal Ranking

1. CiteScore: It was introduced in 2016. It is a measure to analyze the publication influence of serial titles. CiteScore metrics are a family of 8 indicators, include:

- CiteScore
- CiteScore Tracker
- CiteScore Percentile
- CiteScore Quartiles
- CiteScore Rank
- Citation Count
- Document Count and
- Percentage Cited.

CiteScore metrics offer more robust, timely and accurate indicators of a serial title's impact. CiteScore is the number of citations received by a journal in one year to documents published in the three previous years, divided by the number of documents indexed in Scopus published in those same three years.

CiteScore for 2015 counts the citations received in 2015 to documents published in 2012, 2013 or 2014, and divides this by the number of documents published in 2012, 2013 and 2014.

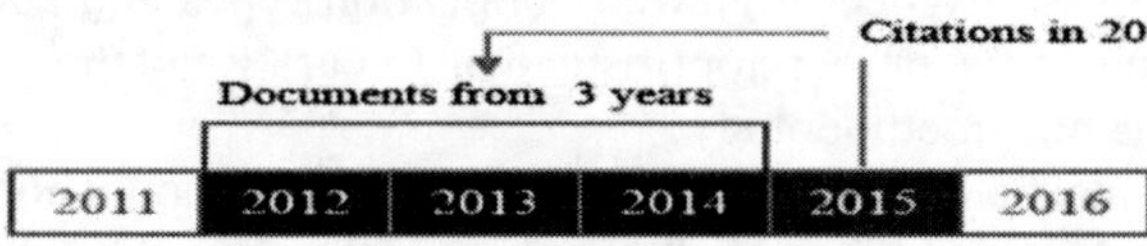

CiteScore is a family of eight indicators that offer complementary views to analyze the publication influence of serial titles of interest. Derived from the Scopus database, CiteScore metrics offer a more transparent, current, comprehensive and

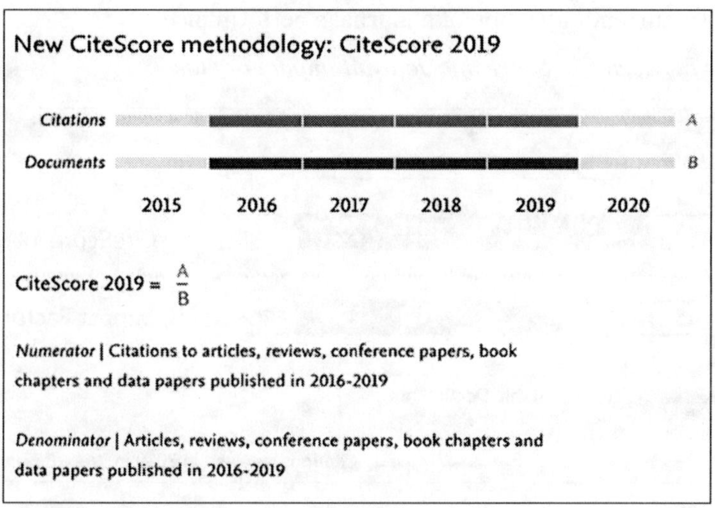

accurate indication of a serial's impact. CiteScore metrics are available for all active journals.

As of June 2020, the definition of CiteScore has changed, now only including typically peer-reviewed research: articles, reviews, conference papers, data papers and book chapters, covering 4 years of citations and publications. Historical data back to CiteScore 2011 have been recalculated and are displayed on Scopus.

CiteScore is a metric for measuring journal impact in Scopus. The calculation of CiteScore for the current year is based on the number of citations received by a journal in the latest 4 years (including the calculation year), divided by the number of documents published in the journal in those four years. This is how CiteScore of 2019 is calculated:

Calculation of CiteScore in the Year 2019:

$$\text{CiteScore in 2019} = \frac{\text{No. of citations received in 2016-2019 to documents published in 2016-2019}}{\text{No. of documents published in 2016-2019}}$$

Note:

- Document types include: articles, reviews, conference papers, data papers and book chapters.
- CiteScore 2019 were released in Jun 2020 with a new methodology. The new CiteScore counts only peer-reviewed publication types and adopts a 4-year citation window in the numerator (instead of 1 year). Read this article to learn more about the new methodology.
- CiteScore is a metric without field-normalization, thus should not be compared between subject fields (different citation practices across disciplines affect the values of the metric). If you wish to compare journals across subject fields, use SNIP or SJR instead, which are field-normalized metrics.
- CiteScore is calculated on an annual basis, showing the average citations for a full calendar year. CiteScore Tracker calculation is updated every month, giving a current indication of a journal's performance.

Difference between CiteScore and Journal Impact Factor

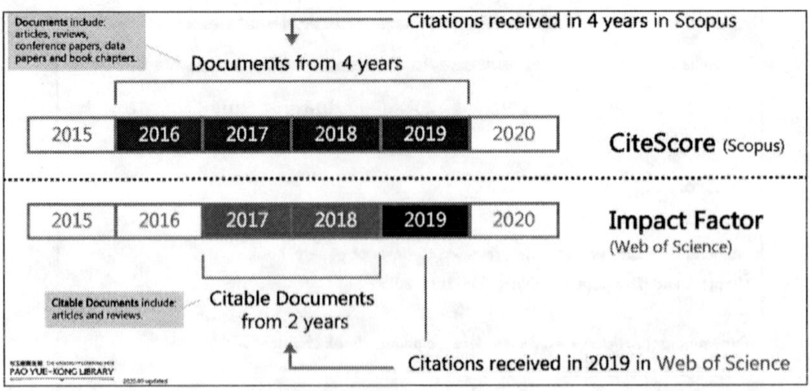

Major difference between CiteScore and Journal Impact Factor are given below:

- CiteScore calculation is based on Scopus data, while Impact Factor is based on Web of Science data.
- CiteScore uses a 4-year window while Impact Factor adopts a 2-year window.
- CiteScore includes more document types indexed by Scopus, including articles, reviews, conference papers, data papers and book chapters; while Impact Factor only includes "citable documents" which are articles and reviews.

Find CiteScore and Journal Ranking in Scopus

1. *Find CiteScore for a specific journal*:
   - ▶ Step 1. Go to Scopus and click *"Sources"* at the top of the page.
   - ▶ Step 2. Under *"Title"*, type in the journal title in the search box and click *"Find sources"*.

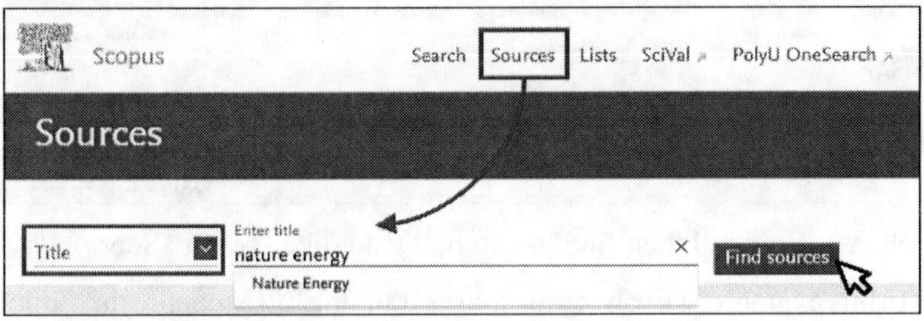

   - ▶ Step 3. You will find the CiteScore of the journal on the page.

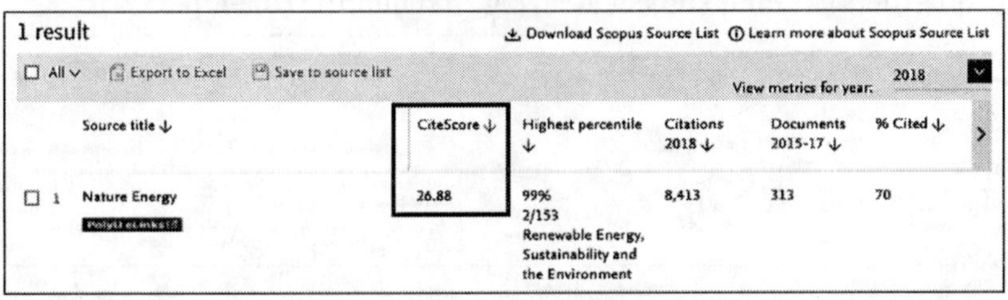

You may also click on the journal title to see more details, e.g., how the journal's CiteScore is calculated, the ranking of this journal in relevant subject categories.

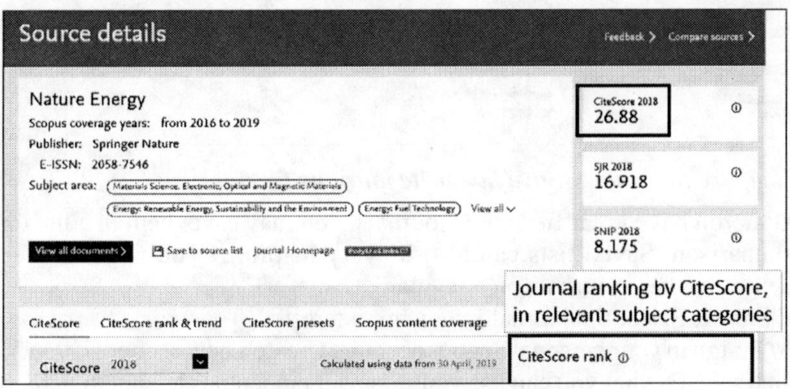

2. *Check journal ranking by CiteScore in a specific subject category*:
   ▸ Step 1. Go to Scopus and click *"Sources"* at the top of the page.
   ▸ Step 2. Under *"Subject area"*, search a subject area, check relevant subject area(s), and click *"Apply"*.

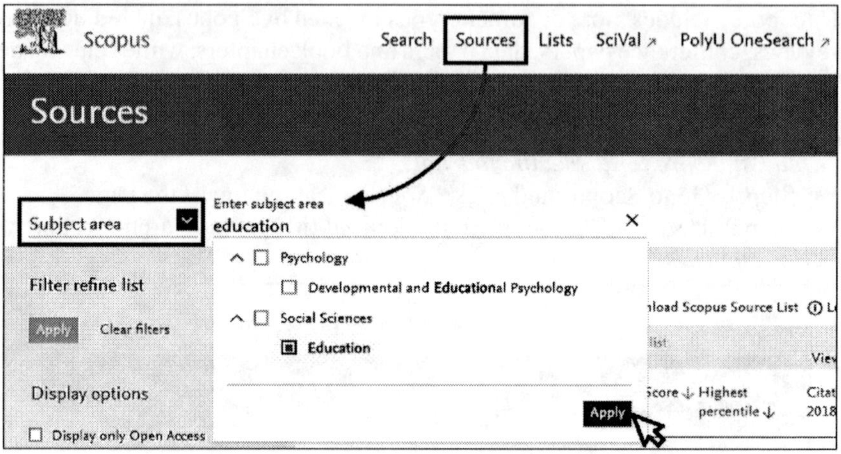

▸ Step 3. You will then find the journal list ranked by CiteScore.

In this example, we can see the journal ranking by CiteScore in *"Education"* field. You may further limit results to only those journals listed in certain quartile(s) of their subject area, e.g., 1st quartile (the top 25%).

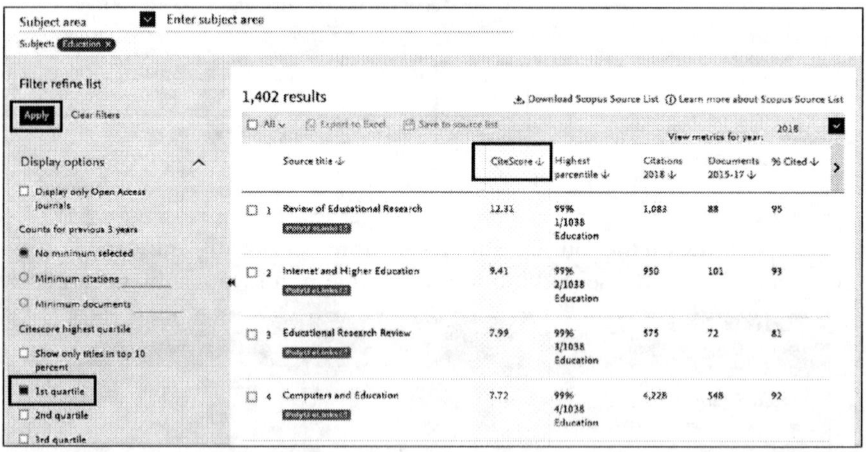

3. *Compare journals & Save favourite journals for future use*:

   After you have identified some journals, you may save them in a list for easy comparison. Saved lists can also be very helpful if you need to check the metrics of these journals on a regular basis.
   ▸ Step 1. Select the journal(s) you are interested. Then click *"Save to source list"*. Sign in your personal Scopus account. Create a new account if you haven't done so. Note that you can use your Elsevier credentials to sign in Scopus.

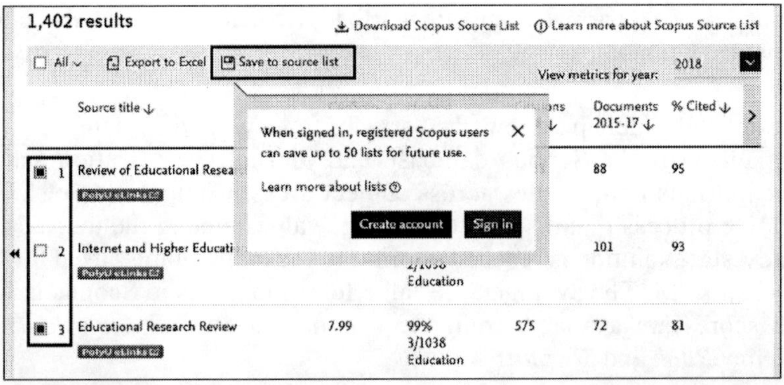

▶ Step 2. Enter name of a new list, or select an existing list from your saved lists. Then click *"Save list"*.

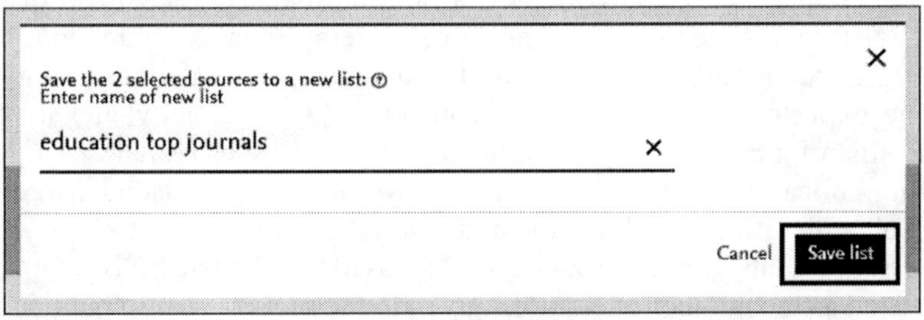

▶ Step 3. Click *"Lists"* from the top menu. Then switch to *"Sources"* to find all your saved lists. You may edit the name of the list or delete the list from this page.

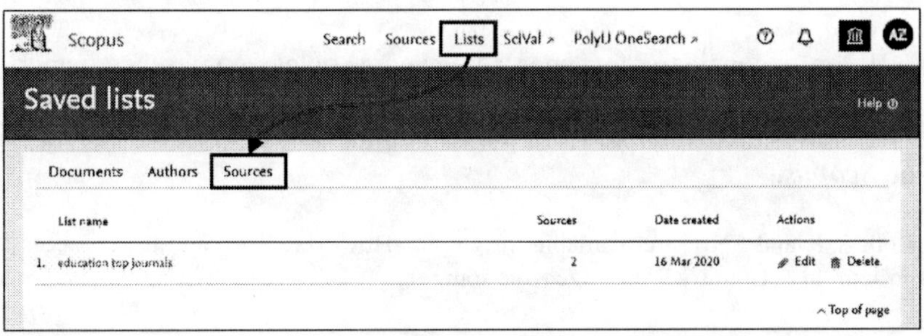

2. SCImago Journal Rank (SJR): Scimago Journal Rank (SJR) is a measure of the prestige of scholarly journals. SJR scores are computed using network analysis of citations received by journals. The methodology accounts for number of citations as well as the source of citations, with citations from high prestige journals being worth more than those from journals with lower prestige. The prestige value depends on the field, quality and reputation of the source journals that citing article is published in.

By incorporating citation behaviour in different disciplines into account, SJR can be used to make comparisons between journals in different disciplines. The effect of SJR is to flatten differences between fields i.e., citations in high cite fields (e.g., neuroscience, pharmacology) are worth less than a citation in a low cite fields (mathematics, humanities).

Note:

- SJR only considers peer reviewed articles, reviews and conference papers.
- Scimago uses the Scopus database and journal classification scheme to rank journals by quartiles across subject areas. Computation of SJR is an iterative process that distributes prestige values among the journals until a steady-state solution is reached, similar to the methodology used for Google PageRankTM. The average SJR value for all journals in Scopus is 1.000.
- SJR scores are available from the two databases: *SCIMago Journal and Country Rank* and *Scopus.*

3. Source-Normalized Impact per Paper (SNIP): SNIP is developed by Leiden University's Centre for Science & Technology Studies (CWTS). Source-normalized Impact per Paper (SNIP) is a field normalised assessment of journal impact. SNIP scores are the ratio of a source's average citation count and *'citation potential'*. Citation potential is measured as the number of citations that a journal would be expected to receive for its subject field. Essentially, the longer the reference list of a citing publication, the lower the value of a citation originating from that publication. SNIP therefore allows for direct comparison between fields of research with different publication and citation practices.

The Scopus database is the source of data used to calculate SNIP scores. SNIP is calculated as the number of citations given in the present year to publications in the past three years divided by the total number of publications in the past three years. A journal with a SNIP of 1.0 has the median (not mean) number of citations for journals in that field.

Note:

- SNIP only considers for peer reviewed articles, conference papers and reviews.
- SNIP scores are available from the two databases: *CWTS Journal Indicators* and *Scopus.*

Note: Both SJR and SNIP are available in Scopus. However, SJR can also be accessed via Scimago Journal & Country Rank page (free source).

Use SJR	*Use SNIP*
to enhance position of post-prestigious journals (SJR emphasizes the differences)	if value is less important than rank (SNIP reduces the differences)
if focusing on Life and Health Sciences	if focusing on Engineering, Computer Science, and Social Sciences
if topicality is important in journal performance	if you are focused on subject field normalization
if you want to weight citations based on the status of the citing journal	if you think that impact and topicality are separate and should be considered independently

1. *Find SJR or SNIP for a specific journal*:
   - ► Step 1. Go to Scopus and click *"Sources"* at the top of the page.
   - ► Step 2. Under *"Title"*, type in the journal title in the search box and click *"Find sources"*.

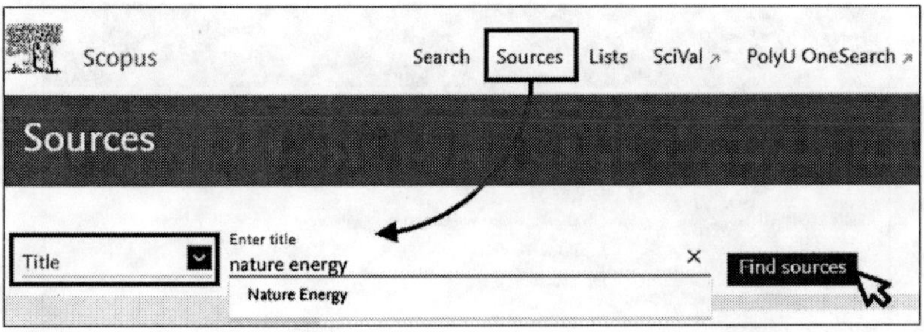

   - ► Step 3. Click on the journal title to find the SNIP and SJR of the journal.

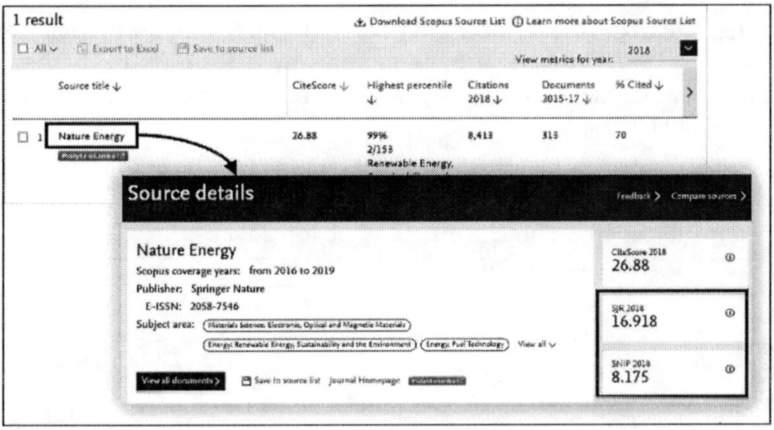

From the result list, you may also expand the header to find SNIP and SJR of the journal.

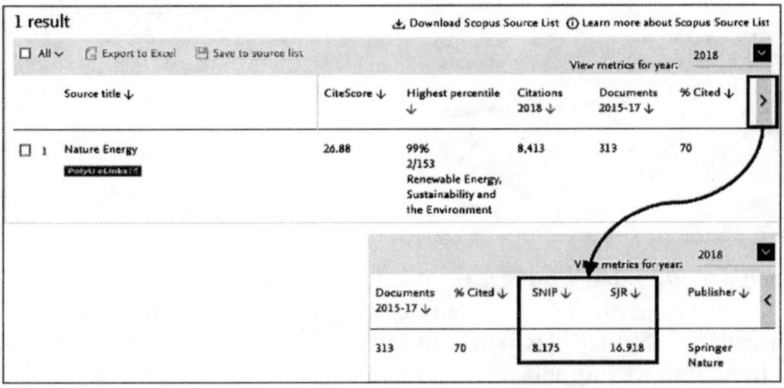

2. *Check journal ranking by SNIP or SJR in a specific subject category*:
   - ► Step 1. Go to Scopus and click *"Sources"* at the top of the page.

▶ Step 2. Under *"Subject area"*, search a subject area, check relevant subject area(s), and click *"Apply"*.

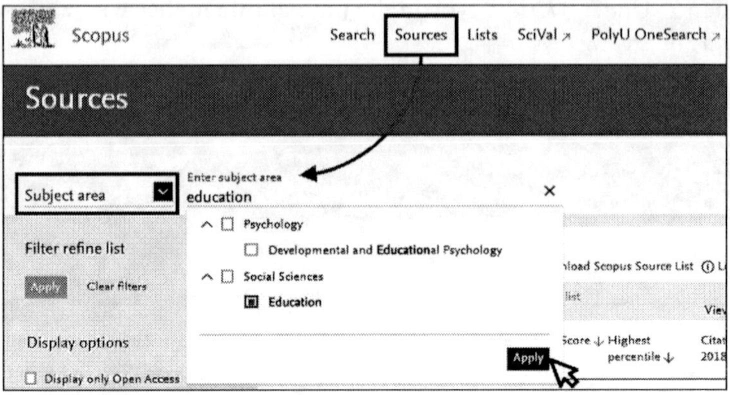

▶ Step 3. Expand the result list to find SNIP and SJR of the journal list. Click *"SJR"* or *"SNIP"* header to rank journals by SJR or SNIP. By default, the journals are ranked by CiteScore, another metric available in Scopus. Learn more about CiteScore here.

In this example, we can see the journal ranking by SJR in *"Education"* field. You may further limit results to only those journals listed in certain quartile(s) of their subject area, e.g., 1st quartile (the top 25%).

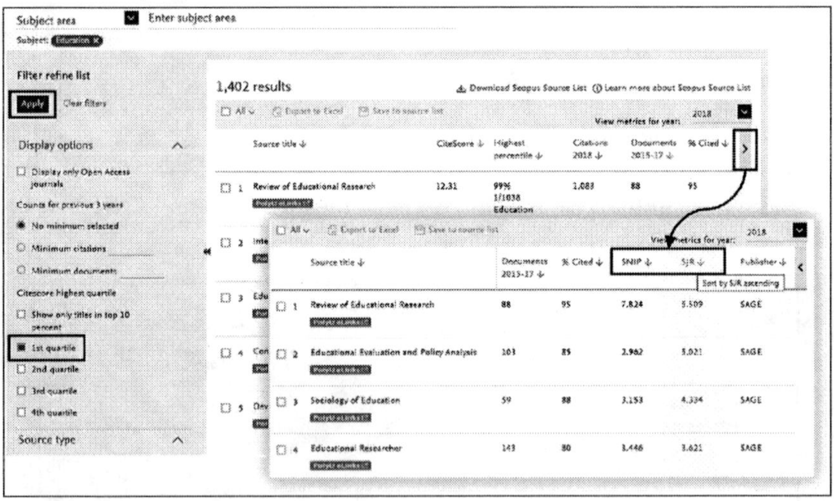

3. *Compare journals & Save favourite journals for future use*:
After you have identified some journals, you may save them in a list for easy comparison. Saved lists can also be very helpful if you need to check the metrics of these journals on a regular basis.
▶ Step 1. Select the journal(s) you are interested. Then click *"Save to source list"*. Sign in with your personal Scopus account. Create a new account if you haven't done so. Note that you can use your Elsevier credentials to sign in Scopus.

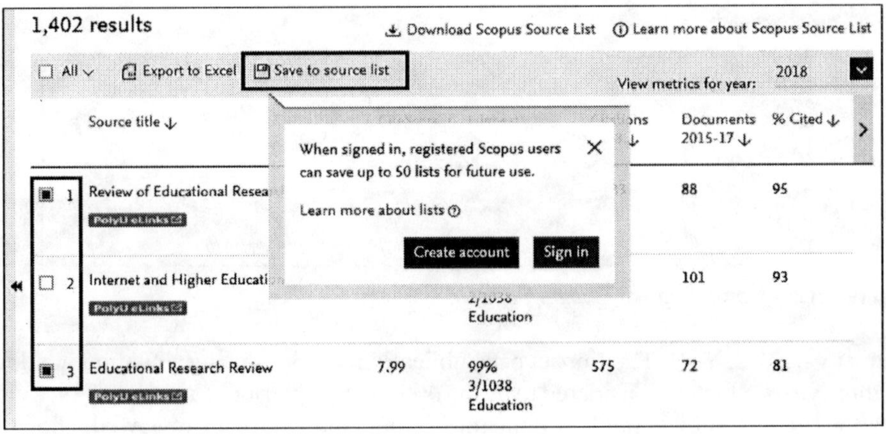

▶ Step 2. Enter name of a new list, or select an existing list from your saved lists. Then click *"Save list"*.

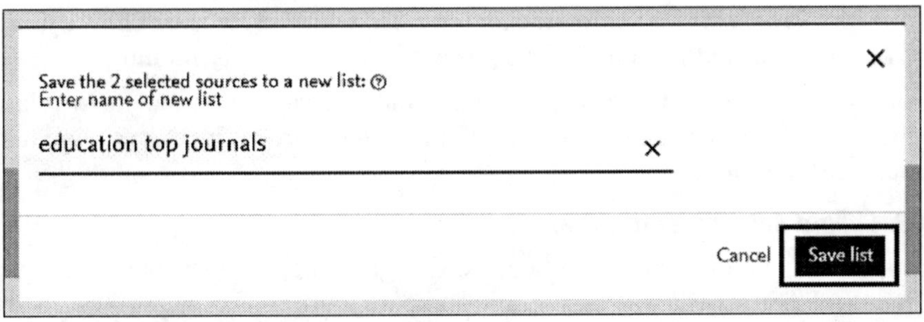

▶ Step 3. Click *"Lists"* from the top menu. Then move to *"Sources"* to find all your saved lists. You may edit the name of the list or delete the list from this page.

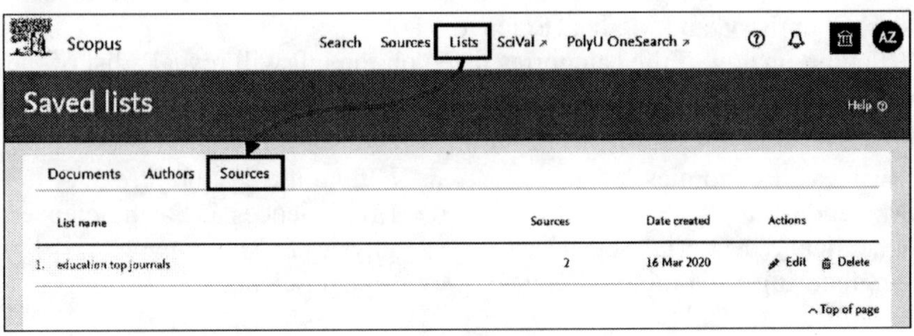

4. Impact per Publication (IPP): The Impact per Publication (IPP) is based on citations in one year to articles, reviews, and conference papers published in the preceding three years, divided by the number of articles, reviews, and conference papers published in those three years. The Impact per Publication measures the ratio of citations in a year (Y) to scholarly papers published in the three previous years (Y-1, Y-2, Y-3) divided by the number of scholarly papers published in those same

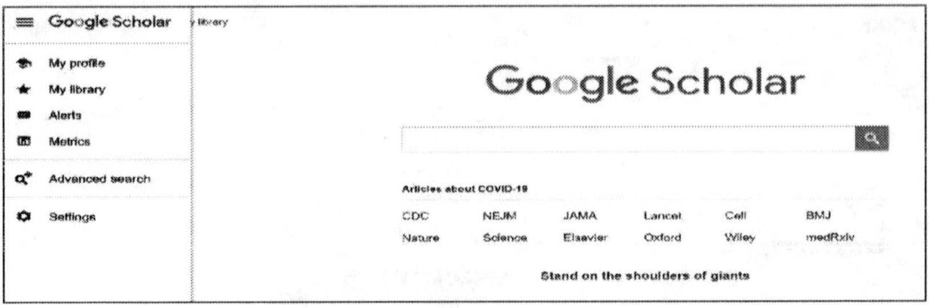

Figure 8.12 *Home Page of Google Scholar*

years (Y-1, Y-2, Y-3). The Impact per Publication metric is using a citation window of three years which is considered to be the optimal time period to accurately measure citations in most subject fields. Taking into account the same peer-reviewed scholarly papers only in both the numerator and denominator of the equation provides a fair impact measurement of the journal and diminishes the change of manipulation.

5. *CiteScore Tracker*: CiteScore Tracker provides a current review of how a journal is performing during the course of the year. It is updated every month.

6. *CiteScore Percentile*: CiteScore Percentile indicates how a journal ranks relative to other journals in the same subject field. (The fields are defined according to the Scopus field definitions).

8.8.3. Google Scholar Journal Metrics

Like Journal Citation Report and Scopus, Google Scholar collects and distributes journal level metrics as a way to rank and compare journals. To access these metrics click on the link on the Google Scholar home page titled "*Metrics.*"

The landing page for Google Scholar Metrics shows a list of the top 100 publications across disciplines in multiple languages, despite the fact that they are labelled English language. Most of these top publications are from the Sciences, Physics, Chemistry, and Medical Science.

Clicking on any of the categories listed on the left will reveal a list of the top 20 publications in that broad subject area. Each of these primary categories offers a list of subcategories within that primary area. There are 8 categories:

- Business, Economics & Management
- Chemical & Material Sciences
- Engineering & Computer Science
- Health & Medical Sciences
- Humanities, Literature & Arts
- Life Sciences & Earth Sciences
- Physics & Mathematics
- Social Sciences

The image below shows the top journals for the main category 'Social Sciences' and shows the subcategories 'Education' for this main category.

8.8.3.1. Metrics of Google Scholar Journal Metrics

1. *h-index*: The h-index was originally developed to measure an author's productivity and impact. In journal ranking the h-index is calculated such that

Categories > Social Sciences > Education ▾

	Publication	h5-index	h5-median
1.	Teaching and Teacher Education	69	93
2.	Review of Educational Research	59	139
3.	British Journal of Educational Technology	59	101
4.	Studies in Higher Education	59	81
5.	Higher Education	54	75
6.	Educational Psychology Review	52	97
7.	The International Review of Research in Open and Distributed Learning	51	83
8.	Learning and Instruction	51	76
9.	Educational Researcher	49	101
10.	American Educational Research Journal	48	75
11.	Contemporary Educational Psychology	48	70
12.	Journal of Research in Science Teaching	48	66
13.	Educational Evaluation and Policy Analysis	46	74
14.	Early Childhood Research Quarterly	45	66
15.	Economics of Education Review	43	65

Figure 8.13 *Top Journals List in Google Scholar*

within a journal with an h-index score of 30, there exists 30 journals that have been cited at least 30 times.

2. *h5-index*: The h5-index is the h-index for articles published in the last 5 complete years. It is the largest number h such that h articles published in 2010-2014 have at least h citations each.

3. *h5-median*: The h5-median for a publication is the median number of citations for the articles that make up its h5-index

8.8.4. CWTS Journal Indicators

CWTS Journal Indicators provides free access to bibliometric indicators on scientific journals. The indicators have been calculated by Leiden University's Centre for Science and Technology Studies (CWTS) based on the Scopus bibliographic database produced by Elsevier. Indicators are available for over 20,000 journals indexed in the Scopus database.

Indicators

CWTS Journal Indicators currently provides four indicators:

- *P*: The number of publications of a source in the past three years.
- *Impact per Publication (IPP)*: The impact per publication, calculated as the number of citations given in the present year to publications in the past three years divided by the total number of publications in the past three years. IPP is fairly similar to the well-known journal impact factor. Like the journal impact factor, IPP does not correct for differences in citation practices

between scientific fields. IPP was previously known as *RIP (raw impact per publication).*

- *Source Normalized Impact per Publication (SNIP)*: A key indicator offered by CWTS Journal Indicators is the SNIP indicator The original version of the SNIP indicator was developed by Henk Moed in 2009 and is documented in a scientific paper (an open access preprint is available here). In 2012, SNIP was revised, leading to some changes in the way it is calculated.
- The source normalized impact per publication, calculated as the number of citations given in the present year to publications in the past three years divided by the total number of publications in the past three years. The difference with IPP is that in the case of SNIP citations are normalized in order to correct for differences in citation practices between scientific fields. Essentially, the longer the reference list of a citing publication, the lower the value of a citation originating from that publication. A detailed explanation is offered in our scientific paper.
- *% Self Citation*: The percentage of self-citations of a source, calculated as the percentage of all citations given in the present year to publications in the past three years that originate from the source itself.

Example of a Source Normalized Impact per Paper (SNIP) Search
To compare journals in a specific subject field, follow the steps:

- ▸ Step 1. Go to CWTS Journal Indicators web site.
- ▸ Step 2. Click on the Indicators tab.
- ▸ Step 3. Make your selections from the drop down menus. In this search, the SNIP Indicators for journals in Psychology are shown below:

8.8.5. SCImago Journal Rank (SJR)

SCImago Journal Rank (SJR) is a portal that includes the journals and country scientific indicators developed from the information contained in the Scopus database (Elsevier). It is also a prestige metric based on the idea that *"all citations are not created equal."* With SJR, the subject field, quality and reputation of the journal has a direct effect on the value of a citation. Using the Google Page Rank algorithm, it was developed by a research group from the Consejo Superior de Investigaciones Científicas (CSIC), University of Granada, Extremadura, Carlos III (Madrid) and Alcalá de Henares.

Map Generator for Subject Citation Relationship
With the SJR tool, researchers can create maps or bubble charts based on a subject citation relationship for a particular country. Below is a map generated for India.

Example of a SCImago Journal & Country Rank (SJR) Search
To compare journals in a specific subject field, follow the steps:

- ▸ Step 1. Go to SCImago Journal & Country Rank web site.
- ▸ Step 2. Click on 'Explore' under 'Journals Ranks'
- ▸ Step 3. Make your selections from the menus- like subject areas, subject categories, all regions/countries etc.

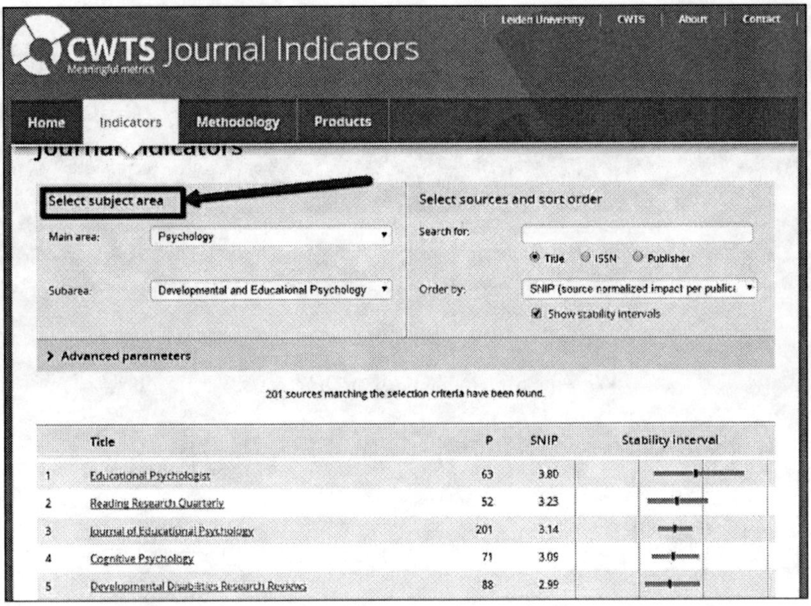

Figure 8.14 *Home Page of CWTS Journal Indicators*

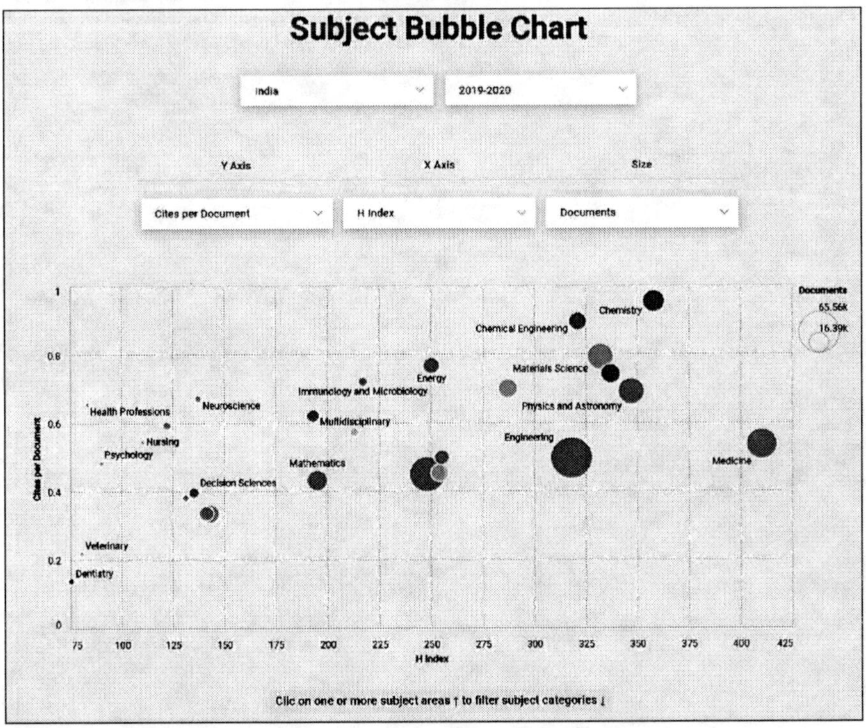

Figure 8.15 *Country Search in SCImago Journal Rank (SJR)*

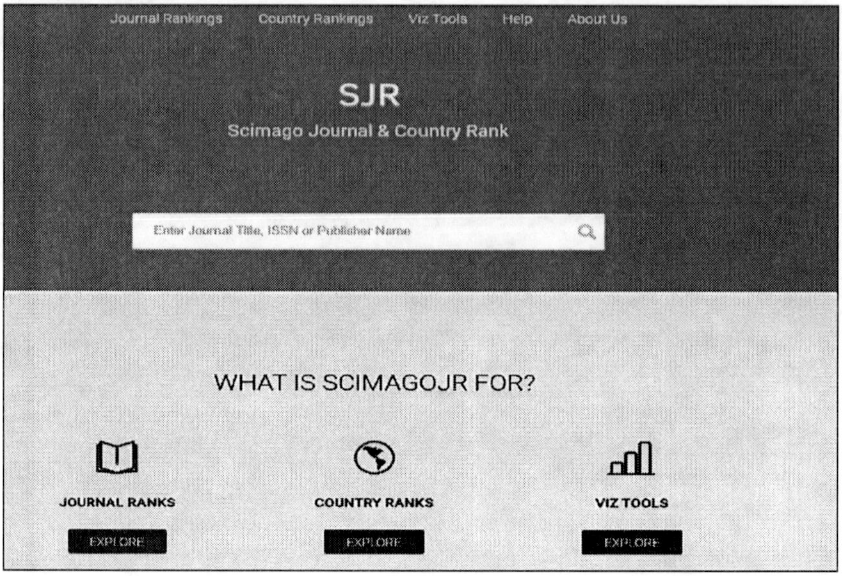

Figure 8.16 *Home Page of SJR*

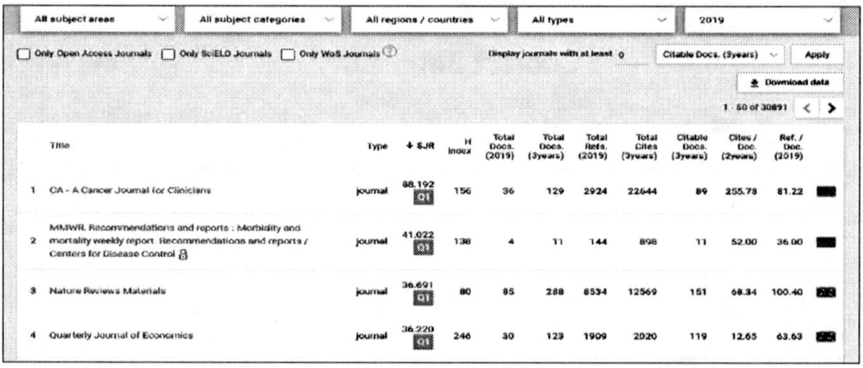

Figure 8.17 *Comparing Journal Rankings*

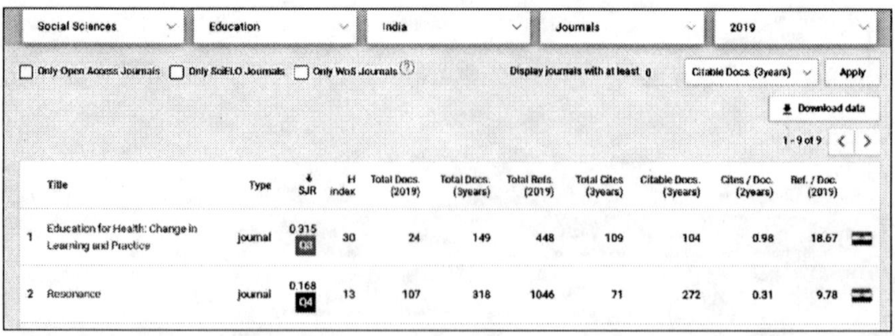

Figure 8.18 *SJR Journal Rankings on different Metrices*

▶ Step 4. Click the 'Apply' button to generate a report comparing journal rankings. You can generate similar reports for comparing different countries:

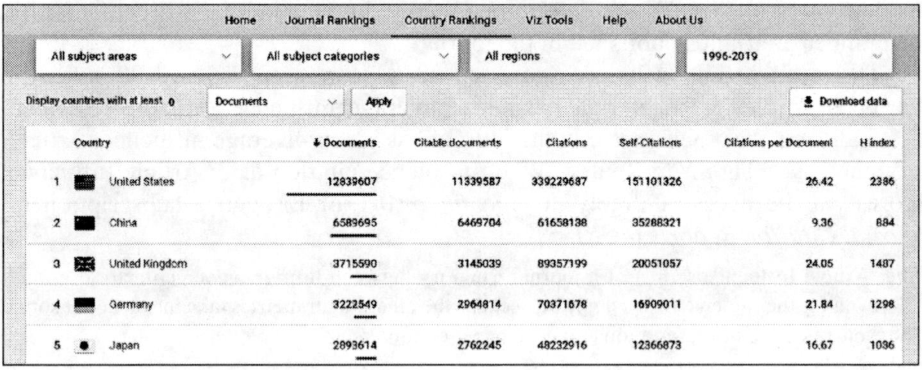

	Country	Documents	Citable documents	Citations	Self-Citations	Citations per Document	H index
1	United States	12839607	11339587	339229687	151101326	26.42	2386
2	China	6589695	6469704	61658138	35288321	9.36	884
3	United Kingdom	3715590	3145039	89357199	20051057	24.05	1487
4	Germany	3222549	2964814	70371678	16909011	21.84	1298
5	Japan	2893614	2762245	48232916	12366873	16.67	1036

Figure 8.19 *Country Rankings*

8.8.6. Eigenfactor

Eigenfactor.org is a project of Bergstrom Lab at the University of Washington. The goal of Eigenfactor is to rate a journal's importance to the scholarly community. Towards that goal, Eigenfactor gathers data from around the web, including Thomson Scientific's Journal Citation Reports. Using the same dataset as "Journal Citation Reports" (JCR), the Eigenfactor metrics try to overcome some problems inherent to the JCR Impact Factor:

- Citation data are gathered for 5 years
- Self-citations are removed
- Quality of the citing journals is considered
- Differences in citation patterns among disciplines are adjusted

The Eigengactor project provides three types of metrics, which are all freely available at their website Eigenfactor.org:

8.8.6.1. Eigenfactor Score (EF)

The Eigenfactor Score measures the number of times articles from the journal published in the past five years have been cited in the Journal Citation Reports (JCR) year. Like the Impact Factor, the Eigenfactor Score is essentially a ratio of number of citations to total number of articles. However, unlike the Impact Factor, the Eigenfactor Score:

- Counts citations to journals in both the sciences and social sciences.
- Eliminates self-citations. Every reference from one article in a journal to another article from the same journal is discounted.
- Weights each reference according to a stochastic measure of the amount of time researchers spend reading the journal.

Eigenfactor scores are scaled so that the sum of the Eigenfactor scores of all journals listed in Thomson's Journal Citation Reports (JCR) is 100. The Eigenfactor uses Thomson Reuters Web of Science citation data.

8.8.6.2. Article Influence (AI)

The Article Influence is the ranking of a journal based on the influence of the articles that journal publishes. This is determined by dividing the journal's Eigenfactor by the number of articles published in the journal.

The mean Article Influence Score is 1.00. A score greater than 1.00 indicates that each article in the journal has above-average influence. A score less than 1.00 indicates that each article in the journal has below-average influence. Article Influence uses Thomson Reuters Web of Science citation data. Article Influence Scores can be accessed freely at *eigenfactor.org* or through a subscription to *Journal Citation Reports (JCR).*

Note: Article Influence scores of a journal can vary between http://www.eigenfactor.org/ and JCR, even for the same year. This may be because the eigenfactor metrics take into account some other sources, such as dissertation and newspaper citations.

8.8.6.3. Normalized Eigenfactor Score (EFn)

The Normalized Eigenfactor Score is the Eigenfactor score normalized, by rescaling the total number of journals in the JCR each year, so that the average journal has a score of 1. Journals can then be compared and influence measured by their score relative to 1. For example, if a journal has a Normalized Eigenfactor Score of 5, that journal is considered to be 5 times as influential as the average journal in the JCR.

How to find the Eigenfactor:

- To find a journal's Eigenfactor score, Article Influence, or Normalized Eigenfactor score, go to the Journal Ranking Search page on the Eigenfactor website.
- From the Journal Ranking search page, you can search for a journal name, ISSN, publisher, year, ISI category or exact journal name.
- Once you do a search and have a list of results, click the journal listing to see additional information on rankings.

The Journal Ranking page may include the name of the journal and ISSN, the Eignfactor score (EF); Article Influence number (AI) and the Normalized Eigenfactor number (EFn). Additional information about the journal, such as publisher, cost, number of articles published, etc. Graphs showing article influence and cost effectiveness of the journal are included.

8.9. Measuring Author Impact

Author-level metrics are citation metrics that measure the bibliometric impact of individual authors, researchers, academics and scholars. Author metrics are measures of the influence and productivity of an author or researcher. Many metrics have been developed that take into account varying numbers of factors (from only considering total number of citations, to looking at their distribution across papers or journals using statistical or graph-theoretic principles).

Author-level metrics help track an individual researcher's impact in an academic discipline. This is traditionally calculated by using the number of times their

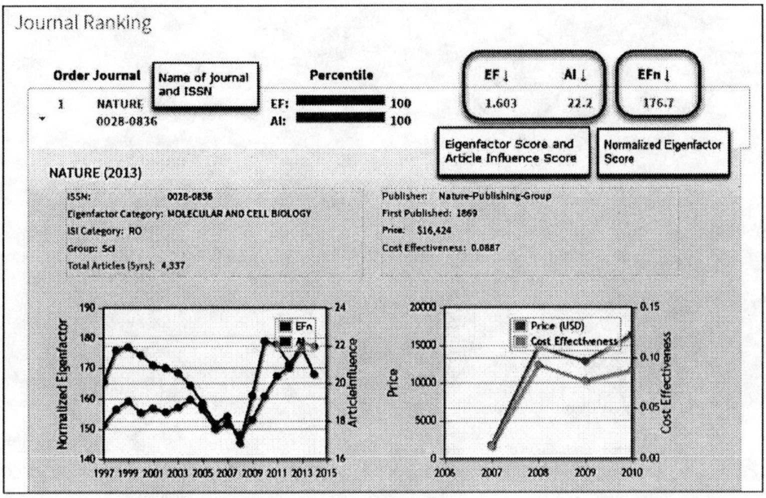

Figure 8.20 *Three Types of Metrics of Eigenfactor*

scholarly publications are cited by other researchers. These impact factors can help in promotion and tenure, as well as aiding in funding and grants.

8.9.1. Author Citation Tracking

Citation tracking looks at the number of times a particular work or author have been cited in the bibliographies of other works. This gives some indication of how the author has been received by the academic community. Large numbers of citations are associated with greater impact and more influence. By demonstrating where and how one's work has been cited, author citation metrics can:

- Identify key authors in a field
- Indicate an author's perceived value in that field
- Discover who is doing related work
- Track the published works of colleagues, collaborators or competitors
- Be used for purposes of hiring, tenure or promotion

Article and author level citation counts are available on Web of Science, Google Scholar, PLoS, BioMed Central and some discipline-specific databases.

8.9.2. Types of Author Metrics

Different algorithms have been created that calculate an author impact 'score' using data on their publications. Below are a few metrics you may encounter:

8.9.2.1. h-Index

The *h*-index was proposed by J.E. Hirsch in 2005 and published in the Proceedings of the National Academy of Sciences of the United States of America. The *h* index is a quantitative metric based on analysis of publication data using publications and citations to provide *"an estimate of the importance, significance, and broad impact of a scientist's cumulative research contributions."* According to Hirsch,

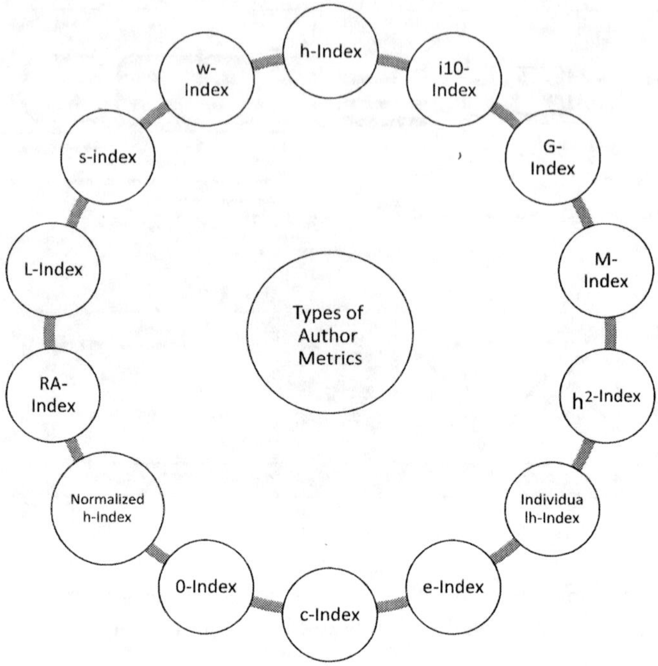

Figure 8.21 *Types of Author Metrics*

the h index is defined as: *"A scientist has index h if h of his or her Np papers have at least h citations each and the other (Np – h) papers have ≤h citations each."*

The *h*-index is an author-level metric that attempts to measure both the productivity and citation impact of the publications of a scientist or scholar. The index is based on the set of the research scholar's most cited papers and the number of citations that they have received in other publications. The *h*-index, originally described in 2005 by Jorge Hirsch, is a measurement that aims to describe the scientific productivity and impact of a researcher. Like all metrics, the h-index is not perfect, however, it addresses many of the problems associated with impact factors and the publication process in general and enables some very interesting analyses. The research index is a measure of the number of highly impactful papers a researcher has published.

The larger the number of important papers, the higher is the h-index, irrespective of where the work is published. To calculate it, only two pieces of information are required: the total number of papers published (Np) and the number of citations (Nc) for each paper. The *h*-index is defined by how many *h* of a researcher's publications (Np) have at least h citations each. *H*-index increases with increase in number of publications and by increase in citations of increased number of papers. By publishing n number of papers each having n number of citations gives *h*-index value *n*.

1. Advantages of h-Index: The h index has several advantages over other metrics:

- It relies on citations to your papers, not the journals, which is a truer measure of quality;

- It is not dramatically skewed by a single well-cited, influential paper (unlike total number of citations would be);
- It is not increased by a large number of poorly cited papers (unlike total number of papers would be);
- It minimizes the politics of publication. A high-impact paper counts regardless of whether your competitor kept it from being published in the top-tier journals;
- It's good for comparing scientists within a field at similar stages in their careers;
- It may be used to compare not just individuals, but also departments, programs or any other group of scientists;
- Since the most highly cited articles contribute to the h-index, its determination is a simpler process;
- The h-index is intended to measure the quality and quantity of scholarly published papers simultaneously.

2. Benefits of h-Index: The important benefits of h-index value of individuals/ institutions are:

- The *h*-index gives an idea on quantity and quality of scholarly published papers simultaneously so that based on h-index value of an individual or organization, one can judge the scientific contribution of individual or organization.
- *H*-index cannot be more than number of publication or number of citations so that an author intended to increase h-index has to continuously increase his publications along with citable papers.
- *H*-index value identifies the ranking of an author/organization in scientific community.

3. Constraints of h-Index

- It counts a highly-cited paper regardless of why it's being referenced- e.g., for negative reasons.
- It does not account for variations in average number of publications and citations in various fields (some traditionally publish and cite less than others).

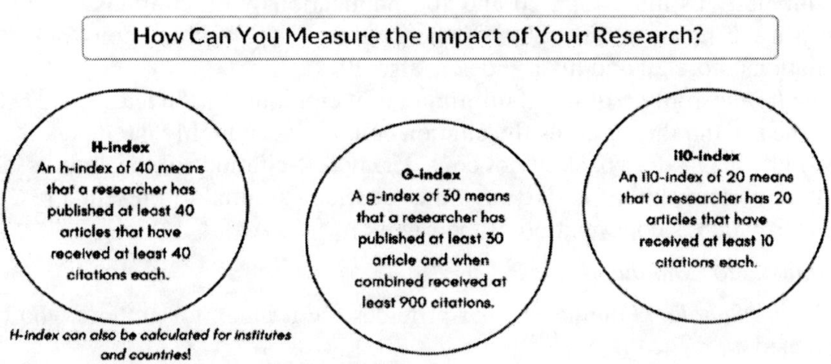

Figure 8.22 *Difference between H-Index, G-Index and i10-Index*

- It ignores the number and position of authors on a paper.
- It limits authors by the total number of publications, so shorter careers are at a disadvantage.
- It has relatively low resolution in that many scientists end up in the same range since it gets increasingly difficult to increase the h-index the higher it gets (an h-index of 100 corresponds to a minimum of 10,000 citations).
- It, like all metrics, is based on data from the past and may not be a valid predictor of future performance. However, in a follow-up publication Jorge Hirsch demonstrated that the h-index is better than other indicators (total papers, total citations, citations per paper) at predicting future scientific achievement.

4. Disadvantages of h-Index: The important disadvantages of *h*-index value of individuals/institutions are:

- The *h*-index does not provide a significantly more accurate measure of total number of papers published by a given scholar.
- The *h*-index does not provide a significantly more accurate measure of impact than the total number of citations for a given scholar.
- The *h*-index only counts the number of papers (n) of an author which have n number of citations. It does not give any idea on the accounting for the rank in the sequence of authors.
- The *h*-index does not provide any idea on total time duration the published papers took to reach current h-index value.
- The scholars researching in a unique area may not get many citations so that even if they publish more papers their citations and hence the h-index may be at low value.
- The scholars with less number of publications but more citations per paper may have low value of h index.
- *H*-index cannot be used to measure the annual research performance of the authors.
- *H*-index value does not give accurate value of author's publications as well as citations and hence confusing. For example, an author has 20 publications with citations more than 20 and 100 publications with citations close to 20 and his h-index is only 20. Another author has 20 publications only with citations more 20 and his h-index is also 20.
- The *h*-index only requires a minimum of n citations for the least-cited article in the set and thus ignores the citation count of very highly cited papers.
- *H*-index has a drawback of not considering self-citations of the authors. Self-citation by an author is like any other citation essential to present a research paper which is continuation of their work.

5. Resources to Find the h-Index

- *Google Scholar*: Google Scholar provides the h index for authors who have created a profile.
- *Publish or Perish*: Publish or Perish is a software program that retrieves and analyzes academic citations from Google Scholar and provides the h index

among other metrics. Publish or Perish is handy for obtaining the h index for authors who do not have a Google Scholar profile.

- *Scopus*: Scopus provides a Citation Tracker feature that allows for generation of a Citation Overview chart to generate a h index for publications and citations from 1970 to current. The feature also allows for removal of self-citations from the overall citation counts.
- *Web of Science*: Web of Science allows for generation of the h index for publications and citations from 1970 to current using the "Create Citation Report" feature.

8.9.2.2. i10-Index

*i*10-Index is the number of publications of an author with at least 10 citations. The *i*10-index indicates the number of academic publications an author has written that have been cited by at least 10 sources. This very simple measure is only used by Google Scholar and is another way to help gauge the productivity of a scholar. It was introduced in July 2011 by Google as part of their work on Google Scholar.

1. Advantages of i10-Index

- Very simple and straightforward to calculate
- My Citations in Google Scholar is free and easy to use
- Authors can identify the important papers out of their publications which have contributed for the continuation of research based on received at least 10 citations.
- *i*10 index gives an idea of quantity and quality of scholarly published papers of an author simultaneously.

2. Benefits of i10-index: The important benefits of i10--index value of individuals/ institutions are:

- Gives an idea of author's research impact in terms of a number of publications reached 10 citations.
- Continuous evaluation method without any timeframe.
- Gives comparative performance of published papers of different researchers in the same field.
- Can be shown along with other indices to show the impact of an author.

3. Constraints of ilo-Index

- Only 10 citations of a publication are counted.
- Citations of the papers lower than 10 are not counted in calculation and hence less specific.
- Total number of publications and total number of citations of an author is not taken into account for calculation of *i*10-index. Thus, it gives a vague idea of authors research productivity.

4. Disadvantages of i10-Index

- Used only in Google Scholar
- *i*10-index becomes stagnant once all published papers reach 10 citations.

- It does not count number of publications or number of total citations of an author.
- It does not signify the position of the author in the sequence of authors of the published paper.
- It does not identify single author papers, annual research contribution of an author.

8.9.2.3. G-Index

G-index is an improved version of *h*-index. In the theory and practice of the *g*-index, the inventor, 'Leo Egghe' (2006) aims to improve on the *h*-index by giving more weight to highly-cited articles. The *g*-index is an index for quantifying scientific productivity based on publications and calculated based on the distribution of citations received by a given researcher's publications. So, given a set of articles ranked in decreasing order of the number of citations that they receive, the *g*-index is the (unique) largest number such that the top *g* articles received (together) at least g^2 (g square) citations. For the citations received and given a number of papers ranked in a decreasing order according to the citations received till now, the *G*-index is the biggest number such that the top *G* articles received (altogether) at least G^2 (G square) citations. This index assists the *h*-index and gives more weight to the highly-cited papers.

1 Advantages of G-Index

- Improved version of *h*-index and hence represents both number of publications and number of citations.
- *G*-index calculation methodology gives more weightage to highly cited papers.
- The *g*-index is an alternative for the *h*-index, which does not average the numbers of citations.
- In a group of authors of the same field, the variance of the *g*-indexes will be much higher than the one of the *h*-indexes which make a comparison between authors concerning their visibility in the world more apparent.

2. Benefits of G-Index

- *G*-index allows citations from higher-cited papers to be used to bolster lower-cited and hence in all cases the *g*-index value is in most cases higher than *h*-index value.
- *G*-index helps to make more apparent the difference between authors' respective impacts. The inflated values of the *G*-Index help to give credit to lowly-cited or non-cited papers while giving credit for highly-cited papers.
- More scientific than *h*-index.

3. Constraints of G-Index

- *G*-index saturates whenever the average number of citations for all published papers exceeds the total number of published papers and hence cannot be used in such cases.
- After introducing in the year 2006, the researchers have still confusion to replace *g*-index with *h*-index and hence not widely accepted.

4. Disadvantages of G-Index

- Like the *h*-index, the *g*-index is a natural number and thus lacks in discriminatory power.
- Like *h*-index, *g*-index failed to give absolute value of a total number of papers published by an author during a given period.
- *G*-index also fails to represent the total citations of an author during a given period.

8.9.2.4. M-Index

The *m*-index, also proposed by Hirsch, is defined as *h*-index divided by the number of years since the Researcher's first publication. The index is meant to normalize the *h*-index so that early- and late-stage scientists can be compared. The *m*-index averages periods of high and low productivity throughout a career, which may or may not be reflective of the current situation of the scientist.

1. Advantages of M-Index

- Improved version of *H*-index and hence can be better than h-index.
- Averages the low and high citations received during the long period of the career.
- Includes the number of years research as the third variable.

2. Benefits of M-Index

- More specific than *h*-index due to the usage of total years of research as a third variable component.
- While comparing the citation values of two or more people, their earlier stage of career or late stage of career can be identified and differentiated.
- Due to averaging of high and low productivity of scientists throughout their career, the low performance of one period may be compensated with high performance during another period.

3. Constraints of M-Index

- Calculation of *m*-index needs time in years as the third variable unlike two variable based *h*-index calculation.
- Determining the first publication time for old researchers is a cumbersome process.
- Determining a number of publications, a number of citations, and a number of years of involvement in research and publications is a bit difficult compared to *h*-index or *i*-10 index calculation.

4. Disadvantages of M-Index

- The m-index averages periods of high and low productivity throughout a career, which may or may not be reflective of the current situation of the scientist.
- *M*-index may give fraction value for a given researcher unlike *h*-index, and *i*-10 index.

8.9.2.5. Individual h-Index

An individual h-index normalized by the number of authors has been proposed: $h_I = h^2/N_a^{(T)}$, with $N_a^{(T)}$ being the number of authors considered in the h papers. It was found that the distribution of the h-index, although it depends on the field, can be normalized by a simple rescaling factor. For example, assuming as standard the hs for biology, the distribution of h for mathematics collapse with it if this h is multiplied by three, that is, a mathematician with $h = 3$ is equivalent to a biologist with $h = 9$. This method has not been readily adopted, perhaps because of its complexity. It might be simpler to divide citation counts by the number of authors before ordering the papers and obtaining the h-index, as originally suggested by Hirsch.

8.9.2.6. h^2

Three additional metrics have been proposed: h^2 lower, h^2 center, and h^2 upper, to give a more accurate representation of the distribution shape. The three h^2 metrics measure the relative area within a scientist's citation distribution in the low impact area, h^2 lower, the area captured by the h-index, h^2 center, and the area from publications with the highest visibility, h^2 upper. Scientists with high h^2 upper percentages are perfectionists, whereas scientists with high h^2 lower percentages are mass producers. As these metrics are percentages, they are intended to give a qualitative description to supplement the quantitative h-index.

8.9.2.7. e-Index

The e-index, the square root of surplus citations for the h-set beyond h^2, complements the h-index for ignored citations, and therefore is especially useful for highly cited scientists and for comparing those with the same h-index.

8.9.2.8. c-Index

The c-index accounts not only for the citations but for the quality of the citations in terms of the collaboration distance between citing and cited authors. A scientist has c-index n if n of [his/her] N citations are from authors which are at collaboration distance at least n, and the other (N − n) citations are from authors which are at collaboration distance at most n.

8.9.2.9. o-Index

The o-index corresponds to the geometric mean of the h-index and the most cited paper of a researcher.

8.9.2.10. Normalized h-Index

The h-index has been shown to have a strong discipline bias. However, a simple normalization $h/\langle h\rangle_d$ by the average h of scholars in a discipline d is an effective way to mitigate this bias, obtaining a universal impact metric that allows comparison of scholars across different disciplines.

8.9.2.11. RA-Index

The RA-index accommodates improving the sensitivity of the h-index on the number of highly cited papers and has many cited paper and uncited paper under the h-core. This improvement can enhance the measurement sensitivity of the h-index.

8.9.2.12. L-Index

L-index combines the number of citations, the number of co-authors, the age of publications into a single value, which is independent of the number of publications and conveniently ranges from 0.0 to 9.9.[31] With c as number of citations, a as number of authors and y as number of years, L-index is defined by the formula:

$$L = ln(\sum_i \frac{c_i}{a_i * y_i}) + 1$$

8.9.2.13. s-Index

An s-index, accounting for the non-entropic distribution of citations, has been proposed and it has been shown to be in a very good correlation with *h*.

8.9.2.14. w-Index

w-index is defined as follows: if w of a researcher's papers has at least 10*w* citations each and the other papers have fewer than 10(*w* + 1) citations, that researcher's w-index is *w*.

8.10. Popular Research Indices Currently Used

Research indices are calculated based on either citation values of research publications of a research scholar or the number of research papers published by a research scholar for a given period. There are many research indices developed in various by many researchers which include H-, i10-, G-, H (2)-, HG-, Q2-, AR-, M-quotient, M-, W-, Hw-, E-, A-, R-, W-, J-index, etc.. Out of these citation-based research indices, h-index, G-index and i10-index are commonly used in some of the Citation databases. Table 8.1, lists some of the popular research indices used based on Citations.

Table 8.1 *Some of the popular research indices used based on Citations*

S. No.	*Research Indices*	*Developer*	*Commonly using in Citation Databases*
1	h-index	Jorge Hirsch (2005)	Web of Science Indexing. Scopus Indexing. Google Scholar Indexing. Chemical Abstracts
2	G-Index	Leo Egghe (2006)	Encyclopedia of Information Science and Technology
3	i10-Index	Google (2011)	Google scholar indexing.
4	R-index	Reserchgate	Reserchgate
5	m-index	Jorge Hirsch	Improvement in H-index

8.11. Comparison of traditional and Alternative Metrics Sites

Besides traditional citation counts, there are many ways of tracking research impacts. They try to capture the presence in new scholarly venues, presence and impact in social media and other forms of online engagement, such as views, downloads, bookmarks etc. Collectively, we refer to these as altmetrics, as opposed to traditional citation measurement using Web of Science, Scopus and other citation enhanced databases.

Metrics	Journal Citation Reports	Scopus	Web of Science	Google Scholar	Google Scholar Citation	Microsoft Academic Search	Mandeley	Impact Story	PLoS	Altmetric	Plum Analytics
Metrics For:											
Article		√	√	√	√	√	√[a]	√[a]	√	√	√
Author		√	√		√	√		√[a]		√[b]	√
Journal											
Institution		√	√			√	√[b]			√[b]	√
Country		√	√								
Traditional Metrics:											
Citations	√	√	√	√	√	√		√	√		√
Altmetrics:											
Views/downloads								√[c]	√		√
Reads/bookmarks/tags							√	√	√	√	√
Comments									√		
News media							√			√	
Blogs								√	√	√	√
Facebook								√	√	√	√
Twitter								√	√	√	√
Coverage:											
Transparency	√	√	√						√		
Multidisciplinary	√	√	√	√	√	√	√	√	√[c]	√	√

Access:											
Free access				√	√	√	√	√[d]	√	√[d]	
Registration necessary					√		√	√			
Paid service	√	√	√				√[b]	√		√[b]	√
Advanced options:											
Data download/ management	√	√	√	√[c]	√[c]	√[c]		√[c]	√	√[b]	√[b]
Data standardization/ cleaning	√	√	√			√[c]					
Normalization	√	√	√					√[c]	√[c]		
API possibilities	√[c]	√[c]	√[c]			√[c]	√	√	√	√	√

Notes:

[a] Only items/persons/users included in the system (depends on data collected/uploaded by the users)

[b] Paid services: Mendeley Institutional Edition / Altmetric Institutional Edition / Altmetric Explorer

[c] With restrictions/limitations

[d] Article level metrics (Mendeley, Altmetric) and author profiles (ImpactStory) free to view.

9

Open Access Publishing

Open access began as a serious scholarly communications movement in the early 2000s, when developments in information and communications technology increasingly allowed research publications to be accessed online. Its goal is to make this material openly available online without restriction to all readers, free from the barriers imposed by subscription access

Open access (OA) means free access to information and unrestricted use of electronic resources for everyone. Any kind of digital content can be OA, from texts and data to software, audio, video, and multi-media. While most of these are related to text only, a growing number are integrating text with images, data, and executable code. OA can also apply to non-scholarly content, like music, movies, and novels.

9.1. Meaning of Open Access (OA)

Open access means that research results are made freely accessible on the internet in digital form, which promotes the dissemination of research results both within the scientific community and to the public at large. The reader can read free of charge, use, copy, print, and link to the OA publications.

A publication is considered open access if:

- its content is universally and freely accessible, at no cost to the reader, via the Internet or otherwise;
- the author or copyright owner irrevocably grants to all users, for an unlimited period, the right to use, copy, or distribute the article, on condition that proper attribution is given;
- it is deposited, immediately, in full and in a suitable electronic form, in at least one widely and internationally recognized open access repository committed to open access.

Publishing in Open Access:

- avoids duplication of research effort, and the resulting financial and time waste
- enhances the transparency of scientific research funding and fosters wider understanding of outstanding scientific questions
- increases the accountability of public institutions
- facilitates the search of information through metadata
- helps people to better appreciate scientists and their work
- closes gaps in the access to knowledge
- enables the building of knowledge databases and re-using published results

The promotion of scientific knowledge and their wide dissemination has clear benefits not only for researchers but also for society as a whole. It serves the interests of many groups, such as:

- *Authors*: it gives them a worldwide audience and increases the visibility and impact of their work;
- *Universities*: it increases the visibility of their faculties and research, reduces their expenses for journals, and advances their mission to share knowledge;
- *Teachers and students*: It puts rich and poor on an equal footing by eliminating the need for payments or permissions to reproduce and distribute content;
- *Libraries*: with Open Access, librarians can help users find the information they need, regardless of the budget-enforced limits on the library's own collection;
- *Citizens*: it informs on decisions that are important to everyone. It gives them access to research documents, most of which is unavailable in public libraries and for which they have paid through their taxes;
- *Readers*: it gives them barrier-free access to the literature they need;
- *Journals*: it makes their articles more visible, discoverable, retrievable, and useful. This visibility enables to effectively attract submissions, subscriptions and advertising;
- *Donors*: it increases the return on their investment in research, making the results more widely available. It also provides a fundamental fairness to taxpayers or public access to the results of publicly-funded research;
- *Governments*: it also promotes democracy by sharing non-classified government information as widely as possible.

9.2. Definitions of Open Access

- According to The Berlin Declaration on Open Access to Knowledge in the Sciences and Humanities, *"By 'open access' to the literature, we mean its free availability on the public internet, permitting any users to read, download, copy, distribute, print, search, or link to the full texts of these articles, crawl them for indexing, pass them as data to software, or use them for any other lawful purpose, without financial, legal, or technical barriers other than those inseparable from gaining access to the internet itself."*
- Open Letter to the US Congress signed by Nobel Prize winners, *"Open access truly expands shared knowledge across scientific fields — it is the best path for accelerating multi-disciplinary breakthroughs in research."*

9.3. Benefits of Open Access

- *Visibility, Impact and Quality*: It is easier for a larger audience to find open access publications than articles published in subscription-based journals. Previous research has concluded that articles that are freely accessible are read and cited more. An article deposited in the institutional repository is easily found also in search engines services such as Google Scholar. When an article is easily accessible, it is more used and cited, which adds to the visibility and impact of the author. Open access also increases the transparency of research, the possibility of repetition, and therefore, the reliability of the research rises.

- *Research available for All*: Research results made openly available benefits the whole research community and make it possible also for developing countries with limited resources for database licenses to access research. Research results made freely accessible democratize science, improve scientific communication and smooth out differences between various countries' research institutions. Publicly funded research is accessible also to the business sector as well as the general public. Making research open access produces increased downloads and citations. It also ensures that taxpayers can access the results of publicly-funded research.

Apart from the above, the following are the benefits of open access:

- Provides readers with quicker, more direct access to research results
- Research is equally accessible to all academics, not just those at the richest institutions
- Researchers in low and middle-income countries will be able to keep up-to-date and be competitive with world-class research
- Universities can't teach what they can't access. This gives everyone an educational leg-up

Figure 9.1 *Benefits of Open Access (OA)*

- Increased visibility, impact, and citations - Increased access is positively correlated with the number of citations and an author's impact
- Ability to retain copyright of your work so can make it available via different routes and avenues.
- Available for data and text mining so researchers can find new purposes and directions for your work.
- Global reach - Improve knowledge circulation for everyone.
- Accelerates the pace of research, discovery and innovation
- *Research funders require open research*: Many research funders, national as well as international, requires research results to be openly available. In some cases, also the research data may be published open access. Research results may be published in an open access journal or self-archived in an institutional repository.

9.4. Characteristics of Open Access

Open Access has the following characteristics:

- Greater visibility and impact of research
- Increased opportunity for collaboration
- Easier access to information for anyone
- Takes advantage of technology - text mining and the digital environment
- Better return on investment for research sponsors
- Encourages and enables greater innovation
- Faster than traditional publishing
- Contributes to education's mission of advancing knowledge
- Reducing cost barriers to research
- Expediting wider sharing of research and related data
- Faster publication and increased visibility of research
- Providing public access to publicly funded research
- Free availability of scholarly publication.
- Free of copyright and licensing restrictions
- Materials are available online or on the Internet.
- Material is full text.
- Material can be accessed by anybody from anywhere without any discrimination.
- Material can be freely used by anyone.
- Open Access contents can be in any format from texts and data to software, audio, video, and multi-media, scholarly articles and their preprints.

9.5. Open Access Publication

An open access publication is a publication that provides immediately free online access to all users worldwide. There are many web sites (directories) which list open access journal collections and individual journals. Open access publications are freely and permanently available online to anyone with an internet connection. Unrestricted use, distribution and reproduction in any medium is permitted,

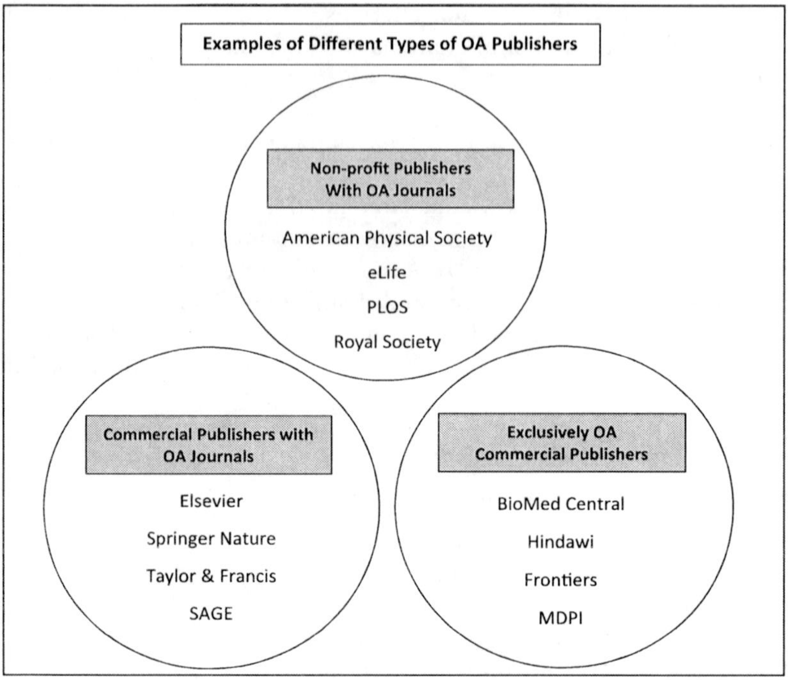

Figure 9.2 *Types of Open Access (OA) Publishers*

provided the author/editor is properly attributed. Open access is a broad international movement that seeks to grant free and open online access to academic information, such as publications and data. A publication is defined 'open access' when there are no financial, legal or technical barriers to accessing it - that is to say when anyone can read, download, copy, distribute, print, search for and search within the information, or use it in education or in any other way within the legal agreements.

Open access is a publishing model for scholarly communication that makes research information available to readers at no cost, as opposed to the traditional subscription model in which readers have access to scholarly information by paying a subscription (usually via libraries).

9.6. Conditions of Open Access Publication

An Open Access Publication is one that meets the following two conditions:

- The author(s) and copyright holder(s) grant(s) to all users a free, irrevocable, worldwide, perpetual right of access to, and a license to copy, use, distribute, transmit and display the work publicly and to make and distribute derivative works, in any digital medium for any responsible purpose, subject to proper attribution of authorship as well as the right to make small numbers of printed copies for their personal use.
- A complete version of the work and all supplemental materials, including a copy of the permission as stated above, in a suitable standard electronic

format is deposited immediately upon initial publication in at least one online repository that is supported by an academic institution, scholarly society, government agency, or other well-established organization that seeks to enable open access, unrestricted distribution, interoperability, and long-term archiving.

9.7. Benefits of Open Access Publishing

- *Free availability thanks to unrestricted online access*: Open access publications are freely available online to anyone. This maximizes visibility, and thus the uptake and use of the work published
- *Authors retain copyright*: The use of a Creative Commons License enables authors/editors to retain copyright to their work. Publications can be reused and redistributed as long as the original author is correctly attributed.
- *High quality and rigorous peer review*: Open access publications run through the same peer review, production and publishing processes similar to journals and books published under the traditional subscription-based model do.
- *Rapid publication*: A streamlined and easy to use online submission and production process enables quick review, approval and publication.
- *No space constraints*: Publishing online means unlimited space for supplementary material including figures, extensive data and video footage.
- *Compliance with open access mandates*: Open access publications can comply with open access mandates from funding sources or academic institutions in the fastest and easiest way. Final articles can be deposited into bibliographic databases and institutional repositories without any embargo periods
- *Citation tracking and inclusion in bibliographic databases*: Open access journals are tracked for impact factors and are deposited into bibliographic databases and institutional repositories without any embargo period just as traditional journals.

9.8. Types of Open Access

There are three basic types of open access publishing. These are Green Open Access, Gold Open Access, and Hybrid Open Access

9.8.1. Green Open Access

"Green" open access occurs when the publisher of a subscription journal allows the author to keep the non-commercial rights to his/her article so it can be posted in open internet archives. Archives may be institutional repositories or discipline-specific archives maintained by scholarly associations.

Green Open access publishing refers to the self-archiving of published or pre-publication works for free public use. Authors provide access to preprints or post-prints of their works with publisher permission in an institutional or disciplinary digital repository. Thus, Green open access refers to the practice of republishing a publication in an open access institutional or disciplinary repository. In this case the publication is first published in a traditional, closed-access journal. These materials are then made available to all via the internet, without restrictions or pay walls. In the "Green Route" of open access, institutions create repositories for their own research which is made open after an appropriate embargo period agreed upon with commercial publishers. As such Green Open Access generally refers to the post-print of an article. In this context, there are three basic version types that can be self-archived in repositories: These are:

- *Pre-Prints* – The author's copy of article before it has been reviewed by the publisher, or pre-reviewed.
- *Post-Prints* – The author's copy of article after it has been reviewed and corrected, but before the publisher has formatted it for publication, or post-reviewed.
- *Publisher's Version* – The version that is formatted and appears in print or online.

9.8.2. Gold Open Access

"Gold" open access refers to journals in which all articles and content are open access — available to anyone on the internet without any subscription fees or sign-in. These journals are either supported by their organizations or funded by fees charged to the author or institution to cover organization, review, formatting and archiving expenses.

Gold open access publishing refers to works published in an open access journal and accessed via the journal or publisher's website. The Gold Route involves publishing in an open access journal, which then provides the dissemination and curation services in the same way as current proprietary publishers. This form of publishing is funded through government, society or institutional grants, and sometimes through charging authors a fee for deposit, known as an article processing charge (APC). However, the latter practice is implemented by a minority of open access journals and most journals do not charge any fees at all.

9.8.3. Hybrid Open Access

"Hybrid" open access means that one or more articles in a subscription journal may be open to anyone on the internet even though all the rest of the content is available only to people and institutions with paid subscriptions. Anyone who can discover these open access articles can use them. This is better than a closed subscription journal but makes the freely-accessible articles hard for faculty and students to know about. These journals often offer their authors a choice of paying the fee to make their article freely accessible or leaving it behind the subscription barrier.

Hybrid open access publishing is mostly associated with gold open access. It takes place in journals that offer authors the option of making their articles open access, for a fee. Hybrid journals are subscription-based journals that make individual articles openly available in return for a fee. The hybrid route has been suggested as a means for traditional publishers to make a transition to open access publishing without significantly decreasing revenue, by charging fees for open access articles equal to the average subscription revenue per article. In the Hybrid Open Access publishing type, sometimes called Paid Open Access, the fee is paid to the publisher or journal by the author, the author's organization, or the research funder.

There are a number of other variations of these major types of open access publishing types. These include the Diamond Open access and the Platinum Open Access.

- *Diamond Open access*: The Diamond Open access journals provide scholarly publishing free of fees and access charges. They have direct or indirect subsidies from institutions like universities, research centres, government agencies etc.
- Platinum open access: Platinum model of open access publishing refers to the situation in which journals are published directly by the research or funding institutions themselves.

9.9. Creative Commons Licences (CCL)

Open access papers sometimes have lenient copyright and licensing restrictions depending on the open access route they have been published through, allowing anyone on the internet to read, download, copy and distribute material within reasonable use. Derivative work can also be produced using some open access papers, providing the original author is credited. Creative Commons licences help authors to share scholarly material legally online with standardized copyright licences.

9.9.1. Types of CCL

Below, is a brief explanation of the different Creative Commons licences available.

Table 9.1 *Types of CCL*

Conditions and Licence Type	*Definition*
Attribution (CC BY)	Every Creative Commons licence requires anyone using your work to credit you in the way you see fit. Their credit cannot suggest that you have endorsed their use of your work. People using your work who do not wish to credit you must get permission from you before using it. *Attribution (CC BY):* This is the most lenient of Creative Commons licences, and allows users to share, edit and build on your work, even for commercial uses. Users must credit you if they wish to use your work.
ShareAlike (CC BY-SA, CC BY-NC-SA)	You allow other people to use, copy, share, show and change your work if they share any modified versions of your work under the same conditions that you originally shared it. Permission must be sought from you if users wish to share it under different conditions. *Attribution ShareAlike (CC BY-SA):* Users can share, edit and build on your work, including for commercial purposes. All derivative works created from your work must also be shared under the Attribution ShareAlike licence.

NonCommercial (CC BY-NC, CC BY-NC-SA)	You allow other people to copy, share, show and change your work, unless you have chosen NoDerivatives, in which case no modifications can be made without your permission. Other people can use your work for any purpose other than commercial uses, unless permission has been given. *Attribution-NonCommercial (CC BY-NC):* Your work can be edited and built upon for non-commercial purposes. Any derivative works created from your work must credit you as the original author. Users of your work do not have to use the same CC BY-NC licence for their derivative works. *Attribution-NonCommercial-ShareAlike (CC BY-NC-SA):* Users can edit and build upon your work for non-commercial purposes. They must credit you as the author and any derivative works must use the same licence as the original work.
Attribution-NoDerivs (CC BY-ND, CC BY-NC-ND)	The NoDerivatives condition allows others to copy, share, and show original copies of your work. No changes to your work may be made unless you give prior permission. *Attribution-NoDerivs (CC BY-ND):* Credit must be given to you when your work is used. Anyone using your work may use your work for any purpose, but it cannot be changed from its original form. *Attribution-Non-Commercial-NoDerivs (CC BY-NC-ND):* This is the most restrictive Creative Commons licence. Your work cannot be changed in any way, and users must credit you if they download and share your work. Commercial use is not allowed with this licence.

9.10. Who Benefits from Open Access?

Researchers

- Improving reach of research
- Helping to provide evidence for impact
- Improved reputation for researchers and their host institution through increased citations
- Improved quality of research through open, transparent and reproducible research practices
- Increases readers' ability to find use relevant literature
- Increases the visibility, readership and impact of author's works
- Creates new avenues for discovery in digital environment
- Enhances interdisciplinary research
- Accelerates the pace of research, discovery and innovation

Educational Institutions

- Contributes to core mission of advancing knowledge
- Democratizes access across all institutions – regardless of size or budget
- Provides access to important materials
- Increases competitiveness of academic institutions
- Enriches the quality of their education
- Ensures access to all learners need to know, rather what they can afford
- Contributes to a better-educated workforce

Research Funders

- Leverages return on research investment
- Creates tool to manage research portfolio
- Avoids funding duplicative research
- Creates transparency
- Encourages greater interaction with results of funded research

Businesses

- Access to cutting-edge research encourages innovation
- Stimulates new ideas, new services, new products
- Creates new opportunities for job creation

Public

- Provides access to previously unavailable materials relating to health, energy, environment, and other areas of broad interest
- Creates better educated populace
- Encourages support of scientific enterprise and engagement in citizen science

9.11. Open Access Tools

Open access tools are pointers to information obtained in databases and repositories. We can define access tools as bibliography, catalog, database, or other information source, which leads us to information on our topic. An access tool helps a researcher, student or librarian gain access to relevant documents located on the web. Some of the Open Access tools as discussed in this chapter are: DOAJ, DOAR, ROAR, SHERPA-ROMEO, and SPARC.

9.11.1. Directory of Open Access Journals (DOAJ)

The Directory of Open Access Journals (http://www.doaj.org/) is a website that lists Open Access journals and is maintained by Infrastructure Services for Open Access (IS4OA). Until January 2013, the DOAJ was maintained by Lund University. The project defines Open Access journals as scientific and scholarly journals that meet high quality standards by exercising peer review or editorial quality control and *'use a funding model that does not charge readers or their institutions for access.'* The Budapest Open Access Initiative's definition of Open Access is used to define required rights given to users, for the journal to be included in the DOAJ, as the rights to *'read, download, copy, distribute, print, search, or link to the full texts of these articles*. Open Access journals are defined by DOAJ as *'journals that use a funding model that does not charge readers or their institutions for access'* (Wikipedia, 2013a).

DOAJ is the most recognized and most authoritative list of scholarly, peer-reviewed, fully Open Access journals. More than 10 percent of the world's peer-reviewed journals are now included in DOAJ, making DOAJ among the world's largest collections of peer reviewed scholarly journals, period. There are more peer-reviewed journals in DOAJ than Science Direct; more non-embargoed, peer reviewed journals in DOAJ than in EBSCO's Academic Search Premiere or Gale's One File. Full Open Access means no journals are embargoed, and articles are available for use, a significant strength of DOAJ. The DOAJ vetting process involves querying journal editors to ensure that peer-review or equivalent quality controls are in place and that journals meet the criterion of true Open Access as per the Budapest Open Access Initiative definition. To be included in DOAJ, a journal must have an ISSN. Journals included in DOAJ go through a periodic review process to ensure that the journal continues to meet the criteria for inclusion.

The aim of the DOAJ is to increase the visibility and ease of use of Open Access scientific and scholarly journals, thereby promoting their increased usage and impact. The DOAJ aims to be comprehensive and cover all Open Access scientific and scholarly journals that use a quality control system to guarantee the content. In short, the DOAJ aims to be the one stop shop for users of Open Access journals.

Selection Criteria

- Coverage:
  - *Subject*: All scientific and scholarly subjects are covered
  - *Types of resource*: Scientific and scholarly periodicals that publish research or review papers in full text.
  - *Acceptable sources*: Academic, government, commercial, non-profit private sources are all acceptable.
  - *Level*: The target group for included journals should primarily be researchers.
  - *Content*: A substantive part of the journal should consist of research papers. All content should be available in full text.
  - All languages
- Access:
  - All content freely available.
  - Registration: Free user registration
  - online is acceptable.
  - Open Access without delay (e.g., no embargo period).

DOAJ Services

DOAJ offers the 'Search' and 'Browse' interfaces, which offer users opportunity to gain access to all the journals available in the directory (See Figure 9.3).

This 'search' interface is a service that enables researchers search the directory by journals or articles by typing a desired title or subject. This is similar to a library user who visits the library for research, needing a material without knowing the author or name of the book or journal he/she is looking for. Therefore, the user consults the access tool (catalog) using either the subject or title catalog, especially when the author is unknown. There is also the 'advanced search' option whereby journals can be searched for using either the title, ISSN, author, keyword, abstract, publisher (See Figure 9.4).

9.11.2. Directory of Open Access Repositories (OpenDOAR)

OpenDOAR is an authoritative directory of academic Open Access repositories. Each OpenDOAR repository has been visited by project staff to check the information that is recorded here. This in-depth approach does not rely on automated analysis and

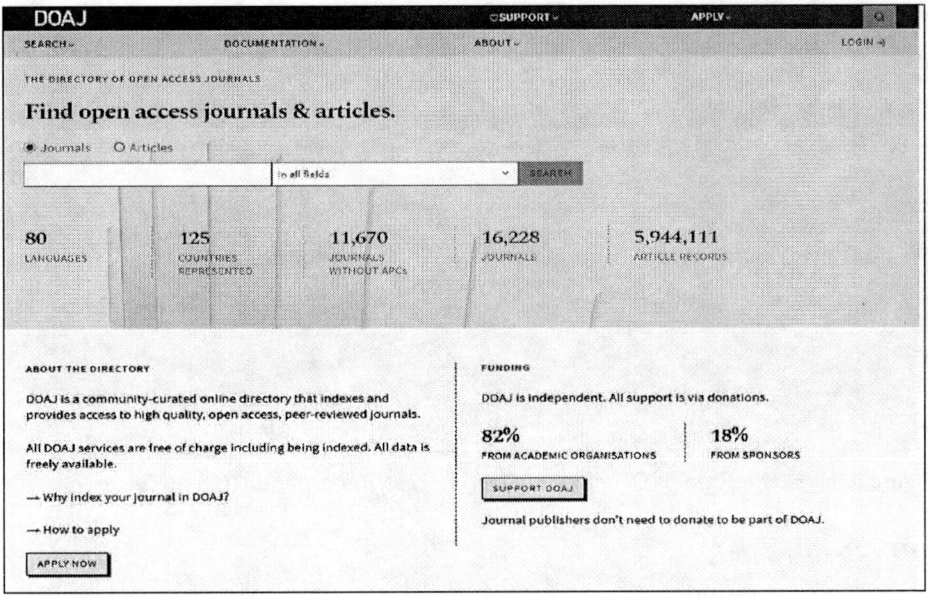

Figure 9.3 *'Search' and 'Browse' interfaces of DOAJ*

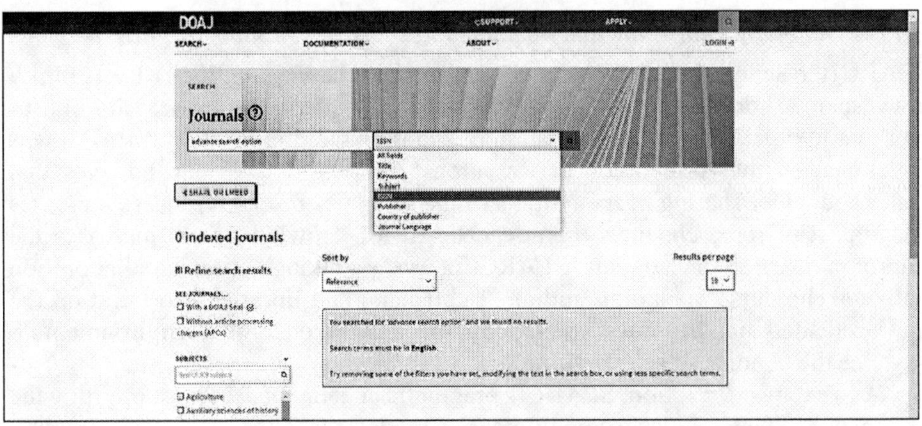

Figure 9.4 *Advanced Search in Directory of Open Access Journals (DOAJ)*

gives a quality-controlled list of repositories. As well as providing a simple repository list, OpenDOAR lets you search for repositories or search repository contents. OpenDOAR is one of the SHERPA Services including RoMEO and JULIET, run by the Centre for Research Communications (CRC). OpenDOAR has also been identified as a key resource for the Open Access community and identified as the leader in repository directories in a study by Johns Hopkins University. OpenDOAR was one of the services, which contributed to SHERPA being awarded the 2007 SPARC Europe Award for Outstanding Achievements in Scholarly Communications.

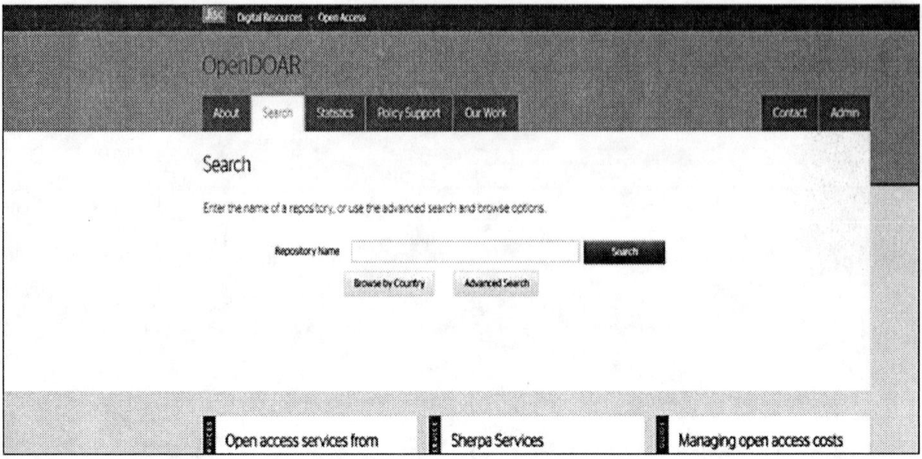

Figure 9.5 *Home Page of Directory of Open Access Repositories (OpenDOAR)*

DOAR's Strengths

- It is user-friendly
- It offers Open Access to over 2200 listings
- It gives a quality-controlled list of repositories.

9.11.3. Scholarly Publishing and Academic Resources Coalition (SPARC)

SPARC (the Scholarly Publishing and Academic Resources Coalition), URL: http://www.sparc.arl.org is an international alliance of academic and research libraries working to create a more open system of scholarly communication. SPARC was developed by the Association of Research Libraries in 1998 and believes that faster and wider sharing of the outputs of the scholarly research process increases the impact of research, fuels the advancement of knowledge, and increases the return on research investments. SPARC focuses on taking action in collaboration with stakeholders - including authors, publishers, and libraries - to build on the unprecedented opportunities created by the networked digital environment to advance the conduct of scholarship.

As a catalyst for action, SPARC's pragmatic agenda focuses on supporting the emergence of new scholarly communication models that expand the dissemination of scholarly research and reduce financial pressures on libraries and create a more open system of scholarly communications.

SPARC's Strategy

Reducing barriers to the access, sharing, and use of scholarship and their highest priority is in advancing the understanding and implementation of policies and practices that ensure Open Access to scholarly research outputs. SPARC's primary focus is on journal literature, but their evolving strategy reflects an increasing focus on Open Access to research outputs of all kinds – including digital data and open educational resources (OER).

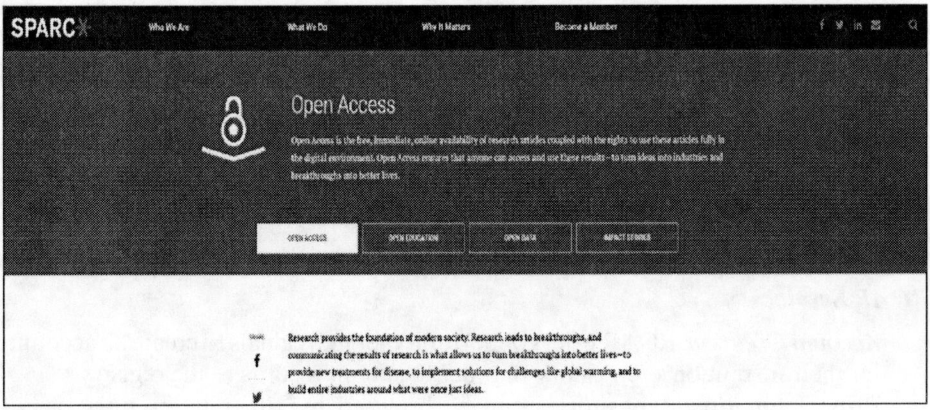

Figure 9.6 *Home Page of Scholarly Publishing and Academic Resources Coalition (SPARC)*

What Does SPARC Do?

SPARC's activities will advance acceptance and long-term sustainability of an open system for scholarly communication. SPARC will promote changes to both the infrastructure and culture needed to make 'open' the default mode in scholarly communication. SPARC's activities are centered on the following broad issue areas:

- *Open Access to Scholarly and Scientific Research Articles*: SPARC supports the immediate, barrier-free online availability of scholarly and scientific research articles, coupled with the rights to reuse these articles fully in the digital environment, and supports practices and policies that enable this.
- *Open Data*: SPARC recognizes that the conduct of scientific and scholarly research is increasingly digital, and that its advancement is predicated on being able to access, comment on, build upon and reuse data. SPARC supports practices and policies that promote broad, Open Accessibility and utility of scholarly and scientific research data.
- *Open Educational Resources (OER)*: SPARC believes that Open Education makes the link between teaching, learning and the collaborative culture of the Internet. SPARC supports the open creation and sharing of materials used in teaching, as well as new approaches to learning where people create and shape knowledge openly together, and supports practices and policies to advance this vision.

SPARC's role in stimulating change focuses on the following:

- Educating stakeholders about challenges in the scholarly communication system and the opportunities for change;
- Advocating for policy changes that leverage technology to advance scholarly communication and that explicitly recognize that dissemination is an essential, inseparable component of the research process;
- Incubating demonstrations of business and publishing models that leverage openness for the benefit of scholarship and academe.

9.11.4. Registry of Open Access Repositories (ROAR)

The aim of ROAR is to promote the development of Open Access by providing timely information about the growth and status of repositories throughout the world. Open Access to research maximizes research access and thereby also research impact, making research more productive and effective. ROAR is hosted at the University of Southampton, UK and is made possible by funding from the JISC. ROAR is part of the EPrints.org network. See Figure 9.7 for ROAR homepage: (Website: http://roar.eprints.org/)

ROAR Services

- *Account Creation*: ROAR offers opportunity for individuals to create an account for their institution's repository in order to submit records to the registry.
- *Browse Facility*: Repositories can be browsed by either by country, year, repository type, or repository software (See Figure 9.8 and 9.9).

9.11.5. SHERPA Services

The original SHERPA partnership was formed for the SHERPA project (2002-2006) and drew from research-led universities with an active interest in establishing an example of a then-new concept - an Open Access institutional repository. (Website:

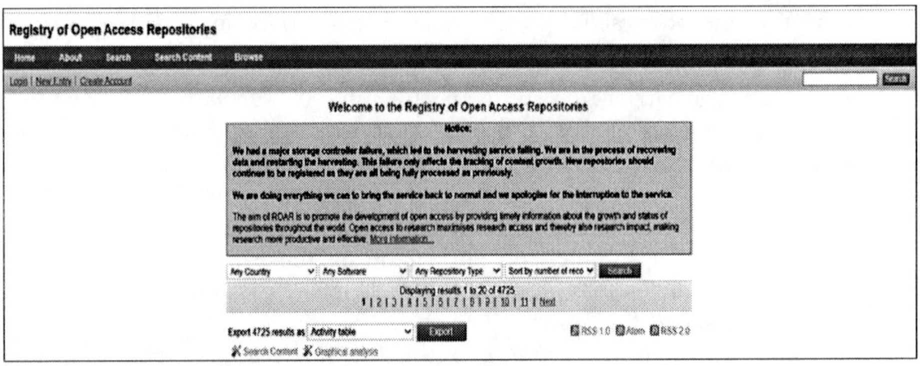

Figure 9.7 *Home Page of Registry of Open Access Repositories (ROAR)*

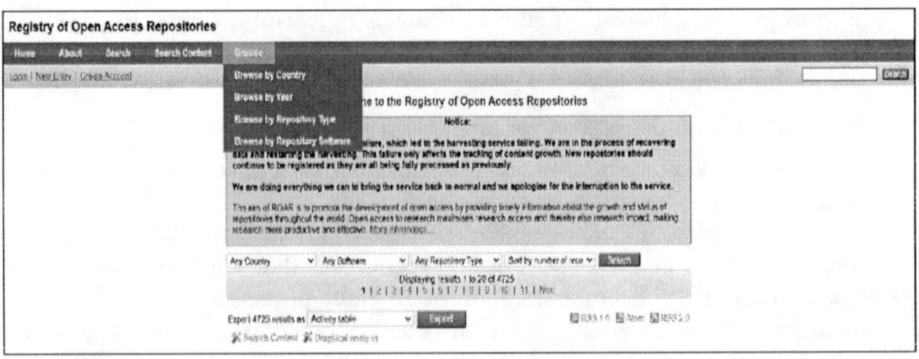

Figure 9.8 *ROAR Browse Interface*

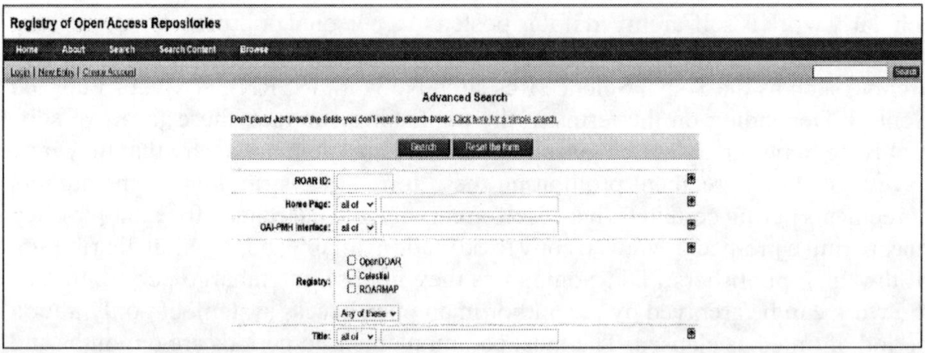

Figure 9.9 *ROAR Search Facility*

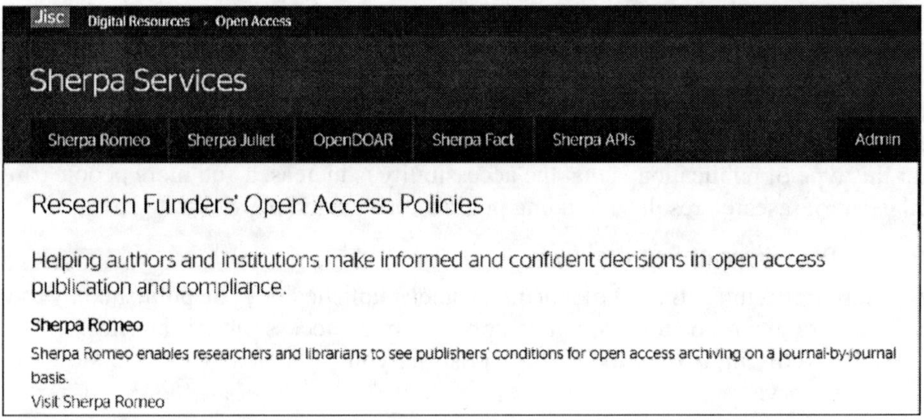

Figure 9.10 *Home Page of Sherpa Services*

http://www.sherpa.ac.uk/) SHERPA is investigating issues in the future of scholarly communication. It is developing Open Access institutional repositories in universities to facilitate the rapid and efficient worldwide dissemination of research.

SHERPA services and the SHERPA Partnership are both based at the Centre for Research Communications at the University of Nottingham. SHERPA services include:

- *Sherpa Romeo*: Publisher's copyright & archiving policies
- *Sherpa Juliet*: Research funder's archiving mandates and guidelines
- *OpenDOAR*: Worldwide Directory of Open Access Repositories
- *Sherpa Fact*: Checking for funder open access policies
- *Sherpa REF*: Checking for compliance of OA REF policies.

9.12. Self-Archiving

Self-archiving is a strategy used by authors to make their scholarly works available on the open web–to provide open access. In this context, the contents are usually journal articles, conference or technical reports, dissertations, or data sets. A scholarly work is self-archived if it is posted to a personal or professional web site, deposited in an institutional repository, or contributed by the author to a disciplinary archive such as the Social Science Research Network (SSRN), arXiv, or PubMed Central. Depending on the terms in the publishing contract, these forms of self-archiving may or may not be permitted; authors are often not aware that they may have signed an agreement prohibiting these forms of distribution. Some authors agreements permit certain forms of self-archiving, but not others: for example, they may permit a pre-peer reviewed copy to be made available, but prohibit distribution of the final, publishers PDF. Sometimes they impose an embargo period, that is: the work can be archived by the author in an open access system, but only after a period of time has elapsed. The most common embargo periods are 6 months and 12 months, but there is some variation by publisher.

Self-archiving, also called green open access, is a way of providing free access to a published or accepted research publication, and means that a full text version of the publication is uploaded to an institutional or other open archive. Self-archiving means that a copy of a published work is uploaded in full text in an open archive. Full text publication of the reviewed, accepted version of an article meets most research funders' requirements for making research results publicly available. A good reason for this type of publication is that the accessibility is increased and more people can take part of research results, including publications behind paywalls.

9.12.1. Definitions of Self-Archiving

- Self-archiving is the act of storing articles published or to be published by the authors in a repository which can provide open access to their articles.
- Self-archiving is the process of depositing your scholarly work into a digital repository.

9.12.2. Advantages of Self-Archiving

Self-archiving refers to open-access filing of an article (published in publication channel, e.g., a journal, an edited book or conference proceedings) to a publication archive of the organisation or the discipline. The filed version of the article can be either the published article or a manuscript. Some advantages of self-archiving are given below:

- By self-archiving, researchers can make their scientific work freely and easily accessible to the world at large.
- Making a research article accessible by self-archiving will significantly increase the article's visibility. Greater visibility also increases the number of potential citations.
- Self-archiving saves the researcher's time and effort: When an article is freely available, it decreases personal requests for the article.
- Self-archiving usually meets the openness criteria of research financers. It is recommended for researchers to mention the openness of their previous publications in their funding applications.
- Making the world a better place is always worth the effort. Every self-archived item brings one more research publication available to a great

number of researchers who would otherwise be partially excluded from such scientific knowledge because of the high price of journals. At the same time, scientific knowledge becomes available to larger audiences, both nationally and internationally.

9.12.3. Self-Archiving the Research Work

Self-Archiving (also known as Green Open Access) refers to the practice of sharing scholarly works in an open access repository. You can include your works that have been published in an Open Access journal, works you have published in traditional journals, and works that you do not plan on publishing at all (such as conference posters and white papers). Self-archiving is an attractive option if you want to publish your research in a traditional, commercial journal and still share your work openly after it is published. However, some commercial journal publishers do not allow self-archiving immediately after publication. In these cases, you should consider negotiating your publication contract to allow for self-archiving. They may have a wait period or embargo of a certain number of months. Negotiating your publishing contract can be relatively easy, and some publishers have self-archiving rights built into their work by default

9.12.3.1. Know Your Self-Archiving Rights

Sherpa Romeo is a unique database that helps you know the rights that specific journals will allow you as an author to retain. Just search your journal by name in Sherpa / Romeo. You will quickly see if you can retain copyright, and which version(s) of your work (pre-print, post-print, publisher's version) you can post ("self-archive") and where, plus any special conditions you will need to follow. You can use the information you find to guide your decision on which journals to choose for your publications. With the help of 'Sherpa Romeo', researchers can analyse the publishers open access policies.

9.12.3.2. How to Self-Archive

Self-archiving means that you first publish your article in a journal. After that you deposit a manuscript copy of the article in an open archive. In this way your research becomes freely available and you fulfil any open access requirements from your research funder, without any additional costs. If you have published an article in a subscription journal, you can self-archive a manuscript copy in an open archive to make it available open access.

9.12.3.3. Terms and Conditions from Publishers when Self-Archiving

When you publish an article in a traditional subscription journal, in most cases you sign an agreement with the publisher. Therefore, if you plan to self-archive a copy of the article, you should check the publisher's terms and conditions for self-archiving.

9.12.3.4. Version and Embargo

The publisher's terms and conditions may state restrictions for when a copy of the article can be published and what version the copy should be. Some publishers only allow self-archiving after an embargo, that is, with a delay since the article was first published in the journal. The publishers conditions regarding version usually mean that the copy you self-archive must be a so called post-print, a peer reviewed manuscript without any connection to the journal's layout.

9.12.3.5. Check the Conditions in Sherpa Romeo

To find out what applies to self-archiving specifically for your article, you can look up your journal in the database Sherpa Romeo. The database holds information about terms and conditions from many journals and publishers. If the journal is not listed in Sherpa Romeo you can find information about copyright and terms and conditions for self-archiving on the journal's website.

9.13. How to Find your Publishing Agreement and Permissions

As an author, you generally hold the copyright to your work. However, when you publish a book or paper, publishers usually ask you to transfer some or all of your copyright to them. This is done through a publishing contract, usually called a publication agreement or copyright transfer agreement. For previously published works, if copyright ownership rests with the publisher, you'll need to ensure you have permission to deposit your work in the repository. It is important to look carefully at your agreement. Many authors do not realize what rights they are signing away or that they can negotiate the terms of their publishing contracts. We strongly encourage exploring your options for negotiating with publishers. Check their websites for copyright and archiving policies, and keep a copy of your publications agreement so you can easily verify terms for sharing your work. Another tool for locating permissions is SHERPA/RoMEO (sherpa.ac.uk/romeo), which provides details of the self-archiving rights given by the various publishers.

Publishers' policies vary on whether you can deposit your work in a digital repository. They may also have different policies for different versions of the same work. Authors should be familiar with three publication versions: pre-print, post-print and published. Most publishers do not allow authors to self-archive the final, published version of a work. However, many do allow you to self-archive earlier versions (pre-prints and post-prints). Note that many publishers only allow self-archiving a work after an embargo period, typically 6 to 12 months.

9.14. RoMEO (Publishers' Copyright and Archiving Policies)

RoMEO (http://www.sherpa.ac.uk/romeo/) is part of SHERPA Services based at the University of Nottingham. As an author of an article if you are in doubt of which journal supports self-archiving, you should always consult RoMEO. The link to RoMEO is http://www.sherpa.ac.uk/romeo/. RoMEO is a searchable database of publisher's policies regarding the self-archiving of journal articles on the web and in Open Access repositories. Sherpa Romeo is an online resource that aggregates and analyses publisher open access policies from around the world and provides summaries of publisher copyright and open access archiving policies on a journal-by-journal basis.

RoMEO is a searchable database of publisher's policies regarding the self-archiving of journal articles on the web and in Open Access repositories. If an academic author wants to put their research articles on-line, they are faced with an increasingly complex situation. Evidence shows that citations to articles made openly accessible in this way are taken up and cited more often than research that is simply published in journals. Also, some funding agencies require Open Access archiving for their research, to increase the use of the information generated. However, some publishers prohibit authors from using their own articles in this way. Others allow it, but only under certain conditions, while others are quite happy for authors to show their work in this way. Authors can be left confused: RoMEO helps to clarify the situation. RoMEO contains publishers' general policies on self-archiving of journal articles and certain conference series. Each entry provides a summary of the publisher's policy, including what version of an article can be deposited, where it can be deposited, and any conditions that are attached to that deposit. RoMEO Services are as follows:

9.14.1. Search Options and Publishers' Policy

This offers a platform where publishers' copyright policies and self-archiving can be looked up. The title, ISSN, publisher, etc. of a particular journal can be used as a key term to search for the archiving policy. When reading a SHERPA RoMEO record or the publisher's policy, pay particular attention to the version of the paper you may self-archive and any embargo periods you are expected to adhere to. On this page, the keys to the archiving policy can be viewed too.

9.14.2. Author Deposit / Self-Archiving Policy in Sherpa Romeo

Self-archiving is the act of the author depositing an electronic copy of a published article on their website or in an online repository to maximize the article's accessibility, usage and citation impact. Journals need to make their self-archiving policies clear on their website so that authors or their institutions know whether they are permitted to make a copy available via personal websites, institutional or subject repositories and whether there are any restrictions or conditions associated with such sharing.

Having a defined self-archiving policy in Sherpa Romeo or a similar database is one of the requirements for a Directory of Open Access Journals (DOAJ) application.

Sherpa Romeo is an online resource that aggregates publisher/journal open access policies and self-archiving policies. The following is the policy page for Nature Communications, an open access journal.

9.14.3. Getting Started with Sherpa Romeo

Sherpa Romeo is an online service that aggregates and presents publisher and journal open access policies from around the world. The service is used by researchers, repository staff and research support teams across the world, to help users understand complex publisher and journal open access policies.

Every registered publisher or journal held in Romeo is carefully reviewed and analyzed by Sherpa Romeo's specialist team who provide summaries of self-archiving permissions and conditions of rights given to authors on a

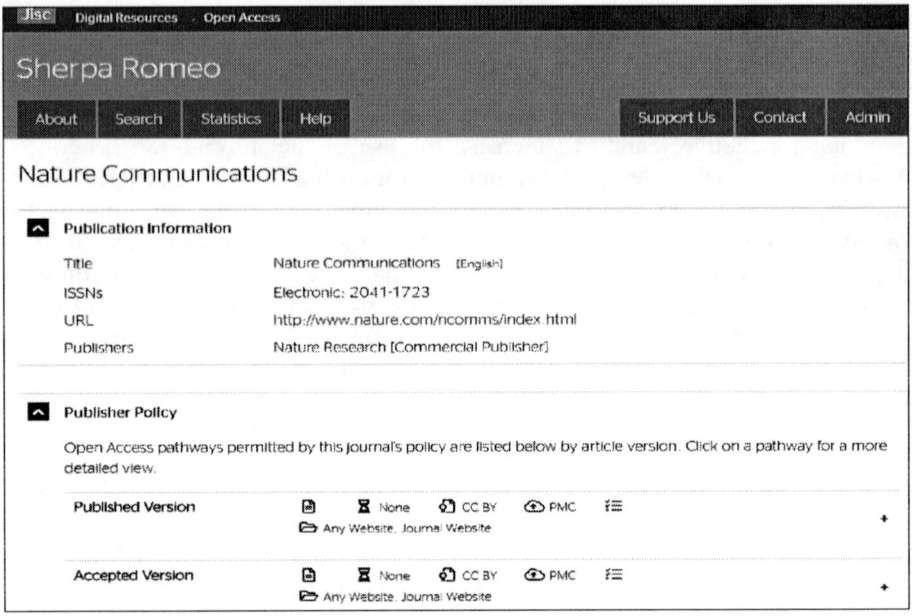

Figure 9.11 *Screenshot of Sherpa Romeo record for Nature Communications journal*

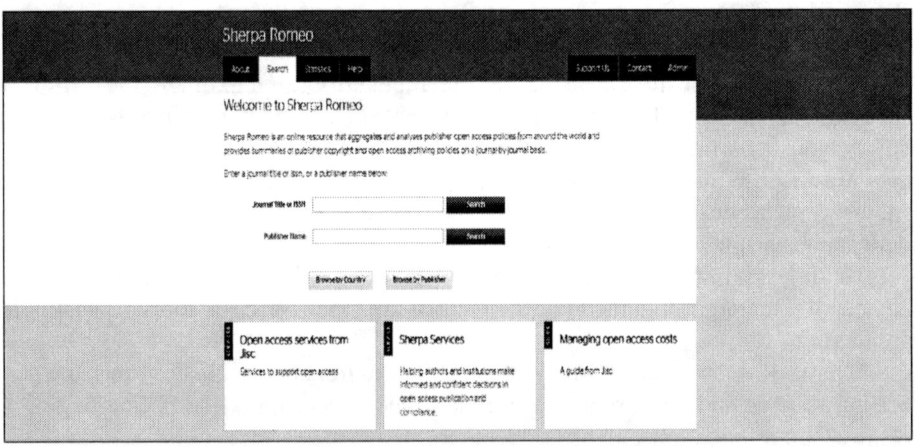

Figure 9.12 *Home Page of Sherpa Romeo*

journal-by-journal basis. The policy information provided through this service primarily aims to serve the academic research community.

9.14.3.1. Searching and Browsing

Sherpa Romeo now contains more options for searching and browsing than the previous version, to help you find the information you need more quickly and reflecting the requirements of different users of the service.

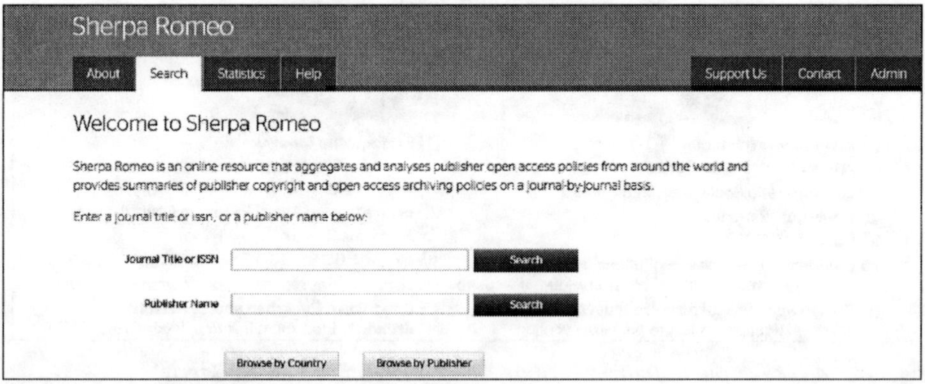

Figure 9.13 *'Search Bars' in Sherpa Romeo*

9.14.3.2. Options for Searching and Browsing

You can search for the information you need from the Sherpa Romeo landing page, and the Sherpa Romeo search page. The new options for searching and browsing now include:

- Search by:
  - Journal title
  - ISSN
  - Publisher
- Browse publications by publisher

9.14.3.3. How to Read a Publisher Policy

Policy records contain information on how articles can be made open access for the published, submitted and accepted versions of an article.

Policies are stored on Sherpa Romeo as a set of pathways, each pathway presenting a way in which a document can become open access.

Authors can refer to these pathways to understand how to make their article open access.

Properties within pathways are represented by icons to give users a condensed summary of publisher policies

9.14.3.4. Understanding Pathways

Each version of an article contains one or more *pathways* through which the article can be made open access, which can depend on factors such as funders, publisher requirements, or the availability of the article. In the example below, there are *two pathways available for the accepted version* of an article, through which the article can be made open access. The author may follow *Pathway a* or *Pathway b*, depending on who the article is funded by.

- *Pathway a* requires the article to be funded by the Arts and Humanities Research Council and Economic and Social Research Council. This pathway will then include a 2-year embargo, and a CC BY-NC licence will apply to

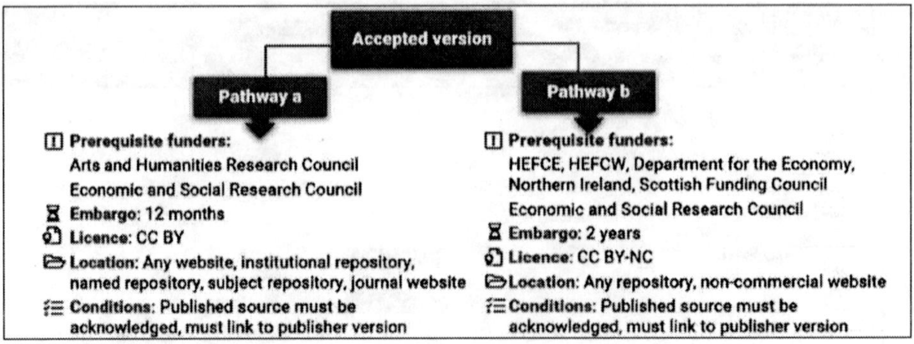

Figure 9.14 *Example of Pathways from 'Child and Family Law Quarterly'*

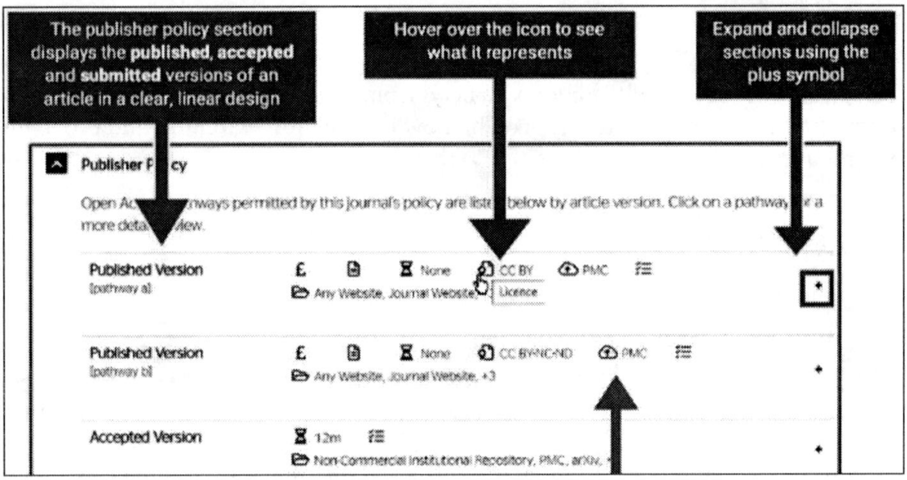

Figure 9.15 *Example of Publisher Policy Layout*

the article. The article will be available on any repository, or non-commercial website. Two conditions also apply to this pathway.

- *Pathway b* requires the article to be funded by HEFCE, HEFCW, Department for the Economy, Northern Ireland, Scottish Funding Council, or the Economic and Social Research Council. With this pathway, there is a 2-year embargo. A CC BY-NC licence will be applied, and the article can be available in any repository or a non-commercial website, and there are two conditions that apply to the pathway.

9.14.3.5. Publisher Policy Icons

Sherpa Romeo now contains an iconography scheme that represents aspects of publisher policy. Publisher policies are stored in Sherpa Romeo as a set of pathways. Each pathway represents a different way in which a document can become open access. Pathways have different policies, and the icons represent the properties within the pathways. The icons were selected by Jisc's team of open access specialists and were user tested with a sample of industry professionals.

Icon Key

Icon	Name	Description
	**Open access publishing**	The pathway includes open access publishing
	**Additional open access fee**	The pathway requires the payment of a fee (in addition to any normal publication fees that may be required) to make the article open access
	**Not permitted**	No open access pathway exists for the article version
	**Copyright owner**	The copyright owner that the pathway requires
	**Conditions**	Conditions that apply to the pathway
	**Licence**	The licence that the pathway requires
	**Prerequisites**	Requirements that must be met to allow the pathway to be used. These may include prerequisite funders, subjects, or permissions from the publisher
	**Location**	The websites on which the pathway allows the article version to be available. This includes self-archiving and publisher-deposit locations, including the website of the journal
	**Notes**	Additional notes on the policy
	**Publisher deposit**	The publisher will deposit on your behalf in the location specified
	**Embargo**	The embargo that the pathway requires. Unless stated otherwise, the embargo starts on the date of publication

Figure 9.16 *Types of Publisher Policy Icons*

9.15. Predatory Publishing

Predatory publishing is an unethical scholarly practice that exploits the "author-pays" publishing model to earn revenue. The ultimate goal of predatory publishing is monetary gain, not the promotion and preservation of the scholarly record. Predatory publishing means deceptive publishing or to write only for the purpose of publishing. It is a problematic academic publishing mechanism that involves charging huge publication fees to writers without properly checking articles for quality and legitimacy and without providing the other editorial and publishing services that standard and legitimate journals provide. These journals are considered predatory journals because scholars are forced into publishing with them, although some authors may be aware that the journal is of poor quality or predatory. New scholars from developing countries are said to be especially at risk of being misled by predatory publishers.

9.15.1. Definition of "Predatory Publishing"

- Coined by Jeffrey Beall, a former librarian at the Auraria Library, University of Denver, *"the term 'predatory publishing' refers to a questionable business practice of charging fees to authors to publish their articles without standard editorial and publishing services provided by legitimate scholarly journals."*
- *"Predatory journals and publishers are entities that prioritize self-interest at the expense of scholarship and are characterized by false or misleading information, deviation from best editorial and publication practices, a lack of transparency, and/or the use of aggressive and indiscriminate solicitation practices."*

9.15.2. Predatory?

- **P**rimary goal: to make money
- **R**eputation: questionable
- **E**mails: flattering, persuasive, and repetitive
- **D**atabases: none of them included the title
- **A**uthor is targeted by website, not the reader
- **T**itle: suggests a vague or broad scope
- **O**pen Access, but publisher retains copyright
- **R**evision: not required, instant publication guaranteed
- **Y**es, it's predatory!

9.15.3. Basics of Predatory Publishing

Predatory publishing is an academic publishing model that charges author fees to publish in a journal that does not undergo the traditional scholarly editorial process of checking the validity and quality of an article prior to publication.

Common signs of predatory publishing:

- Mimicry of other respected journals, such as a similar name;
- Incorrect use of a proper ISSN;
- Fake editorial boards- either incorrectly listing an academic board member or listing one with fake credentials
- Accepting articles quickly without signs of peer review or quality control;
- Notification of fees after a paper is accepted;
- Not a member of COPE;
- Not indexed in a well-established database;
- Journal uses poor language.

9.15.4. Why is Predatory Publishing Harmful?

- Threatens the integrity of scholarly communication
- Results in loss of knowledge (predatory journals could disappear at any time and with them could disappear all previously published research)
- Corrupts the open access publishing model

- Encourages the unethical behavior of authors who seek to publish research of questionable quality and plagiarized or self-plagiarized work
- Hurts researcher's academic credibility and career advancement

9.16. Predatory Journals

The term *'predatory journal'* was coined by Jeffrey Beall, a librarian at the University of Colorado. These journals act as predators. Authors feel attracted by the promise to get published quickly and are willing to pay for this service. Some authors might feel compelled to take the irresistible offer, despite assuming or even knowing that it is a false promise.

Predatory journals (also called deceptive or scamming journals) are accused of applying poor academic standards and practices in their editorial and peer-review processes. They apply poor ethical procedures by claiming to live-up to the established quality control standards in peer-review, but do so only on a superficial level. They simply exploit the situation that researchers (in particular young and inexperienced ones), are under pressure to publish in journals.

9.16.1. Characteristics of Predatory Journals

Predatory journals:

- do not apply a standardized peer-review process
- may not send your paper to peer-reviewers or may not apply any editing or improvement of them before publishing
- publish a high number of low-quality papers
- are more likely to publish fake or hoax papers, as they do not identify them as such due to their poor-quality control
- send spam emails to thousands of researchers asking them to contribute to the journal
- list members on editorial boards without those people agreeing or knowing of it
- make up names of editorial board members or authors
- copy material, design and advertise as established and legitimate journals
- may even hijack established journals by setting up journals with identical names and similar websites
- inappropriately or fraudulently use ISSN
- make up or fake journal metrics such as impact factors and others
- state wrong or misleading information about the size and the location of the publisher

9.16.2. Characteristics of Predatory Publications

The most common complaints about predatory publishing are as follows:

- Accepting articles very soon with little or no peer review and quality control.
- Informing fees only after papers accepting the article for the journal.
- A huge and too much campaigning for academics to submit the articles.
- Mentioning the list of academics as members of editorial boards without getting their permission, and also, not allowing academics to resign from editorial boards.

- Appointing false academics to their editorial board.
- Copying the name of the journal and website style of more established and popular journals.
- Making misleading claims about the publishing operation, such as a false location.
- Using ISSN improperly.
- Citing or non-existent impact factors.
- Boasting about being "indexed" by academic social networking sites such as Research Gate and standard identifiers such as ISSNs and DOIs as if they were prestigious or reputable bibliographic databases.

9.16.3. Warning Signs / Red Flags of Predatory Journals

- *Flattering email* to invite you to submit an article or serve on the editorial board of a "scholarly" journal
  - poor language with typos and awkward style
  - vocabulary below industry standard with multisyllabic words
  - offer sounds too good to be true
- *Journal title*
  - sounds similar to a reputable publication (words are in different order or mixed from several other titles)
  - contains prestigious-sounding but potentially vague terms such as "advanced", "global", "international", "universal", "world", "open", (although these words are also used by reputable journals)
  - might be hijacked from a legitimate academic journal: a bogus website offers rapid publication for a fee
- *Website* with information on the journal, editorial board, and publisher
  - site looks amateurish and unprofessional (layout, typos, poor quality pictures, flashy ads, dead links, abundance of well-known logos)
  - multiple pages "under construction", including current and past issues, editorial board
  - missing, scarce, or contradictory information on "About Us" page (claiming a US address - check with Google Maps)
  - contact information is missing, incomplete, or leads to unavailable links
  - unclear or falsely claimed affiliation to scholarly associations or reputable organizations
  - same publisher publishes multiple journals with a broad scope and from different disciplines
  - editors and editorial board members are from all over the world and have no academic credentials (or are unaware that they are listed!)
- *Metrics and indexing*
  - no ISSN, no DOI
  - invented or fake metrics (sounding similar to established metrics used by reputable journals)
  - Impact Factor can't be verified in Journal Citation Reports
  - falsely claimed to be indexed, e.g., in DOAJ
  - not listed in reputable sources such as Ulrich's Periodical Directory

- *Article processing and peer review*
  - lack of clear instructions to authors
  - lack of transparency or policies about fees related to publishing
  - article processing fees look below that of reputable open access journals
  - peer review process is not clearly explained
  - peer review seems to be extremely fast (i.e., days) - may be non-existent
  - articles are to be submitted via email (some predatory publishers use legitimate editorial manager systems - it doesn't make them legitimate)
- *Negative reputation*
  - journal and/or publisher is already listed on Beall's list
  - listed on Cabell's Blacklist
- *Common Features in Predatory Invitations*
  - Awkward language
  - Copycat syndrome
  - False information
  - Flattering
  - Language is boastful, editorialized
  - Missing standards: ISSN, DOI, IF
  - New business
  - Overly polite, but clumsy
  - Persuasive
  - Promises
  - Urgency

9.17. Evaluation Tools for Identifying Predatory Journals and Publishers

With an exponentially growing number of articles being published every year, scientists can use some help in determining which journal is most appropriate for publishing their results, and which other scientists can be called upon to review their work. Authors can use the following websites and tools to evaluate the reputation and reliability of particular journals and publishers. If authors have doubts about a particular publisher, please proceed with caution. Use a critical eye, make use of the tools below; reflect on whether these publishers or journals meet the criteria for credibility.

- OASPA (Open Access Scholarly Publishers Association)
- Eriksson and Helgesson's 25 Criteria
- Beall's (2015) Criteria
- Think. Check. Submit. Checklist
- AMWA–EMWA–ISMPP Joint Position Statement on Predatory Publishing
- Consortium for Academic and Research Ethics (CARE) List

9.17.1. OASPA Principles of Transparency and Best Practice in Scholarly Publishing (Warning Signs of Predatory Publishing)

Committee on Publication Ethics (COPE), the *Directory of Open Access Journals (DOAJ)*, the *Open Access Scholarly Publishers Association (OASPA)*, and the *World Association of Medical Editors (WAME)* are scholarly organizations that have collaborated to identify principles of transparency and best practice for scholarly publications. These Principles of Transparency and Best Practice in Scholarly Publishing is given by OASPA.

Warning signs based on the 16 Principles of transparency are suggested by OASPA:

1. *Website*: The journal's website contains misleading or false information (e.g., indexing, metrics, membership of scholarly publishing organizations), lacks an ISSN or uses one that has already been assigned to another publication, mimics another journal/publisher's site, or has no past or recent journal content.
2. *Name of journal*: The journal name is the same as or easily confused with that of another in scope, or association.
3. *Peer review process*: Peer review and peer review process and model are not mentioned, or manuscript acceptance or a very short peer review time is guaranteed. Submitted manuscripts receive inadequate or no peer review.
4. *Ownership and management*: Information about the ownership and/or management is missing, unclear, misleading, or false.
5. *Governing body*: Information on the editorial board is missing, misleading, false, or inappropriate for the journal; full names and affiliations of editorial board members are missing.
6. *Editorial team/contact information*: Full names and affiliations of the journal's editor/s and full contact information for the editorial office are missing, the editor-in-chief is also the owner/publisher, or the editor-in-chief is also the editor of many other journals, especially in unrelated fields.
7. *Copyright and licensing*: Policies and notices of copyright (and publishing license and user license) are missing or unclear.
8. *Author fees*: Mandatory fees for publication are not stated or explained clearly on the journal website, submission process, or the letter of acknowledgment and/or are revealed only in the acceptance letter, as a condition of acceptance.

Figure 9.17 *Home Page of Open Access Scholarly Publishing Association (OASPA)*

9. *Process for identification of and dealing with allegations of research misconduct*: There is no description on how cases of alleged misconduct are handled.
10. *Publication ethics*: There are no policies on publishing ethics (e.g., authorship/contributorship, data sharing and reproducibility, intellectual property, ethical oversight, conflicts of interest, corrections/retractions). See: publicationethics.org.
11. *Publishing schedule*: The periodicity of publication is not indicated and/or the publishing schedule appears erratic from the available journal content.
12. *Access*: The way(s) in which content is available to readers, and any associated costs, is not stated, and in some cases listed articles are not available at all.
13. *Archiving*: There is no electronic backup and preservation of access to journal content (despite such claims).
14. *Revenue sources*: Business models, business partnerships/agreements, or revenue sources are not stated; publishing fees or waiver status are linked to editorial decision making.
15. *Advertising*: Advertising policy is not given, or advertisements are linked to editorial decision making or are integrated with published content.
16. *Direct marketing*: Direct marketing is obtrusive and gives misleading or false information.

9.17.2. Eriksson and Helgesson's 25 Criteria for Identifying Predatory Publishing

In 2016, scientists and researchers Stefan Eriksson and Gert Helgesson identified 25 features of predatory publishing. The complete list is as below:

1. The publisher is not a member of any recognized professional organization committed to best publishing practices (like COPE or EASE)
2. The journal is not indexed in well-established electronic databases such as MEDLINE or Web of Science.
3. The publisher claims to be a *"leading publisher"* even though it just got started the journal
4. The journal and the publisher are completely unfamiliar to you and all your colleagues
5. The papers of the journal are of poor research quality, and may not be academic at all
6. There are some basic errors in the titles and their abstracts, or frequent and repeated typographical or factual errors throughout the published papers.
7. The journal website is not professional in look and feel.
8. The journal website does not present an editorial board or gives insufficient data on names and affiliations.
9. The journal website does not display the journal's editorial office location or uses an incorrect address
10. The publishing schedule is not clearly stated
11. The journal-title claims a national affiliation that does not match its location (such as "American Journal of …" while being located on another continent) or includes "International" in its title while having a single-country editorial board

12. The journal copies another journal title or the website
13. The journal provides an impact factor in spite of the fact that the journal is new which means that the impact cannot yet be calculated
14. The journal claims an unrealistically high impact based on false alternative impact factors such as 7 for a bioethics journal, which is far beyond the top notation
15. The journal website posts non-related or non-academic advertisements
16. The publisher of the journal has released an overwhelmingly large suite of new journals at one occasion or during a very short period of time
17. The editor in chief of the journal is editor in chief also for other journals
18. The journal includes articles outside its stated scope
19. The journal sends you an unsolicited invitation to submit an article for publication while making it deliberately clear that the editor has absolutely no idea about your field of expertise
20. Emails from the journal editor are written in poor language, include exaggerated flattering (everyone is a leading profile in the field), and make contradictory claims such as *"You have to respond within 48 hours"* while later on saying "You may submit your manuscript whenever you find convenient"
21. The journal charges a submission or handling fee, instead of a publication fee which means that you have to pay even if the paper is not accepted for publication
22. The types of submission/publication fees and what they amount to are not clearly stated on the journal's website
23. The journal gives unrealistic promises regarding the speed of the peer review process
24. The journal does not describe copyright agreements clearly
25. The journal displays no strategies

9.17.3. Beall's (2015) Criteria for Identification of Predatory Journals and Publishers

Editor and Staff

- The publisher's owner is identified as the editor of each and every journal published by the organization.
- No single individual is identified as any specific journal's editor.
- The journal does not identify a formal editorial / review board.
- No academic information is provided regarding the editor, editorial staff, and/or review board members.
- Evidence exists showing that the editor and/or review board members do not possess academic expertise to reasonably qualify them to be publication gatekeepers in the journal's field.
- Two or more journals have duplicate editorial boards (i.e., same editorial board for more than one journal).
- The journals have an insufficient number of board members (e.g., 2 or 3 members), have concocted editorial boards (made up names), name scholars on their editorial board without their knowledge or permission or have

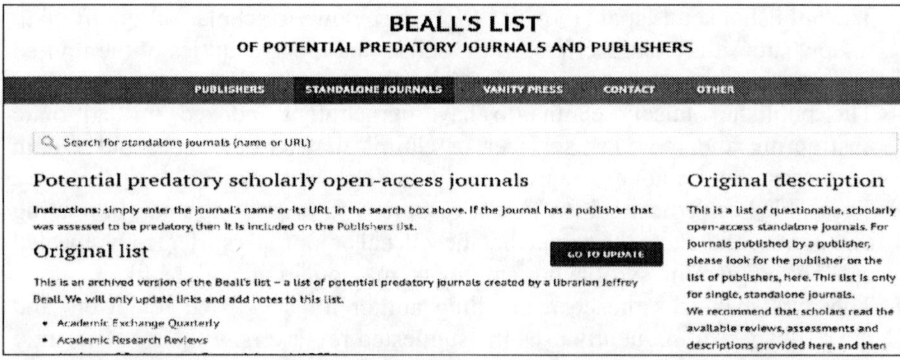

Figure 9.18 *Home Page of Beall's List of Potential Predatory Journals and Publishers*

board members who are prominent researchers but exempt them from any contributions to the journal except the use of their names and/or photographs.

- There is little or no geographical diversity among the editorial board members, especially for journals that claim to be international in scope or coverage.
- The editorial board engages in gender bias (i.e., exclusion of any female members).

Business Management

The publisher:

- Demonstrates a lack of transparency in publishing operations.
- Has no policies or practices for digital preservation.
- Begins operations with a large fleet of journals, often using a common template to quickly create each journal's home page.
- Provides insufficient information or hides information about author fees, offering to publish an author's paper and later sending an unanticipated "surprise" invoice.
- Does not allow search engines to crawl the published content, preventing the content from being indexed in academic indexes.
- Copy-proofs (locks) their PDFs, thus making it harder to check for plagiarism.

Integrity

- The name of a journal is incongruent with the journal's mission.
- The name of a journal does not adequately reflect its origin (e.g., a journal with the word "Canadian" or "Swiss" in its name when neither the publisher, editor, nor any purported institutional affiliate relates whatsoever to Canada or Switzerland).
- In its spam email or on its website, the publisher falsely claims one or more of its journals have actual (Thomson-Reuters) impact factors or advertises impact factors assigned by fake "impact factor" services, or it uses some made up measure (e.g., view factor), feigning/claiming an exaggerated international standing.

- The publisher sends spam requests for peer reviews to scholars unqualified to review submitted manuscripts, in the sense that the specialties of the invited reviewers do not match the papers sent to them.
- The publisher falsely claims to have its content indexed in legitimate abstracting and indexing services or claims that its content is indexed in resources that are not abstracting and indexing services.
- The publisher dedicates insufficient resources to preventing and eliminating author misconduct, to the extent that the journal or journals suffer from repeated cases of plagiarism, self-plagiarism, image manipulation, and the like.
- The publisher asks the corresponding author for suggested reviewers and the publisher subsequently uses the suggested reviewers without sufficiently vetting their qualifications or authenticity.

Other

A predatory publisher may:

- Re-publish papers already published in other venues/outlets without providing appropriate credits.
- Use boastful language claiming to be a "leading publisher" even though the publisher may only be a startup or a novice organization.
- Operate in a Western country chiefly for the purpose of functioning as a vanity press for scholars in a developing country (e.g., utilizing a mail drop address or PO box address in the United States, while actually operating from a developing country).
- Provide minimal or no copyediting or proofreading of submissions.
- Publish papers that are not academic at all, e.g. essays by lay people, polemical editorials, or obvious pseudo-science.
- Have a "contact us" page that only includes a web form or an email address, and the publisher hides or does not reveal its location.

9.17.4. Think. Check. Submit. Checklist for Identification of Predatory Journals and Publishers

Think. Check. Submit. Checklist helps researchers identify trusted journals and publishers for their research. Through a range of tools and practical resources, this international, cross-sector initiative aims to educate researchers, promote integrity, and build trust in credible research and publications. The checklist is a tool that will help researchers discover what they need to know when assessing whether or not a journal is a suitable venue for their research.

The checklist given below is a tool that will help you discover what you need to know when assessing whether or not a journal is a suitable venue for your research:

Think

Are you submitting your research to a trusted journal? Is it the right journal for your work?

- More research is being published worldwide.
- New journals are launched each week.
- Many researchers have concerns about predatory publishing.

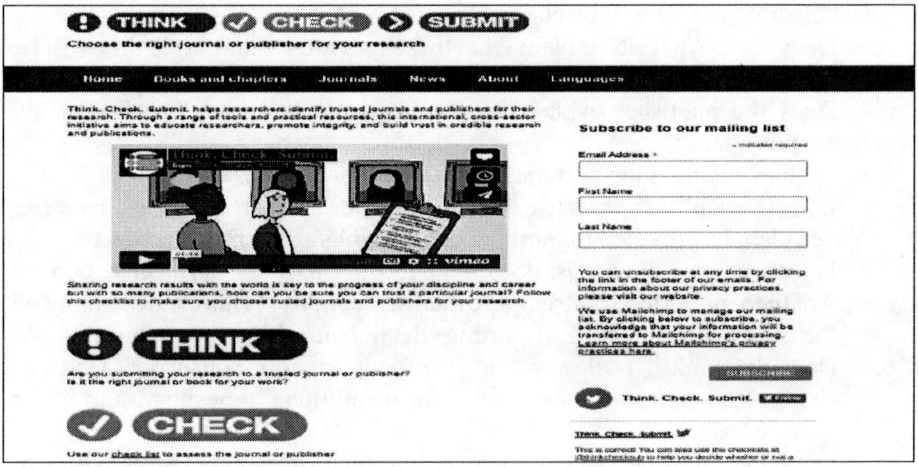

Figure 9.19 *Home Page of Think. Check. Submit. Checklist for Identification of Predatory Journals and Publishers*

- It can be challenging to find up-to-date guidance when choosing where to publish.
- How can you be sure the journal you are considering is the right journal for your research?

Check

Reference this list for your chosen journal to check if it is trusted.

- Do you or your colleagues know the journal?
  - Have you read any articles in the journal before?
  - it easy to discover the latest papers in the journal?
  - Name of journal: is the journal name the same as or easily confused with that of another?
  - Can you cross check with information about the journal in the ISSN portal?
- Can you easily identify and contact the publisher?
  - Is the publisher's name clearly displayed on the journal website?
  - Can you contact the publisher by telephone, email, and post?
- Is the journal clear about the type of peer review it uses?
  - Does the website mention whether the process involves independent/external reviewers, how many reviewers per paper?
  - Is the publisher offering a review by an expert editorial board or by researchers in your subject area?
  - Does the journal guarantee acceptance or a very short peer review time?
- Are articles indexed and/or archived in dedicated services?
  - Will your work be indexed/archived in an easily discoverable database?
  - Does the publisher ensure long term archiving and preservation of digital publications?
  - Does the publisher use permanent digital identifiers?

- Is it clear what fees will be charged?
  - Does the journal site explain what these fees are for and when they will be charged?
  - Does the publisher explain on their website how they are financially supported?
  - Do they mention the currency and amount of any fees?
  - Does the publisher website explain whether or not waivers are available?
- Are guidelines provided for authors on the publisher website?
  - For open access journals, does the publisher have a clear license policy? Are there preferred licenses? Are there exceptions permitted depending on the needs of the author? Are license details included on all publications?
  - Does the publisher allow you to retain copyright of your work? Can you share your work via, for example, an institutional repository, and under what terms?
  - Does the publisher have a clear policy regarding potential conflicts of interest for authors, editors and reviewers?
  - Can you tell what formats your paper will be available in? (e.g., HTML, XML, PDF)
  - Does the journal provide any information about metrics of usage or citations?
- Is the publisher a member of a recognized industry initiative?
  - Do they belong to the Committee on Publication Ethics (COPE)?
  - If the journal is open access, is it listed in the Directory of Open Access Journals (DOAJ)?
  - If the journal is open access, does the publisher belong to the Open Access Scholarly Publishers' Association (OASPA)?
  - Is the journal hosted on one of INASP's Journals Online platforms (for journals published in Bangladesh, Nepal, Sri Lanka, Central America and Mongolia) or on African Journals Online (AJOL, for African journals)?
  - Is the publisher a member of another trade association?

Submit
If you can answer 'yes' to most or all of the questions on the list.

Complete the check list and submit your article only if you can answer 'yes' to most or all of the questions above.

9.17.5. AMWA–EMWA–ISMPP Joint Position Statement on Predatory Publishing

The *American Medical Writers Association (AMWA)*, the *European Medical Writers Association (EMWA)* and the *International Society for Medical Publication Professionals (ISMPP)* recognize the challenges to scientific publishing being posed by predatory journals and their publishers, which employ practices undermining the quality, integrity and reliability of published scientific research. This joint position statement complements several other sets of guidelines that have helped define the characteristics of a predatory journal. Some certain characteristics have been identified as being typical of predatory journals and their publishers:

1. publishers or journals sending emails that aggressively solicit researchers;
2. a journal name that sounds somewhat familiar—but is actually a devious permutation of a legitimate journal name;
3. a website that appears unprofessional, with poor graphics, misused language, dead links and aggressive advertising;
4. no street address or in-country telephone number noted on the journal or publisher's website, or a fake address/phone number provided;
5. a lack of journal indexing in a recognized citation system such as *PubMed* or within a legitimate online directory such as the *Directory of Open Access Journals (DOAJ)*;
6. promises of unrealistically quick peer review, or no information provided about a journal's peer-review process;
7. article processing charges that are not transparent (and may be either very high or very low) or are payable on submission (that is, not dependent on the outcome of peer review);
8. claims made of broad coverage across multiple specialties in medicine or across multiple subspecialties in a particular discipline;
9. a large stable of journals that have been started very recently and/or that contain no or few published articles, are inaccessible or are of obviously poor quality;
10. an editorial board consisting of members from outside the specialty or outside the country in which the journal is published, or board members who are unknown to someone experienced in publishing in the field;
11. a submission system that is overly simple with few questions asked and no conflict-of-interest or authorship qualification information requested.

9.17.6. DOAJ (Directory of Open Access Journals) Criteria for Receipt of the DOAJ Seal

To receive the DOAJ Seal, journals must meet all of the following criteria:

1. provide permanent identifiers [e.g., DOIs] in the papers published;
2. provide DOAJ with article metadata;
3. deposit content with a long-term digital preservation or archiving program;
4. embed machine-readable CC licensing information in articles;
5. allow generous reuse and mixing of content, in accordance with a CC BY, CC BY-SA or CC BY-NC license;
6. have a deposit policy registered with a deposit policy registry;
7. allow the author to hold the copyright without restrictions.

9.17.7. WAME's (World Association of Medical Editors) Warning Sign for Identifying Predatory or Pseudo-Journals

Because existing initiatives do not provide error-proof methods for determining the status of a particular journal, individuals who aim to gain a high level of assurance about a journal's status need to investigate further. This WAME document aims to provide guidance to help editors, researchers, funders, academic institutions and other stakeholders distinguish predatory journals from legitimate journals. WAME developed the framework illustrated in Figure 9.20 for such investigation. This framework begins with assessing whether the journal has any of the characteristics Beall viewed as potentially problematic *(See Beall's Criteria)*, its presence in the DOAJ, and presence of *Think. Check. Submit.* features, with further investigation guided by these initial indicators. Assessment remains subjective, but reviewing the journals' website and practices/policies for evidence of the *"warning sign"* features (given below) will help inform this judgment. The more "red flags" that are present, the more hesitant one should be to consider the journal a desirable publication venue.

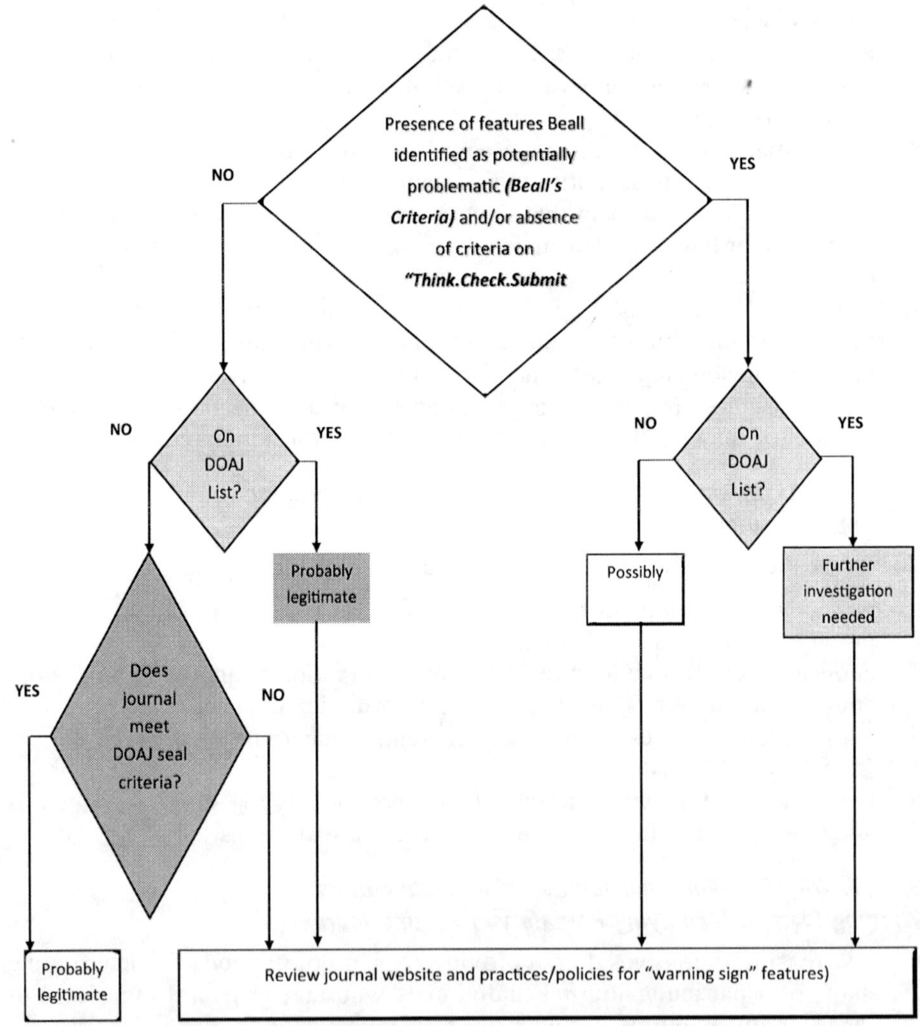

Figure 9.20 *WAME's Flowchart for Identifying predatory or Pseudo-Journals*

Table 9.2 *Beall's Criteria for Identification of Predatory Journals and Publishers*

Editor and Staff

- The publisher's owner is identified as the editor of each and every journal published by the organization.
- No single individual is identified as any specific journal's editor.
- The journal does not identify a formal editorial / review board.
- No academic information is provided regarding the editor, editorial staff, and/or review board members.
- Evidence exists showing that the editor and/or review board members do not possess academic expertise to reasonably qualify them to be publication gatekeepers in the journal's field.
- Two or more journals have duplicate editorial boards (i.e., same editorial board for more than one journal).
- The journals have an insufficient number of board members (e.g., 2 or 3 members), have concocted editorial boards (made up names), name scholars on their editorial board without their knowledge or permission or have board members who are prominent researchers but exempt them from any contributions to the journal except the use of their names and/or photographs.
- There is little or no geographical diversity among the editorial board members, especially for journals that claim to be international in scope or coverage.
- The editorial board engages in gender bias (i.e., exclusion of any female members).

Business management, the publisher...

- Demonstrates a lack of transparency in publishing operations.
- Has no policies or practices for digital preservation.
- Begins operations with a large fleet of journals, often using a common template to quickly create each journal's home page.
- Provides insufficient information or hides information about author fees, offering to publish an author's paper and later sending an unanticipated "surprise" invoice.
- Does not allow search engines to crawl the published content, preventing the content from being indexed in academic indexes.
- Copy-proofs (locks) their PDFs, thus making it harder to check for plagiarism.

Integrity

- The name of a journal is incongruent with the journal's mission.
- The name of a journal does not adequately reflect its origin (e.g., a journal with the word "Canadian" or "Swiss" in its name when neither the publisher, editor, nor any purported institutional affiliate relates whatsoever to Canada or Switzerland).
- In its spam email or on its website, the publisher falsely claims one or more of its journals have actual (Thomson-Reuters) impact factors, or advertises impact factors assigned by fake "impact factor" services, or it uses some made up measure (e.g. view factor), feigning/claiming an exaggerated international standing.

- The publisher sends spam requests for peer reviews to scholars unqualified to review submitted manuscripts, in the sense that the specialties of the invited reviewers do not match the papers sent to them.
- The publisher falsely claims to have its content indexed in legitimate abstracting and indexing services or claims that its content is indexed in resources that are not abstracting and indexing services.
- The publisher dedicates insufficient resources to preventing and eliminating author misconduct, to the extent that the journal or journals suffer from repeated cases of plagiarism, self-plagiarism, image manipulation, and the like.
- The publisher asks the corresponding author for suggested reviewers and the publisher subsequently uses the suggested reviewers without sufficiently vetting their qualifications or authenticity.

Other

- Re-publish papers already published in other venues/outlets without providing appropriate credits.
- Use boastful language claiming to be a "leading publisher" even though the publisher may only be a startup or a novice organization.
- Operate in a Western country chiefly for the purpose of functioning as a vanity press for scholars in a developing country (e.g., utilizing a mail drop address or PO box address in the United States, while actually operating from a developing country).
- Provide minimal or no copyediting or proofreading of submissions.
- Publish papers that are not academic at all, e.g. essays by lay people, polemical editorials, or obvious pseudo-science.
- Have a "contact us" page that only includes a web form or an email address, and the publisher hides or does not reveal its location.

Poor journal standards/practice (do not equal predatory criteria, but authors should consider these items prior to manuscript submissions)

- The publisher copies "authors guidelines" verbatim (or with minor editing) from other publishers.
- The publisher lists insufficient contact information, including contact information that does not clearly state the headquarters location or misrepresents the headquarters location (e.g., through the use of addresses that are actually mail drops).
- The publisher publishes journals that are excessively broad (e.g., Journal of Education) in order to attract more articles and gain more revenue from author fees.
- The publisher publishes journals that combine two or more fields not normally treated together (e.g., International Journal of Business, Humanities and Technology).
- The publisher charges authors for publishing but requires transfer of copyright and retains copyright on journal content. Or the publisher requires the copyright transfer upon submission of manuscript.

- The publisher has poorly maintained websites, including dead links, prominent misspellings and grammatical errors on the website.
- The publisher makes unauthorized use of licensed images on their website, taken from the open web, without permission or licensing from the copyright owners.

Table 9.3 *Criteria for Receipt of the DOAJ Seal*

To receive the DOAJ Seal, journals must meet all of the following criteria:
• provide permanent identifiers [e.g., DOIs] in the papers published;
• provide DOAJ with article metadata;
• deposit content with a long term digital preservation or archiving program;
• embed machine-readable CC licensing information in articles;
• allow generous reuse and mixing of content, in accordance with a CC BY, CC BY-SA or CC BY-NC license;
• have a deposit policy registered with a deposit policy registry;
• allow the author to hold the copyright without restrictions.

Table 9.4 *Checklist from Think. Check. Submit. Initiative*

1. Do you or your colleagues know the journal?
   - Have you read any articles in the journal before?
   - Is it easy to discover the latest papers in the journal?
2. Can you easily identify and contact the publisher?
   - Is the publisher name clearly displayed on the journal website?
   - Can you contact the publisher by telephone, email, and post?
3. Is the journal clear about the type of peer review it uses?
4. Are articles indexed in services that you use?
5. Is it clear what fees will be charged?
   - Does the journal site explain what these fees are for and when they will be charged?
6. Do you recognise the editorial board?
   - Have you heard of the editorial board members?
   - Do the editorial board members mention the journal on their own websites?
7. Is the publisher a member of a recognized industry initiative?
   - Do they belong to the Committee on Publication Ethics (COPE)?
   - If the journal is open access, is it listed in the Directory of Open Access Journals (DOAJ)?
   - If the journal is open access, does the publisher belong to the Open Access Scholarly Publishers Association (OASPA)?
   - Is the publisher a member of another trade association?

Table 9.5 *"Warning Sign" Features that Should Increase Suspicion that a Journal is Predatory (although features may be absent even in a predatory journal)*

- Someone you know listed on the editorial board or journal staff, when you query them about the journal, is unaware of their supposed affiliation with the journal.
- No information as to whether there are author fees in the Instructions for Authors.
- Peer review is not mentioned in the Instructions for Authors.
- Little or no information is provided regarding the editor or editorial board.
- No location is listed for the journal offices, or location is very different than the location of the editors and editorial board.
- The journal website is not easily accessible in an internet search (could be a problem in a legitimate journal in a low or middle income locale).
- The journal publishes either an unusually small, unusually large, or markedly variable numbers of articles each year.
- You or your colleagues have received formulaic e-mail solicitations for submissions that do not specify an interest in particular projects or areas that you are working on.
- Promised routine turnaround times for review and publication are so rapid that they seem "too good to be true" and would be unlikely to encompass the time necessary for true peer review.
- You do not receive a response to e-mail or telephone messages sent to the editor or journal office within a few days.
- The name of the journal is very similar to the name of a well-known, established journal with a good reputation.
- The publication fees are atypical for the scholarly publishing industry (much higher or much lower fees can both signal problems [with recognition that journals in low or middle income countries may have legitimately low fees]).
- It is difficult to identify articles published in the journal when searching Google Scholar or other databases (with recognition that new journals or those in low or middle income countries may face lags in indexing).
- Information about author affiliations and/or contact information is not present in published articles.

9.17.8. Consortium for Academic and Research Ethics (CARE)

The *"Quality Mandate"* of the University Grants Commission (UGC) emphasizes importance of promoting high quality research and creation of new knowledge by faculty members. For this purpose, efforts to distinguish between standard and predatory/ dubious/deceptive journals and ensure that Indian academic work appears only in globally recognized and acceptable journals, the UGC has set up a Consortium for Academic and Research Ethics (CARE), as announced vide the UGC's notification of 14 January 2019 to continuously monitor and identify quality journals across disciplines. The main task of the CARE is to improve the quality of research in Indian Universities and to promote academic and research integrity as well as publication ethics.

9.17.8.1. Objectives of CARE

- To promote the quality research by the faculty members and creating credible research
- To promote academic and research integrity as well as publication ethics.
- To promote high quality publications in reputed journals that would help in achieving higher global ranks and overall improvement of the quality of research and education.
- To Develop an approach and methodology for identification of good quality journals.
- To prevent publications in dubious / sub-standard journals which reflect adversely and tarnish the image of research work and thus lead to a long-term academic damage.
- To create and maintain a *"CARE Reference List of Quality Journals"* for various academic evaluations.

9.17.8.2. Need for UGC-CARE List

- The credibility of research publications is extremely important because it represents the academic image of not just an individual, but of the institution and the entire nation.
- The number of research articles published in reputed journals is one of the globally-accepted indicators considered for various academic purposes such as institutional ranking, appointments, promotions of faculty members, membership of academic committees, award of research degrees etc.
- The problem of predatory / dubious / sub-standard journals has become a cause of serious concern all over the world.
- The percentage of research articles published in poor quality journals is reported to be high in India, which has adversely affected its image.
- Publications in dubious / sub-standard journals reflect adversely leading to long-term academic damage and a tarnished image of an individual, institution and the nation.

9.17.8.3. Scope of the UGC-CARE List

- UGC-CARE has taken the responsibility of preparing the *"UGC-CARE Reference List of Quality Journals"* (UGC-CARE List).
- A list of Indian journals, especially from disciplines of Arts, Humanities, Languages, Culture and Indian Knowledge Systems is being prepared and updated quarterly (UGC-CARE Group I).
- The UGC-CARE List includes journals from all disciplines indexed in globally accepted databases, such as indexed in *Scopus* (Source list) or *Web of Science* (Arts and Humanities Citation Index Source Publication, Science Citation Index Expanded Source Publication, Social Science Citation Index Source Publication). These journals are to be considered for all academic purposes. Journals indexed in Scopus and / or Web of Science are part of UGC-CARE List Group II.

9.17.8.4. UGC-CARE Initiative for Identifying Cloned/Predatory Journals

Worldwide there is an increase in deceptive publications in predatory journals which are usually online and offer the incentive of immediate/overnight publications/free/or at low cost. Due to the academic pressure to publish or perish many researchers take this short cut route and the number of such predatory journals is increasing exponentially. Most of the academic and research organizations give considerable weight to number of research publications in a year while assessing them for promotions. In India, ICMR, UGC and other agencies have recommended academic as well as scientific community to avoid publication in predatory journals and conferences.

UGC has released in a public notice on Academic Integrity dated 14th June 2019 stated that *"Any publication in predatory/dubious journals or presentations in predatory/dubious conferences should not be considered for academic credit for selection, confirmation, promotion, performance appraisal, award of scholarship or academic degrees or credits in any form. Vice Chancellors, selection committees, research supervisors/guides and such other experts involved in academic evaluation/assessment are hereby advised that they must ensure that their decisions are primarily based on quality of research work and not merely on number of publications".*

The Consortium for Academic and Research Ethics (UGC-CARE) has listed legitimate and good quality journals and also reported about the increase in number of publications in these journals within a very short span of time without valid peer review and editorial board in last consecutive years. By doing so, these journals are accepting poor quality scientific research without any peer review and charging payment fees for publication. A good initiative is that 'UGC-CARE' provides the *'List of Cloned Journals for UGC-CARE listed Journals of Group I and Group II'* at his website (https://ugccare.unipune.ac.in/apps1/home/index). A good thing is that 'UGC- CARE' regularly updates the cloned list of journals.

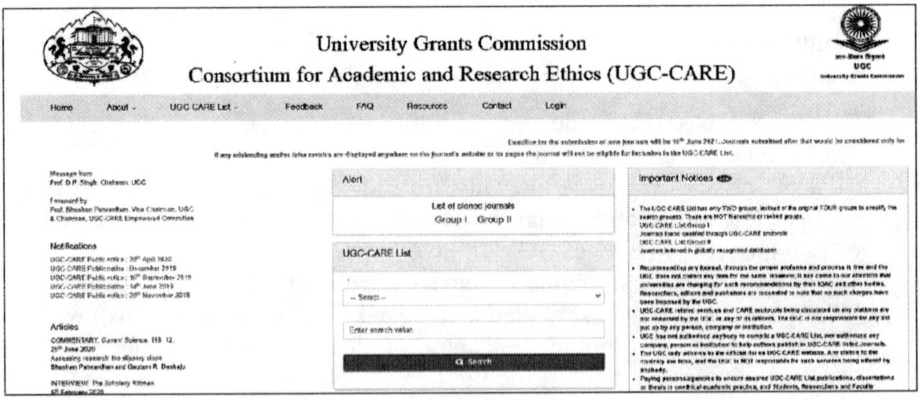

Figure 9.21 *List of Cloned Journals (Group I and Group II) on Home Page of UGC-CARE Website*

Figure 9.22 *List of Cloned Journals: Group II (UGC-CARE Website)*

9.18. COPE's Suggestions to Avoid Predatory Journals and Publishers

Below are some COPE's suggested actions for selected stakeholders to take so as to tackle, avoid, and raise awareness of the problem of predatory journals.

Authors, Professional Societies and Institutions

1. Educate researchers, supervisors, librarians, and administrators in publishing literacy and about fake journals (see the list of warning signs above based on the 16 Principles of transparency).
2. Identify trustworthy journals through the *'Think.Check.Submit.'* campaign. (https://thinkchecksubmit.org/)
3. Create and continually update community and discipline-specific journal whitelists/safelists using clear criteria, similar to the 'Directory of nursing journals' jointly maintained by Nurse author & editor and the International academy of nursing editors. (https://nursingeditors.com/journals-directory/)
4. Verify spam invitations, made by email, text message, or telephone call, to submit manuscripts (e.g., research papers or invited reviews) or attend conferences. Consider using the DNS Checker to check the Internet Protocol of suspected spam. (https://dnschecker.org/ip-blacklist-checker.php)
5. Check journal names, ISSN codes, and URLs are real ones; verify any claimed metrics, indexed status, and organisational membership. Check that researcher profiles on institutional websites or LinkedIn mention claimed editorship of journals.
6. Read a sample of archived articles from potential target journals to check quality. Avoid citing predatory journal articles and beware when performing systematic and meta-analyses.
7. Beware of paying author fees, especially those that are suddenly demanded as a condition of acceptance, without checking what they are for, and assigning copyright to a predatory journal. Demand manuscript withdrawal if payment has not yet been made and/or copyright has not yet been assigned as a condition of acceptance.

Funders and Institutions

1. Discourage publication in predatory journals and discourage citation of articles in predatory journals.
2. Exercise caution in the use of journal metrics during research assessments and staff appraisals. Consider using peer review, as well as the following guidelines and recommendations:
    i. San Francisco declaration on research assessment (DORA). (https://sfdora.org/)
    ii. Leiden manifesto for research metrics. (https://www.leidenmanifesto.org/)
    iii. The metric tide. (https://responsiblemetrics.org/the-metric-tide/)
    iv. The Hong Kong principles for assessing researchers: Fostering research integrity. (https://osf.io/m9abx/)

Journals and Publishers

1. Check that your journals adhere to the COPE/DOAJ/OASPA/WAME Principles of transparency and best practice in scholarly publishing (https://bit.ly/2lZNPYU) and COPE's Core practices. (https://bit.ly/2m2kFrN).
2. Trademark journals if possible. Periodically perform online searches of your journal and articles to check if they are being misappropriated. Consider legal action and issue cease and desist letters in cases of trademark or copyright breech.
3. Consider making use of publicly visible platforms for open review or publishing 'open reports' (peer review reports with or without reviewers' names) for transparency.
4. Write editorials to promote the *'Think.Check.Submit.'* campaign and inform readers/indexes if you identify predatory versions of your journal/s.
5. Discourage citation of articles published in fake journals.

Reviewers and Editors

1. Periodically perform online searches of yourself to check if you appear on any journal or conference editorial boards without your knowledge or permission. Demand removal of your name if necessary.
2. Verify spam invitations, made by email, text message, or telephone call, to join reviewer panels or editorial boards. Consider using the DNS Checker to check the Internet Protocol of suspected spam. (https://dnschecker.org/ip-blacklist-checker.php).
3. Check journal names, ISSN codes, and URLs are real ones; verify any claimed metrics, indexed status, and organisational membership.
4. Discourage citation of articles published in fake journals

9.19. Journal Selector/Finder/Matcher Tools

Finding a good match between the manuscript and a peer-reviewed academic journal is the key to getting published efficiently and effectively. A good match will not only minimize the chances of manuscript rejection, but also maximize the chances that the paper is read and cited. These tools given below provide help for how to select and shortlist appropriate target journals. The tools below could help researchers to identify journals that might be interested in publishing your article. Researchers will need to enter a title and a description (abstract) of his/her paper in order to receive a list of suggestions. Some important journal selector tools are listed below:

- Elsevier Journal Finder
- JANE (Journal/Author Name Estimator)
- Springer Journal Suggester
- Directory of Open Access Journals (DOAJ)
- Master Journal List (MJL)
- Edanz Journal Selector
- JournalGuide
- Open Journal Matcher
- Enago Open Access Journal Finder

The above Journal Finder Tools

- Helps inexperienced authors to select the correct journals for their papers
- Helps authors working in multidisciplinary fields identify possible journals
- Highlights journals that offer open-access options

9.19.1. Elsevier Journal Finder (URL is http://journalfinder.elsevier.com.)

Rejection is the norm in academic publishing. One of the main reasons for rejections is that the topics of the submitted papers are not relevant to the scope of the journal, even when the papers themselves are excellent. Submission to a journal that fits well with the publication may avoid this issue. A system that is able to suggest journals that have published similar articles to the submitted papers may help authors choose where to submit. The Elsevier journal finder, a freely available online service, is one of the most comprehensive journal recommender systems, covering all scientific domains and more than 2,900 per-reviewed Elsevier journals. The procedure is to paste text, such as an abstract, and get a list of recommend journals and relevant metadata.

The tool is designed to:

- Help less experienced authors select suitable journals for their papers
- Enable authors working across multidisciplinary fields to identify possible journals
- Highlight journals that offer open access options, and provide information on publication speeds and impact factors

9.19.1.1. How to find best journal through 'Elsevier Journal Finder' for the publication of paper

Step-1: First of all, open the website of Elsevier Journal Finder (URL is http://journalfinder.elsevier.com.). The home page (Figure-9.23) of the 'Elsevier Journal Finder' will be as follows:

Here, we can see the three (Figure-9.24) windows namely:

- Paper title
- Paper abstract
- Keywords and
- Field of research

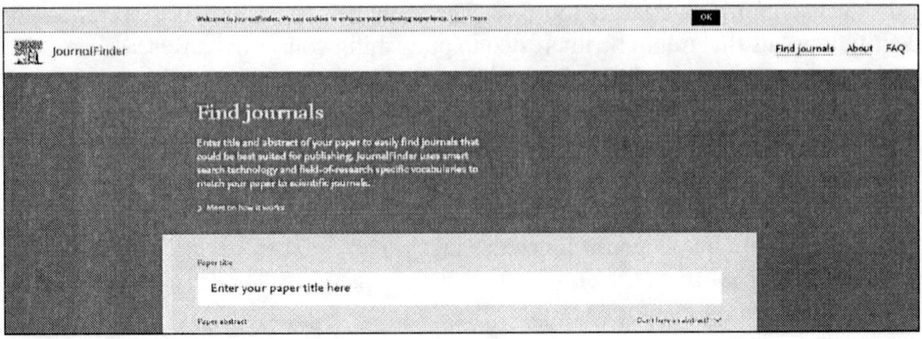

Figure 9.23 *'Home Page' of 'Elsevier Journal Finder'*

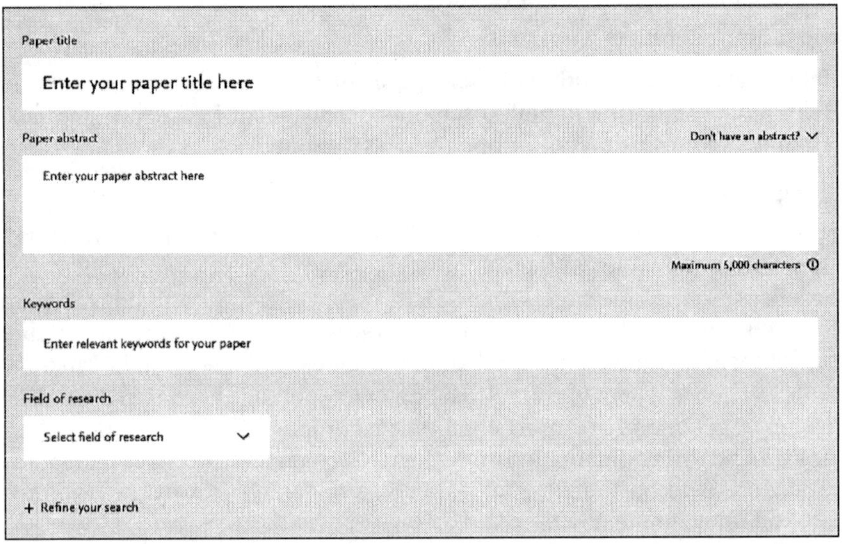

Figure 9.24 *Entering Windows*

Step-2: Now, enter the paper title, enter your paper abstract and relevant keywords of the paper for which you are finding the best journal for publication.

Step-3: You can also refine your searches with the help of 'Select field of research'. For this purpose, you can select the appropriate field of your research paper. You can select one or more than one fields of research (See figure 9.25).

Step-4: You can also refine the scope of your search to get more relevant journals. For this, you have to click on 'Refine your search'. When you click on this button then a new window will pop-up like this (Figure 9.26)

Here, you will be provided three options as follows:

- Publication type
- Journal impact and
- Review and publication time

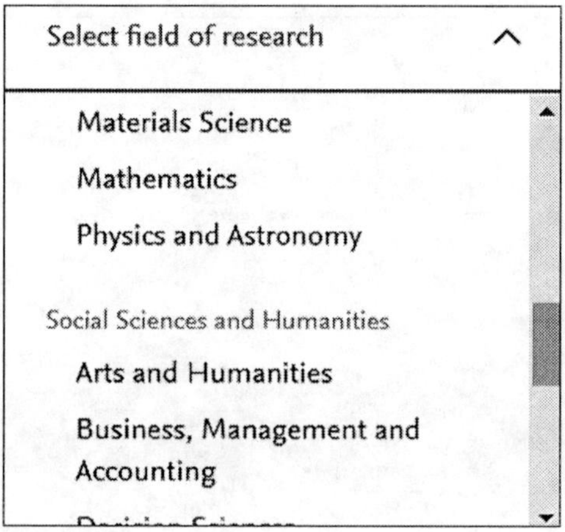

Figure 9.25 *Using 'Select field research' Option for Refining the Results*

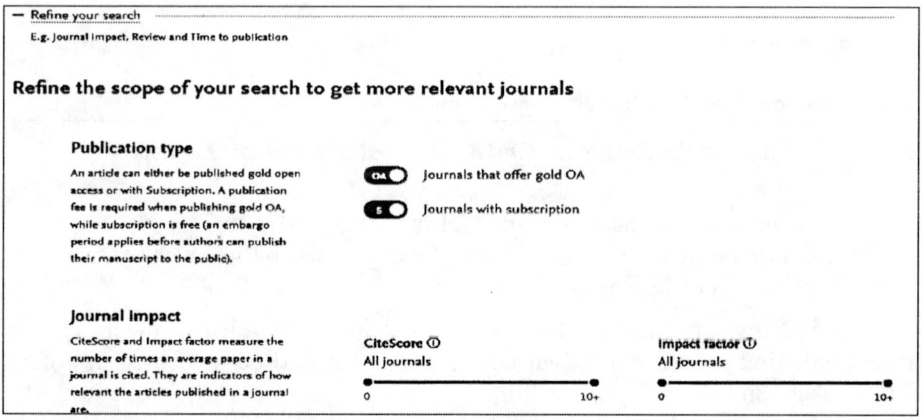

Figure 9.26 *Sorting Journals by 'Best match' Option*

Step-5: You can select 'journals that offer gold open access' or 'journals with subscription'; 'cite score', 'impact factor' and 'time of first decision' and 'time to publication' as per your requirement of the publication in the journal. You can select filters as per your need. Then click on 'Find journal' button.

Suppose we have entered the following entries for finding the best journal for publication of my article/paper (Figure 9.27):

- *Paper title*: 'Role of ICT in Research'
- *Paper abstract*: There is a growing need to understand the importance of ICT in the field of research.
- *Keywords*: ICT Skills, Research Collaboration
- *Field of research*: Social Sciences, Arts and Humanities
- *Publication type*: 'Journals that offer gold OA' and 'Journals with subscription'

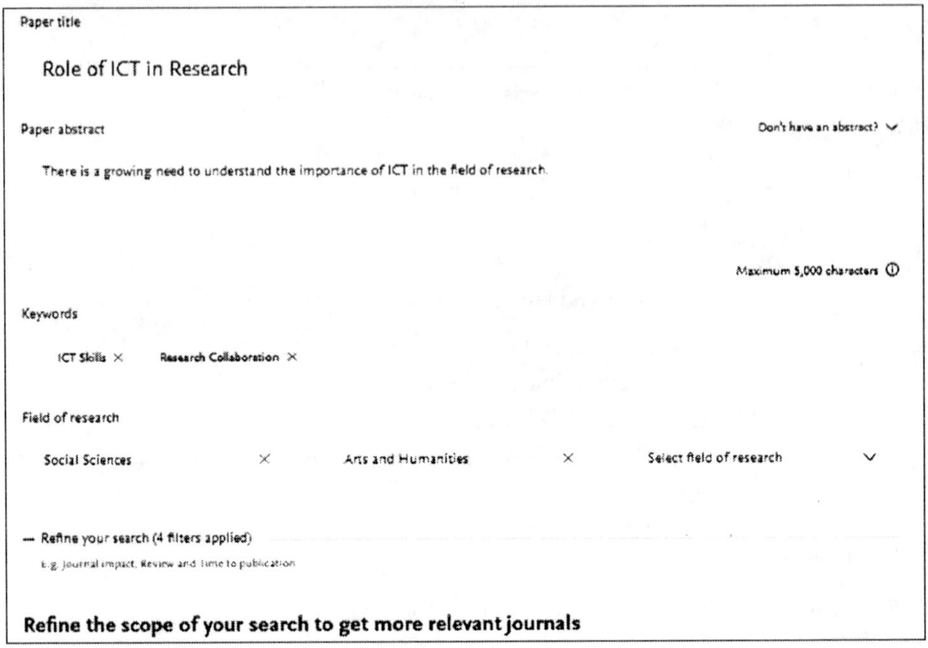

Figure 9.27 *Entering the Details for Find out the List of Matching Journals*

- *Journal impact*: 'CiteScore-Up to 9'; 'Impact factor-Up to 7'
- *Review and publication time*: 'Time to 1st decision-Up to 49 weeks'; 'Time to publication-Up to 16 weeks'

Step-6: Now, on clicking the button 'Find journals', the 'Elsevier Journal Finder' will find the matching journals for us and it will be presented in a new window as given below (Figure-9.28):

Here you can see that the matching journals for our publication of our paper is 20 according to our manuscript.

Step-7: By clicking on the arrow button, we can see the full details of the journal. Suppose we have to find the full details of the second journal 'Information and Organization'. For this purpose, we have to click on the arrow button given list of journals. See figure 9.29

We can also sort the journals for paper by 'Best match'. See figure 9.30

9.19.1.2. Features of Elsevier Journal Finder

In the search list authors will get information about:

- *Match*: matching (in per cent, if you hold the cursor above the matching icon)
- *Impact*: an Impact Factor is shown if the journal is indexed in Journal Citation Report (Web of Science)
- *Editorial Times*: the time between the submitted manuscript and a first decision to send it further for peer review or rejection
- *Acceptance*: the share of manuscripts in percentage that are accepted for publication in the journal

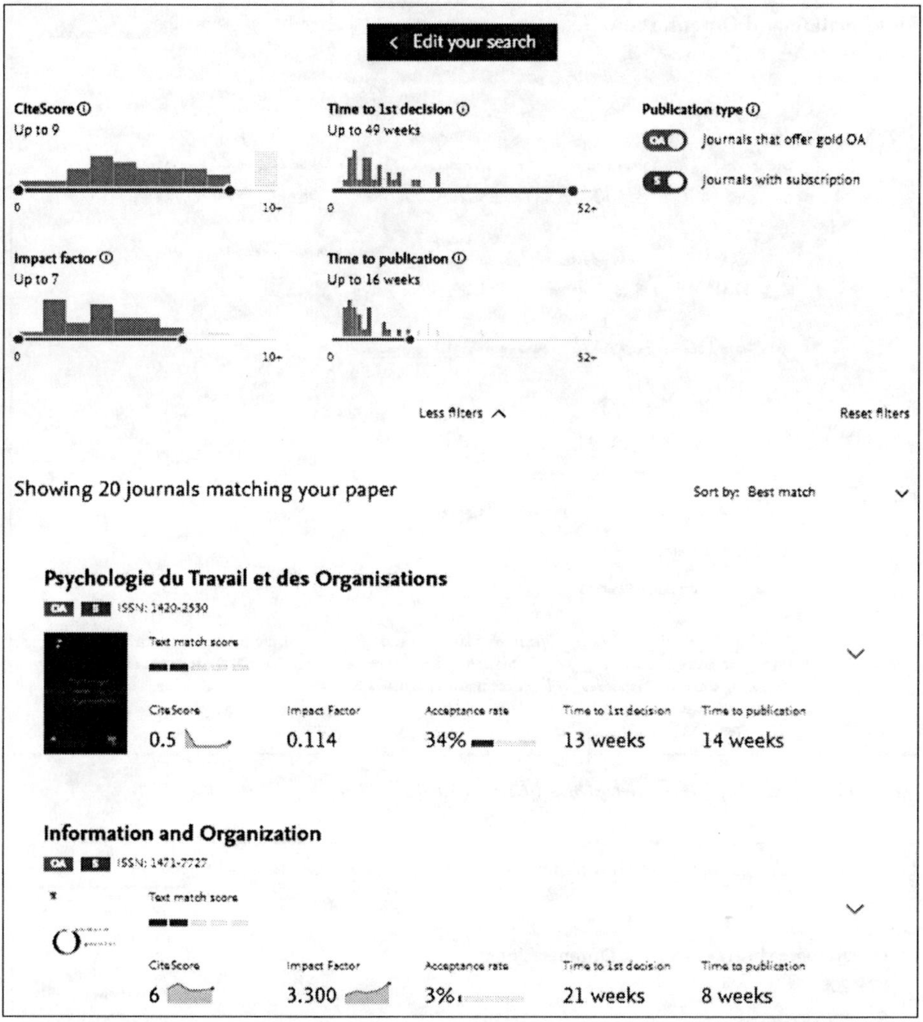

Figure 9.28 *List of Matching Journals for the Paper*

- *Production Times*: time in weeks from acceptance to online posting of the article on the journal's website
- *Open Access*: open access options where:
  - *Yes*: means that it is an open-access journal
  - *Optional*: means that you can make your article open access for a fee stated in the heading Open Access Fee (also known as APC — Article Processing Charge)
  - – [a dash]: means that no open access options are available for the journal
- *Embargo period*: the amount of time after having published the article in the journal before you are allowed to share your peer-reviewed accepted

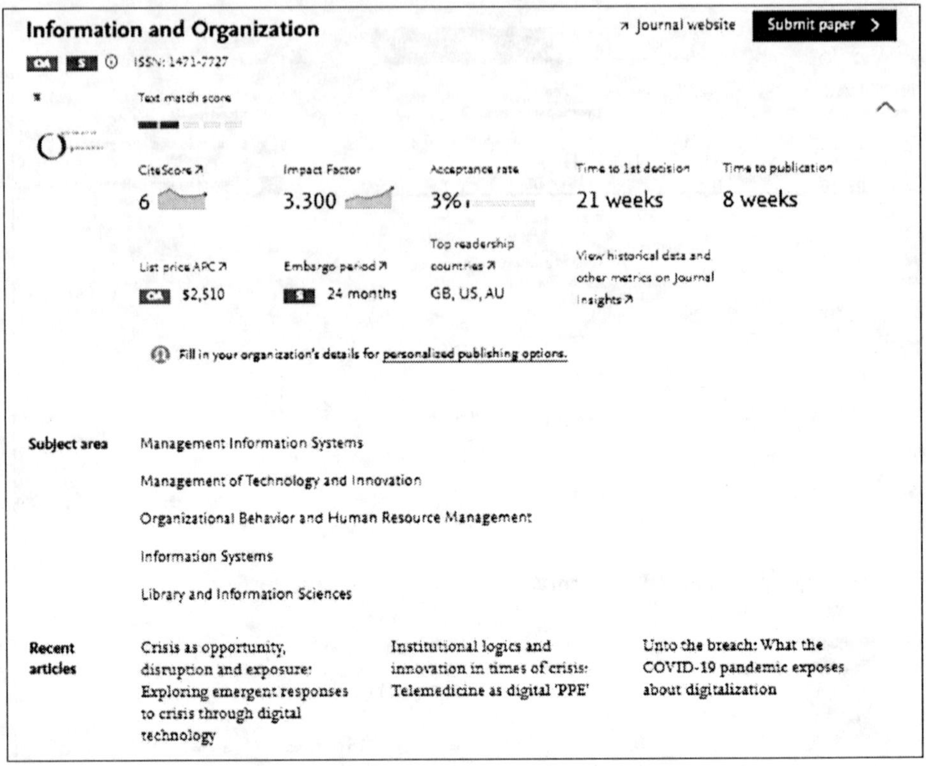

Figure 9.29 *Seeing the Full Details of the Journal*

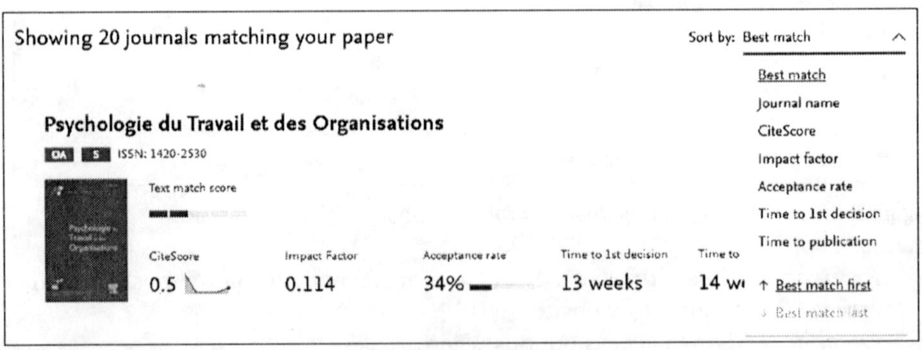

Figure 9.30 *Sorting Journals by Best Match Option*

manuscript in a digital repository (such as DiVA). Read more about this so-called *green open access* option.

- *Open Access Fee*: the author fee (APC) to make the article open access
- *User License*: icons that describe what others can do with the article based on *Creative Commons*

9.19.2. JANE (Journal/Author Name Estimator)

JANE: Journal/Author Name Estimator, a freely available Web-based tool, to identify suitable journals. In addition to locating journals, JANE can also locate relevant articles to cite in your paper and even help find manuscript reviewers. This is supported by the Biosematics Group; created and maintained by Martijn Schuemie. The system would match the information you entered with the journals in PubMed. This tool does not search for journals outside the collection of PubMed.

Jane (Journal/Author Name Estimator) is a freely available web-based application that, on the basis of a sample text (e.g., the title and abstract of a manuscript), can suggest journals and experts who have published similar articles. The Journal/Author Name Estimator (JANE) is a free online bibliographic journal selection tool. Journal selection tools, also known as journal matching or journal comparison tools, are popular resources that help authors determine the most appropriate in scope journal to publish their manuscripts. JANE is one of the earliest journal selection tools, debuting in 2007. The resource is web-based and allows users to input keywords, abstract text, or author names and view related articles based on user-supplied terms.

To search in JANE, enter the title, author, and/or abstract of the paper in the search box, and click on "Find journals," "Find authors," or "Find articles." JANE will then compare your document to millions of documents in MEDLINE to find the best matching journals, authors or articles. JANE can also be searched by keyword.

JANE is updated monthly and includes papers with abstracts that were published in the last 10 years. The database works by searching for the 50 articles that are most similar to your input. For each of these articles, a similarity score between that article and your input is calculated. The similarity scores of all the articles belonging to a certain journal or author are summed to calculate the confidence score for that journal or author. The results are ranked by confidence score.

JANE also calculates an Article Influence (AI) score. The AI measures how often articles in the journal are cited within the first five years after its publication. These citations are weighted based on the influence of the journals from which citations are received: being cited in an article in Science can boost a journal's AI more than being cited in an article in an obscure journal. Jane states that citations included contain an abstract, were published in the last 10 years, and did not belong to one of these categories: "comment, editorial, news, historical article, congresses, biography, newspaper article, practice guideline, interview, bibliography, legal cases, lectures, consensus development conference, addresses, clinical conference, patient education handout, directory, technical report, festschrift, retraction of publication, retracted publication, duplicate publication, scientific integrity review, published erratum, periodical index, dictionary, legislation or government publication."

9.19.2.1. How does Jane work?

Jane first searches for the 50 articles that are most similar to your input. For each of these articles, a similarity score between that article and your input is calculated.

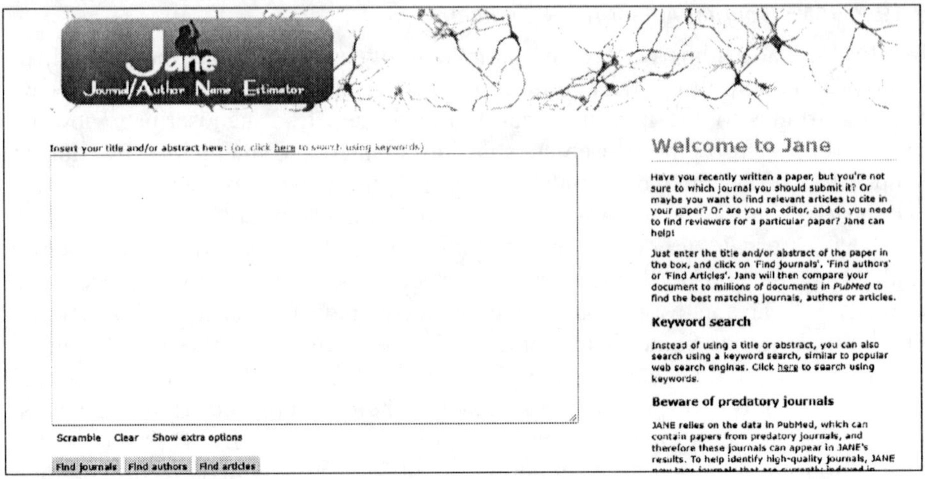

Figure 9.31 *Home Page of 'Jane'*

The similarity scores of all the articles belonging to a certain journal or author are summed to calculate the confidence score for that journal or author. The results are ranked by confidence score.

9.19.2.2. Search Methods of JANE

Jane has three basic search methods; by journal, by article, and by author (Figure-9.31).

Jane analyzes only first 50 results in active journals.

Search by 'Find Journals'

- Typing in a search term, for *"Teacher Education,"* and then clicking the Find Journals button returns a page with journal titles ranked from the most to least number of articles on 'Teacher Education' (Figure-8.32). This results page has four columns:
- Confidence level
- Journal Title
- Article Influence and
- Articles

The article influence score is calculated using 'Eigenfactor' (http://www.eigenfactor.org) which uses data from 'Thomson Scientific's Journal Citation Reports (JCR)'. The score itself is hyperlinked to the Eigenfactor page where the details about the journal's scores and publication history may be found. The blue bar indicates the percentage of journals in MEDLINE that have a lower Article Influence score, according to Eigenfactor. Some journals may not show an article influence score because they are not listed in the JCR or because they must "be cited in the last 5 years by some journal that is listed in the JCR." Journals may also not be listed because they are "those publications that are smaller than a threshold size of 12 articles per year averaged over 5 years, … or those journals that do not cite other journals listed in the JCR."

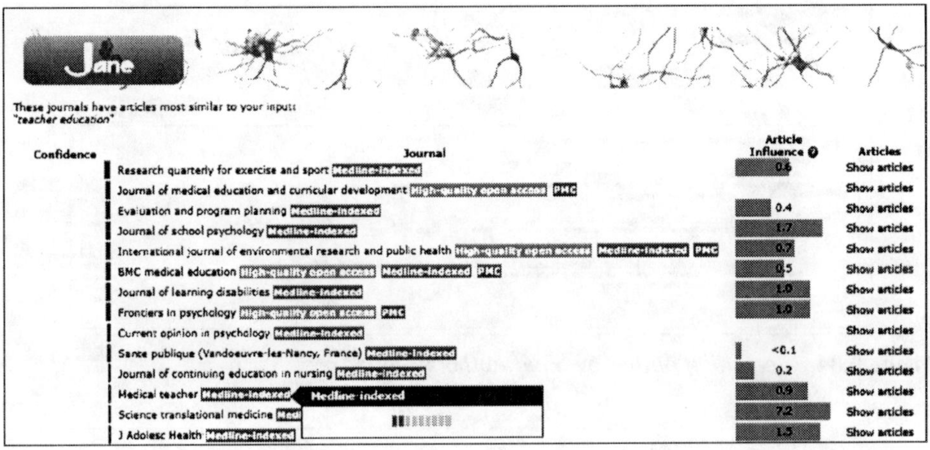

Figure 9.32 *Searching Journals by 'Find Journal' Option*

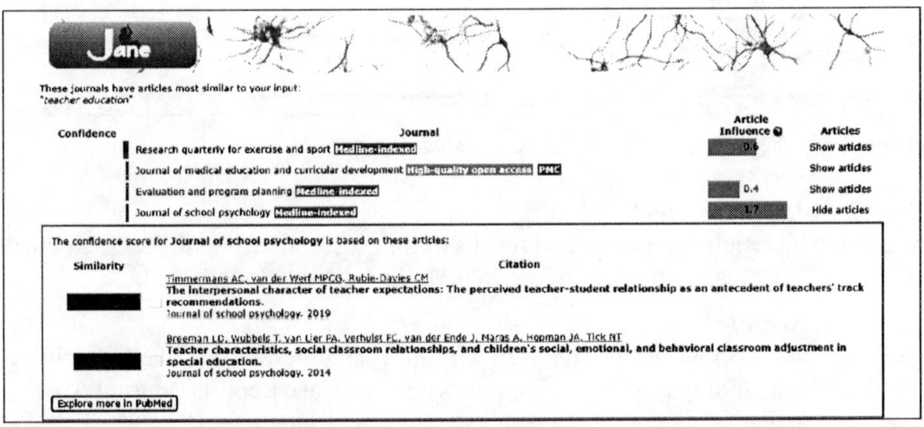

Figure 9.33 *'Show Article' Option for view of citations from the Journal*

Clicking on 'Show Articles' opens a view of citations from that journal that are hyperlinked to the PubMed abstract (Figure-9.33). There is also an "Explore More in PubMed" link that goes to PubMed and shows those citations and others from that journal (a maximum of 20 articles are displayed). There are no additional ways to sort the results, such as by publication date, but the once the "Explore More in PubMed" link is clicked results may be sorted in PubMed.

Search by 'Find Authors'

The Author Search (Figure-9.34) returns in descending order authors who have written repeatedly about the topic searched for. In these results you may click on Show Articles to view additional citations of related articles written by that author. The author names in the citations are hyperlinked directly to PubMed. E-mail addresses may be available as well.

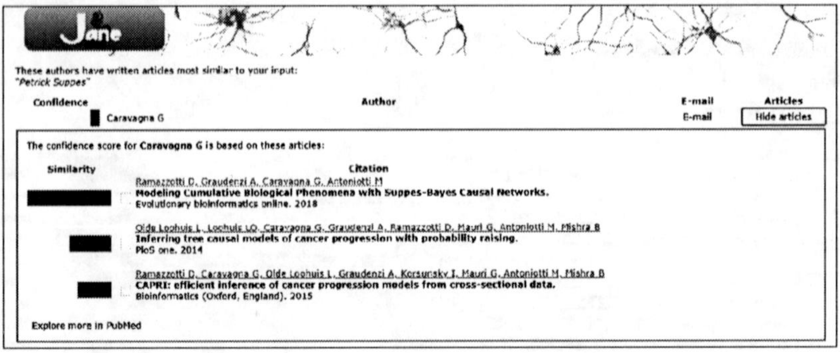

Figure 9.34 *Searching Author by 'Find Authors' Option*

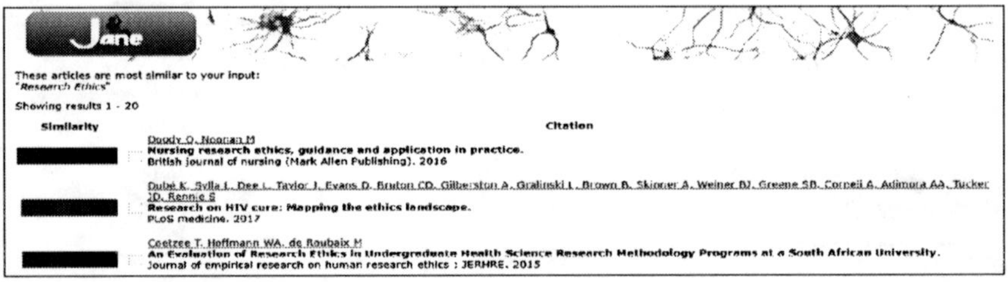

Figure 9.35 *Searching Article by 'Find Articles' Option*

Search by 'Find Articles'

Searching by article returns ranked results of the closest match to the text searched (Figure-8.35). Again, all citations are hyperlinked directly to PubMed.

Advanced Search

Clicking the *"Show Extra Options"* button (Figure-8.36) unveils refining capabilities, including type of publication type (e.g., Case Reports, Journal Article, Classical Article, Review, Meta-Analysis etc.), and language (English, French, German etc.). In the journal search only, Open Access or PubMed Central published

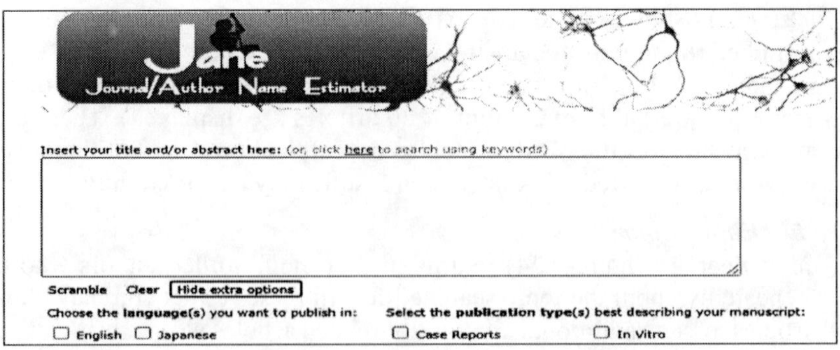

Figure 9.36 *'Show Extra Options' in 'Jane'*

journals may be chosen as limiters. Users should note that boxes remain checked off from search to search so be sure to clear your choices.

9.19.2.3. Features of Jane

In the search list you will get information about:

- *Confidence*: the confidence level shows the accuracy of the match between your search and the journal - hold the cursor above the blue line to see the percentage
- *Open Access*: indicates if it is an open-access journal
- *PubMed Central*: if the journal is indexed in PubMed Central and if there is a time embargo before an article is posted there
- *Article Influence*: *Article Influence* is a bibliometric indicator based on how often articles are cited within a five-year period
- *Show articles*: you can look at the articles that the matching is built upon. Instead of journals, you can look at the authors or articles that match your title/abstract search. In the author search (Find authors) you will get the following information in the search list:
- *Confidence*: the confidence level shows the accuracy of the match between your search and the author (based articles that she/he has published and are included in the match) - hold the cursor above the blue line to see the percentage
- *E-mail*: the e-mail address to the author if it is registered in any of the articles included in the search results
- *Show articles*: you can look at the articles that the matching is built upon. In the article search (Find articles) you will get the following information in the search list:
- *Similarity*: the similarity level shows the accuracy of the match between your search and the article in the search list - hold the cursor above the blue line to see the percentage
- You can also mark single articles by clicking a box in front of the title or all with the option Select all at the bottom of the page and report them as references to for example EndNote

9.19.3. Springer Journal Suggester

The Springer journal suggester tool allows researchers to do a search where you must indicate title and abstract. In addition, the search can be refined by selecting the research field, the impact factor, the percentage of acceptance of articles, the period of response of the journal and indicate if you want an Open Access or subscription journal. The results you can obtain are the titles of journals, the impact factor, if the journal publishes in Open Access, the period of response and the percentage to acceptance of articles.

The Springer Journal Suggester is an academic research tool that enables users to select the best-suited journal for their research. The automated process can enable journal selection from a database of over 2,600 Springer publications. The web-based semantics technology refines a list of relevant journals, based on inputs of

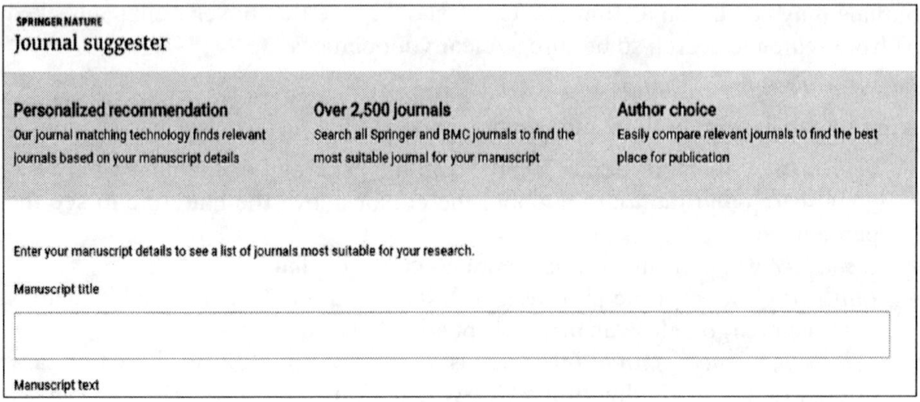

Figure 9.37 *Home Page of 'Journal Suggester'*

manuscript title, abstract and publishing model. The personalized recommendation process will search Springer and BioMed Central to find the best publication that suits the author's choice. A refined list of potential journals can thereby assist authors to delineate a core publication for their final manuscript submission.

9.19.3.1. Structure of Springer Journal Suggester

Springer Journal Suggester is easily accessible, requiring only an abstract/description of the unpublished manuscript to find matching journals. The structure is as follows:

- *Choosing the theme*: Focus on the research discipline best suited for the unpublished manuscript. Consider the best fit of the study within research models of—applied science, clinical research, basic research, or translational research. Browse a list of journals by subject area.
- *Choosing the audience*: Consider the target audience. Choose a specialized journal or a broader publication covering a range of topics for accessibility of the study outlined.
- *Type of article*: Ensure the possibility of publishing the article in your journal of choice. Depending on the study and journal publication guidelines, submit the manuscript as an original research article, a review, or a case study.
- *Impact Factor*: This is not a key requisite for publication. However, enquire about the metrics as a measure of the journal's reputation, in alignment with the quality of your impending publication.
- *Publication timeline*: Estimate the timeline for peer review and the turnaround time for publication in the journal of interest. To reach a broader audience, consider options from open access journals

Authors can further refine the web-based recommendations tool by including the following parameters to the semantics analysis:

- Minimum impact factor sought
- Article acceptance rate

- Time to first decision
- Indexing services
- View (choice of all journals, fully open access journals only, or subscription journals).

9.19.3.2. Key Features of Springer Journal Suggester

In the search list you get information about:

- *Subscription*: is stated if it is a subscription-based journal
- *Open Access*: is stated if it is an open-access journal (so-called *gold open access*)
- *Subscription & Open Access*: is stated if it is a subscription-based journal with paid open access options (so-called *hybrid open access*)
- *Impact Factor*: the journal's Impact Factor if it is indexed in Web of Science
- *Time to first decision*: how long it will take to get a first decision whether the manuscript will get peer review or not
- *Acceptance rate*: the share of submitted manuscripts that will be accepted for publication

9.19.4. Directory of Open Access Journals (DOAJ)

Many predatory journals are claiming they are indexed by DOAJ and JCR Master List, while they are not. Researchers should always check whether a journal they want to publish in is telling the truth. If a journal is indexed by JCR or/and DOAJ, that is usually a very good indicator that the journal is not predatory.

Searching DOAJ database is quite easy – researchers and authors just need to enter the journal's name, ISSN or the journal's publisher. Their search engine is quite flexible. Make sure to search through journals only, unless you want to find an open-access article.

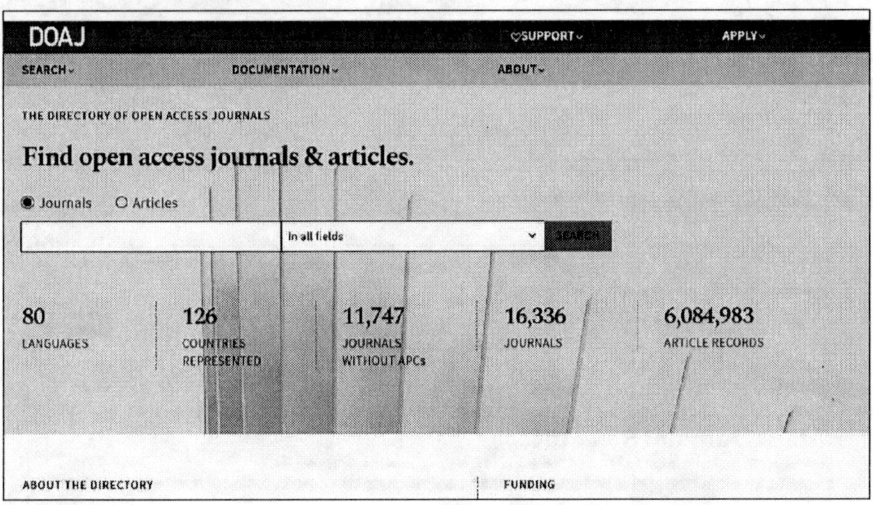

Figure 9.38 *Home Page of 'DOAJ'*

9.19.5. Master Journal List (MJL)

Searching the Web of Science Master Journal List has improved in recent years. The website now allows you to search quite flexibly, however it requires a login to view the detailed record of the journal. MJR recently also introduced a service where if you upload your manuscript, they can tell you which MJR-indexed journals match the topics within your article. Always make sure that the journal you found has the same website and ISSN as the journal you are looking for.

9.19.6. Edanz Journal Selector

Edanz journal selector is an online tool, that helps researchers enter their unpublished abstract and will find the best possible journals that have published relevant papers. Researchers and authors can filter results by field of study, impact factor range, SCI-E index and Open Access options.

9.19.6.1. Features of Edanz

When you click on a journal-title you will get information on:

- *Publisher*: information about which publisher owns the journal
- *Article-processing charges (APC)*: the author fee you have to pay to publish in the journal (open access journals and paid open access)

Figure 9.39 *Home Page of 'Master Journal List'*

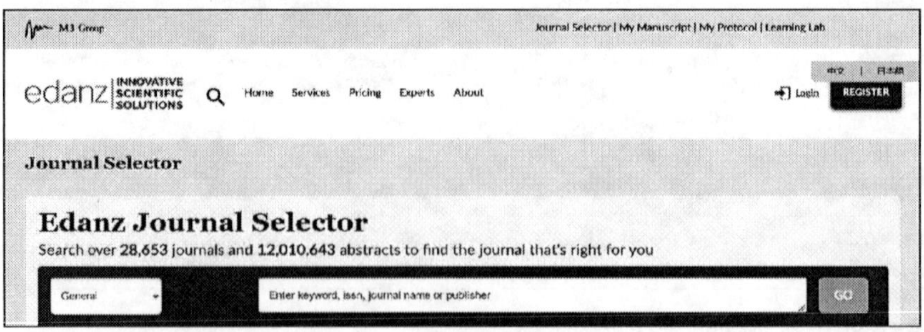

Figure 9.40 *Home Page of 'Edanz Journal Selector'*

- *Embargo time*: the amount of time after having published the article in the journal before you are allowed to share your peer-reviewed accepted manuscript in a digital repository (such as DiVA). Read more about this so-called green open access option.
- *SJR (SCImago Journal Rank)*: the database Scopus' equivalent to Web of Science's Impact Factor
- *SNIP (Source normalized impact per paper)*: another journal indicator used in Scopus
- *IPP (Impact per publication)*: another journal indicator used in Scopus
- *CC licenses*: any Creative Commons licenses describing how others may use an article in the journal
- *h-index*: an indicator that describes the number of citations to the journal in relation to the number of articles published by the journal in the same time period (see more about the h-index here)
- *SCI (Science Citation Index)*: indicates if the journal is included in Web of Science's index SCI which indexes journals within science
- *SCI-E (Science Citation Index - Expanded)*: indicates if the journal is included in Web of Science's index SCI which indexes journals within science (actually the same as above)
- *SSCI (Social Sciences Citation Index)*: indicates if the journal is included in Web of Science's index SSCI which indexes journals within the social sciences
- *A&HCI (Arts & Humanities Citation Index)*: indicates if the journal is included in Web of Science's index SCI which indexes journals within art and humanities

9.19.6.2. How to Use the Edanz Journal Selector

1. Type in the secure text box of the Journal Selector tool (www.edanzediting.com/Journal-Selector) to find target journals that match your:
   - Draft title, keywords, notes, outlines, or abstract
   - Field of study
   - Preferred publisher
   - Journal names or ISSNs (international standard serial numbers)
2. Filter your search results by:
   - Field of study
   - Whether a journal is indexed in Science Citation Index (SCI) or SCI Expanded
   - Whether open access options are available
   - Publication frequency
   - Range of Journal Impact Factors
3. Find journals with recent papers similar to yours, and make a shortlist:
   - Match your criteria and publishing goals to journal features
   - Note that some journals ask if your manuscript has previously been rejected
   - Ask for advice from a colleague or an Edanz expert

9.19.6.3. Factors to Consider in Journal Selection

1. *Aims and Scope*
   - Topics (multidisciplinary, interdisciplinary, unidisciplinary, or subdisciplinary)?
   - Focus (e.g., theory or practice, basic or applied, laboratory or clinical)?
   - Evidence levels or study types (meta-analyses, prospective studies, retrospective studies, quantitative or qualitative studies)?
   - Selectivity (% acceptance rate)?
   - Are novelty and potential impact important?
2. *Readership*
   - Depends on Aims & scope (e.g., generalists or specialists; international, regional, or national?)
   - Researchers, academics, educators, practitioners, or policy-makers?
   - May depend on publication mode
3. *Article Type*
   - Which article types are accepted (e.g., some journals accept only reviews or methods papers or short communications), and which are not accepted (e.g., some journals do not accept case reports or reviews)?
   - Are there limits on length (word count) or number of illustrations or references?
   - Are supplementary files allowed?
   - Is prior inclusion of a preprint (un-submitted draft) in a preprint server, such as arXiv or bioRxiv, allowed?
4. *Peer Review*
   - Model of peer review?
     - Before or after publication
     - Closed (single- or double-blind) or open
     - Collaborative (reviewers may discuss with each other, or reviewers/editors may discuss with the authors)
     - Cascading/transferable (manuscript with or without reviews may be passed to another journal in the publishing group or consortium)
     - Portable (a review service organizes peer review before journal submission)
     - Transparent (reviews are published, with or without reviewer names)
   - Speed of peer review? Are requests for fast-track review allowed?
   - Are pre-submission inquiries allowed (thus saving time, and sometimes allowing you to receive advice or journal suggestions from an editorial office)?
5. *Production*
   - Publication frequency: how many issues per year?
   - Is there continuous online publication?
   - How many articles per issue?
   - Publication speed: time from submission to first/final decision, first online publication, final (online) publication?

6. *Publication Mode and Rights*
    - Print only, subscription- or membership-based: who is the audience and what is the circulation number?
    - Print plus online version, which may be a longer version, with or without
        - Early view ("early online", "online first", or "ahead of print") version
        - Supplementary materials/media and relevant links
        - Links to supplementary materials in an online repository
        - PDF version
    - Online only: based on pay-per-view, site license, or subscription?
    - Open access:
        - Green open access (free access to preprint or accepted manuscript [final draft] on personal website, institutional website, or nonprofit repository, with or without a time delay before uploading [embargo])?
        - Gold open access (free access to final published version [version of record])?
    - Hybrid open access (some content is open access and some is subscription-based; can depend on authors' choice or on journal policy, which may include "delayed open access" after an embargo)?
    - Open access available to authors of manuscripts based on studies whose institution or funder mandates open access?
    - Author or journal or publisher/owner owns copyright?
    - Creative Commons license available?
7. *Cost and Services*
    - Submission fee, production fee (color/page charges), article-processing charge for open access?
    - Editing/illustration service, news release service, marketing, and social media promotion included in publication charge?
    - Post-publication commenting and altmetrics (article-level metrics) tracking provided?
    - Free batch of reprints or online copies, or (limited) free online access to published article for authors?
8. *Journal Reputation*
    - Is the journal/publisher well known?
    - Is the journal affiliated with a professional society?
    - Are the editor/s and editorial board well known?
    - Is the journal recommended by your library/society?
    - Have you or your colleagues read/cited the journal?
    - Have your peers or colleagues published in the journal and say they value its peer review process?
    - Is the journal known for quality content, language, and production?
    - Is the journal included in respected general or specific indexes?
    - Does the journal have a long history and a permanent online archive?
    - What are the journal's bibliometric scores (e.g., Journal Impact Factor)?

9.19.7. JournalGuide

JournalGuide (https://www.journalguide.com/) is a free tool created by a group of software developers, former researchers and scholarly publishing veterans at Research Square. Goal for JournalGuide is to bring all sources of data together in one place to give authors a simple way to choose the best journal for their research. It also can help tracking down open access titles. Data sources include major industry data sets, public resources, information submitted directly by journal editors, and even real-life publishing experiences submitted by authors.

9.19.7.1. How to Find Best Journal for Your Research

JournalGuide is a free tool that helps researchers to evaluate scholarly journals. In addition to searching by journal name, category, or publisher, authors can use the title and abstract of a paper to discover journals that have already published articles on similar topics. By matching journals to a paper's content, researchers can see which journals would be most likely to have interest in their story.

Use your abstract or top keywords to receive journal recommendations, or search the comprehensive database of journal information to make data-driven decisions about which journal to choose. JournalGuide allows authors to effectively search, sort, filter, and compare journals. JournalGuide also offer a robust Journal Recommendation service for more personal evaluation by experts.

9.19.7.2. Features of Journal Guide

In the search list you will get quick information about the following aspects:

- *Score*: shows the accuracy of the match between your search and the journal
- *Journal name*: click on the journal name to get complete information about the journal. Here you can also see if the journal is included in JournalGuide's *whitelist*, i.e., a list of reputable journals (compare *blacklists*).

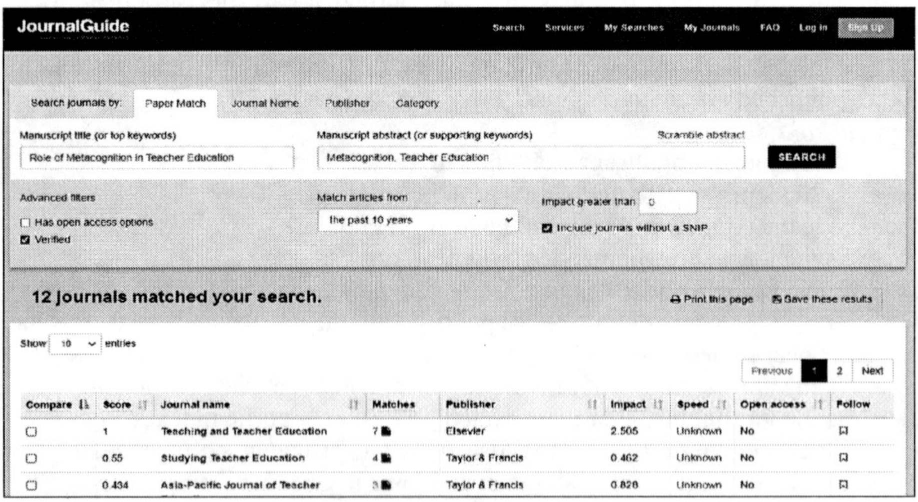

Figure 9.41 *Searching Results in 'JournalGuide'*

- *Matches*: the number of articles that matches your search criteria. Click on the number to get a list of these articles.
- *Publisher*: the publisher that publishes the journal
- *Impact*: uses one of Scopus' journal impact indicators, SNIP (Source Normalized Impact per Paper)
- *Speed*: indicate the journal's information on its (estimated) time from submitted manuscript to publication. However, it is not always that information about this can be indicated ('Unknown').
- *Open access*: indicates Yes or No whether the journal has an open access policy. Please note! This information is questionable, though. It is better to check this on the journal's website or the database *SHERPA/RoMEO*.
- *Compare*: by clicking the box in front of up to three journals you can compare these by bringing up a table based on the aspects above, as well as in which databases the journals are indexed.

9.19.8. Open Journal Matcher

This application suggests open access journals based on their similarity to a draft abstract submitted by the user. It is meant for authors who are trying to discover

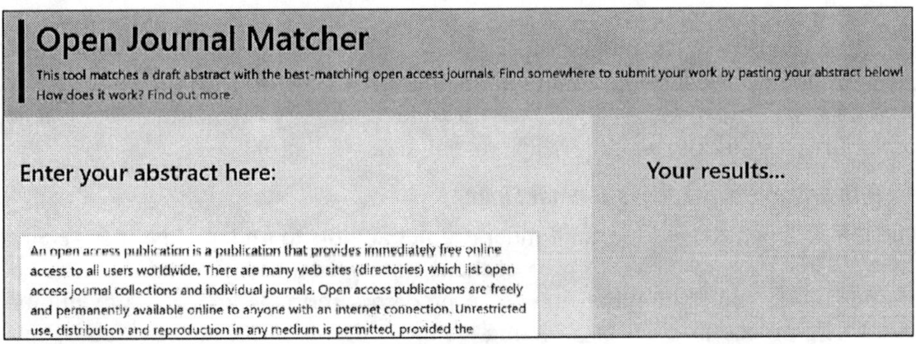

Figure 9.42 *Home Page of 'Open Journal Matcher'*

Figure 9.43 *Journal Search results in 'Open Journal Matcher'*

Figure 9.44 *Home Page of 'enago'*

suitable target journals for their work. The results are meant to be serendipitous; the goal is to uncover unexpected but relevant journals.

The application is built with Flask, combined with "serverless" infrastructure for data analysis. The Flask application calls a Google Cloud Function asynchronously. Most of the computationally intensive work is done by the Cloud Function. Specifically, the Cloud Function does similarity calculations use spaCy and returns a similarity score for each potential target journal.

9.19.9. Enago Open Access Journal Finder

The Enago Open Access Journal Finder enables authors to find quality open access journals that are pre-vetted to protect them from predatory publishers. This free journal finder solves common issues on predatory journals, journal authenticity and article processing fees by utilizing a validated journal index provided by the Directory of Open Access Journals (DOAJ). Enago's proprietary search algorithm helps authors to shortlist journals that are most relevant to their manuscript and research objectives, thus giving them the best chance of publication.

10

Scientific Research Misconduct and Best Practices

Education in responsible conduct is essential because unethical or compromised behaviors on the part of researchers lead the public to lose trust in the research community. When trust is lost, credibility is lost. When credibility is lost, the opportunity to improve human well-being and protect the environmental is lost. When belief that science can make a difference is lost, funding for research is lost.

The publication of an article in a peer-reviewed journal or conference proceedings is an essential building block in the development of a coherent and respected network of knowledge. It is a direct reflection of the quality of the work of the Authors and the institutions that support them. Peer-reviewed articles support and embody the scientific method. It is therefore important to agree upon standards of expected ethical behavior for all parties involved in the act of publishing: Authors, Editors, Reviewers, Publishers and Societies or Institutions for society-owned or institutionally-owned journals and/or sponsored journals.

10.1. Why to Publish?

A scientific paper is an organized description of hypothesis, data, and conclusions, intended to instruct the readers. Research conducted has to be published or documented; otherwise, it is considered not done. Publication of paper is critical for the evolution of modern science, in which the work of one scientist builds upon that of others. The roots of scholarly, scientific publishing can be traced to 1665, when Henry Oldenburg of the British Royal Society established the journal Philosophical Transactions of the Royal Society. The aim of the journal was to create a public record of original contribution to knowledge and also to encourage scientists to *"speak"* directly to others. Documentation of research work followed by publication helps in the dissemination of observations and findings. This flow of knowledge guides and contributes towards research coalition. Established and budding researchers do get benefited by published literature and consolidates their research.

Publication of research in peer-reviewed journal not only validates the research and boosts confidence of the authors but also gives national and international recognition to an author, department, university, and institution. Unfortunately, in some establishments, the most compelling reason for publication is to fulfil specific job requirements by employers. It may include promotion to an academic position and improving prospects of success in research grant application. The importance of publication in the career is further emphasized by the adage *"Publish or perish"* i.e., publish your research or lose your identity.

10.2. Scientific Research Misconduct

Scientific misconduct is the violation of the standard codes of scholarly conduct and ethical behavior in the publication of professional scientific research. Research misconduct means fabrication, falsification, plagiarism and violation of authorship rules in proposing, performing, or reviewing research, or in reporting research results. This may occur every stage of the research process (Data generation, recording, review and publication/ dissemination of scientific knowledge) Scientific misconduct can be described as a deviation from the accepted standards of scientific research, study and publication ethics. Scientific misconduct is the violation of the standard codes of scholarly conduct and ethical behavior in the publication of scientific research. Misconduct in the scientific publication process by the authors is detrimental for integrity of the whole system and is considered unethical. Falsification or fabrication of data is the gravest form of scientific misconduct wherein authors either manipulate skewed data to look favorable or generate data where no data exists. Different forms of scientific misconduct are plagiarism or misappropriation of the ideas of others, improprieties of authorship, simultaneous publications, duplicate publications, salami slicing, and non-declaration of conflict of interest (COI). Conducting research without informed consent or ethics approval and not maintaining data confidentiality is a form of scientific misconduct. Editors or publication houses do take disciplinary action as per COPE recommendations against scientific misconduct. Authors are blacklisted or banned to submit articles in the respective journal in the future.

Scientific misconduct has to be both wilful and intentional. There are several different examples of scientific misconduct. These can include altering data, adjusting calculations, or not being completely truthful about the scientific process that you are engaged in. The implications of such misconduct can be significantly damaging to public health, and publication of dubious research findings can affect the professional scientific community in a negative manner.

10.3. Research Misconduct

Research misconduct is defined as fabrication, falsification or plagiarism in proposing, performing or reviewing research or in reporting research results.

Table 10.1 *Difference between Research Misconduct and Publication Misconduct*

Research Misconduct	*Publication Misconduct*
Fabrication	Plagiarism
	Biased/selective Reporting
Falsification	Authorship Abuse
Unethical Research	Redundant Publication
	Undeclared Conflict of Interest (CoI)
	Reviewer Misconduct
	Abuse of position

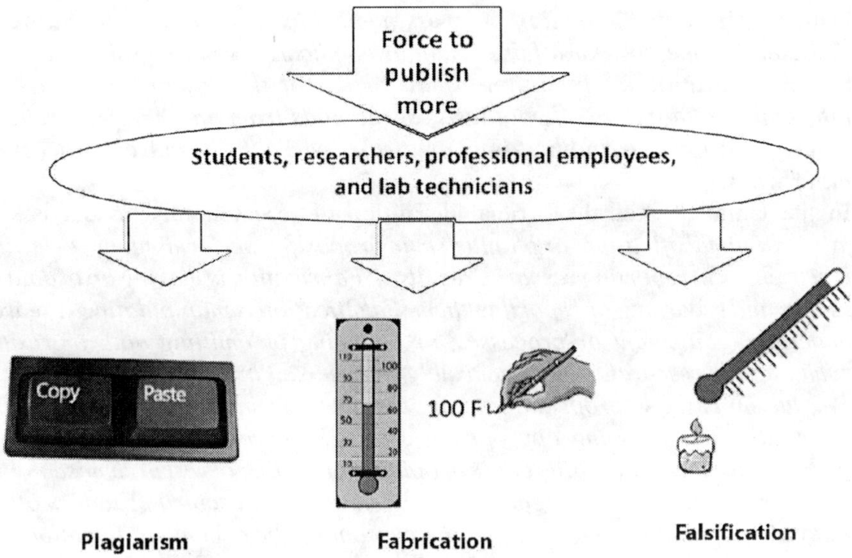

Figure 10.1 *Factors leads to Research Misconduct*

However, the KU Leuven (Katholieke Universiteit Leuven) definition of research misconduct is broader than that. It also includes practices that seriously deviate from those that are commonly accepted within the research community for proposing, conducting or reporting research. These practices are often called Questionable Research Practices (QRPs). The most important point here is the intention, which leads to the misconduct and unethical publication (Figure 10.1).

Research misconducts can be divided into two major categories; research integrity violations and publication ethics violations.

- Research integrity violations include fabrication, falsification and plagiarism.
- Publication ethics violations include duplicate publication and/or self-plagiarism and inappropriate authorship.

10.4. Definitions of Scientific Research Misconduct

- Committee on Publication Ethics (COPE) defines misconduct as *"intention to cause others to regard as true that which is not true."*
- Federal Research Misconduct Policy (2018), *"Research misconduct is defined as fabrication, falsification, or plagiarism in proposing, performing, or reviewing research, or in reporting research results"*.
- Smith (2006), "any behavior by a researcher, whether intentional or not, that fails to scrupulously respect high scientific and ethical standards."
- According to Office of Science and Technology Policy (OSTP, Washington, DC, USA) *"Research misconduct is defined as fabrication, falsification, or plagiarism in proposing, performing, or reviewing research, or in reporting research results"*

- Danish definition: *"Intention or gross negligence leading to fabrication of the scientific message or a false credit or emphasis given to a scientist"*
- Swedish definition: *"Intention[al] distortion of the research process by fabrication of data, text, hypothesis, or methods from another researcher's manuscript form or publication; or distortion of the research process in other ways."*
- In the United States the official definition of research misconduct is: *"... fabrication, falsification, or plagiarism in proposing, performing, or reviewing research, or in reporting research results. ... Fabrication is making up of data or results and recording or reporting them. Falsification is manipulating research materials, equipment or processes, or changing or omitting data or results such that the research is not accurately represented in the research record. ... Plagiarism is the appropriating of another person's ideas, processes, results, or words without giving appropriate credit. Research misconduct does not include honest error or differences of opinion. A finding of research misconduct requires that: There be a significant departure from accepted practices of the relevant research community; and the misconduct be committed intentionally, or knowingly, or recklessly; and the allegation be proven by a preponderance of the evidence. (Science and Technology Policy 2000, p. 76262)."*
- The Wellcome Trust, Britain's largest biomedical charity, defines misconduct as: *"Fabrication, falsification, plagiarism or deception in proposing, carrying out, or reporting results of research or deliberate, dangerous or negligent deviations from accepted practices in carrying out research. It includes failure to follow established protocols if this failure results in unreasonable risk or harm to humans, other vertebrates, or the environment and facilitating of misconduct in research by collusion in, or concealment of, such actions by others. It also includes intentional, unauthorized use, disclosure, or removal of or damage to research related property of another including apparatus, materials, writings, data, hardware or software or any other substances or devices used in the conduct of research. It does not include honest error or honest differences in the design, execution, interpretation or judgment in evaluating research methods or results or misconduct unrelated to the research process. Similarly, it does not include poor research unless this encompasses the intention to deceive."*
- According to British Consensus Panel (1999): *"Research misconduct is significant misbehavior that improperly appropriates the intellectual property or contributions of others, that intentionally impedes the progress of research, or that risks corrupting the scientific record or compromising the integrity of scientific practices. Such behaviors are unethical and unacceptable in proposing, conducting, or reporting research, or in reviewing the proposals or research reports of others."*
- Medical Research Council (MCR), United Kingdom defines scientific misconduct as: *"fabrication, falsification, plagiarism, or deception in proposing, carrying out, or reporting results of research and deliberate, dangerous, or negligent deviations from accepted practice in carrying out research. It includes failure to follow established protocols if this results*

in unreasonable risk or harm to human beings, other vertebrates, or the environment and also the facilitating of misconduct by collusion in, or concealment of, such actions by others. Misconduct does not include honest error or honest differences in the design, execution, interpretation, or judgment in evaluating research methods or results of misconduct (including gross misconduct) unrelated to the research process."

10.5. Motivation to Scientific Research Misconduct

According to David Goodstein (2002) of Caltech, there are motivators for scientists to commit misconduct, which are briefly summarised here:

Career Pressure
Science is still a very strongly career-driven discipline. Scientists depend on a good reputation to receive ongoing support and funding, and a good reputation relies largely on the publication of high-profile scientific papers. Hence, there is a strong imperative to *"publish or perish"*. Clearly, this may motivate desperate (or fame-hungry) scientists to fabricate results.

Ease of Fabrication
In many scientific fields, results are often difficult to reproduce accurately, being obscured by noise, artifacts, and other extraneous data. That means that even if a scientist does falsify data, they can expect to get away with it – or at least claim innocence if their results conflict with others in the same field. There are no *"scientific police"* who are trained to fight scientific crimes; all investigations are made by experts in science but amateurs in dealing with criminals. It is relatively easy to cheat although difficult to know exactly how many scientists fabricate data.

Monetary Gain
In many scientific fields, professionals make the most money by selling their expert opinions. Corporations can pay experts to support products directly or indirectly through conferences. Psychologist can make money by repeatedly acting as an expert witness in custody proceedings for the same law firms.

10.6. Classification of Scientific Research Misconduct

Classification-I
Fabrication, Falsification and Plagiarism (FFP) and Questionable Research Practice (QRP) have been used worldwide in the classification of research misconduct. However, FFP comprises two distinct categories of misconduct: FF is extreme research misconduct that betrays truth, while P undermines trust of science community. Irreproducibility and inadequate practice of research also betray trust. Research misconduct has the potential to cause serious risk of safety in daily life. The proposed classification system is outlined as follows:

- *Class I misconduct*: *Betrayal of the truth*: (1) Fabrication and (2) Falsification.
- *Class II misconduct: Betrayal of trust*: (1) Plagiarism of text; Irreproducibility; and (3) Inadequate research practice.
- *Class III misconduct: Risk to safety of health and industrial products*: (1) Risk to safety of health and (2) Risk to safety of industrial products.

The proposed classification reflects deeper values of truth, trust, and risk more directly than the previous classification and elucidates issues about nature and significance of misconduct.

Classification-II

Misconduct that distorts scientific knowledge

- Fabrication – reporting of non-existent data
- Falsification – selective reporting of data

Misconduct that misleads the scientific community

- Authorship: Plagiarism, 'Guest' authors, 'Ghost' authors
- Duplicate publication
- Abuse of the peer-review process

Misconduct relating to human subjects

- Consent issues
- Exploitation issues (inc. financial)

Other issues

- Conflicts of Interest
- Poor record-keeping
- Failure to obtain necessary ethical approval
- Incidental findings?

10.7. Taxonomy of Scientific Research Misconduct Ranked by Seriousness

Seriousness Level I

- *Fabrication*: invention of data or cases
- *Falsification*: willful distortion of data
- *Plagiarism*: copying of ideas, data or words without attribution
- Failing to get consent from an ethics committee for research

Seriousness Level II

- Not admitting that some data are missing
- Ignoring outliers without declaring it
- Not including data on side effects in a clinical trials
- Conducting research in humans without informed consent

Seriousness Level III

- Publication of post hoc analysis without declaration that they were post hoc
- Gift authorship
- Not attributing other authors
- Redundant publication
- Not disclosing a conflict of interest

Seriousness Level IV

- Not attempting to publish completed research
- Failure to do adequate search of existing research before beginning new research

10.8. Forms of Scientific Research Misconduct

10.8.1. Fabrication

Fabrication is the invention of data or information. Fabricating data involves creating a new record of data or results. Most commonly fabricated documents are informed consent forms and patient diaries. Fabrication is the second most common form of scientific misconduct. Fabrication is making up data or results and recording or reporting them. Fabrication comprises the creation of false data or other aspects of research, including documentation and participant consent. Fabrication is making up results and recording or reporting them. This is sometimes referred to as *"drylabbing"*. A more minor form of fabrication is where references are included to give arguments the appearance of widespread acceptance, but are actually fake, or do not support the argument.

Examples of Fabrication

- Completing a questionnaire for a fictitious subject that was never interviewed.
- Creating a data set for an experiment that was never actually conducted.
- Adding fictitious data to a real data set collected during an actual experiment for the purpose of providing additional statistical validity.
- Insertion of a clinical note into the research record to indicate compliance with an element of the protocol.

10.8.2. Falsification

Falsification is the alteration of the observed result of a scientific experiment. This is the practice of manipulating research materials, equipment, or processes, or changing or omitting data or results such that the research is not accurately represented in the research record. Falsification is the most common form of scientific misconduct. Falsification involves making changes for example in the set up or results of an experiment in a way that cannot be scientifically justified. Most commonly with the intention of improving the results or removing results that do not fit the hypothesis.

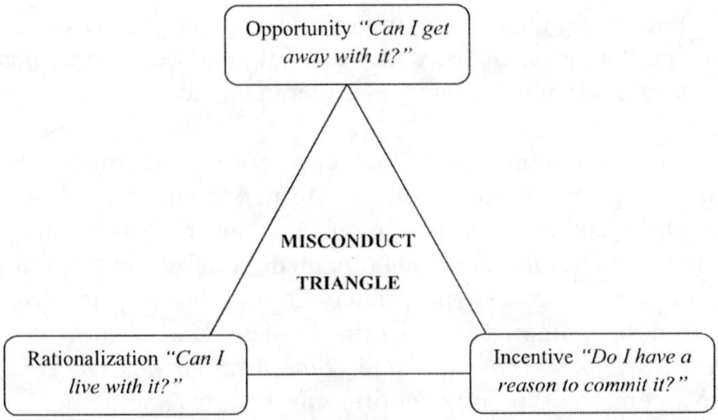

Figure 10.2 *Research Misconduct Triangle*

Falsification is manipulating research materials, equipment, or processes or changing or omitting data or results such that the research is not accurately represented in the research record. Falsification involves manipulation of research materials, equipment or processes, or changing or omitting data/results such that the research is not accurately represented in the research record. Falsification comprises inappropriate manipulation and/or selection of data, images and/or other contents. Falsification means manipulating research materials, equipment, or processes, or changing or omitting/suppressing data or results without scientific or statistical justification, such that the research is not accurately represented in the research record. This would include the *"misrepresentation of uncertainty"* during statistical analysis of the data. *"Falsification is manipulating research materials, equipment, or processes, or changing or omitting data or results such that the research is not accurately represented in the research record."*

Examples of Falsification

- Alteration of data to render a modification of the variances in the data
- Falsifying dates and experimental procedures in the study notebook
- Misrepresenting results from statistical analysis
- Misrepresenting the methods of an experiment such as the model used to conduct the experiment
- The addition of false or misleading statements in the manuscript or published paper.
- Misrepresenting the materials or methods of a research study in a published paper
- Providing false statements about the extent of a research study
- Falsificying telephone call attempts to collect data for a survey study

10.8.3. Plagiarism

Plagiarism is presenting someone else's work or ideas as your own, with or without their consent, by incorporating it into your work without full acknowledgement. All published and unpublished material, whether in manuscript, printed or electronic form, is covered under this definition. Plagiarism may be intentional or reckless, or unintentional. Plagiarism means copying of other people's work (ideas, writings, structures, designs, images, plans, code, etc.) or one's own previously written work, without adequate source references either in an identical or slightly adjusted fashion.

Plagiarism is the appropriation of another person's ideas, processes, results, or words without giving appropriate credit. One form is the appropriation of the ideas and results of others, and publishing as to make it appear the author had performed all the work under which the data was obtained. A subset is citation plagiarism – wilful or negligent failure to appropriately credit other or prior discoverers, so as to give an improper impression of priority. This is also known as, *"citation amnesia"*, the *"disregard syndrome"* and *"bibliographic negligence"*. Arguably, this is the most common type of scientific misconduct. Sometimes it is difficult to guess whether authors intentionally ignored a highly relevant cite or lacked knowledge of the prior work. Discovery credit can also be inadvertently reassigned from the original discoverer to a better-known researcher. This is a special case of the *Matthew effect*.

Types of Plagiarism

- *Direct Plagiarism*: This includes the complete or partial direct copying or word by word copying of a someone's work without acknowledging the original author.
- *Self-Plagiarism*: A situation where the person duplicates his previous works or sentences used in a new project or new publications. This is also considered an unethical practice in case of publication in journals
- *Mosaic Plagiarism*: Copying of idea and general structure of the concept of someone by changing the phrases and words like using synonyms and without quoting.
- *Accidental Plagiarism*: When the author neglects or forget to cite the original source or refer to a wrong source or unintentionally paraphrases someone's idea by using similar words, groups of words, and/or sentence structure without attribution.
- *Redundant Publications* ('salami' publications): This refers to publishing many very similar manuscripts/reports based on the same experiments and same work design.

Why Does Plagiarism Matter?

Plagiarism is a breach of academic integrity. It is a principle of intellectual honesty that all members of the academic community should acknowledge their debt to the originators of the ideas, words, and data which form the basis for their own work. Passing off another's work as your own is not only poor scholarship, but also means that you have failed to complete the learning process. Plagiarism is unethical and can have serious consequences for your future career; it also undermines the standards of your institution and of the degrees it issues.

Avoiding Plagiarism

Plagiarism is a serious offense. It can not only have legal implications but also damage the credibility and reputation of the author. In academic publishing, plagiarism can lead to retraction of the published work and loss of academic positions or jobs. Read through the figure-10.3 below for effective tips to avoid plagiarism when drafting your manuscript. Authors can also use plagiarism checkers such as *Turnitin, Duplichecker, PaperRater, Copyleaks, PlagScan, Plagiarisma, Plagiarism Checker, Quetext, PlagScan, iThenticate*, etc. to avoid text plagiarism.

10.8.4. Questionable Research Practices

Examples of 'QRPs' are:

- guest, gift or ghost authorship
  - guest authors are those who do not meet accepted authorship criteria but are listed because of their seniority, reputation or supposed influence

- ◆ gift authors are those who do not meet accepted authorship criteria but are listed as a personal favour or in return for payment
- ◆ ghost authors are those who meet authorship criteria but are not listed
- duplicate publication and 'salami slicing' publication
- dropping observations or data points from analyses based on a gut feeling that they were inaccurate
- inadequate record keeping related to research projects
- failure to disclose conflicts of interest

10.8.5. Other Types of Research Misconduct

Research misconduct includes:

- Publishing the same paper in two different journals without telling the editors
- Submitting the same paper to different journals without telling the editors
- Not informing a collaborator of your intent to file a patent in order to make sure that you are the sole inventor
- Including a colleague as an author on a paper in return for a favor even though the colleague did not make a serious contribution to the paper
- Discussing with your colleagues confidential data from a paper that you are reviewing for a journal

Quoting

- When using word-to-word (verbatim) text from any source, use quotation marks for the extract and cite the source.
- For longer extracts, some style guides recommend using block quotes.

Summarizing

- When summarizing, use your own words to convey the main message/idea of the original work in an abridged form.
- Make sure to cite the original source.

Paraphrasing

- When paraphrasing original work, make sure to use your own words and sentence structures to convey the same meaning.
- Always cite the original source.

Common knowledge

- Universal truths or facts expected to be known to readers need not be cited.
- Cite statistical information or lesser-known facts. When in confusion whether the fact or statement is a common knowledge or not, always cite to remove any doubt!

Figure 10.3 *Techniques of avoiding Plagiarism*

- Using data, ideas, or methods you learn about while reviewing a grant or a papers without permission
- Trimming outliers from a data set without discussing your reasons in paper
- Using an inappropriate statistical technique in order to enhance the significance of your research
- Bypassing the peer review process and announcing your results through a press conference without giving peers adequate information to review your work
- Conducting a review of the literature that fails to acknowledge the contributions of other people in the field or relevant prior work
- Stretching the truth on a grant application in order to convince reviewers that your project will make a significant contribution to the field
- Stretching the truth on a job application or curriculum vita
- Giving the same research project to two graduate students in order to see who can do it the fastest
- Overworking, neglecting, or exploiting graduate or post-doctoral students
- Failing to keep good research records
- Failing to maintain research data for a reasonable period of time
- Making derogatory comments and personal attacks in your review of author's submission
- Promising a student a better grade for sexual favors
- Using a racist epithet in the laboratory
- Making significant deviations from the research protocol approved by your institution's Animal Care and Use Committee or Institutional Review Board for Human Subjects Research without telling the committee or the board
- Not reporting an adverse event in a human research experiment
- Wasting animals in research
- Exposing students and staff to biological risks in violation of your institution's bio-safety rules
- Sabotaging someone's work
- Stealing supplies, books, or data
- Rigging an experiment so you know how it will turn out
- Making unauthorized copies of data, papers, or computer programs
- Deliberately overestimating the clinical significance of a new drug in order to obtain economic benefits
- Inappropriate development of research protocols;
- Failure to disclose or take action on declared conflict of interest;
- Inadequate management of a research project;
- Sabotage – intentionally damaging, destroying, obstructing or otherwise harming a research project;
- Piracy – the deliberate exploitation of data from others without authorization;
- Failure to follow accepted procedures or exercise due care for avoiding unreasonable risk of harm to humans, animals or the environment. Mismanagement or inadequate preservation of data and/or primary materials;
- Misappropriation of data;
- Improper conduct in peer review;

- Misrepresentation of interests, qualifications, and experience;
- Misrepresentation of involvement or authorship;
- Failure to protect or the inappropriate use or disclosure of confidential or proprietary information, or the misuse of intellectual property;
- Improper dealing with allegations of wrongdoing;

10.9. Varieties of Scientific Research Misconduct and its Consequences

A wide range of misbehaviours by scientists can be labelled "misconduct". Clarity and consistency in defining misconduct are prerequisites to establishing or evaluating an administrative system for processing misconduct allegations, and for understanding the underlying causes and effective remedies. A variety of administrative mechanisms and modalities (including prevention and investigation/enforcement) may be needed to deal correctly with the diversity of inappropriate

Table 10.2 *Varieties of Scientific Research Misconduct*

Core "Research Misconduct" Fabrication of data Falsification of data Plagiarism FFP normally includes: • Selectively excluding data from analysis • Misinterpreting data to obtain desired results (including • inappropriate use of statistical methods) • Doctoring images in publications • Producing false data or results under pressure from a sponsor	**Research Practice Misconduct** • Using inappropriate (e.g., harmful or dangerous) research methods • Poor research design • Experimental, analytical, computational errors • Violation of human subject protocols • Abuse of laboratory animals
Data-related Misconduct • Not preserving primary data • Bad data management and storage • Withholding data from the scientific community	**Publication-related Misconduct** • Claiming undeserved authorship • Denying authorship to contributors • Artificially proliferating publications ("salami-slicing") • Failure to correct the publication record
Personal Misconduct • Inappropriate personal behaviour, harassment • Inadequate leadership, mentoring, counselling of students • Insensitivity to social or cultural norms	**Financial and other Misconduct** • Peer review abuse e.g., non-disclosure of conflict of interest, unfairly holding up a rival's publication • Misrepresenting credentials or publication record • Misuse of research funds for unauthorised purchases or for personal gain • Making an unsubstantiated or malicious misconduct allegation

behaviours. In particular, it is important to identify instances of misconduct that can be remediated via education, or that merit a full investigation, including procedures for establishing innocence or guilt.

Research misconduct is very harmful for researcher, institution, discipline, society and for country. Misconduct in research not only damages science but its consequences also extend into the broader societal sphere. The following are the general areas where negative impact of research misconduct has been identified:

- ***Harm to Individuals and to Society:*** If fraudulent research results in the release of an unsafe product or process (e.g., a drug or a therapy) then it will be very harmful to the individuals as well as for society. Society may be harmed if false results become widely known and believed. The formal responsibility for protecting the public lies mostly outside the research administration system and is assured by a well-developed structure of national laws, regulations, and institutions (e.g., the drug approval process). Even so, research administrations must assume responsibility for not burdening the regulatory process.
- ***Damage to Society:*** Direct damage to science itself, by creating false leads for other scientists to follow, and/or forcing others to waste time, effort and money to reproduce fraudulent results. Fortunately, the research record is inherently self-correcting, since repeatability, verifiability and consistency are hallmarks of the scientific method. However, incorrect results can persist and mislead for extended periods of time.
- ***Degradation of Relations:*** The degradation of relations among scientists, between senior researchers and students, and between researchers and agency programme managers.
- ***Damage to Science:*** Damage to science through the undermining of the public's trust in science, and of the government's ability to foster and promote research in a competent and responsible manner. A possible consequence is a decline in the credibility of scientific analysis and advice on issues that have important implications for society. These issues (in such areas as health, environment, energy, national security) often have a major scientific component, and science-based laws and regulations may be needed to address them

10.10. At What Stages can Misconduct Occur?

Misconduct can be at the level of planning, wherein ideas may be borrowed in a wrong way. It could be at the level of application of permission for conducting the research. Moreover, it could be that research is being done without appropriate permissions. There could be misconduct in the way of collection of data, with deviations from approved protocols. It should be stated here that mere obtaining of permission is not enough, but the protocols approved by the institutional ethics committee should be followed. There could be misconduct in the management of the data. The collection, storing and transmission can lead to many possibilities. Inadequate measures to ensure authenticity of data can itself construed to be misconduct. Data obtained from the subjects should be converted to analysis with good amount of fidelity. Inability to ensure can be viewed upon as misconduct. Hence, it is easy to acknowledge that the ways in which misconduct can occur are multiple, and all researchers must actively guard against it.

10.11. Measures to Maintain Research Ethics and Avoid Scientific Research Misconduct

Table 10.3 *Research Misconduct and Publication Misconduct*

Before conduction of research	*During conduction of research*	*After research*
• Develop clear research plan • Submit protocol to ethical review • Prepare well with your research community • Agree on authorship	• Follow the approved protocol • Gain consent • Involve the community • Protect yourself, your team and your participants • Regularly check your data	• Share your study report • Return 'something' back to the researched community • Follow publication ethics • Use reference management software

10.12. Ethical Behavior in Professional Scientific Research

In order to understand the nature of scientific misconduct, it is necessary to understand the general guidelines associated with research in the field. Some of the universal ideas incorporated into the umbrella of thought about ethics and scientific research include:

- Maintaining the highest level of integrity for all research and experiments
- Appropriate treatment of human subjects
- Publishing results and research in journals and other forms of media
- Granting access to others in order to reproduce the testing results
- Acknowledging the contributions of others

These are the most important factors that should be incorporated into a general understanding of appropriate ethical behavior in scientific research. The responsibility of scientific journals for recording and reporting scientific research is critical and has been recognized by the Committee on Publication Ethics (COPE).

10.13. Avoiding Scientific Misconduct

Although scientific misconduct is generally intentional in nature, it is a good idea for early-stage researchers to review the general guidelines and ethical standards before engaging in any scientific research project. This helps to ensure the quality of your data and your results, as well as increases the awareness of publication ethics among the entire scientific community. In today's publish-or-perish environment, scientific and academic misconduct is increasingly being noticed with the continuous increase in the number of retractions and the prevalence of "predatory" publishers. Work with integrity and promote valuable results by upholding standards in your own work and also reporting concerns if you suspect another person is engaging in scientific misconduct.

10.14. What is Publishable or not Publishable?

Writing for publication is an important yet challenging form of knowledge dissemination. Journals like to publish articles that present an exhaustive meaningful research. It should contribute towards the knowledge building and awareness of readers. At the very minimum, a publishable article needs to be original. It should be conducted and drafted with robust methodology and significant findings, well organized, well written, and concise yet clear. It should be drafted with clear explanation of how the article addresses the existing knowledge gap. Conclusion drawn should be relevant to the audience or readers with a comprehensive list of up-to-date references. Papers that are poorly organized, cluttered with unnecessary information, and consist of routine extension of previous reports or fragmentary reports of research results are not accepted for publication. Violation of ethical or legal norms, including plagiarism, duplicates publication led to immediate rejection of the paper.

10.15. Committee on Publication Ethics (COPE) Guidelines on Good Publication Practice

10.15.1. Why the Guidelines were developed?

COPE was founded in 1997 to address breaches of research and publication ethics. A voluntary body providing a discussion forum and advice for scientific editors, it aims to find practical ways of dealing with the issues, and to develop good practice. These guidelines are essential to attempt to define best practice in the ethics of scientific publishing. These guidelines should be useful for authors, editors, editorial board members, readers, owners of journals and publishers. Intellectual honesty should be actively encouraged in all medical and scientific courses of study, and used to inform publication ethics and prevent misconduct. It is with that in mind that these guidelines have been produced.

10.15.2. How the Guidelines were developed?

The guidelines were developed from a preliminary version drafted by individual members of the committee, which was then submitted to extensive consultation. They address: study design and ethical approval, data analysis, authorship, conflict of interests, the peer review process, redundant publication, plagiarism, duties of editors, media relations, advertising, and how to deal with misconduct.

10.15.3. What Guidelines aim to do?

These guidelines are intended to be advisory rather than prescriptive, and to evolve over time. We hope that they will be disseminated widely, endorsed by editors, and refined by those who use them.

I. Study Design and Ethical Approval

Definition

Good research should be well justified, well planned, appropriately designed, and ethically approved. To conduct research to a lower standard may constitute misconduct.

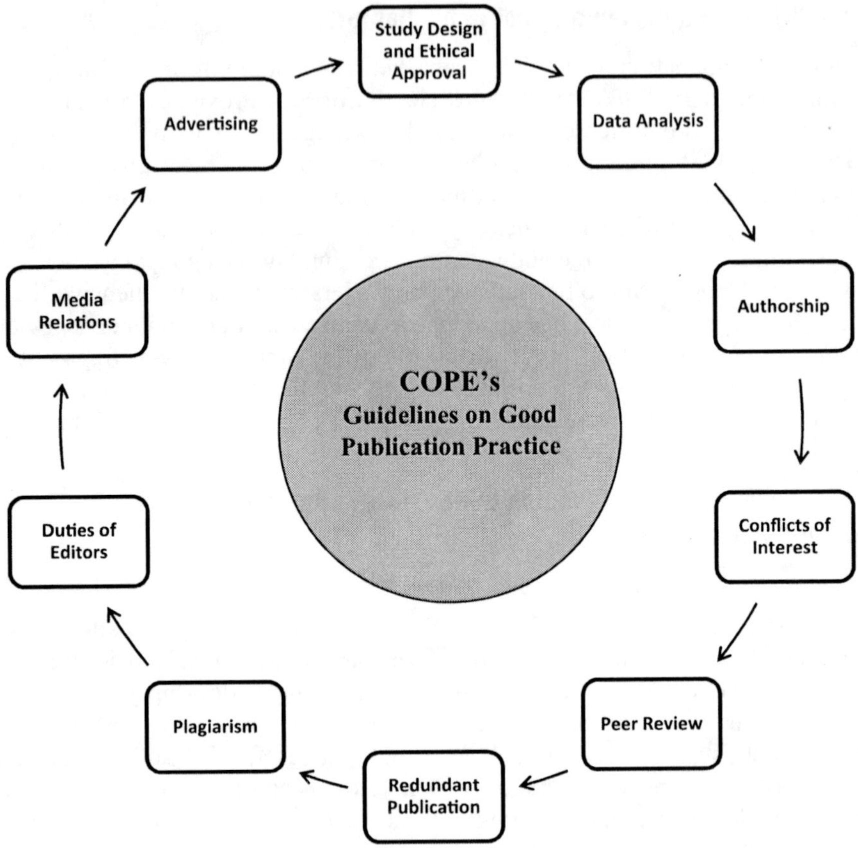

Figure 10.4 *COPE's Guidelines on Good Publication Practice*

Action

1. Laboratory and clinical research should be driven by protocol; pilot studies should have a written rationale.
2. Research protocols should seek to answer specific questions, rather than just collect data.
3. Protocols must be carefully agreed by all contributors and collaborators, including, if appropriate, the participants.
4. The final protocol should form part of the research record.
5. Early agreement on the precise roles of the contributors and collaborators, and on matters of authorship and publication, is advised.
6. Statistical issues should be considered early in study design, including power calculations, to ensure there are neither too few nor too many participants.
7. Formal and documented ethical approval from an appropriately constituted research ethics committee is required for all studies involving people, medical records, and anonymized human tissues.

8. Use of human tissues in research should conform to the highest ethical standards, such as those recommended by the Nuffield Council on Bioethics.
9. Fully informed consent should always be sought. It may not always be possible, however, and in such circumstances, an appropriately constituted research ethics committee should decide if this is ethically acceptable.
10. When participants are unable to give fully informed consent, research should follow international guidelines, such as those of the Council for International Organizations of Medical Sciences (CIOMS).
11. Animal experiments require full compliance with local, national, ethical, and regulatory principles, and local licensing arrangements. International standards vary.
12. Formal supervision, usually the responsibility of the principal investigator, should be provided for all research projects: this must include quality control, and the frequent review and long-term retention (may be up to 15 years) of all records and primary outputs.

II. Data Analysis

Definition

Data should be appropriately analyzed, but inappropriate analysis does not necessarily amount to misconduct. Fabrication and falsification of data do constitute misconduct.

Action

1. All sources and methods used to obtain and analyze data, including any electronic pre-processing, should be fully disclosed; detailed explanations should be provided for any exclusions.
2. Methods of analysis must be explained in detail, and referenced, if they are not in common use.
3. The post hoc analysis of subgroups is acceptable, as long as this is disclosed. Failure to disclose that the analysis was post hoc is unacceptable.
4. The discussion section of a paper should mention any issues of bias which have been considered and explain how they have been dealt with in the design and interpretation of the study.

III. Authorship

Definition

There is no universally agreed definition of authorship, although attempts have been made. As a minimum, authors should take responsibility for a particular section of the study.

Action

1. The award of authorship should balance intellectual contributions to the conception, design, analysis and writing of the study against the collection of data and other routine work. If there is no task that can reasonably be attributed to a particular individual, then that individual should not be credited with authorship.

2. To avoid disputes over attribution of academic credit, it is helpful to decide early on in the planning of a research project who will be credited as authors, as contributors, and who will be acknowledged.
3. All authors must take public responsibility for the content of their paper. The multidisciplinary nature of much research can make this difficult, but this can be resolved by the disclosure of individual contributions.
4. Careful reading of the target journal's "Advice to Authors" is advised, in the light of current uncertainties.

IV. Conflicts of Interest

Definition

Conflicts of interest comprise those which may not befully apparent and which may influence the judgment of author, reviewers, and editors. They have been described as those which, when revealed later, would make a reasonable reader feel misled or deceived. They may be personal, commercial, political, academic or financial. "Financial" interests may include employment, research funding, stock or share ownership, payment for lectures or travel, consultancies and company support for staff.

Action

1. Such interests, where relevant, must be declared to editors by researchers, authors, and reviewers.
2. Editors should also disclose relevant conflicts of interest to their readers. If in doubt, disclose. Sometimes editors may need to withdraw from the review and selection process for the relevant submission.

V. Peer Review

Definition

Peer reviewers are external experts chosen by editors to provide written opinions, with the aim of improving the study. Working methods vary from journal to journal, but some use open procedures in which the name of the reviewer is disclosed, together with the full or "edited" report.

Action

1. Suggestions from authors as to who might act as reviewers are often useful, but there should be no obligation on editors to use those suggested.
2. The duty of confidentiality in the assessment of a manuscript must be maintained by expert reviewers, and this extends to reviewers' colleagues who may be asked (with the editor's permission) to give opinions on specific sections.
3. The submitted manuscript should not be retained or copied.
4. Reviewers and editors should not make any use of the data, arguments, or interpretations, unless they have the authors' permission.
5. Reviewers should provide speedy, accurate, courteous, unbiased and justifiable reports.

6. If reviewers suspect misconduct, they should write in confidence to the editor.
7. Journals should publish accurate descriptions of their peer review, selection, and appeals processes.
8. Journals should also provide regular audits of their acceptance rates and publication times.

VI. Redundant Publication

Definition

Redundant publication occurs when two or more papers, without full cross reference, share the same hypothesis, data, discussion points, or conclusions.

Action

1. Published studies do not need to be repeated unless further confirmation is required.
2. Previous publication of an abstract during the proceedings of meetings does not preclude subsequent submission for publication, but full disclosure should be made at the time of submission.
3. Re-publication of a paper in another language is acceptable, provided that there is full and prominent disclosure of its original source at the time of submission.
4. At the time of submission, authors should disclose details of related papers, even if in a different language, and similar papers in press.

VII. Plagiarism

Definition

Plagiarism ranges from the unreferenced use of others published and unpublished ideas, including research grant applications to submission under "new" authorship of a complete paper, sometimes in a different language. It may occur at any stage of planning, research, writing, or publication: it applies to print and electronic versions.

Action

1. All sources should be disclosed, and if large amounts of other people's written or illustrative material are to be used, permission must be sought.

VIII. Duties of Editors

Definition

Editors are the stewards of journals. They usually take over their journal from the previous editor(s)and always want to hand over the journal in good shape. Most editors provide direction for the journal and build a strong management team. They must consider and balance the interests of many constituents, including readers, authors, staff, owners, editorial board members, advertisers and the media.

Actions

1. Editors' decisions to accept or reject a paper for publication should be based only on the paper's importance, originality, and clarity, and the study's relevance to the remit of the journal.

2. Studies that challenge previous work published in the journal should be given an especially sympathetic hearing.
3. Studies reporting negative results should not be excluded.
4. All original studies should be peer reviewed before publication, taking into full account possible bias due to related or conflicting interests.
5. Editors must treat all submitted papers as confidential.
6. When a published paper is subsequently found to contain major flaws, editors must accept responsibility for correcting the record prominently and promptly.

IX. Media Relations

Definition
Medical research findings are of increasing interest to the print and broadcast media. Journalists may attend scientific meetings at which preliminary research findings are presented, leading to their premature publication in the mass media.

Action

1. Authors approached by the media should give as balanced an account of their work as possible, ensuring that they point out where evidence ends and speculation begins.
2. Simultaneous publication in the mass media and a peer reviewed journal is advised, as this usually means that enough evidence and data have been provided to satisfy informed and critical readers.
3. Where this is not possible, authors should help journalists to produce accurate reports, but refrain from supplying additional data.
4. All efforts should be made to ensure that patients who have helped with the research should be informed of the results by the authors before the mass media, especially if there are clinical implications.
5. Authors should be advised by the organisers if journalists are to attend scientific meetings.
6. It may be helpful to authors to be advised of any media policies operated by the journal in which their work is to be published.

X. Advertising

Definition
Many scientific journals and meetings derive significant income from advertising. Reprints may also be lucrative.

Action

1. Editorial decisions must not be influenced by advertising revenue or reprint potential: editorial and advertising administration must be clearly separated.
2. Advertisements that mislead must be refused, and editors must be willing to publish criticisms, according to the same criteria used for material in the rest of the journal.
3. Reprints should be published as they appear in the journal unless a correction is to be added. Guidelines on good publication practice

10.15.4. Dealing with Misconduct

Principles

- The general principle confirming misconduct is intention to cause others to regard as true that which is not true.
- The examination of misconduct must therefore focus, not only on the particular act or omission, but also on the intention of the researcher, author, editor, reviewer or publisher involved.
- Deception may be by intention, by reckless disregard of possible consequences, or by negligence. It is implicit, therefore, that "best practice" requires complete honesty, with full disclosure.

(4) Codes of practice may raise awareness, but can never be exhaustive.

Investigating Misconduct

1. Editors should not simply reject papers that raise questions of misconduct. They are ethically obliged to pursue the case. However, knowing how to investigate and respond to possible cases of misconduct is difficult.
2. COPE is always willing to advise, but for legal reasons, can only advise on anonymized cases.
3. It is for the editor to decide what action to take.

Serious Misconduct

1. Editors must take all allegations and suspicions of misconduct seriously, but they must recognize that they do not usually have either the legal legitimacy or the means to conduct investigations into serious cases.
2. The editor must decide when to alert the employers of the accused author(s).
3. Some evidence is required, but if employers have a process for investigating accusations—as they are increasingly required to do—then editors do not need to assemble a complete case. Indeed, it may be ethically unsound for editors to do so, because such action usually means consulting experts, so spreading abroad serious questions about the author(s).
4. If editors are presented with convincing evidence—perhaps by reviewers—of serious misconduct, they should immediately pass this on to the employers, notifying the author(s) that they are doing so.
5. If accusations of serious misconduct are not accompanied by convincing evidence, then editors should confidentially seek expert advice.
6. If the experts raise serious questions about the research, then editors should notify the employers.
7. If the experts find no evidence of misconduct, the editorial processes should proceed in the normal way.
8. If presented with convincing evidence of serious misconduct, where there is no employer to whom this can be referred, and the author(s) are registered doctors, cases can be referred to the General Medical Council.
9. If, however, there is no organization with the legitimacy and the means to conduct an investigation, then the editor may decide that the case is

sufficiently important to warrant publishing something in the journal. Legal advice will then be essential.

10. If editors are convinced that an employer has not conducted an adequate investigation of a serious accusation, they may feel that publication of a notice in the journal is warranted. Legal advice will be essential.
11. Authors should be given the opportunity to respond to accusations of serious misconduct.

Less Serious Misconduct

1. Editors may judge that it is not necessary to involve employers in less serious cases of misconduct, such as redundant publication, deception over authorship, or failure to declare conflict of interest. Sometimes the evidence may speak for itself, although it may be wise to appoint an independent expert.
2. Editors should remember that accusations of even minor misconduct may have serious implications for the author(s), and it may then be necessary to ask the employers to investigate.
3. Authors should be given the opportunity to respond to any charge of minor misconduct.
4. If convinced of wrongdoing, editors may wish to adopt some of the sanctions outlined below.

Sanctions

Sanctions may be applied separately or combined. The following are ranked in approximate order of severity:

1. A letter of explanation (and education) to the authors, where there appears to be a genuine misunderstanding of principles.
2. A letter of reprimand and warning as to future conduct.
3. A formal letter to the relevant head of institution or funding body.
4. Publication of a notice of redundant publication or plagiarism.
5. An editorial giving full details of the misconduct.
6. Refusal to accept future submissions from the individual, unit, or institution responsible for the misconduct, for a stated period.
7. Formal withdrawal or retraction of the paper from the scientific literature, informing other editors and the indexing authorities.
8. Reporting the case to the General Medical Council, or other such authority or organization which can investigate and act with due process. The COPE Report 1999

10.16. How to Prevent Scientific and Research Misconduct

Below are there ways to prevent misconduct:

1. Institutions should establish clear guidelines for responsible conduct in research, not only for students but all faculties and scientists in the institution. Only including research and publication ethics courses in the syllabus is not enough.

2. Active mentoring should be compulsory. Investigators and mentors should not only talk to their researchers and trainees about the importance of good scientific practices but should also present model good behaviour. There should be an appropriate training for mentors.
3. Create a zero tolerance environment. There should be a provision of clear and stringent penalties for violations of guidelines in the institutions.
4. Clear system for reporting suspected cases of misconduct. Institutions should have a transparent mechanism by which faculties and scientists can bring to light potential misconduct situations. Protection of informants or "whistle blowers" is needed.
5. Create visible oversight committees at institutions for fair investigation. Findings of committees should be made public when possible.
6. Institutions need to prepare clear retraction statements and distinguish between frauds vs. "honest errors." Consider scale of act.
7. Better mechanisms for linking/updating papers, so retracted papers do not continue to be referenced and cited.
8. Develop institute-level standards for record keeping and education of researchers at all levels of training. There should be a centralized storage of data/records?
9. Carefully consider reward systems that may contribute to poor practices or focus on short term gains.

10.17. Role and Responsibilities of the Editor in dealing with Research Misconduct

1. Editors have a duty to act if they suspect misconduct or if an allegation of misconduct is brought to them. This duty extends to both published and unpublished papers.
2. Editors should not simply reject papers that raise concerns about possible misconduct. They are ethically obliged to pursue alleged cases.
3. Editors should follow the COPE flowcharts14 where applicable.
4. Editors should first seek a response from those suspected of misconduct. If they are not satisfied with the response, they should ask the relevant employers, or institution, or some appropriate body (perhaps a regulatory body or national research integrity organization) to investigate.
5. Editors should make all reasonable efforts to ensure that a proper investigation into alleged misconduct is conducted; if this does not happen, editors should make all reasonable attempts to persist in obtaining a resolution to the problem. This is an onerous but important duty.

10.18. Ethical Requirements for Researchers

Shamoo and Resnik (2007) have effectively summarized the important ethical requirements for researchers:

Integrity: Fulfil your promises and obligations of your agreements. Show sincerity and consistency in your actions and thoughts.

Honesty: Communicate and report your research data, results, methods, procedures, and publication status honestly. Strictly avoid falsification, fabrication, and misrepresentation of research output.

Objectivity: Avoid bias in experiment/ study design, data analysis, data interpretation, peer review, personnel decisions, and grant writing. Disclose both personal and financial interests.

Competence: Strive to improve your expertise and take effective steps to advance competence in your field.

Carefulness: Maintain a good record of your research activities including data collection and correspondences with journals. Examine your work thoroughly with peers to avoid errors.

Openness: Share your data, results, tools, resources, and ideas.

Legality: Adhere to required governmental and institutional laws/policies.

Confidentiality: Maintain confidentiality of important information such as patient records, trade or military secrets, grant applications, and papers submitted for publication.

Non-discrimination: Avoid discrimination against colleagues or students based on gender, sex, ethnicity, race, or religion.

Respect for Intellectual Property: Do not use published or unpublished material without permission. Avoid plagiarism. Acknowledge and credit the original author/ creator. Follow obligations related to a patent, copyright, trademark, and more.

Responsible Publication: Avoid duplicate publication. Follow publication ethics to advance science and not just your career.

Responsible Mentoring: Encourage, educate, mentor, and advise students.

Social Responsibility: Advocate and advance public interests and health through your research.

Animal Care: Show respect and care for animals in a study by avoiding bad study designs and experiments.

Human Subjects Protection: Maintain respect, confidentiality, welfare, and dignity of human subjects involved in clinical studies. Minimize any risk/harm to the study population.

References

About Sherpa. (2006). Sherpa: University of Nottingham; http://www.sherpa.ac.uk/about.html . [Google Scholar]

Abraham, P. (2000). Duplicate and salami publications. *Journal of Postgraduate Medicine*, 46: 67.

Adie, E., and W. Roe (2013). *Altmetric: Enriching scholarly content with article-level discussion and metrics*. Learned Publishing 26 (1): 11–17.

Aguinis, H., Hill, N.S., and Bailey, J.R., (2019). "Best Practices in Data Collection and Preparation: Recommendations for reviewers, editors, and authors." *Organizational Research Methods.*

All European Academies, The European Code of Conduct for Research Integrity (2017). https://ec.europa.eu/research/participants/data/ref/h2020/other/hi/h2020-ethics_code-of-conduct_en.pdf

ALLEA (2017). The European Code of Conduct for Research Integrity. https://allea.org/code-ofconduct.

American Psychological Association (APA). (2020). Ethical Principles of Psychologists and Code of Conduct. Retrieved from https://www.apa.org/ethics/code/index

American Psychological Association (APA). (2020). Publication Manual of the American Psychological Association (7th ed.). Washington, DC: American Psychological Association.

American Sociological Association (ASA) (2018). Code of Ethics. Washington, D.C.: American Sociological Association.

Anderson, M. S., & Steneck, N. H. (Eds.). (2010). *International Research Collaborations: Much to Be Gained, Many Ways to Get in Trouble*. Routledge. ISBN: 978-0415999639

Angell M, Relman, A.S. Redundant publication. N Engl J Med 1989; 320:1212-1214

Asim, Z. and S. Sorooshian (2019). "Clone Journals: A threat to medical research." *Sao Paulo Medical Journal* 137 (6): 550–551.

Association of Ideas. *Science* Vol:122 July 15 (3159): 108–111.

Australian National University (ANU) (2020). Policy: Code of research conduct, viewed 29 July, 2020. https://policies.anu.edu.au/ppl/document/ANUP_007403.

Barnes, John Arundel (1977). *The Ethics of Inquiry in Social Science: Three Lectures*. Oxford, UK: Oxford University Press.

Baykoucheva, Svetla (2015). "Managing Scientific Information and Research Data." *Science Direct*.

Beall, J. (2012). "Predatory Publishers are Corrupting Open Access." *Nature* 489 (7415): 179–179.

Beall, J. (2016). Best Practices for Scholarly Authors in the Age of Predatory Journals. The Annals of The Royal College of Surgeons of England 98(2): 77–79.

Beall's List of Predatory Publishers http://openscience.ens.fr/ABOUT_OPEN_ACCESS/BLOGS/2017_01_23_Jeffrey_Beall_last_list_of_predatory_journals.pdf [Google Scholar]

Bellah, R.N. (1983). The Ethical Aims of Sociological Inquiry. Social Science as Moral Inquiry.

Bellé, N. and P. Cantarelli (2017). "What Causes Unethical Behaviour? A meta-analysis to set an agenda for public administration research." *Public Administration Review* 77: 327–339.

Benatar, S. R., & Singer, P. A. (Eds.). (2010). *A Companion to Bioethics*. Wiley-Blackwell. ISBN: 978-1405170057

Berger M. Everything you ever wanted to know about predatory publishing but were afraid to ask. http://www.ala.org/acrl/sites/ala.org.acrl/files/content/conferences/confsandpreconfs/2017/EverythingYouEverWantedtoKnowAboutPredatoryPublishing.pdf [Google Scholar]

Bjork, B.C. and D. Solomon (2015). "Article Processing Charges in OA Journals: Relationship between price and quality." *Scientometrics* 103(2): 373–385.

Bohannon, J. (2013). Who's Afraid of Peer Review? American Association for the Advancement of Science.

Bornmann, L. (2014). Measuring the societal impact of research. EMBO Reports, 15(6), 540-544. doi: 10.15252/embr.201438464

Bornmann, L. and W. Marx (2016). The Journal Impact Factor and Alternative Metrics: A variety of bibliometric measures has been developed to supplant the impact factor to better assess the impact of individual research papers. EMBO reports 17(8): 1094–1097. doi.10.15252/embr.201642823.

Boseley, Sarah and Melissa Davey (2020). "Covid 19: Lancet retracts paper that halted hydroxychloroquine trials." *The Guardian*.

Braun, T., Glänzel, W., & Schubert, A. (1989). "Scientometric Indicators: A 32-Country Comparative Evaluation of Publishing Performance and Citation Impact." *Springer Netherlands*. doi: 10.1007/978-94-011-6921-7

Brembs, B. (2018). "Prestigious Science Journals Struggle to Reach Even Average Reliability." *Frontiers Human Neuroscience* 12: 37. doi:10.3389/fnhum.2018.00037

British Sociological Association (BSA) (2017). *Statement of Ethical Practice*. BSA Publications. https://www.britsoc.co.uk/media/24310/bsa_statement_of_ethical_practice.pdf

Bryman, A. (2012). *Social Research Methods*, 4th Edn., Oxford University Press, New York.

Bryman, A. and Bell, E. (2011). *Business Research Methods*. 3rd ed. Oxford: Oxford University Press.

Chubin, Daryl E. (1985). *Misconduct in Research: An Issue of Science Policy and Practice*. Minerva 23(2): 175–202.

Citation Index. https://www.en.wikipedia.org/wiki/Citation_index.

Clarivate Analytics (2018). The Impact Factor. https://clarivate.com/webofsciencegroup/essays/impact-factor/

Clarivate Analytics (2019). Journal Selection Process. https://clarivate.com/webofsciencegroup/journal-evaluation-process-and-selection-criteria.

Cobey, K.D., Lalu, M.M., Skidmore, B., et al. (2018). "What is a predatory journal? A scoping review." Version 2. F1000Res. 7:1001.

Cokol, M., Iossifov, I., Rodriguez-Esteban, R., Rzhetsky, A. (2007). "How Many Scientific Papers Should Be Retracted?" EMBO Reports, 8(5), 422-423. doi: 10.1038/sj.embor.7400976

Collberg, C. and S. Kobourov (2005) "Self-plagiarism in computer science" Communications of the ACM 48(4), pp. 88-94

Collis, J. and Hussey, R. (2014). *Business Research*. 4th edn. Basingstoke: Palgrave Macmillan.

Colnerud, Gunnel (2013). "Brief Report: Ethical problems in research practice." *Journal of Empirical Research on Human Research Ethics* (8), 4: 37–41. http://dx.doi.org/10.1525/jer.2013.8.4.37

Commission on Research Integrity (CORI). (1995). Integrity and Misconduct in Research. Washington, DC: U.S. Department of Health and Human Services, Public Health Services.

Committee on Publication Ethics (COPE) (2005). *Cases*, Salami Publication. Available at: publicationethics.org/search/site/ salami.

Committee on Publication Ethics (COPE). (2020). "Code of Conduct and Best Practice Guidelines for Journal Editors." Retrieved from https://publicationethics.org/resources/code-conduct

Committee on Publication Ethics (COPE). (n.d.). "Best Practice Guidelines for Journal Editors." Retrieved from https://publicationethics.org/resources/guidelines-new/cope-editorial-roles/best-practice-guidelines-journal-editors

Committee on Publication Ethics (COPE). Guidance from COPE. https://publicationethics.org.

Conflict of Interest (2020). Responsible Conduct of Research. https://ori.hhs.gov/education/products/columbia_wbt/rcr_conflicts/foundation/index.

Cope, B. and A. Phillips (2014). *The Future of the Academic Journal*. Oxford: Chandos Publishing.

Council of Canadian Academies Expert Panel on Research Integrity (2010). Honesty, Accountability and Trust: Fostering research integrity, Electronic Resource. http://www.frqnt.gouv.qc.ca/documents/10191/186011/Report+on+Research+integrity.p.

Council of Science Editors (CSE). (2019). White Paper on Publication Ethics. Retrieved from https://www.councilscienceeditors.org/resource-library/editorial-policies/white-paper-on-publication-ethics/

Council of Science Editors (CSE). (n.d.). Editorial Policies. Retrieved from https://www.councilscienceeditors.org /resource-library/editorial-policies/

Council of Science Editors. Predatory or Deceptive Publishers – Recommendations for Caution. https://www.councilscienceeditors.org/resource-library/editorial-policies/cse-policies/approved-by-the-cse-board-of-directors/predatory-deceptive-publishers-recommendations-caution [Google Scholar]

Cress, P.E. and D.B. Sarwer (2019). "Predatory Journals: An ethical crisis in publishing." *Aesthetic Surgery Journal Open Forum* 1 (1): 1–3.

Cromey, D.W. (2010). "Avoiding Twisted Pixels: Ethical guidelines for the appropriate use and manipulation of scientific digital images." *Science and Engineering Ethics*, 16(4): 639–667.

Dadkhah, M. and G. Borchardt (2016). *Hijacked Journals: An emerging challenge for scholarly publishing*. Oxford, UK: Oxford University Press.

Das, A.K. (2019). Research Integrity in the Context of Responsible Research and Innovation Framework. DESIDOC *Jour. Library Inf. Technology* 39: 82–86. doi:10.14429/djlit.39.2.13892

Das, A.K. (2015). "Research Evaluation Metrics." UNESCO.

Dattalo, Patrick (2010). "Ethical Dilemmas in Sampling." *Journal of Social Work Values and Ethics* Volume 7 (1).

De Groote, S., n.d. Subject and Course Guides: Measuring Your Impact: Impact Factor, Citation Analysis, and other Metrics: Journal Impact Factor (IF). https://researchguides.uic.edu/if/impact.

Demir, S. B. (2018). "Predatory Journals: Who publishes in them and why?" *Journal of Informetrics* 12 (4): 1296–1311.

Directory of Open Access Journals (2020). Frequently Asked Questions. https://doaj.org/faq#definition.

DORA (2012). San Francisco Declaration on Research Assessment. https://sfdora.org/read//

Du.ac.in. (Delhi University). (2018). UGC Regulations for Promotion of Academic Integrity and Prevention of Plagiarism in Higher Educational Institutions. http://www.du.ac.in/du/uploads/19092018_noti.pdf.

Economic and Social Research Council (ESRC) (2015). ESRC Framework for Research Ethics https://esrc.ukri.org/files/funding/guidance-for-applicants/esrcframework-for-research-ethics-2015/. Accessed May 3, 2021.

Edwards, M. A. and S. Roy (2017). "Academic Research in the 21st Century: Maintaining scientific integrity in a climate of perverse incentives and hyper competition." *Environmental Engineering Science* 34: 51–61.

Egghe, L. "Theory and practice of the g-index." *Scientometrics* 69, 131–152 (2006). https://doi.org/10.1007/s11192-006-0144-7

Elliott, D. (2016). *White Coat, Black Hat: Adventures on the Dark Side of Medicine*. Beacon Press. ISBN: 978-0807061429

Emerson, J. (2017). "Don't Give Up on Unconscious Bias Training—Make it better." *Harvard Business Review*, 28.

Emmerich, Nathan (2016). "Reframing Research Ethics: Towards a professional ethics for the social sciences." *Sociological Research Online*. December 6, Vol 21: Issue 4: 16–29.

European Code of Conduct for Research Integrity. (2017). Retrieved from https://ec.europa.eu/research/participants/data/ref/h2020/other/hi/h2020-ethics_code-of-conduct_en.pdf

European Science Foundation (2011). The European Code of Conduct for Research Integrity. https://www.allea.org/wpcontent/uploads/2015/07/Code_Conduct_ResearchIntegrity.pdf.

Eykens, J., Guns, R., Rahman, A.J., and Engels, T.C. (2019). "Identifying Publications in Questionable Journals in the Context of Performance-based Research Funding." *PloS one*, 14(11): p.e0224541.

Falagas, M.E., V.D. Kouranos, et al. (2008). "Comparison of SCImago Journal Rank Indicator with Journal Impact Factor." *The FASEB Journal* 22: 2623–2628.https://doi.org/10.1096/fj.08-107938.

Fanelli, D. (2009). "How Many Scientists Fabricate and Falsify Research? A Systematic Review and Meta-Analysis of Survey Data." *PLoS one*, 4(5), e5738. doi: 10.1371/journal.pone.0005738

Fang, F. C., Steen, R. G., & Casadevall, A. (2012). Misconduct accounts for the majority of retracted scientific publications. Proceedings of the National Academy of Sciences, 109(42), 17028–17033. doi: 10.1073/pnas.1212247109

Fang, F.C., Steen, R.G., and Casadevall, A. (2012). Misconduct Accounts for the Majority of retracted Scientific Publications. Proceedings of the National Academy of Sciences, 109(42): 17028–17033.

Federal Research Misconduct Policy. https://ori.hhs.gov/ federal-research-misconduct-policy.

Fischer, P. (2012). New research misconduct policies. https://web.archive.org/web/20120910021419/https://www.nsf.gov/oig/session.pdf.

Fives, Allyn, Daniel W. Russell, et al. (2014). The Ethics of Randomized Controlled Trials in Social Settings: Can social trials be scientifically promising, and must there be equipoise? *International Journal of Research & Method in Education* April, Pp. 56–71.

Frankel, Mark S. (1993). "Professional Societies and Responsible Research Conduct." In *Responsible Science: Ensuring the Integrity of the Research Process*, Vol. 2. Washington, DC: National Academy Press.

Gall, M. D., Borg, W. R., & Gall, J. P. (1996). *Education Research: An Introduction*. New York: Longman Publishers.

Gallin, J. I., & Ognibene, F. P. (2018). *Principles and Practice of Clinical Research* (4th ed.). Academic Press. ISBN: 978-0128499054

Garfield E. (1970). Citation indexing for studying science. *Nature*; 227:669–71.

Garfield E. (2007). The evolution of the science citation index. *Int Microbiol*. 10:65–9.

Garfield, E. (1955). Citation Indexes for Science: A New Dimension in Documentation through

Garfield, E. (1979). *Its Theory and Application in Science, Technology, and Humanities*. New York: John Wiley and Sons.

Garfield, E. (1993). "Citation Searches Can Be Powerful Tools in Combating Redundant Publication." *The Scientist*, 7(8): 12

Garfield, E. (1999). "Journal Impact Factor: A brief review." *CMAJ* 161: 979–980.

Gilligan Carol (1982). "In A Different Voice: Psychological Theory and Women's Development." Publisher: Harvard University Press. ISBN: 9780674445444.

Goodstein, David (Jan-Feb 2002). "Scientific Misconduct." *Academe*, v88 n1 p28–31.

Goundar, S. (2012). "Research Methodology and Research Method." In *Cloud Computing*, Chapter 3.

Graf, C., & Wager, E. (Eds.). (2017). "Finding and evaluating evidence: Systematic reviews and evidence-based practice." Elsevier. ISBN: 978-0702066008

Grants.nih.gov. (2018). What is Research Integrity. https://grants.nih.gov/policy/research_integrity/what-is.htm

Greenwald, Howard P. (2020). Ethics in Social Research. https://www.encyclopedia.com/social-sciences/encyclopedias-almanacs-transcripts-and-maps/ethics-social-research (Accessed October 1, 2020).

Grey, A., Avenell, A., Klein, A.A., and Gunsalus, C.K. (2020). "Check for publication integrity before misconduct." *Nature*, 577(7789): 167.

Grudniewicz, A., D. Moher, K.D. Cobey, G.L. Bryson, S. Cukier, K. Allen, et al. (2019). "Predatory Journals: no definition, no defence." *Nature* 576: 210–212.

Grudniewicz, A., D. Moher, K.D. et al. (2019). Predatory Journals: No definition, no defence. 210–212. Available online at https://www.nature.com/articles/d41586-019-03759-y?sf225811500=1.

Guanine, Louis M. (2005). "Candor in Science: Intellectual honesty." *Synthese.* 145 (2): 179.

Guenin, L.M. (2005). "Intellectual Honesty." *Synthese*. 145, 177–232. https://doi.org/10.1007/s11229-005-3746-3

Guthrie, S., C.A. Lichten, J. Van Belle, S. Ball, A. Knack, and J. Hofman (2018). "Understanding Mental Health in the Research Environment: A rapid evidence assessment." *RAND Health Care* Q. 7: 2. PMC5873519.

Hames, I. (Ed.). (2014). *Peer Review and Manuscript Management in Scientific Journals: Guidelines for Good Practice*. Wiley-Blackwell. ISBN: 978-0470758717

Hansoti, B., M.I. Langdorf, and L.S. Murphy (2016). "Discriminating between Legitimate and Predatory Open Access Journals: Report from the International Federation for Emergency Medicine Research Committee." *Western Journal of Emergency Medicine* 17(5): 497.

Hari Dass, S. (2019). Sowing the Seeds of a Long-term Mental Health Study in an Indian Population. https://indiabioscience.org/columns/indian-scenario/sowing-the-seeds-of-a-long-term-mentalhealth-study-in-an-indian-population.

Harnad, S. (2010). "Gold Open Access Publishing Must Not Be Allowed to Retard the Progress of Green Open Access Self-archiving." *Logos* 21(3–4): 86–93.

Hicks, D., Wouters, P., Waltman, L., De Rijcke, S., and Rafols, I. (2015). "Bibliometrics: the Leiden Manifesto for research metrics." *Nature*, 520(7548): 429–431.

Hirsch, J.E. (2005), An index to quantify an individual's scientific research output. Proceedings of the National Academy of Sciences of the United States of America, 102 (46), 16569–16572. accessible via http://arxiv.org/abs/physics/0508025).

Holm, S., & Williams-Jones, B. (2017). *Global Perspectives on Research Ethics*. John Wiley & Sons. ISBN: 978-1118471086

Horkoff, T. (2015). Citations and Referencing. Writing for Success. https://opentextbc.ca/writingforsuccess/chapter/chapter-9-citations-and-referencing/

Index Copernicus. https://www.en.wikipedia.org/wiki/Index_Copernicus .

Index Medicus. https://www.en.wikipedia.org/wiki/Index_Medicus.

Indian Academy of Sciences (2018). Scientific Values: Ethical guidelines and procedures. https://www.ias.ac.in/About_IASc/Scientific_Values:_Ethical_Guidelines_And_Procedures.

Indian Citation Index. https://www.en.wikipedia.org/wiki/Indian_Citation_Index .

Indian National Science Academy (2018). Policy Statement on Dissemination and Evaluation of Research Output in India. https://www.insaindia.res.in.

Institute of Medicine / National Research Council. (2002). *Integrity in Scientific Research: Creating an Environment That Promotes Responsible Conduct*. Washington, DC: National Academies Press.

International Committee of Medical Journal Editors (ICMJE) (2006). Uniform Requirements for Manuscripts Submitted to Biomedical Journals: Writing and editing for biomedical publication. www.icmje.org.

International Committee of Medical Journal Editors (ICMJE). (2020). Recommendations for the Conduct, Reporting, Editing, and Publication of Scholarly Work in Medical Journals. Retrieved from http://www.icmje.org/recommendations/

International Committee of Medical Journal Editors (ICMJE). (2021). Recommendations for the Conduct, Reporting, Editing, and Publication of Scholarly Work in Medical Journals. Retrieved from http://www.icmje.org/icmje-recommendations.pdf

International Committee of Medical Journal Editors. "Fake," "Predatory," and "Pseudo" Journals: Charlatans Threatening Trust in Science. http://www.icmje.org/news-and-editorials/fake_predatory_pseudo_journals_dec17.html [Google Scholar]

International Committee of Medical Journal Editors. Responsibilities in the Submission and Peer-Review Process. http://www.icmje.org/recommendations/browse/roles-and-responsibilities/responsibilities-in-the-submission-and-peer-peview-process.html [Google Scholar]

Iphofen, R. (2011). Ethical Decision Making in Social Research: A practical guide. https://www.palgrave. com/gp/book/9780230210356.

Jain, N. and M. Singh. (2019). "The Evolving Ecosystem of Predatory Journals: A case study in Indian perspective." In: *Digital libraries at the crossroads of digital information for the future*. Springer International Publishing. DOI: 10.1007/978-3-030-34058-2-9.

Jenny T. van der Steen, Cornelis A. van den Bogert, Mirjam C. van Soest-Poortvliet, Soulmaz Fazeli Farsani5, Rene' H. J. Otten, Gerben ter Riet, Lex M. Bouter (2018). Determinants of selective reporting: A taxonomy based on content analysis of a random selection of the literature. PLOS ONE. https://doi.org/10.1371/journal.pone.0188247.

Johansen, Michal Wiik, Knut-Brede Kaspersen, and Aste Marie Bergseng Skullerud (2001). Personal Data Act. Norske Serier, Capellen Damm.

Journal Indexing: What it is, and What It's Not. http://www.scholarlyoa.com/2012/11/20/journal-indexing-what-it-is-and-what-its-not/

Kakamad, F.H., S.H. Mohammed, et al. (2020). "Kscien's List: A new strategy to discourage predatory journals and publishers." *International Journal of Surgery Open* 23: 54–56. https://doi.org/10.1016/j.ijso.2019.11.001.

Kaldas, M., S. Michael, J. Hanna, and G.M. Yousef (2020). "Journal Impact Factor: A bumpy ride in an open space." *Journal of Investigative Medicine* 68: 83–87. https://doi.org/10.1136/jim-2019-001009.

Kalichman, M.W. (2013). *Research Ethics in Practice: A Guide for the Social Sciences*. Routledge. ISBN: 978-1412994737

Kalichman, M.W. (2018). *Ethics and the Conduct of Business* (8th edn.). Pearson. ISBN: 9780134167657

Kant, Immanuel (1797/1996). *The Metaphysics of Morals*. New York: Cambridge University Press. Edited by Mary J. Gregor.

Kassirer, J.P., Angell M. Redundant publication: a reminder. N Engl J Med 1995; 333:449-450

Kennedy, Donald. (2000). "Reflections on a etraction." *Science* 289: 1137.

Klyce, W. and E. Feller (2017). "Junk Science for Sale: Sham journals proliferating online." *Rhode Island Medical Journal* 100 (7): 27–29.

Koenig, Robert. (2001). "Wellcome Rules Widen the Net." *Science* 293: 1411–1413.

Kohlberg, Lawrence (1981). *The Philosophy of Moral Development: Moral Stages and the Idea of Justice*. San Francisco: Harper & Row.

Kornfeld, D.S. (Ed.). (2018). *Responsible Conduct of Research in Health Sciences*. CRC Press. ISBN: 978-1498779480

Krause, Heather (2020). Equity and Ethics in Data Journalism: Hands-on approaches to getting your data right. Knight Centre for Journalism in the Americas.

Laine C, Winker MA. Identifying Predatory or Pseudo-Journals [Internet]. World Association of Medical Editors.http://www.wame.org/identifying-predatory-or-pseudo-journals

Lakhotia, S.C. (2013). 'National' versus 'International' Journals. *Current Science* 105: 287–288.

Lakhotia, S. C. (2011). The Damaging Impact of "Impact Factor". https://indiabioscience.org/columns/opinion/the-damaging-impact-of-impact-factor.

Lakhotia, S.C. (2014). Research, Communication and Impact. Proc. Indian Natn. Sci. Acad. 80: 1–3.

Lakhotia, S.C. (2017a). The Fraud of Open Access Publishing. Proc. Indian Natn. Sci. Acad. 83: 33–36.doi: 10.16943/ptinsa/2017/48942.

Lakhotia, S.C. (2017b). Mis-conceived and Mis-implemented Academic Assessment Rules Underlie the Scourge of Predatory Journals and Conferences. Proc. Indian Natn. Sci. Acad. 83: 513–515. doi:10.16943/ptinsa/2017/49141.

Lakhotia, S.C. (2015). "Predatory Journals and Academic Pollution." *Current Science*. 108: 1407–1408.

Lakhotia, S.C. (2018). "Why Are Indian Research Not Making a Mark? – The enemy is within." *Current Science*. 115: 2187–2188.

Lariviere, V. and C.R. Sugimoto (2019). The Journal Impact Factor: A brief history, critique, and discussion of adverse effects. In: W. Glanzel, H.F. Moed, U. Schmoch, and M. Thelwall. (eds.). *Springer Handbook of Science and Technology Indicators*. Springer Handbooks, Springer, Cham. https://doi.org/10.1007/978-3-030-02511-3-1.

Leo Egghe, 2006. "Theory and practise of the g-index," *Scientometrics*, Springer; Akadémiai Kiadó, vol. 69(1), pages 131–152, October.

Linacre, S., M. Bisaccio, and L. Earle (2019). "Publishing in an Environment of Predation: The many things you really wanted to know but did not know how to ask." *Journal of Business-to-Business Marketing* 26 (2): 217–228.

Mackinnon, S., B.A. Drozdowska, et al. (2018). Are Methodological Quality and Completeness of Reporting Associated with Citation-based Measures of Publication Impact? A secondary analysis of a systematic review of dementia biomarker studies. BMJ Open 8, e020331. https://doi.org/10.1136/bmjopen-2017-020331.

MacRae DA. (2015). *Indexing: Myths and Realities*, Editor Newsletter Series I. Georgia, United States: Wolters Kluwer Medknow Publications.

Macrina, F.L. (2005). *Scientific Integrity: An Introductory Text with Cases* (2nd ed.). ASM Press. ISBN: 978-1555813182

Macrina, F.L. (2014). *Scientific Integrity: Text and Cases in Responsible Conduct of Research* (4th edn.). ASM Press.

Macrina, F. L. (2016). *Scientific Integrity: An Introductory Text with Cases* (3rd edn.). ASM Press.

Mandal, Jharna, Srinivas Acharya, and Subhash Chandra Parija (2011). "Ethics in Human Research." *Tropical Parasitology* Jan-Jun 1(1): 2–3. doi: 10.4103/2229-5070.72105

Martin, B.R. (2013). "Whither Research Integrity? Plagiarism, Self-Plagiarism and Coercive Citation in an Age of Research Assessment." *Research Policy*, 42(5).

Martyn, J. (1964). "Unintentional Duplication of Research." *New scientist*, 21(377): 338.

Massachusetts Institute of Technology (MIT) (2020). Responsible Conduct of Research. Medical Research Council, 2012. MRC Ethics Series, Good Research Practice: Principles and guidelines. https://research.mit.edu/integrity-and-compliance/responsible-conduct-research

Mayer, T., & Steneck, N. H. (Eds.). (2013). *Promoting research integrity in a global environment.* World Scientific Publishing.

Medical Council of India. (2015). Clarification with Regard to Research Publications in the Matter of Promotion for Teaching Faculty in Medical Colleges/Institutions (Dated Sept 3, 2015 and No. MCI-12 (1)/2015-TEQ/131880). http://www.mciindia.org/circulars/Circular03-09-2015-TEQ-Promotion-Publication.pdf.

Medical Research Council (2012). MRC Ethics Series, Good Research Practice: Principles and guidelines. https://mrc.ukri.org/publications/browse/good-research-practice-principles-and-guidelines/methodspace.com/125795-2/.

Mitcham, Carl. (2003). "Co-Responsibility for Research Integrity." *Science and Engineering Ethics* 9: 273–290.

Mizera K. What is Gold Open Access — useful links. https://openscience.com/what-is-gold-open-access/ [Google Scholar]

Moed, H.F. (2010). Measuring Contextuality of Citations in Scientific Literature. arXiv:1003.4390

Moed, H.F., Burger, W.J.M., Frankfort, J.G., & Van Raan, A. F. J. (1985). "The Use of Bibliometric Data for the Measurement of University Research Performance." *Research Policy*, 14(3), 131–149. doi: 10.1016/0048-7333(85)90012-5

Moher, D., Avey, M., Antes, G., Altman, D.G., Schulz, K. F., Stefan, K., ... & Shekelle, P. (2017). "The National Institutes of Health and guidance for reporting preclinical research." *BMC Medicine*, 15(1), 1–5. doi:10.1186/s12916-017-0785-4

Moher, D., L. Shamseer, K.D. Cobey, M.M. Lalu, J. Galipeau, et al. (2017). "Stop This Waste of People, Animals and Money." *Nature News* 549 (7670): 23.

Molyneux, Catherine, Jane Goudge, et al. (2009). "Conduct of Health-related Social Science Research in Low-income Settings: Ethical dilemmas faced in Kenya and South Africa." *Journal of International Development*: 21: 309–326.

Moore, A. (2020). "Predatory Preprint Servers Join Predatory Journals in the Paper Mill Industry." *BioEssays* 42(11): 2000259. https://doi.org/10.1002/bies.202000259.

National Academies of Sciences, Engineering, and Medicine. (2017). Fostering Integrity in Research. Retrieved from https://www.nap.edu/read/21896/chapter/1

National Academy of Sciences (NAS). (1992). *Responsible Science: Ensuring the Integrity of the Research Process*, Vol. I. Washington, DC: National Academies Press.

National Committee for Ethics in Social Science Research in Health (NCESSRH) (2004). Ethical Guidelines for Social Science Research in Health. http://www.cehat.org/go/uploads/EthicalGuidelines/ethicalguidelines.pdf.

National Institutes of Health (NIH). (2020). Protecting Human Research Participants. Retrieved from https://www.nih.gov/health-information/nih-clinical-research-trials-you/protecting-human-research-participants

Nature Editorial (2019). "The Mental Health of Ph.D. Researchers Demands Urgent Attention." *Nature* 575: 257–258. doi: https://doi.org/10.1038/d41586-019-03489-1.

Nazemian, S., F. Balash, and R. Balash (2017). "Psychological Factors Underlying Unethical Research." Eurasia Proceedings Educational Social Sciences 7: 211–215.

Neuman, W.L. (2013). *Social Research Methods: Qualitative and Quantitative Approaches* (7th edn.). Pearson.

Nicholls, A. (Ed.). (2019). *The Oxford Handbook of Professional Economic Ethics.* Oxford University Press. ISBN: 978-0198793993

Office of Research Integrity. Salami Slicing (i.e., data fragmentation). Available at: ri.hhs.gov/plagiarism-16.

Office of Science and Technology Policy. (2000). Federal Policy on Research Misconduct. Federal Register 65: 76260–76264.

Open Access Scholarly Publishers Association – Code of Conduct. https://oaspa.org/membership/code-of-conduct [Google Scholar]

Owens, E., n.d. Research Guides: Scholarly Research and Publishing: Early Career Researcher Edition: Citation-Based Journal Metrics (Impact Factor & Beyond). https://shsulibraryguides.org/publish-early/journalmetrics.

Panda, S. (2020). "Predatory Journals." *Indian J. Dermatol. Venereol. Leprol.* 86:109–114.

Pascal, Chris B. (1999). "The History and Future of the Office of Research Integrity: Scientific Misconduct and Beyond." *Science and Engineering Ethics* 5: 183–198.

Patnaik, Ila (2017). "Why India Needs Ethical Guidelines for Social Science Trials after Abhijit Banerjee Nobel." *The Print*, 27 December. https://theprint.in/ilanomics/why-india-needs-ethical-guidelines-forsocial-science-trials-after-abhijit-banerjee-nobel/341314/

Patwardhan, B. and A. Thakur (2019). "UGC-CARE Initiative to Promote Research Quality, Integrity and Publication Ethics." *Current Science* 117: 918–919.

Patwardhan, B., S. Nagarkar, S.R. Gadre, S.C. Lakhotia, V.M. Katoch, and D. Moher (2018). "A Critical Analysis of the UGC-approved List of Journals." *Current Science* 114: 1299–1303. doi: 10.18520/cs/v114/i06/1299–1303.

Paul, H. (2018). "The Scientific Self: Reclaiming its place in the history of research ethics." *Science Engineering Ethics* 24: 1379 –1392. doi:10.1007/s11948-017-9945-8.

Petrisor, A.I. (2018). "Predatory Publishers Using Spamming Strategies for Call for Papers and Review Requests: A case study." *DESIDOC Jour. Library Info. Technology* 38: 199–207. doi: 10.14429/djlit.38.3.12551.

Piaget, J. (1932). "The Moral Judgment of the Child." *The Free Press*, New York.

Pimple, K.D. (2002). "Six Domains of Research Ethics: A Heuristic Framework for the Responsible Conduct of Research." *Science and Engineering Ethics*, 8(2), 191–205. doi:10.1007/s11948-002-0044-3

Plagiarism in Higher Education Institutions. https://www.ugc.ac.in.

PSA (Office of the Principal Scientific Advisor to the Government of India). https://www.psa.gov.in.

PubMed. https://www.ncbi.nlm.nih.gov/pubmed [Google Scholar]

Reitz, Joan M. (2013). Online Dictionary for Library and Information Science: http://www.abc-clio.com/ODLIS/searchODLIS.aspx.

Research Output in India. Proc. INSA 84 No. 2 June: 319–329.

Resnik, D. 2007. *The Price of Truth: How Money Affects the Norms of Science.* Oxford University Press, New York.

Resnik, D.B. (2015). "Retraction in Science: The Bad, The Ugly, and The Good." *Science and Engineering Ethics*, 21(4), 843–846. doi: 10.1007/s11948-014-9618-0

Resnik, D.B. (2015). What is Ethics in Research & Why is it Important? National Institute of Environmental Health Sciences. https://www.niehs.nih.gov/research/resources/ bioethics/whatis/index.cfm

Resnik, D. B., & Dinse, G. E. (Eds.). (2015). *Scientific Integrity: Text and Cases in Responsible Conduct of Research* (4th edn.). Wiley. ISBN: 978-0470671555

Resnik, D.B., & Shamoo, A.E. (2017). *Responsible Conduct of Research* (3rd edn.). Oxford University Press.

Resnik, David B. (2015). What is Ethics in Research and Why is it Important? https://www.niehs.nih.gov/research/resources/bioethics/whatis/index.cfm.

Roemer, Robin Chin and Rachel Borchardt (2015). Meaningful Metrics: A 21st Century Librarian's Guide to Bibliometric and Research Impact. ala.org

Roig, M. (2001). Plagiarism and Paraphrasing Criteria of College and University Professors. Ethics and Behavior, 11, 307323. http://dx.doi.org/10.1207/S15327019EB1103_8

Rousseau, R., Leo Egghe, and Raf Guns (2018). "Becoming Metric-wise: A bibliometric guide for researchers." *Science Direct.*

Sadeghi R. (2015). Self archiving of the scientific publications: Legal and ethical issues. Self-Archiving. https://www.linkedin.com/pulse/self-archiving-scientific-publicationslegal-ethical-issues-sadeghi .

Salmons, Janet (2019). *Ethics and Your Literature Review*. Methodspace: Sage. https://www.

SATORI. 2015. Ethics Assessment in Different Fields of Social Sciences. A report.

Saunders, M., Lewis, P. and Thornhill, A. (2012). *Research Methods for Business Students*. 6th edn. Harlow: Pearson Education Limited.

Schmid, S.L. (2017). Five Years Post-DORA: Promoting best practices for research assessment. Mol. Biol. Cell 28: 2941–2944.

Science Citation Index. https://www.en.wikipedia.org/wiki/Science_Citation_Index.

Self-Archiving Repository goes online. (2009). URL: https://www.researchgate.net/ blog/post/self- archiving-repository-goes-online.

Sen, Amartya K. (1989). *On Ethics and Economics*. Pp. 148, New Jersey: Wiley Blackwell.

Shamoo, A.E., & Resnik, D.B. (2009). *Responsible Conduct of Research* (2nd edn.). Oxford University Press. ISBN: 978-0195368246

Shamoo, A.E., & Resnik, D. B. (2015). *Responsible Conduct of Research* (2nd edn.). Oxford University Press. ISBN: 978-0190249597

Shamoo, A.E., and Woeckner, E. (2007). "Ethical Flaws in the TeGenero Trial." *American Journal of Bioethics* 7(2): 90–92.

Shen, C., Bjork, B.C. (2015). "'Predatory' open access: a longitudinal study of article volumes and market characteristics." *BMC Med.* 13:230.

Sherpa, RoMeo Wikipedia, the free encyclopedia. https://en.wikipedia.org/wiki/SHERPA/RoMEO.

Shils, S.E. (1980). *The Calling of Sociology and Other Essays on the Pursuit of Learning*. P. 76. Chicago, USA: University of Chicago Press.

Sim, Julius. 2010. "Conflicts in Research Ethics: Consent and risk of harm." *Physiother. Res. Int.* 15(2), 80–87.

Simpson, G.G. (1950). *The Meaning of Evolution: A study of the history of life and of its significance for man*. New Haven/London: Yale University Press.

Singapore Statement on Research Integrity. (2010). Retrieved from https://www.singaporestatement.org/

Singh, Yogendra. 1973. "The Role of Social Sciences in India: A Sociology of Knowledge."

Smith R. (2006). "Research misconduct: the poisoning of the well." *J R Soc Med*; 99(5):232–7

Smith, J.W. (1999). *The Deconstructed Journal — A New Model for Academic Publishing.* Learned Publishing 12(2): 79–91.

Sociological Bulletin. https://doi.org/10.1177/0038022919730103

Solomon, D.J., & Bonham, A.C. (2014). *Ethical and Regulatory Aspects of Clinical Research: Readings and Commentary*. The Johns Hopkins University Press. ISBN: 978-1421415643

Sommer, T.J. (2001). "Suppression of scientific research: bahramdipity and mulltiple scientific discoveries." *Science and Engineering Ethics*, 7, 77–104. doi:10.1007/s11948-001-0025-7

Sovacool, B.K. (2008). "Exploring Scientific Misconduct: Isolated individuals, impure institutions, or an inevitable idiom of modern science?" *Journal Bioethical Inquiry* 5: 271–282.

Stark, L. (2011). *Behind Closed Doors: IRBs and the Making of Ethical Research*. University of Chicago Press. ISBN: 978-0226770864

Steen, R.G. (2011). "Retractions in the Scientific Literature: Is the Incidence of Research Fraud Increasing?" *Journal of Medical Ethics*, 37(4), 249–253. doi: 10.1136/jme.2010.040923

Steen, R.G., Casadevall, A., & Fang, F. C. (2013). "Why Has the Number of Scientific Retractions Increased?" *PLoS one*, 8(7), e68397. doi: 10.1371/journal.pone.0068397

Steneck, N.H. (2006). "Fostering integrity in research: Definitions, current knowledge, and future directions." *Science and Engineering Ethics*, 12(1), 53–74. doi: 10.1007/s11948-006-0006-y

Steneck, N.H. (2007). Introduction to the Responsible Conduct of Research. Office of Research Integrity. Retrieved from https://ori.hhs.gov/sites/default/files/rcrintro.pdf

Steneck, N.H. (2007). ORI Introduction to the Responsible Conduct of Research. Retrieved from https://ori.hhs.gov/sites/default/files/rcrintro.pdf

Strasser, B.J. (Ed.). (2016). *Ethics in Science: Ethical Misconduct in Scientific Research*. Academic Press. ISBN: 978-0124200733

Swaner, L.E. (2005). *Educating for Personal and Social Responsibility: A Review of the Literature*. Liberal Education, 91(3), pp. 14–21. ISBN: 59904868X.

TheDanishCodeofConductforResearchIntegrity.(2017).Uddannelses-ogForskningsministeriet. Ufm.dk. https://ufm.dk/en/publications/2014/the-danish-code-of-conduct-for-research-integrity. (Ministry of Higher Education, Dansk).

The Danish Committee on Research Misconduct. https://ufm.dk/en/research-and-innovation/councils-and-commissions/The-Danish-Committee-on-Research-Misconduct.

"The Declaration of Helsinki — Ethical Principles for Medical Research Involving Human Subjects." (2013). *Journal of the American Medical Association*, 310(20), 2191–2194. doi:10.1001/jama.2013.281053

The Metric Tide: Report of the Independent Review of the Role of Metrics in Research Assessment and Management (2015). doi: 10.13140/RG.2.1.4929.1363

The Office of Research Integrity (2020a). Definition of Research Misconduct. https://ori.hhs.gov/definition-misconduct >

The Office of Research Integrity (2020b). Research Misconduct Case Summary. https://ori.hhs.gov/content/case-summary-yakkanti-sudhakar

The Office of Research Integrity (2020c). Roles and Relationships. Ufm.dk. (Ministry of Higher Education, Dansk), 2017. (Ministry of Higher Education, Dansk), 2014.

Thorp, H.H. (2020). Underpromise, Overdeliver. Science 367: 1405. doi:10.1126/science.abb8492.

Titus, S. L., & Wells, J. A. (2008). Repairing Research Integrity. Nature, 453(7198), 980–982. doi: 10.1038/453980a

Tri-Council (1998). Medical Research Council of Canada, Natural Sciences and Engineering Research Council of Canada, Social Sciences and Humanities Research Council of Canada.

Tri-Council Policy Statement, Ethical Conduct for Research Involving Humans. August. http://www.bcmhsus.ca/Documents/tri-council-policy-statement-ethical-conduct-for-research-involving-humans.pdf.

UGC (2017). The UGC Draft Regulations — Promotion of Academic Integrity and Prevention of UGC (2018). (Promotion of Academic Integrity and Prevention of Plagiarism in Higher Educational Institutions) Regulations. https://www.ugc.ac.in/ugc_notices.aspx?id=MjA3OQ.

UGC (2020). Summary: Good Research Practices, in Good Academic Research Practices (GARP), p. 8. New Delhi: University Grants Commission.

UGC Public Notice (2019). CARE: Reference List of Quality Journals. https://www.ugc.ac.in/pdfnews/8378640_Public-Notice-CARE-14-01-2019.pdf.

UGC-CARE. Reference List of Quality Journals. https://ugccare.unipune.ac.in/apps1/home.

UGC-CARE. Savitribai Phule Pune University. https://ugccare.unipune.ac.in.

UK Research Integrity Office (2020). Questionable Research Practices. https://ukrio.org/research-integrity-resources/#Questionable-Research-Practices

Universities UK (2019). The Concordat to Support Research Integrity. https://www.universitiesuk.ac.uk/policy-and-analysis/reports/Documents/2019/theconcordat-to-support-research-integrity.pdf.

University Grants Commission (UGC) (2019). Public Notice on Academic Integrity. https://www.ugc.ac.in/pdfnews/6315352_UGC-Public-Notice-CARE.pdfUniversity of Cambridge, 2020. Research Integrity and Good Research Practice Checklist, viewed 29 July, 2020.https://research.mit.edu/integrity-and-compliance/responsible-conduct-research.

University of Cape Town (2020). Office of Research Integrity and Good Research Practice Checklist. http://www.researchsupport.uct.ac.za/office-researchintegrity. University of Delhi, 2020. Academic Integrity and Ethical Guidelines, viewed 29 July 2020.

University of Delhi (2020). Academic Integrity and Ethical Guidelines. http://du.ac.in/du/index.php?page=academic-integrity-and-ethical-guidelines

US Office of Science and Technology Policy Federal Policy on research misconduct. http://www.ostp.gov/html/001207_3.html (accessed on December 14, 2007).

Uzun, A., & Çakmak, T. (2015). "Altmetrics: Complement or replacement for traditional metrics?" *Journal of the Medical Library Association*, 103(3), 160–163. doi: 10.3163/1536-5050.103.3.010

Van Noorden, R. (2020). "Hundreds of Scientists Have Peer-reviewed for Predatory Journals." *Nature Mar*. DOI: 10.1038/d41586-020-00709-x.

Van Raan, A.F.J. (2005). Measuring Science: Capita Selecta of Current Main Issues. In: N. Cronin & B. Atkins (Eds.), *The Web of Knowledge: A Festschrift in Honor of Eugene Garfield*. Information Today Inc. ISBN: 978-1573872235

Von Elm E, Poglia G, Walder B, Tramèr, M.R. "Different Patterns of Duplicate Publication: An Analysis of Articles used in Systematic reviews." *JAMA* 2004; 291: 974–980.

Von Schomberg, R. (2012). Prospects for Technology Assessment in a Framework of Responsible Research and Innovation. In Technikfolgen abschätzen lehren. VS Verlag fur Sozialwissenschaften, pp. 39–61.

Wager, E. and Kleinert, S. (2012). "Cooperation between Research Institutions and Journals on Research Integrity Cases: Guidance from the Committee on Publication Ethics (COPE)." *Maturitas*, 72(2): 165–169.

Wager, E., & Kleinert, S. (Eds.). (2011). *Responsible Research Publication: International standards for editors*. Committee on Publication Ethics (COPE). ISBN: 978-0-9568157-0-4

Wager, E., & Williams, P. (2011). "Why and How Do Journals Retract Articles? An Analysis of Medline Retractions 1988–2008." *Journal of Medical Ethics*, 37(9), 567–570. doi: 10.1136/jme.2010.040964

Waltman, L., & van Eck, N. J. (2015). "Field-normalized citation impact indicators and the choice of an appropriate counting method." *Journal of Informetrics*, 9(4), 872–894. doi: 10.1016/j.joi.2015.08.006

Wassenaar, D.R. and N. Corbella (2005). Ethical Issues in Social Science Research. Paper presented at a social science and ethics conference in Kilifi, Kenya.

Weiner, G. (2001). The Academic Journal: Has it a future? Education Policy Analysis Archives 9: 9.

Wellcome Trust Guidance Document (2020). Good research practice guidelines, viewed 29 July, 2020. https://wellcome.ac.uk/grant-funding/guidance/good-research-practice-guidelines.

Wellcome Trust. (2013). The Misconduct Allegations in Research: The Hinxton Group Consensus Statement. Retrieved from https://wellcome.org/sites/default/files/wtp056877.pdf

Williams, Malcolm (2003). The Ethics of Social Science Research. Chapter 4. In Making Sense of Social Research. https://www.sagepub.com/sites/default/files/upm-binaries/34088_Chapter4.pdf] In SAGE Research.

World Association of Medical Editors (WAME). (2021). WAME's Policy Statement on Geopolitical Intrusion on Editorial Decisions. Retrieved from http://www.wame.org/news/2021/4/1/wames-policy-statement-on-geopolitical-intrusion-on-editorial-decisions

World Association of Medical Editors (WAME). (n.d.). Publication Ethics Policies for Medical Journals. Retrieved from http://www.wame.org/policies/

World Association of Medical Editors (WAME). (n.d.). WAME Publication Ethics Policies for Medical Journals. Retrieved from http://www.wame.org/publications/policies

World Medical Association. (2013). Declaration of Helsinki: Ethical Principles for Medical Research Involving Human Subjects. Retrieved from https://www.wma.net/policies-post/wma-declaration-of-helsinki-ethical-principles-for-medical-research-involving-human-subjects/

Wouters, Paul (1999). Historical details pertaining to the creation of ISI, Ph.D. Thesis, University of Amsterdam.

Yuh-Shan H. (2013). "Science citation index expanded." *Scientometrics*. 94:1297–312.

Zitt, M., Ramanana-Rahary, S., & Bassecoulard, E. (2005). Relativity of citation performance and excellence measures: From cross-field to cross-scale effects of field-normalisation. Scientometrics, 63(2), 373–401. doi: 10.1007/s11192-005-0222-4